D1544132

From Generation
to Generation

A HISTORY OF ST. LUKE'S EPISCOPAL PARISH

Salisbury, North Carolina

The handsome Gothic Revival-style altar and reredos in St. Luke's was installed in 1910 as a memorial to the Rev. Dr. Francis Johnstone Murdoch (1846-1909), the longest-serving rector in the history of the parish. Photograph by Robert Bailey

From Generation to Generation

A HISTORY OF ST. LUKE'S EPISCOPAL PARISH

Salisbury, North Carolina

DAVYD FOARD HOOD

Copyright © 2006 St. Luke's Episcopal Parish
All Rights Reserved

Printed in Korea
Library of Congress Catalog Card Number: 2006932706
ISBN 0970675348

Spirit Publishing, Raleigh, NC (919)828-7774

COVER PHOTOGRAPH

In his Book of Raphael's Madonnas, *published in 1860, James P. Walker described the "Madonna of the Chair" as "without exception, the best known of Raphael's Madonnas, and that from which the greatest number of copies have been taken. It is, therefore, incontestably the favorite with the public...." The popularity of the iconic painting increased through the nineteenth century and, not surprisingly, it was chosen as the subject for the stained glass window above St. Luke's altar. Although the firm of R. Geissler of New York submitted a design for a "rose window" for the baptistry in spring 1909, that design apparently did not figure in the deliberations of December 1909, when the decision was made to relocate the three-part "bishops' window" from the apse to the baptistry as part of the scheme for the Murdoch memorial altar and reredos. The vestry turned to the Montague Castle Company of New York, the makers of the Ascension Window, for this critical part of the new altar decoration. The window was installed in the late fall or early winter of 1910.*

The window is self-framed within a decorative circular band identifying it as "The Children's Birthday Memorial & James Clyde Jackson Memorial." The death of the young Jackson boy on 14 May 1907 deeply affected many in Salisbury. The Salisbury Post carried a long report of the accident leading to his death on the fifteenth; however, the account penned by Dr. Murdoch and recorded in his register reflects its singular effect on the aging rector of St. Luke's.

James Clyde Jackson
Clyde who was nine and a half years old went out on Thursday May 9th 1907 with another boy to the creek; by accident the boy shot him in the leg. He was taken to the Sanitorium and treated with the greatest skill but died May 14th and was taken to Hillsboro for interment. He was baptized in infancy and was a regular attendant at Sunday School which he never missed. He had expressed to his parents his desire to be confirmed as soon as they would let him. He was a model of love and obedience to his parents and has left a sweet memory of only good behind him.

Photograph by Robert Bailey

iv

James Shober Brawley
1918–1981

Thanks be to God for the love and generosity of James Shober Brawley, noted historian and author of *The Rowan Story*, who left a special bequest in 1983 to St. Luke's Church for the purpose of updating Dr. William S. Powell's Bicentennial history published in 1953;

Thanks be to God for Mary Robena Nicolson, a member of this Parish for four score and twelve years who greatly loved her Church, and whose generous gift in 2000 enabled a special committee chosen by the wardens and vestry to appoint Davyd Foard Hood for the research and writing of this history in celebration of St. Luke's 250th anniversary in the year 2003;

Mary Robena Nicolson
1908–2002

and

Thanks be to God for the generous benefactors of this book whose donations, encouragement and great patience have made this publication a reality at last.

IN MEMORY OF

Della Murdoch Carlton
(Nancy Murdoch Carlton)

Ruth Miller Clement
(Donald Clement Jr.)

Louis H. Clement and Mary
Johnson Clement
(Nancy Clement Boyd)

Louis H. Clement and
Mary Johnson Clement
(Mary Shaw Clement Schulte)

James Allan Dunn and
Lois Sanford Dunn
(Mr. and Mrs. James A. Dunn Jr.)

Doctor Paul Green
(Joan Allen Green)

The Joseph Family
(Hannah Joseph and
Virginia Joseph)

Liza Murdoch Lang
(Harriett Lang Hornthal)

Dr. Frank Baker Marsh and
Martha Jenkins Marsh
(John and Jane Riley)

Claudius Stedman Morris and
Emma Lewis Speight Morris
(Lewis Morris)

Wilson Warren Moser and Frances
Sohmer Moser
(Mr. and Mrs. William F. Moser,
Mr. and Mrs. Robert P. Moser,
Mr. and Mrs. David Safrit,
Mr. and Mrs. David Beaver)

The Rev. Francis Johnstone
Murdoch and Eliza Marsh
Murdoch
(Major General Francis
Murdoch III)

Francis Johnstone Murdoch Jr. and
Josephine Speight Murdoch
(Della Murdoch Carlton)

Alice Caldwell McKenzie
(Miss Lorraine Wallenborn)

Doctor Harold Hastings
Newman Jr.
(Mrs. Harold Hastings
Newman Jr.)

Edward Overman Norvell
(Edward P. and Susan L.
Norvell)

Edward E. Proctor and
Lucile S. Proctor
(Patricia Proctor Rendleman)

Abner M. Rice and Linda H. Rice
(Peggy Horton Cox)

Julian Hart Robertson and
Blanche Spencer Robertson
(Blanche Robertson and Zack H.
Bacon Jr.)

Julian Hart Robertson and Blanche
Spencer Robertson
(Wyndham G. Robertson)

Joseph John Summerell and
Berta Allen Russ Summerell
(The Edward Taylor Family)

Edward Tennent Taylor Jr.
(Marye Taylor Wagner, Lisa
Taylor Towell and Kate Taylor
Hill)

Bate Carpenter Toms and
Lily Bernhardt Toms
(Doctor Bate Toms Jr.)

Robert L. Waddell
(Betty Waddell)

Charles Herbert Wentz and
Carolyn May Wentz
(Barbara Wentz Welch)

Vernon Frederick Wilkerson
(Carolyn C. Wilkerson)

Chester David ZumBrunnen
(Betty Jean ZumBrunnen)

IN HONOR OF

Bryan Scott Arthur and
Ashley Arthur Taylor
(Mr. and Mrs. Karl A. Arthur)

Stephanie Marie, Thomas Robert
and Nathaniel James Bartlett
(Deanne Thurber)

Donald Clement Jr.
(Edward H. and Nancy H.
Clement)

Edward H. Clement
(Nancy Hundley Clement,
Thomas Gardiner Thurston IV,
Harrison Hundley and Tatyana
Celine Thurston)

Edward H. Clement
(William and Nancy Stanback)

Peggy Horton Cox and
Naomi Sheets
(Betty Price Gregory)

Saint Luke's Episcopal Church
Women
(Sarah Kellogg)

Elizabeth Hardin Taylor
(Marye Taylor Wagner, Lisa
Taylor Towell, Kate Taylor Hill)

The Rev. Herbert Stevenson Wentz
(Barbara Wentz Welch)

The Rev. I. Mayo Little and
Elizabeth Hill Little
(The Edward Taylor Family)

DONORS

William Chambers Coughenour

William and Shari Graham

Gerry and Brenda Wood

CONTRIBUTIONS

Tomme and Charlene Gamewell

Kathryn Nicolson Bentowski

Mark and Barbara Perry

Elinor B. Reynolds

Joe and Barbara Small

TABLE OF CONTENTS

A MESSAGE FROM THE BISHOP

July 7, 2006

My dear friends in Christ:

Grace to you and peace from God our Father and the Lord Jesus Christ.

It is with great joy that I write on the occasion of 253 years of faith, service and witness to the loving, liberating and life-giving Gospel of our Lord Jesus Christ. We, your diocesan family here in North Carolina, give thanks to Almighty God for your witness to his goodness and love.

The first Bishop of North Carolina, the Rt. Rev. John Stark Ravenscroft, was elected Bishop in Salisbury on April 12, 1823. The Rt. Rev. Henry Beard Delany, father of the venerable Delany sisters, was elected Suffragan Bishop of North Carolina for Colored Work at Convention in Salisbury in 1918. Yours is a remarkable heritage and history. But yours is a history with a legacy that continues to this day.

The Rt. Rev. Michael Bruce Curry, Bishop of North Carolina, made his annual visit to the parish for Confirmation Sunday on 13 November 2005. He appears here with Barbara Setzer.
Photograph by David Setzer

As your bishop I am so aware of the many ways you have supported the global mission of the church and diocese through grants and labors of time. The hungry are being fed, clean water and health care is being provided, young people are experiencing mission work in far and distant lands because of your continued generosity and missionary zeal. Your Rector, the Rev. Whayne Hougland, is one of the leading voices among the clergy of our diocese. Your lay leaders have long continued to be active and positive voices in the life of this diocese.

I thank God for your witness. In times of war and days of peace, in moments of great change and periods of quiet rest, St. Luke's, like Luke the evangelist and physician in the Bible, has been and will continue to be an instrument of God's healing and reconciliation.

As the old hymn says so well:

Through many dangers, toils and snares,
I have already come.
'Tis grace that brought me safe thus far,
And grace will lead me home.

May the Grace of God which has sustained you in the past, guide, direct, uphold and encourage you as we face the future before us, following Jesus as his disciples, witnessing to God's love, healing and reconciliation in the world. I remain,

Your brother in Christ,

+Michael Bruce

The Rt. Rev. Michael B. Curry
11th Bishop of North Carolina

FOREWORD

A church is more than the walls that form to create a physical structure. Yes, a church building is important. And yes, a church is a place of holiness, indeed a sanctuary of the Holy. But a church, properly defined, is the people who endeavor to worship within the physical structure. A church is a living, breathing organism—a gathering of people striving to live faithful lives. A church is made up of blood and tears and sweat. It is built on prayer, sacrifice and forgiveness. A church represents the earthly presence of a living God who focuses on a living Christ filled by the power of a living Spirit. It is beautiful in its diversity and in its complexity. It is recognized by how its people act in the world and it is alive as it acts for justice, freedom and peace.

St. Luke's Salisbury is a church—in the truest sense of the word. For more than 250 years, faithful people have gathered in the home of God to live and love for the glory of God. And they have done so with great humility, grace and joy.

Within the covers of this book you will read about the lives of real people of God; people who have built a beautiful church of bricks and mortar and stained glass through which real lives have been fashioned and formed into vessels of more exceeding beauty than any four walls could contain. It is the people of St. Luke's—their triumphs and tribulations, their starts and their stops and their ongoing struggle to live the Gospel that makes the history of St. Luke's worth the telling and worth the reading.

So read well the story of lives well-lived at the corner of Church and Council streets, Salisbury, NC. Read and enjoy and offer prayers of thanksgiving for a place and her people who have faithfully worshiped, faithfully given and faithfully built a church—a real church.

May you be blessed by this history and may you be encouraged to love and pray and share as beautifully and freely as those who call themselves the people of St. Luke's, Salisbury.

The Rev. Whayne M. Hougland Jr., Rector
March, 2006

PREFACE

The research for this book began in winter 2000. The work has been exhilarating, sometimes frustrating, but never lacking in satisfaction. Soon after beginning my research, William S. Powell turned over to me his notes, both those from his original publication of 1953 and his work on the proposed revision of the 1980s. I am deeply grateful to him for this characteristic act of generosity and his good counsel through the years.

This history of St. Luke's Parish reflects the melding of documentation from many sources. The account of the parish in the long period from the formation of Rowan County in 1753 to the admission of the reorganized church to the Diocese of North Carolina in 1824 is based principally on two sources: public records, and *The Episcopal Church in North Carolina, 1701-1959*. The record of frustrated attempts to plant the Church of England in colonial Rowan County appears in the letters of clergymen and royal governors published in *The Colonial Records of North Carolina*, together with other public documents. For the period after the Revolutionary War, *The State Records of North Carolina*, local public records, the diocesan history edited by Lawrence London and Sarah Lemmon, and accounts of the life and tireless ministry of the Rev. Robert Johnston Miller illuminate our understanding of events leading up to the formal organization of the Diocese in 1817.

In 1819 the Diocese of North Carolina began yearly publication of the *Journal of the Proceedings of the Annual Convention*. These slim but priceless volumes provide invaluable insight into the progress of the parish from its rebirth in 1824, through the course of the nineteenth century, and the relationship of St. Luke's to the revival of the Episcopal Church in North Carolina. Later, *The Carolina Churchman*, published from 1909 to 1935 by the Diocese, also provided information on the life of the church not available elsewhere.

St. Luke's Archives, housed in the vault, the library and the Canterbury House, include the surviving parish registers that begin in 1839, after the arrival of Thomas Frederick Davis; the surviving vestry minutes that date from the last months of Mr. Tillinghast's tenure as rector in 1872 to the present; and a group of other account books, journals, and record books among which are those of Dr. Murdoch. The records for the twentieth century are more numerous and comprise an increasing tide of reports, copies of bulletins, church newsletters, financial records, building plans and quantities of miscellaneous materials that together provide a comprehensive record of church life, particularly for the period since World War II.

xi

William S. Powell's bicentennial history *St. Luke's Episcopal Church*, and John Steele Henderson's essay, "Episcopacy in Rowan County," are foremost among a group of published books and pamphlets listed in the bibliography. These include histories of St. John's Lutheran Church, First Presbyterian Church, Salisbury; Christ Church, Cleveland; and those of other North Carolina churches that have associations with this parish. Through St. Luke's existence, its rectors have sometimes come from or relocated to parishes in the neighboring states of Virginia, Tennessee and South Carolina. Thomas Wright, the first rector of the reorganized parish, left St. Luke's in 1832 for Memphis, Tennessee, where he was the first rector of Calvary Church. Thomas Frederick Davis, who came to St. Luke's in 1836, departed Salisbury in 1846 for Grace Church, Camden, and seven years later was elected Bishop of South Carolina. In 1872 John Huske Tillinghast resigned from St. Luke's after a rectorate of five years, accepting a call to South Carolina, where he had a long career as a clergyman that closed with his death in 1933. Histories of churches in these states proved useful, particularly Dr. Albert Sidney Thomas's comprehensive history of the Episcopal Church in South Carolina from 1820 to 1957.

Frances Wheat Shober, the infant daughter of Francis Edwin and Josephine May (Wheat) Shober and the granddaughter of Dr. John Thomas Wheat, was baptized in St. Luke's on 17 November 1867 by Mr. Tillinghast. Dr. Murdoch married Miss Shober to Isaac E. Haviland on 18 November 1896. After dying in 1905 she was remembered in 1908 with the gift of this imposing brass eagle lecturn.
Photograph by Robert Bailey

The St. Luke's History Book Committee was appointed originally in 1982 by the Rev. Mayo Little. Members of that committee worked through the 1980s with William S. Powell to revise his 1953 history. When that effort stalled, the project languished until Mary Nicolson's gift enabled it to advance, with me as the author. The composition of the committee has changed through the years, and new members have joined its circle: Betsy Detty, Philip Acree Cavalier, Emily Ford, Mayo and Betty Little, Tim Messinger, Barbara Perry and George Simons. Miss Nicolson and Dr. Marsh have died and so, too, has Betsy Detty. However, Edward Clement, Jim Dunn and Lib Taylor, members of the original committee, have continued steadfast in their commitment to St. Luke's. Since winter 2000 when I met with the revived, expanded committee, first in the church library and more often around the dining table at 632 Hobson Road, I have been grateful for its guidance. The committee members are wealthy in their knowledge of St. Luke's, and they have generously shared the benefit of their wisdom, experience and insight as this book has advanced to publication. They are critical to whatever success *From Generation to Generation* comes to enjoy.

A number of individuals have also made important contributions to this work. Standing at the head of the class are Elizabeth Hardin "Lib" Taylor and Mary Jane Fowler. As every communicant of St. Luke's can attest, this history would not have found its way into print without the selfless efforts of Lib Taylor, who readers will learn follows in the footsteps of her father and her grandfather, Archdeacon Hardin, who came to Salisbury in 1912. Many in St. Luke's will also know Mary Jane Fowler, whose extraordinary knowledge of Salisbury's history and its families is unique. So, too, has been her patience with my many questions, posed in dozens of telephone calls and letters. Readers of this book will find themselves as indebted to her as I am for a surer understanding of the many links between people and place. George Stevenson, private manuscripts archivist at the State Archives, was generous also with his knowledge and counsel, as was Canon Elmer Taylor "Ted" Malone Jr., who facilitated my research at the Diocesan House. Many calls were placed to reference librarians in this state and beyond, and none responded more often or with more sympathy than Wanda Rozzelle of the Catawba County Public Library in Newton.

Another, larger group responded either individually or on behalf of their institutions to more particular questions. These generous people include: Sterling P. Anderson Jr., of Richmond, Virginia; Eliza Frazier Bishop of Lenoir, a great-great-great-granddaughter of Robert Johnston Miller; Barbara Buckingham-Hayes of Portland, Oregon; Robin Copp and Henry G. Fulmer of the University of South Carolina Library; Betsy Crusel of New Orleans; Peter Graham Fish of Durham; the Rev. N. Brooks Graebner, Rector of St. Matthew's Church, Hillsborough; Keenan Grigg of The Citadel, Charleston; Harriett Lang Hornthal of Elizabeth City, a great-granddaughter of Dr. Murdoch; Jessica Lacher-Feldman and Merrily Harris of the University of Alabama Library; Arthur D. Leiby, archivist of the Diocese of Easton; Janie C. Morris of Duke University Library; William Speight Murdoch, a grandson of Dr. Murdoch; Sally Reeves, formerly of the New Orleans Notarial Archives; Kevin Reynolds of the Jessie Ball duPont Library at the University of the South, Sewanee; Zoe Rhine of the Asheville-Buncombe Library; the Rt. Rev. John Shelby Spong; and Marcus Corry, Emily Ford, Ann Kemp, Tim Messinger, Nancy Mott, George Simons, Jennie Sparks and Ralph Wagoner of St. Luke's.

While this preface precedes the history of the parish herein, it was actually the last part of the book to be written. As long years of work on this project come to a close, I am mindful of another friend and colleague without whose participation it would not have come to fruition. When computers and word processing equipment were introduced in the State Historic Preservation Office in the 1980s, I continued to use my state-issued IBM Selectric II typewriter. Since late 1989 I have used another trusty Selectric II typewriter for correspondence, National Register nominations, National Historic Landmark designation reports, book reviews, and to produce the manuscripts for published works including *From Generation to Generation*. This typescript, often heavily revised in type and by hand, was transformed into readable text by Sondra Ward who also saw the manuscript through its successive revisions. With her collaboration, and that of Lib and Mary Jane, and the generosity of Miss Mary Nicolson, I come to the end of my work. And you, the reader, are about to begin the history of a church which Mr. Drage determined to plant in the heart of Salisbury when North Carolina was still a colony of Great Britain and its sovereign King George III.

Davyd Foard Hood
Isinglass
Vale, North Carolina
10 January 2006

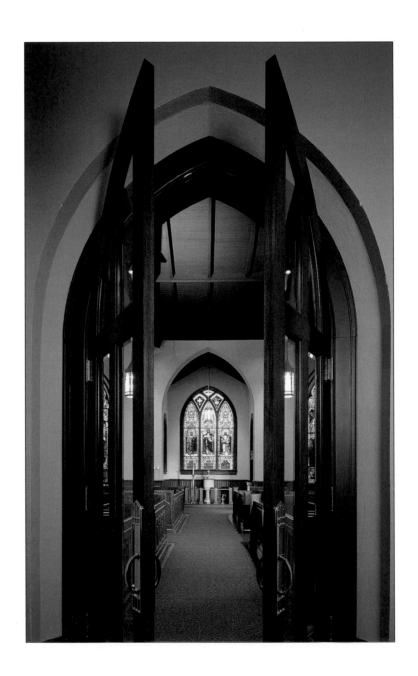

The architectural axis linking the narthex with the baptistry, which gives St. Luke's its cross plan, gained a bold emphasis in 2003 with the installation of new doors. Crafted and installed by James William Hollifield and Dowd Temple, they are set in a lancet arch frame that echoes the shape of the bishops's window.
Photograph by Robert Bailey

1755-1756	William Miller	Rector
1766	George Micklejohn	Curate
1769	Charles Cupples	Visitor
1769-1771	Theodorus Swaine Drage	Rector
1786-1825	Robert Johnston Miller	Acting Rector
1826-1832	Thomas Wright	Rector
1832-1834	John Morgan	Rector
1835	William Wallace Spear	Rector
1835	Moses Ashley Curtis	Visitor
1836-1846	Thomas Frederick Davis	Rector
1846-1858	John Haywood Parker	Rector
1858-1866	Thomas Goelet Haughton	Rector
1867-1872	John Huske Tillinghast	Rector
1872-1909	Francis Johnstone Murdoch	Rector
1909-1910	Thaddeus Ainsley Cheatham	Rector
1910-1914	Frank James Mallett	Rector
1914-1918	Warren Wade Way	Rector
1918-1938	Mark Hemingway Milne	Rector
1939-1942	Edward Brailsford Guerry	Rector
1944-1952	William Moultrie Moore Jr.	Rector
1952-1957	Thom Williamson Blair	Rector
1954-1956	Urban Tigner Holmes, III	Curate
1956-1957	Claude Ward Courtney	Curate
1958-1969	O'Kelley Whitaker	Rector
1965-1968	Harvey Gerald Cook	Assistant
1969-1981	Uly Harrison Gooch	Rector
1970-1977	Kenneth Rosier Terry	Assistant
1978-1979	Jack Glenn Flintom	Assistant
1982-1993	Ichabod Mayo Little	Rector
1984-1987	Paul Dennis Tunkle	Assistant
1988-1992	Virginia Norton Herring	Assistant
1992-1994	Gary David Steber	Assistant and Interim
1995-1999	Clifford A.H. Pike	Rector
1996-1997	C. Roger Butler	Assistant
1999-2000	John Southern Jr.	Interim
2000-2003	Stephen Burnum Morris	Rector
2002-2003	Robert B. Cook Jr.	Associate
2003-2005	Sarah Darnell Hollar	Assistant
2004-2005	Douglas L. Holmes	Interim
2005-	Whayne M. Hougland Jr.	Rector

The memory of Miss Louise Neave (1878-1966) is honored in this small window fitted in the transom over the baptistry door. Designed to complement the earlier Milne memorial on the opposite wall, it takes as its theme the conversion of St. Paul on the road to Damascus.
Photograph by Robert Bailey

The left panel of this window honors the service of the Rev. Theodorus Swaine Drage as rector of St. Luke's Parish. Mr. Drage was actually the third rector of the parish and not its first as he is mistakenly identified in the lower register of the window. Dr. Murdoch's studied choice of St. Aidan (d. 651), an Irish-born monk, for this memorial is marked by poignant irony. King (and later Saint) Oswald asked Aidan to leave the monastery at Iona and come to Northumbria to re-establish the Christian church that had lapsed among his subjects. Aidan was made bishop there in 635 and established his see at Lindisfarne, which became a center of Christian England. Aidan's great achievement came to a crushing personal end in 651, when his second patron, Oswin, King of Deira, was killed through treachery. Aidan is said to have died of grief twelve days later. Mr. Drage enjoyed no like degree of royal support despite his appeals to the governor. The actions of Rowan County's Scotch-Irish citizens proved to be the bane of his tenure here and eventually forced Mr. Drage's removal to Camden, South Carolina, where he died impoverished.

The panel on the right, featuring St. Augustine who led the conversion of the English to Christianity and was named Archbishop of Canterbury in 601, is a memorial to the Rt. Rev. Theodore B. Lyman, the fourth bishop of the Diocese of North Carolina.

Photograph by Robert Bailey

FROM GENERATION TO GENERATION

CHAPTER 1

St. Luke's

A Parish in the Province of North Carolina
1753–1776

Visitors to Salisbury, and particularly those who come to see its historic buildings, are drawn to St. Luke's Church, tucked behind the antebellum court house and set back from Council Street on tree-shaded grounds. Its Gothic detailing and rich purple-brown brick appeal to the mind and eye. Its modesty and quietude seem to set it apart from the city's other, highly visible churches that mostly stand near the street or otherwise trumpet their location. This repose and feeling of separateness, of being of a time apart, has long been appreciated by townspeople and visitors alike. Hope Summerell Chamberlain expressed a view of St. Luke's shared by many when she wrote of the church in the 1930s for her memoir *This Was Home*.

This repose and feeling of separateness, of being of a time apart, has long been appreciated by townspeople and visitors alike.

> St. Luke's Church...was planned after the venerable pattern of some English parish church. It had a truncated square tower with pinnacles, and a raftered interior. Even when half finished it gave an impression of permanence with dignity and was like a stray bit of antiquity which had wandered into new-made surroundings. With all the passing of the years it has never gone out of fashion. My mother possessed no Catholic tradition whatever and had only a literary interest in the Prayerbook, but she admired this church building and said of it, "By grace ye are saved," although by that she meant only the outward appearance rather than any great gift of invisible inwardness as mentioned by St. Paul.[1]

This Salisbury native's perceptive words appear even more apt today, some 70 years after she endorsed the appreciation held by her mother. In this passage of time, one after another of the churches she knew here as a child, young woman and as an adult have been replaced by newer, ever larger edifices, including her own Presbyterian church.

Today, St. Luke's remains not simply the oldest church building in Salisbury, but also the only 19th Century church building to remain the home of its congregation. Even so, the character of antiquity is relative. In fact, the building consecrated by Bishop Ravenscroft in July 1828 is 75 years younger than its namesake, St. Luke's Parish, which was created with the formation of Rowan County in 1753. Then, when North Carolina was a colony of Great Britain, the Church of England was the established state church. The idea of separation between church and state was a concept that grew with the rise toward independence, culminating with the declaration of July 4th, 1776. Thus, in its first quarter century of existence, and until nationhood was assured by the surrender of Lord Cornwallis at Yorktown, Virginia, on 19 October 1781, the history of St. Luke's Parish, the antecedent of St. Luke's Church, is inseparable from the political and social history of Rowan County.

St. Thomas Church, Bath, erected in 1734-35, is the oldest surviving Episcopal church in North Carolina. This view, one of the earliest known, dates to the turn of the 20th Century and shows the building before restoration efforts.
Courtesy of the North Carolina State Archives

This status of co-equalness with the county was a pattern seen throughout colonial North Carolina, where parishes of the Church of England shared boundaries with counties and precincts. Rowan County and St. Luke's Parish were the westernmost in North Carolina, and at a far remove from the coastal settlements where the church thrived. The oldest surviving church buildings in the state housed these eastern North Carolina congregations. St. Thomas Church at Bath, Beaufort County, the oldest church building in North Carolina of any denomination, was erected in 1734-1735. St. Paul's Church, Edenton, Chowan County, was begun in 1736; however, it was not completed until 1774. St. Philip's Church at Brunswick, Brunswick County, the home church of several of the colony's royal governors, was the most elegant of the known Anglican churches in North Carolina. Dating to the mid-18th Century, it survives today as a stabilized ruin with handsome arched door and window openings in its thick brick walls. St. John's Church, at Williamsboro in today's Vance County, was begun in 1771 and survives as the oldest, if also substantially restored and enhanced, frame church in the state.

The delays experienced at St. Paul's, Edenton, reflect the general fortunes of the church throughout the colony in the late Colonial Period when a growing political restlessness was paralleled by the rising visibility and power of colonists who held other religious affiliations. Whether Quakers in northeastern North Carolina and the central Piedmont, Baptists or Anabaptists, Lutherans, Presbyterians or members of the German Reformed Church, those who worshiped apart from the Church of England were seen as dissenting from its doctrines and earned the appellation "Dissenters." North Carolina was not unique in this regard; dissenters were found throughout colonial North America, and especially in areas settled by emigrants from continental Europe. Some of these, especially in Maryland, held to the Catholic Church. All opposed taxation for the support of the Anglican Church and its clergymen and the payment of marriage fees. Political opposition in North Carolina found its expression in the Regulator movement. Although Governor William Tryon defeated the Regulators at the Battle of Alamance in 1771, the revolutionary spirit was not quelled but instead, as history proves, it found new means of opposing British colonial rule.

Because settlement was relatively thin across colonial North Carolina, where cities did not develop as quickly as in neighboring South Carolina and Virginia, and the number of Dissenters was sizable, both the Church of England and a body of native-born clergy to serve it were slow to develop. In his excellent account of the Anglican Church in North Carolina during the Proprietory and Royal periods, appearing in *The Episcopal Church in North Carolina, 1701-1959*, Hugh Talmadge Lefler explains the problems attending the support of clergy and, in turn, the Anglican Church. Ecclesiastical jurisdiction of the American colonies was held by the Bishop of London whose office was represented by commissaries in South Carolina, Virginia and Maryland. North Carolina did not have a commissary, and both the church and its clergy experienced greater difficulties than those seen in the neighboring colonies. The majority of clergymen in colonial North Carolina, 33 of the 46 known Church of England ministers, were dispatched to North Carolina by the Society for the Propagation of the Gospels in Foreign Parts.[2] Of those who came to St. Luke's Parish, George Micklejohn was sponsored by the Society.

North Carolina did not have a commissary, and both the church and its clergy experienced greater difficulties than those seen in the neighboring colonies.

The pattern of settlement seen in the interior of North Carolina in the mid-18th Century, with settlers traveling on the Great Wagon Road from Pennsylvania through Virginia, presented even further obstacles to the development of the church here. The fact that the great majority of those who came to colonial Rowan County were Scotch-Irish and German-speaking immigrants who embraced the Presbyterian, Lutheran and Reformed doctrines, guaranteed these Dissenters a real measure of influence in the political life of Salisbury and Rowan County. Because of their number and prominence, they likewise exercised a controlling interest in the election of the vestry for St. Luke's Parish and effectively stymied the advancement of the church here. They continually elected their friends to the vestry who refused to take the necessary step for qualification. And here, at the edge of the Carolina frontier, the means were not available to enforce the qualification of the vestry. Then, too, there was the matter of the fees that should have been enjoyed by the Anglican clergymen who performed marriage ceremonies. Time and again, those who took out licenses for marriage in St. Luke's Parish were encouraged surreptitiously to have their rites performed by public magistrates or

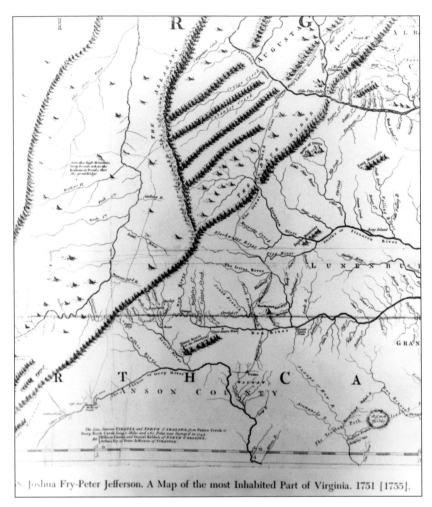

Joshua Fry-Peter Jefferson. A Map of the most Inhabited Part of Virginia. 1751 [1755].

Most of those who settled in St. Luke's Parish in the Colonial period came into the region by way of the Great Wagon Road. Its path through Virginia and into North Carolina is traced on this portion of "A Map of the Most Inhabited Part of Virginia" by Joshua Fry and Peter Jefferson, 1751 (1755). Courtesy of the North Carolina State Archives

dissenting clergyman, and even this means of financial support for the Anglican minister was denied him. Mr. Lefler noted that "North Carolina was one of the least desirable assignments"[3] in the American colonies. That being the case, St. Luke's Parish was the least desirable of the least. But still, three clergymen came to St. Luke's, including the remarkable Mr. Drage.

The record of this struggle to establish the church and the history of St. Luke's Parish appear in a series of letters exchanged between clergymen, the governor and officials of the Society for the Propagation of the Gospels in Foreign Parts (hereinafter SPG). Their formal language and composition may appear abstruse in this age; however, their syntax and rhythm gain appreciation and ease of understanding with reading. As will be seen, the first church building in Salisbury was erected by the town's Lutheran congregation. It stood alone until it was replaced on its site in the 1810s through the efforts of both the Lutheran and Episcopalian residents of Salisbury. That second church also stood alone for some 15 or so years. As late as 1823, when it was the site of the diocesan convention at which Mr. Ravenscroft was elected the first Episcopal Bishop of North Carolina, it was known simply as "The Church at Salisbury." Those churches stood on the site that survives today as the Old Lutheran Cemetery, and housed virtually all of the public worship services here until the construction of a brick Presbyterian church in 1827 and the construction of St. Luke's in 1827-1828. But the building of St. Luke's, Salisbury's second brick church, came 75 years after the creation of St. Luke's Parish in 1753. An account of the ill-fated efforts to plant the Church of England in the red clay soils of colonial Rowan County follows.

And that the upper part of said County, so laid off and divided be erected into a County and Parish, by the Name of Rowan County, and St. Luke's Parish.

On 2 April, 1753, "the Petition of several Persons, whose Names are thereunto subscribed, in behalf of themselves, and the rest of the Inhabitants of the Upper and Frontier Parts of Anson County setting forth the great hardships they undergo in travelling great distances to the Court House of Anson County, Praying an Act may pass, to divide the said County of Anson, etc. and signed with the names of three hundred and forty Eight Persons" was read in the North Carolina House of Burgesses.[4] Action was swift. On 4 April an act for creating a county and parish "on the Head of Anson County" was read for the first time and passed.[5] When the bill was read again on the 9th of April, the name of the county was first identified as "Rowan," and "St. Luke's Parish" first appeared in the language of the act.[6] The bill was read the necessary three times, passed and signed into law by Matthew Rowan, acting governor of North Carolina and president of the Council. The act specified "That Anson County be divided by a Line, to begin where Anson Line was to cross Earl Granville's Line, and from thence, in a direct Line, North, to the Virginia Line, and that the said County be bounded to the North by the Virginia line, and to the South by the southernmost line of Earl Granville's Land: And that the upper part of said County, so laid off and divided be erected into a County and Parish, by the Name of Rowan County, and St. Luke's Parish."[7]

The county was named as a courtesy to Matthew Rowan (d. 1760), an Irish-born colonial official of Scottish descent, serving as acting governor between the death of Governor Nathaniel Rice on 29 January 1753 and the arrival of the newly-appointed governor, Arthur Dobbs, at Newbern on 31 October 1754.[8] The question of why the parish was named St. Luke's remains unanswered. Following by only three years the creation of Anson County out of Bladen County in 1750, the formation

Approximate county divisions within present state boundaries

AT THE BEGINNING OF
1760

AT THE BEGINNING OF
1775

AT THE BEGINNING OF
1780

AT THE BEGINNING OF
1800

AT THE BEGINNING OF
1840

of Rowan County reflected a rapidly growing population of new settlers arriving on the western North Carolina frontier. This influx of immigrants to the Piedmont would continue through the colonial period, resulting in the creation of Guilford County in 1770 from portions of Rowan and Orange counties, Surry County from Rowan in 1771, and Burke County from Rowan in 1777. With the creation of Burke County the boundaries of Rowan County were reduced to an area comprising today's Rowan, Iredell, Davidson and Davie counties. The last three of these, respectively, were separated from their mother county in 1788, 1822 and 1836. Rowan County's boundary has remained intact since 1836.

Efforts to establish a county seat and erect a court house for Rowan County proceeded quickly. They are treated in detail by Rowan County historians Jethro Rumple and James Shober Brawley and by Robert W. Ramsey in both his *Carolina Cradle, Settlement of the Northwest Carolina Frontier, 1747-1762* and his earlier article, "James Carter: Founder of Salisbury," published in 1962.[9] Mr. Carter (d. 1765), a man of complicated background and character, and

The evolution of St. Luke's Parish boundaries, beginning with the creation of Rowan County in 1753, can be seen in this series of maps, showing the North Carolina counties, taken from David Leroy Corbitt's The Formation of the North Carolina Counties, 1663-1943, *first published in 1950. The maps, drawn by L. Polk Denmark, show the steady reduction of the county from 1760 through 1775, 1780 and 1800, to 1840 by which time the county's present boundary was established.*

FROM GENERATION TO GENERATION

a surveyor for Lord Granville, anticipated the eventual choice of this place as the site of the new county seat. On 11 February 1755, William Churton and Richard Vigers, agents for Lord Granville, conveyed a tract of 635 acres to James Carter and Hugh Forster, trustees,

> **for a township...by the name of Salisbury...that they might and should grant and convey in fee Simple the several lots already taken up and entered...reserving the annual rent of one shilling for each lot...and likewise grant and convey...such lots...as are not already entered to such persons as shall respectively apply for the same on the payment of twenty shillings...**[10]

James Carter was appointed one of the commissioners to lay off lots in the new town.

The 1755 deed was the first instance in which the name of the county seat was given as Salisbury. While the name has traditionally been accepted as an honorific reference to Salisbury, England, a valid counter-assertion can be made that the new town was named for Salisbury, Maryland. The two trustees cited in the deed both had ties to Cecil County, Maryland, as did a third man, John Dunn (ca. 1725-1783), who figured prominently in the early history of Salisbury and Rowan County and for whom Dunn's Mountain is named. The first known description of the town appears in a long letter written on 24 August 1755 by Governor Arthur Dobbs (1689-1765) to the London Board of Trade. Two months earlier, on 17 June, he had set out "to view my Lands, and at the same time the Western Frontier..." observing both the natural resources of the province, the character of its citizens, and the nature of settlement, agriculture, and trade. Approaching Salisbury, Governor Dobbs, like John Lawson some 50 years earlier, was impressed by the Yadkin River and the lands along its waters.

The great Yadkin River was a principal Piedmont waterway and a landmark known to all travelers and settlers in the region. It was called the Sapona River by John Lawson, who visited this area in 1709. In 1733 it was labeled the "Sapona or Yadkin River" on the Moseley map and soon thereafter came to be known simply as the Yadkin River. Since the formation of Davie County in 1836, the Yadkin River has formed the long northeast boundary of Rowan County.

Photograph by Dr. Steve Coggin, courtesy of the Land Trust for Central North Carolina

---

...and all along the Yadkin, is very rich level ground, free from rocks or gravel, but all a rich dark red, and some inclining to yellow of the richest Loams, here they sow barley, wheat rye and oats, and have yards to stack it in. The Yadkin here is a large beautiful river where is a ferry. It is near 300 yards over, it was at this time fordable scarce coming to the horses bellies. At 6 miles distance I arrived at Salisbury the County town of Rowan(.) the Town is but just laid out, the Court House built and 7 or 8 log Houses erected, from this unto the end of Lord Granville's Line which is as yet run no farther, upon cold water Creek on the Catawba's path, is 14 miles, the Lands still very good,...[11]

Later in the letter Governor Dobbs discusses another important purpose of his travels, the need to erect a fort to protect the western edge of the frontier settlements near the lands occupied by the Catawba Indians. He had ordered Captain Hugh Waddell (ca. 1734-1773), the head of a military company, to scout the region and report back so that he could "fix upon a proper and most central place for them to winter at. and erect a Barrack, and afterwards if found proper there to build a Fort:..." Governor Dobbs proceeded to a recommended site on Fourth Creek, due north of present-day Statesville.

Arthur Dobbs, governor of North Carolina from 1754 to 1765, and the first Royal Governor to visit St. Luke's Parish, ordered the Rev. William Miller to Salisbury as the first rector of St. Luke's. This image, made soon after his appointment as governor, is of an engraving made by James McArdell of the painting by William Hoare. The map in Governor Dobbs' left hand is labeled "North Carolina."
Courtesy of the North Carolina State Archives

I found an Eminence and good Springs, and fixed upon that as most central to assist the back settlers and be a retreat to them as it was beyond the well settled Country, only straggling settlements behind them, and if I had placed them beyond the Settlements without a fortification they might be exposed, and be no retreat for the Settlers, and the Indians might pass them and murder the Inhabitants, and retire before they durst go to give them notice.[12]

Governor Dobbs' account is a poignant reminder of historical fact. When St. Luke's Parish was created in 1753, it encompassed lands occupied by both the Catawba and Cherokee Indians. Fort Dobbs, a rectangular log building measuring 53 by 40 feet, standing 24½ feet tall, and fitted with three floors, was built in 1756 by Captain Waddell and his soldiers. It was attacked but once, on the evening of 27 February 1760, by a Cherokee Indian raiding party, which was repulsed. The tide of westward settlement continued unabated through the 1750s, and by the early 1760s it had stretched some 50 miles beyond Fort Dobbs. A new fortification was erected at present-day Old Fort in McDowell County. In 1762 the North Carolina Assembly effectively abandoned Fort Dobbs and ordered it to be dismantled. Meanwhile the first Church of England minister to serve St. Luke's Parish had arrived and quickly left.

Soon after Governor Dobbs arrived in the colony, he had approved a petition by "many inhabitants of Rowan county" to recommend the ordination of William Miller. Mr. Miller, described as a teacher who wished to take up the ministry, sought the governor's endorsement for travel to England for examination and admission to the priesthood. That petition of 1754 marks the first known public discussion of the religious life of the new county and efforts to establish the Church of England within the precincts of St. Luke's Parish. William Miller was licensed by the Bishop of London on 31 March 1755. On his return to North Carolina he was assigned to St. Luke's Parish; however, his tenure was short, lasting only into 1756. The voices of the Dissenters, and their mischief-making in regard to the election of a vestry for St. Luke's and its support of the clergyman, so discouraged the Rev. William Miller that he departed Rowan County. He later served as rector of St. Gabriel's parish, Duplin County, and he was last noted serving in St. Patrick's parish in old Dobbs County, North Carolina, in 1767. Mr. Miller was the first in a series of three Church of England ministers assigned to Rowan County who would leave, discouraged and disappointed by the dissenting citizenry, who resented paying taxes to support the Church of England and its clergymen.

This said, however, differences in religious outlook did not guarantee dissent. In the instance of the Moravian settlement in colonial Rowan County, a certain amity came to define relations with most of their neighbors. In 1755 the Unitas Fratrum (United Brethren), "inhabiting that part of the County of Rowan called and known by the Name of Wachovia," petitioned the colonial Assembly to set them apart in a separate parish. An act was passed creating Dobbs Parish, that would encompass "the Tract of Land in the County of Rowan, called and known by the Name of Wachovia, and the several Surveys of Land to the said United Brethren belonging, contiguous, and adjoining to the said Tract of Land called Wachovia."[13] Thus the Moravian citizens of old Rowan County largely

The earliest known document in which William Miller identifies himself as "rector of St. Lukes" is this promissory note signed by Mr. Miller for the loan of 37 pounds by Thomas Child with which he purchased books for his ministry. It was signed on 10 April, 1755 in London, after his approval by the Bishop of London, and presumably shortly before his return to North Carolina to take up his work in the parish. Thomas Child was attorney and agent to John Carteret, Earl of Granville.
Courtesy of the North Carolina State Archives

avoided the political and civic strife that marked efforts in Salisbury. An entry in the Moravian Records for 4 October 1756 conveys a sympathetic regret for conditions in St. Luke's Parish.

> **In the evening the English Minister Miller arrived with his entire family. He had been appointed by Governor Dobbs as minister of St. Luke's Parish, but the people would not have him; he said he was on his way to Granville County.**[14]

After Mr. Miller's departure in the fall of 1756, a decade passed before another minister of the Church of England is known to have been sent to St. Luke's Parish. The first mention of the Rev. George Micklejohn (ca. 1717-1818) appears in a letter written by Governor William Tryon to the Rev. Daniel Burton, secretary to the SPG. Mr. Micklejohn had been ordained on 16 September 1764 and licensed on 12 March 1766 by the Bishop of London, who then sent him as a missionary to North Carolina.[15]

The handsome stone mansion erected by Michael Brown in 1766 is the only surviving building in Rowan County from the Colonial period, when three successive Church of England ministers attempted to plant the church here. Since 1959, it has been owned by the Rowan Museum, Inc., and operated as a house museum.

Photograph by Jason Williams

Following his arrival that summer, Governor William Tryon wrote to Mr. Burton on 1 October 1766 from Brunswick.

> **I have had the pleasure to receive by Mr. Micklejohn, your letters...; I shall pay the proper attention to our Society's recommendation of the above gentleman. The twenty pounds per annum for two years allowed him is a donation no less necessary than generous....**

> **I have great expectations from Mr. Micklejohn; he is lately gone into Rowan County.**[16]

Five days later, on 6 October, Governor Tryon wrote to the Lord Bishop of London from Wilmington.

> The Rev^d Mr. Micklejohn arrived about three months since, I sent him into the back settlements but have not yet absolutely fixed him. He was three weeks at Brunswick while Mr. (John) Barnett was sick; I own I have great expectations of Micklejohn's being serviceable in his calling. It gave me great pleasure to find the Society for propagating the Gospel in Foreign Parts have considered the two last gentlemen who came in here by temporary salaries; This liberality is really necessary to gent^n who come bare of fortune, as the parishes here seem to expect the parochial duty performed before the stipend is paid. Your Lordship's and the Society's endeavors to supply the parishes vacant in this province with men of character and abilities meet with my warmest acknowledgements,... Men of plain characters and exemplary lives are best adapted for the manners of the people of this country.[17]

For reasons now unconfirmed, but likely those which also plagued the efforts of his predecessor Mr. Miller and his successor Mr. Drage, the Rev. Mr. Micklejohn did not long remain in St. Luke's Parish. By April 1767 he was established in Orange County in St. Matthew's Parish by letters of Presentation from Governor Tryon. He was then one of only 13 Church of England ministers in North Carolina.[18] Two years would pass before another minister would come to St. Luke's Parish.

During this interim, other advances were made in the religious life of Salisbury which would later figure in the history of both the parish and church known as St. Luke's. In his letter recounting his travels through the colony in the summer of 1755, Governor Dobbs had mentioned settlements of "what we call Scotch Irish Presbyterians" and "Germans or Swiss, who are all an industrious people." Members of both communities had established themselves in Rowan County, the parish and here in Salisbury. While the Scotch Irish Presbyterians would first establish a church in the settlement on the lands of western Rowan County, since known as Thyatira, the German Lutherans erected the first church in Salisbury. On 9 September 1768 John Lewis Beard (17__-1788), the progenitor of a family counted as members of St. Luke's Church to the present, executed a deed to Michael Brown, Michael More, Casper Gunther and Peter Reeb, "Trustees of the German Lutheran Congregation in the Township of Salisbury."

> John Lewis Beard...for & in Consideration of the Sum of Five Shillings Sterling Money...Hath Granted, Bargained, Sold,... & Confirm unto the s^d. Trustees of the s^d. Congregation afs^d. and to their Successors in that office forever One Lott or parcel of Land,

During this interim other advances were made in the religious life of Salisbury which would later figure in the history of both the parish and church known as St. Luke's.

situate lying & being in the Township of Salisbury Known & Distinguished in the plan of the s^d. Town by the Number Sixty Seven, in the East Square, Containing One Hundred & forty four Square poles,...To hold the Lott or parcel of Land...unto the s^d. German Lutheran Congregation in & about the s^d. Town of Salisbury, for to Erect and Build thereon a Church or Meeting-house for the Only proper use & Behoof of the s^d. German Lutheran Congregation forever;...that it shall be allowed by the approbation of the Minister, Trustees & Elders of sd. Congregation, That any Lawful Minister of the Gospel of our Lord Jesus Christ shall have Liberty to preach in the s^d. Church if he can & do Show a Sufficient Testimonial in Writing, either from the High Church of England or from the Reformed Calvin Ministers, At such Time as the s^d. Lutheran Minister doth not Want to perform Divine Service in s^d. Church.[19]

The Old Lutheran Cemetery occupies the property set apart by John Lewis Beard in 1768 to the trustees of the German Lutheran Congregation in Salisbury. The first church building erected in Salisbury was located on this property and as late as 1823, when the Diocese of North Carolina held its annual convention here, the then existing building was simply known as "The Church at Salisbury."
Photograph by Jason Williams

Lot 67 in the East Square lay at the extreme east edge of Salisbury, and at some real remove from Mr. Beard's house that stood in the north corner of today's Main and Council streets. Its "remote" location derived from the fact that a daughter of Mr. Beard is said to have been interred here on family property and he wished the grounds preserved. Prior to 1768 there was no known burying ground in the town of Salisbury. This lot became the site of both Salisbury's first cemetery and its first church, a log building which is said to have been built in 1768 or soon thereafter. The churchyard was used as a burying ground and today is known as the Old Lutheran Cemetery.[20]

In 1769 the Rev. Theodorus Swaine Drage (ca. 1712-1774) came to St. Luke's Parish, where he would enjoy the longest tenure of the three Church of England ministers in colonial Rowan County. Mr. Drage had led a varied and colorful life in the years preceding his arrival here. Writing in later years that he was prepared as a youth for the church, he was admitted to Gray's Inn, London, in 1737 to study law. Subsequently he made the acquaintance of Arthur Dobbs, later to be governor of North Carolina, and "served as 'clerk' on a voyage in 1746-47 in search of the Northwest Passage sponsored by Dobbs." This exploration was recounted in *An Account of a Voyage for the Discovery of a North-West Passage by Hudson's Streights*, published in two volumes in London in 1748-49, and *The Great Probability of a North-West Passage*, also published in London in 1748. Mr. Drage is considered the author of both. He next appears in Philadelphia, where he was in business, and by 1758 he was a partner of George Croghan, an Indian trader with a store in Bedford, Pennsylvania. About 1763 he formed a partnership with John Hughes, a merchant of Philadelphia, which continued into 1764. What prompted Mr. Drage, in his mid-fifties in the mid 1760s, to enter (or return to) the ministry is unknown. Whatever the case, he returned to England, where he was ordained deacon and priest in May 1769. Benjamin Franklin is said to have given a testimonial for his ordination. Licensed by the Bishop of London, he sailed to North Carolina and arrived in November.[21]

Governor Tryon introduced Mr. Drage to the vestry of St. Luke's Parish by letter of 12 November 1769.

> Gentlemen,
>
> The Reverend Mr. Drage who is lately arrived from England, warmly recommended to me, waits on you to officiate in your parish for the space of two or three months, at the expiration of which time should he give satisfaction in his sacred calling, and his situation prove agreeable to him I propose to give him Letters of Presentation and Induction to your parish agreeable to the petition of sundry of the Inhabitants of your county delivered to me when I was at Salisbury.[22]

Mr. Drage was welcomed to St. Luke's Parish, and soon two communications were sent to Governor Tryon. The first was an undated petition signed by some 200 men of the Parish concerning the need for a vestry that would support the Church of England.

> We the Subscribers Inhabitants of the County of Rowan members of the established church of England labouring under many burdens in mind and body, both for ourselves and children, in

In 1769 the Reverend Theodorus Swaine Drage (ca. 1712–1774) came to St. Luke's Parish, where he would enjoy the longest tenure of the three Church of England ministers in colonial Rowan County.

having no Gospel ordinances among us, until your Excellency was (out of your wonted goodness) pleased to appoint the Reverend Mr. Drage clerk Rector of this our parish of S[t]. Luke, we humbly pray the further assistance of your goodness in getting a Vestry and that John Ford, John Kimbrough, Morgan Bryan, James McCoy, William Fields, Samuel Bryan, George Magoun, John Cowan, Roger Turner, Evan Ellis, William Giles and William Cowan Sen[r] may be appointed to serve as Vestrymen until there shall be an act of Assembly passed for choosing a Vestry, on the same footing as in England and put it out of the Dissenters power to evoke the Law and thereby prevent there being of a Vestry.[23]

The second communication was a letter addressed to Governor Tryon and signed by seven of the twelve men listed in the above petition, "the rest not being in Town," who had been put up for the vestry but had lost to the slate supported by the Dissenters.

> Your Excellency was kindly pleased to recommend to the Vestry of S[t]. Lukes parish the Reverend Mr. Drage, we, being the majority of the second List voted for Vestry members of the Church of England, therefore in compliance with your Excellencys indulgence, Do certify that the Reverend Mr. Drage doth daily give us infinite satisfaction in his sacred calling, and his situation as he informs us, is agreeable to him, and do humbly pray that you will give him Letters of Presentation and Induction to our Parish which will be the most agreeable indulgence your Excellency can possibly confer upon us.[24]

Mr. Drage appears to have been a man with talent and skills well-suited to the time and place. On 13 March 1770 he wrote to Governor Tryon, described his situation in Salisbury, and expressed his wish to remain here ministering in St. Luke's Parish.

> I found it necessary as the weather would permit me to go into the country, (which) was very agreeable to the people; who were desirous that I should stay amongst them, promised me support; to give them satisfaction in this respect, I made a public declaration at Salisbury, that by a License from the Bishop of London and with your Excellency's approbation and appointment I had fixed on this parish of S[t] Lukes, there to perform the office of a Minister of the Church of England, which met with no opposition.[25]

Mr. Drage continued his letter with a report on the Dissenters in his parish, describing resentments that would soon foment revolution.

Mr. Drage appears to have been a man with talent and skills well-suited to the time and place.

They say not in words only but wishing that as they have opposed England in endeavouring to intrude on their civil rights, they also shall, and have a right to oppose any intrusion on their religious rights, a Maxim I presume dangerous in itself not with respect to this county and the neighboring counties, but to the whole Back Frontier of America, principally settled with Sectaries, and is deserving of the attention of Government, *before power is added to inclination* (author's italics). I plainly perceive if I lose my hold, it would be such a discouragement to the present Members of the Church of England, they would never rally again, many of them would quit and go into those provinces where they could have a free exercise of their religion, others would be absorbed up in, and become of the same principles with the people they stayed amongst. Thus I am, may it please your Excellency, engaged in an affair unforeseen, and which the public service requires me to be steady in,—however disagreeable my situation and mode of living, but as that is personal, I shall pass it over in silence. I

Salisbury was one of the ten towns in North Carolina drawn by the French cartographer Claude Joseph Sauthier (1736-1802) between 1767 and 1771 for Governor William Tryon. By 1770 Salisbury had taken on the appearance of a substantial village with houses lining Corbin (now Main) Street. The court house was located at the crossing of Corbin and Innes streets. The future site of St. Luke's Church appears as an enclosed square behind the Beard house, and its grounds in the north corner of Corbin and today's Council streets.
By permission of the British Library

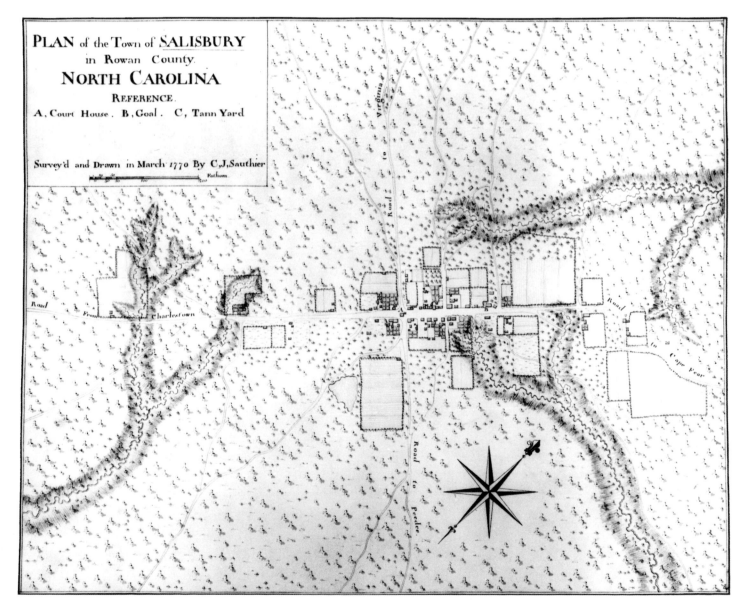

recommend steadfastness and that the Church of England act with coolness, and a christian Temper; the opposites have treated my person with no incivility, my behaviour is studied to give them no offence but they are bitter against my cause.

I enjoy my health and a fine air. I wish your Excellency was equally happy in those two respects.[26]

Mr. Drage's patience and good intentions were soon put to a sore test. On 29 May 1770, Mr. Drage wrote a long letter to Governor Tryon explaining the results of the vestry election on Easter Monday. Despite the best efforts of faithful adherents of the Church of England, the Dissenters prevailed again in electing a slate of twelve men who they knew would make no effort to qualify as elected members of the vestry. In this fashion, now as in preceding years, they effectively manipulated the election process and prevented the lawful election and qualification of a functional vestry for St. Luke's Parish that would support the Church of England and its minister. Nevertheless, the men of the second list, who Mr. Drage described as the "Nominal Vestry," pledged their support in raising his salary, asking of neither "the Dissenters nor the poor" to that end and "That the Congregations of the several preaching Stations, which are no less than six and twenty, should each respectively build their own chapels, with which some are already provided, and others are a providing."[27]

Mr. Drage continued with a description of his ministry, his concern for the future of the church and certain personal observations for the governor's consideration.

> I am so circumstanced as sometimes to preach four times in six days, and do other offices of the church, being desired by the people, I cheerfully do it, Have christened now 370 children, and many yet behind live mean, lye hard, but they do the best for me they can.
>
> ...What prevails with me is, if I quit, it will discourage them so that the Church of England may not for many years be established, if ever, as the power of the opposers will be strengthened, the growing generation will be seduced, and carried away into some Sect or other, so become the worst Subjects, and *there is some shew of latent embers which may in time become a dangerous fire* (author's italics)....
>
> I assure your Excellency I entirely submit to your determination, I have spent a long time here without the satisfaction of my family, and should wish to be at some certainty now, either as to stay or leave while I have the fall before me, and I have not, neither shall I write to England, as to the state of the church, and what I am doing, though they may censure me as indolent and remiss until the affair is settled.[28]

I am so circumstanced as sometimes to preach four times in six days, and do other offices of the church, being desired by the people, I cheerfully do it....

Some six weeks later, and quickly by mid-18th Century standards, Governor Tryon replied to the Rev. Mr. Drage, supporting his approach to the difficulty he was experiencing in the parish.

I lament to find by your Letter of the 29th of May last, that you have met with so unjustifiable an opposition to your Establishment in St. Luke's Parish, while at the same time I congratulate you on the laudable and virtuous support you have experienced from the friends of the Established Church, a Religion that was engrafted upon, and grew up with the Constitution of this colony, A Religion that has ever since been recognized and upheld, and was by Act of the Legislature in 1765 established upon the most solid foundation.

The intemperate zeal of the Dissenters I am inclined to believe arose from mistaken principles. Their Seniors must know their persuasion is a Sect under the Act of Toleration, and the limited powers granted them by the Legislature of this country.—This is ever implied in His Majesty's Instructions to me wherein He commands me to permit a liberty of "conscience to all persons (except Papists) who are contented with a quiet and peaceable enjoyment of the same, not giving offence or scandal to the Government."

I confess I have a pleasure in acknowledging myself greatly obliged by the support the presbyterians have afforded Government in my administration, and it will be a circumstance of peculiar concern to me to have them sully the merit of their late public services, by pursuing measures which are in manifest violation of the rights and liberties of their fellow citizens, by throwing difficulties and obstructions in the way of the maintenance and free exercise of a Religion established by the Laws of their Country. I would appeal to the reason and judgment, and not to the passions of those Gentlemen, how far it may prove impolitic in the issue, to the interests of their persuasion should they carry any further their opposition to the legal Settlement of a Clergyman in S[t] Luke's Parish—I claim no concessions but what are equitable and constitutional, but the Rights of the Country as well as those of the Crown, It is my duty to maintain as long as I am invested with such important trusts.

If after your presentation and Induction, the Letters for which I herewith have the pleasure to send you, you should apprehend the least difficulty would attend the collection of your Salary in the County, the memorials you mention to be presented to the next General Assembly from the Members of the established church, would be a very equitable and expedient measure, and I have not the least doubt but they will meet with proper redress.

I entertain the highest opinion of the temper, moderation and good sense with which you have conducted yourself through this whole business, and which I consider as an earnest of the blessings your parishioners will receive from your Ministry.[29]

Two weeks later, on 22 July, when writing to the secretary of the SPG and giving a report on the status of the society's ministers in the province, he transmitted copies of Mr. Drage's letter and his reply, adding "Mr.

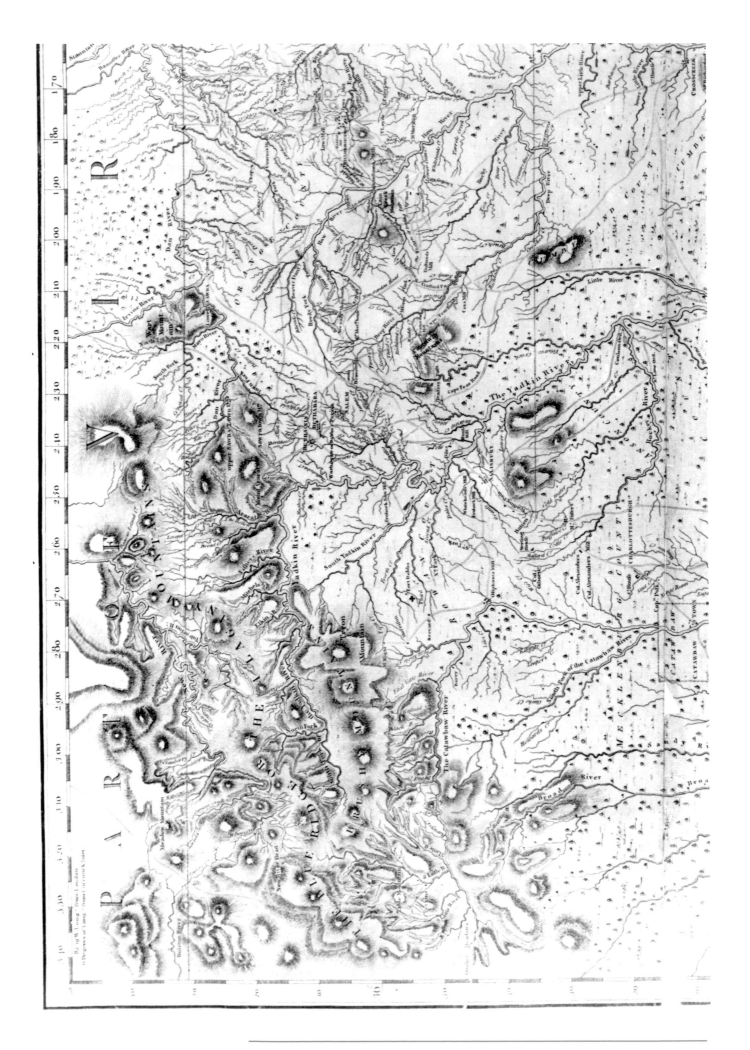

FROM GENERATION TO GENERATION

Drage has met with great difficulties in his Establishment and probably will have many more yet to struggle with."[30] As of July 1770 eighteen ministers of the Church of England, including Mr. Micklejohn in St. Matthew's Parish, Orange County, and Mr. Drage in St. Luke's, were serving the parishes of North Carolina.

Mr. Drage persevered, and on 28 February 1771 he submitted an assessment of conditions in St. Luke's Parish to the secretary of the SPG. It bears quoting at length, as it comprises the last important account of affairs in the parish before its dissolution with the disestablishment of the Church of England in the province of North Carolina in 1776.

Opposite: This image is a reproduction of the upper left quadrant of "A Compleat Map of North Carolina from an actual Survey" by Captain John Collett, 1770. Salisbury appears in the near center of this quadrant. Hillsborough and Charlottesburgh appear on the map, as do Bethania, Bethabra, and Salem in the Wachovia Tract set apart from St. Luke's as Dobbs Parish. Other landmarks, including Frohock's Mill on the waters of Grants Creek and Fort Dobbs, are marked.
Courtesy of the North Carolina State Archives

Salisbury S[t] Lukes Parish,
North Carolina, Feb[y] 28th 1771.

Reverend Sir,

I ask the favor of you to inform the Honorable Society, that I did not before transmit an account relating to my mission by reason of uncertainty of my situation. The place where I reside is named Salisbury in the parish of S[t] Luke in the county of Rowan, Three hundred miles distant from the Seat of Government, and near Four hundred from the Sea, Fine air, temperate climate and a fertile country. It was with his Excellency Governor Tryons approbation I came into these parts having received repeated applications from the people for a church Minister, two thirds of whom are of the church of England, the other a motly mixture, but the most distinguishable are the Irish Dissenters, who had the whole power of Government, as to these parts, invested in them by the late governor: also composed of many different Sects. His Excellency M[r] Tryon was apprehensive there would be an opposition as to my settlement from them.

I found the people of the church of England disheartened, and dispersed like Sheep, but have collected them into about forty congregations, or have as many preaching places where I meet them, consisting upon a moderate calculation of Seven thousand souls men women and children or 900 families inhabiting a country of one hundred and eighty miles in length and one hundred and twenty in breadth of whom I have baptized since the 20th of December 1769 and the 20th of December 1770.—The Reverend Mr Cupples having also baptized many the preceding Summer, being on a visit into these parts—802.

There is a law here, that the freeholders shall annually choose on Easter Monday twelve men as a vestry to manage parish affairs. A Freeholder is properly a person who hath got a Deed or Patent for his land, but for some years past the Lord Carteret, who is proprietor of the Soil in the part where I am, hath granted no patents and the Irish Dissenters being possessed of their Patents before that time, therefore make up the principal number of the Freeholders, and have the power of determining all Elections to their views. On the Election Easter Monday 1770 their list was composed of nine Magistrates, two of whom were members for the county in the Assembly, one Captain of militia, and two senior Elders (all Dissenters) the Election in their favor and then they would not qualify, this had been practiced the year before, declared they could keep out the church by this means, had done it, and always would. The voters further said their purpose in voting, was, not as to whom should compose the vestry, but that there might be none, upon which those of the other List, who were members of the church of England, men of repute and character, excepting one declared they would act as a vestry, met, but proceeded no further, than to answer a Letter from his Excellency the Governor sent by me directed to the Vestry of St Lukes parish which he supposed there was at that time, in which they returned him thanks for the kind provision he made as to a clergyman and desired he would be pleased to give me an immediate Presentation.

I wrote an account to his Excellency of the proceedings,.... His Excellency was pleased to send me a Presentation in July with an approbation of my conduct in very obliging Terms....

It would be supposed...that there are many Dissenting clergy in this Country, there is but one, neither hath there been any regular congregation for Fifteen years, as the Dissenters can not agree in principles. They have only Itinerant preachers, who come from the Northward, preach once in a place, and return, getting considerable contribution from the people of the church of England as well as from others.... I am at a regular conduct, and to be diligent in the discharge of my office, which is disagreeable to them. Being also superior to any little insult and giving no offence, peace is preserved.

I am greatly obliged to the Honorable Society for the honor that hath been done my Draughts, as I have received but few fees taking nothing for Baptism, no burial fees allowed, and excepting their assistance am entirely at my own expence, cannot send for my family, as there is a years salary now due from the parish and no Vestry to assess it, and have little expectation but it will be the same as to the current year, as there is not probability of a Vestry, no great reliance can be had on a free donation of the people, as money is scarce, and it carries a subjection with it.

I have herewith sent you copies of the several papers mentioned in this address.—Pray present my duty to the Honorable Society and assure them of my most faithful services, and zealous discharge of my Function.

I am yours &c.
THEODORUS SWAINE DRAGE,
Rector of St Luke's Parish.[31]

Mr. Drage's letter was carried to the society in London in the hands of two of his parishioners, Germans, "who are commissioned by the Governor to collect in England and Germany, towards a sum which sixty Lutheran families propose to raise as capital, with the Interest of which to maintain a Lutheran Clergyman and a schoolmaster and whom they are to bring from Germany." The two petitioners were Christopher Layrle (Lyerly) and Christopher Reintelmann (Rendleman). Mr. Drage

praised the German Lutherans for their cooperative spirit and encouraged consideration of their
cause to the society.[32] Governor Tryon also supported the efforts of the German-speaking citizens
of the parish and acting "in Consideration of the
loyal and prudent behavior of the Inhabitants of
the said settlement" he, too, endorsed their request
for financial assistance. The petition and the
Governor's testimonial were presented to a general
meeting of the society at Westminster on 19 July
1771 and received a positive consideration. The
necessary funds were raised, and in 1773 Adolphus
Nussmann and Johann Gottfried Arends arrived in
Rowan County to serve as pastor and schoolmaster, respectively.[33]

On Saturday, 2 March 1771, Mr. Drage provided another account of his life and affairs in St.
Luke's Parish, when writing from Salisbury to his
friend Benjamin Franklin in Philadelphia.
Benjamin Franklin (1706-1790), scientist, inven-

*Benjamin Franklin, a friend of
Mr. Drage, received an account of
life in St. Luke's Parish in Spring
1771 from the parish's third rector.
This portrait of the celebrated sci-
entist-statesman was painted in
1785 by Charles Willson Peale.*
Courtesy of the Pennsylvania
Academy of the Fine Arts,
Philadelphia, Pennsylvania. Bequest
of Mrs. Sarah Harrison (The Joseph
Harrison Jr. Collection)

tor, statesman, printer, and publisher of *Poor Richard's Almanac*, was about
midway in a distinguished career that culminated with his role as an
author of the United States Constitution. Mr. Drage's detailed explana-
tions are similar to those he conveyed by letter to the secretary of the
SPG; however, his opening sentences merit reprint here for their evoca-
tive description of Salisbury and Rowan County.

Dear Sir,

**It is not from a want of a sense of pleasure and Honour I have had
in your long acquaintance and Friendship that I have not wrote
since my arrival in these parts. I had nothing to tell you but the
common Occurrences of a voyage, or Inland Journey of near four
hundred miles to a Town called Salisbury, a village of about
Thirty houses, mean in its buildings, but scituated in one of the
finest climates in the world, as I have since experienced.
Temperate in summer, the nights always cool, the winter cold
very moderate, ..., it is the County Town of Rowan, which is
composed of Chiltern and Vales, watered with three fine Rivers;
the Dan, the Yadkin and the Catawba and plenty of streams
makes their course into those Rivers. The soil fertle and capable
with small Industry to produce whatever is desired.[34]**

Mr. Drage continued to experience difficulties in Rowan County, and
he would depart St. Luke's Parish before Mr. Nussmann, the new
Lutheran minister, arrived. One indication of his plight appeared in a
paragraph of Governor Josiah Martin's letter of 7 March 1772 to

Secretary Hillsborough. Mr. Martin, destined to be the last royal governor of North Carolina, had succeeded Governor Tryon in August 1771.

> **I have a recent proof of the collusive malpractices of the Magistrates and County Court Clerks in a complaint from the Rector of St Luke's Parish in Rowan County, who alledges that the Clerk who under a Law of the Province is the dispenser of the Governor's Licences for marriages encourages people who take them to go to Magistrates to solemnize their Marriages in preference to the Rector and that he conceals from him the number of Licenses granted by which means he is deprived of his dues.**[35]

Mr. Drage's situation in Salisbury worsened through 1772, and he was forced to relocate. A confirmation of this decision appears in a short message that Governor Martin conveyed to the provincial assembly on 17 February 1773. "I send herewith a petition of the Rev. Mr. Theodorus Swaine Drage late Rector of St. Lukes Parish in the County of Rowan whose peculiar hard circumstances will I hope recommend him to your benevolence."[36] Unfortunately, Mr. Drage's petition appears to have been lost to history. In any event, it was taken under consideration on the 20th and the following short, dismissive response was transmitted to Governor Martin. "In consequence of your Excellency's Message respecting the petition of the Rev. Theodorus Swaine Drage, The House have taken the same under consideration and are of opinion that the Laws of the Province now in force are sufficient to remove the Grievances complained of."[37]

Writing on 31 March 1773 to Earl Dartmouth, Governor Josiah Martin further expounded on the fate of Mr. Drage and problems attending Presbyterians becoming members of vestries. He "had late convincing proofs that the Admission of Dissenters into Vestries operated as a prohibition to the Establishment of the Church of England, that in the Parish of St. Luke in the County of Rowan, they had actually expelled Mr. Drage the Rector, a very worthy Clergyman, by withholding his Salary, the only means of his subsistence, and forced him to retire to an Asylum, to which he was invited in South Carolina...."[38]

Mr. Drage left Salisbury, apparently in early 1773, and removed to Camden, South Carolina, then in St. Mark's Parish, and ministered to the faithful of the Church of England. His congregation was the predecessor of the body organized as Grace Church in 1830. Mr. Drage's fortunes did not appreciably improve in Camden, where he drafted his will on 5 October, 1774, died soon thereafter, and was buried in an unmarked grave. He was fondly remembered by Joseph Kershaw in 1780 when writing from Camden on 5 January to his friend Henry Laurens.

I have a recent proof of the collusive malpractices of the Magistrates and County Court Clerks in a complaint from the Rector of St. Luke's Parish in Rowan County...

The Letter you forwarded me was from a M^rs. Hannah Swain Drage, the Widow of a very fine Old Gentleman who officiated as Preacher to this district and died here something more than four years ago(.) his Books and apparel was sent by me to the Old Lady(.) his Executor John Rodgers sold his Trifling Household furniture &ca which did not quite pay the demand^s against his Est^e. here; there was due him Six months salary or Fifty pounds Sterling, which I endeavor^d to git from the Publick, but from the Confusion of the times it Could not be got in the usual way so the Account was layd before the Assembly, who thought proper to throw it out, tho it was certainly due to him, I would recommend it to the Executor to renew the application, but as the money is riduced it would scarcely be worth the old Ladys Acceptance(.)[39]

Mrs. Drage was living in Philadelphia at the time of her husband's death, and it is unclear whether she had come South to visit him either in Salisbury or in Camden, or whether he returned to Philadelphia after his arrival here in 1769. Mr. Drage left an estate valued at £312.15.6 in an inventory made in March 1775.[40] His appraisal of his own circumstances and the times of his death matched the view of Mr. Kershaw. Having bequeathed his worldly goods to his wife he wrote "As to what I cou'd devise to my children would be so inconsiderable and difficult to be got to their hands, I recommend them to the blessing of Almighty God."[41] The *Bible, Book of Psalms,* and *Book of Common Prayer* (1764), used by Mr. Drage during services in Camden are said to have descended in the possession of Mr. Kershaw's family into the early 20th Century; their present whereabouts have not been confirmed.[42]

Between Mr. Drage's departure from St. Luke's Parish in 1773 and the Declaration of Independence on 4 July 1776, apparently no Church of England services were held in the parish. If any were held by other ministers of the church resident in North Carolina, the records are not now available. Nonetheless, private devotions continued, as before, and would during the Revolution by those who held to tenets of the Church of England, even after its disestablishment. The Moravians made note of this event in their records.

> Before the year's end, that is on Dec. 18, the Congress at Halifax had drafted and adopted a Constitution for the State, the English Church was no longer the State Church, and with it fell all its Parishes, and so the Brethren ceased to have a Parish of their own.[43]

Thus, as of 18 December 1776, St. Luke's Parish ceased to exist.

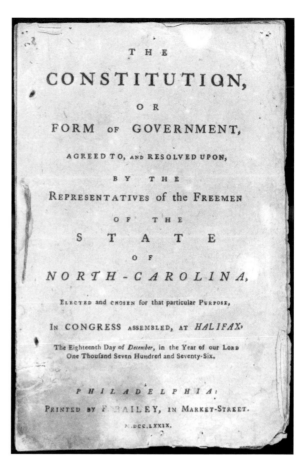

The Constitution...of the State of North Carolina, ratified at the convention meeting in Halifax in 1776, was printed in 1779 in Philadelphia and by others. The only known copy of this printing is held by the Library of Congress.
Courtesy of the North Carolina Collection

ENDNOTES

Endnote Abbreviations

Frequently cited books, journals, and public records have been identified by the following abbreviations in the notes.

CRNC	*Colonial Records of North Carolina*
DNCB	*Dictionary of North Carolina Biography*
ECNC	*The Episcopal Church in North Carolina, 1701-1959*
FPC	*First Presbyterian Church, Salisbury, North Carolina, and Its People, 1821-1995*
HRC	*A History of Rowan County, North Carolina, Containing Sketches...*
JAC	*Journal of the Annual Convention of the Protestant Episcopal Church in the State of North Carolina, 1819-*
NCHR	*North Carolina Historical Review*
RCD	Rowan County Deeds
RCW	Rowan County Wills
RM	*Records of the Moravians in North Carolina*
RS	*The Rowan Story, 1753-1953*
SJLC	*The Heritage and History of St. John's Evangelical Lutheran Church, Salisbury, North Carolina, Through 1983*
SL	*St. Luke's Episcopal Church, 1753-1953*
SRNC	*State Records of North Carolina*

1. Hope Summerell Chamberlain, *This Was Home* (Chapel Hill, The University of North Carolina Press, 1938), 41.

2. ECNC, 26.

3. Ibid.

4. CRNC, V, 59-60.

5. Ibid, 44.

6. Ibid, 48.

7. SRNC, XXIII, 390.

8. For the formation and subsequent division of Rowan County see David Leroy Corbitt, *The Formation of the North Carolina Counties, 1663-1943* (Raleigh, North Carolina Division of Archives and History, 1987), 185-88, hereinafter cited as Corbitt. For Matthew Rowan see H. Kenneth Stephens, "Matthew Rowan," in DNCB, 5, 258.

9. HRC, 47-72, RS, 15-20; CC, 152-70; Robert W. Ramsey, "James Carter: Founder of Salisbury," *North Carolina Historical Review* 39 (Spring 1962), pp. 131-39, hereinafter cited as "James Carter."

10. Land Grant Records of North Carolina, Office of the Secretary of State, Raleigh, Land Grant Book VI, 114.

11. CRNC, V, 355.

12. Ibid, 357. Fort Dobbs is a State Historic Site operated by the North Carolina Department of Cultural Resources.

13. SRNC, XXIII, 438-39.

14. RM, I, 172.

15. DNCB, 4, 264-65.

16. CRNC, VII, 259-60.

17. Ibid, 261-62.

18. Ibid, 457.

19. RCD, 7/13.

20. For a history of this place see Martha W. Agner and Mary Jane Fowler, eds., *The Old Lutheran Cemetery, Salisbury, North Carolina, Since 1768* (Salisbury, Salisbury Printing Company, 1981).

21. See William S. Powell, "Theodorus Swaine Drage," DNCB, 2, 102-03. See also ECNC, 53-54. The most complete account of Mr. Drage's life in Pennsylvania appears in Howard N. Eavenson, *Map Maker & Indian Traders* (Pittsburgh, University of Pittsburg Press, 1949), 85-109, hereinafter cited as Eavenson.

22. CRNC, VIII, 150-51.

23. Ibid, 154-55.

24. Ibid, 155.

25. Ibid, 179.

26. Ibid, 180.

27. Ibid, 207.

28. Ibid, 208-10.

29. Ibid, 217-18.

30. Ibid, 221.

31. Ibid, 502-06. Charles Cupples (d. ca. 1785), mentioned in this letter, was sent by the SPG in 1766 to North Carolina and assigned by Governor Tryon to St. John's Parish, old Bute County. See DNCB, s.v. "Cupples, Charles."

32. Ibid, 506-07.

33. Ibid, 631-33. See also SJLC, I, 59-63. In the event Salisbury and Rowan County were only slightly more hospitable to Messrs. Nussmann and Arends than they were to Mr. Drage. Mr. Nussmann (1739-1794) first settled in Rowan County and served both St. John's, Salisbury, and Zion (Organ) Church, but when members of Zion Church learned he was a convert from the Catholic Church they objected to him as a pastor. In 1774 he relocated to the Buffalo Creek community in Mecklenburg (now Cabarrus) County where he served St. John's Church until his death, and was then buried in its churchyard. In 1775 Mr. Arends (1740-1807), the schoolmaster, became the first person ordained a Lutheran minister in North Carolina. He served St. John's Church, Salisbury, Zion Church, and other churches in the area as an itinerant minister until 1785 when he relocated to Lincoln County, where he died and is buried in Lincolnton. DNCB, s.v. "Arends, John Godfrey," and "Nussmann, Adolph."

34. Eavenson, 99-100.

35. CRNC, IX, 267-68.

36. Ibid, 507.

37. Ibid, 520.

38. Ibid, 622.

39. David R. Chesnutt and C. James Taylor, eds., *The Papers of Henry Laurens*, Volume Fifteen (Columbia, University of South Carolina Press, 2000), 221-222.

40. Ibid, 222.

41. Quoted by William S. Powell in his biographical sketch of Mr. Drage, DNCB, 2, 103.

42. Thomas J. Kirkland and Robert M. Kennedy, *Historic Camden, Part Two, Nineteenth Century* (Columbia, The State Company, 1926), 282, hereinafter cited as Kirkland.

43. RM, III, 1037. Item XXXIV of the Constitution provided "That there shall be no establishment of any one religious church or denomination in this State, in preference to any other; neither shall any person, on any presence whatsoever, be compelled to attend any place of worship contrary to his own faith or judgement, nor be obliged to pay, for the purchase of any glebe, or the building of any house of worship, or for the maintenance of any minister or ministry, contrary to what he believes right...."

The Nativity and the Crucifixion, the two most celebrated events in the Christian Church, are often represented in stained glass and other decorations. The Nativity was chosen by John Steele Henderson as the subject of a memorial window honoring his parents, Archibald Henderson (1811-1880) and Mary Ferrand Henderson (1819-1899). Mrs. Henderson was a granddaughter of John Steele, comptroller of the treasury under Presidents Washington, Adams and Jefferson. The designs of this window, its pendant on the northeast wall of the church, and the Ascension window were approved by the vestry in November 1909. It was installed in 1910.

Photograph by Robert Bailey

CHAPTER 2

The Lost Years

Neither Parish nor Church
1777–1822

The four decades between the disestablishment of the Church of England in December 1776 and the organization of the Episcopal Diocese of North Carolina at New Bern on 24 April 1817 were marked by both extraordinary events and a certain quietude. Following the signing of the Declaration of Independence in Philadelphia on 4 July 1776, battles to gain independence for the American colonies, including the critical battles of Kings Mountain and Guilford Court House, in 1780 and 1781, respectively, culminated in the surrender of Lord Cornwallis and the British forces at Yorktown, Virginia, on 19 October 1781. Military and political events of the period engaged planter and yeoman alike; however, much of the course of everyday life in Salisbury and Rowan County continued largely unchanged, except in one area. The disestablishment of the church removed an important matter of contention between the Dissenters and the supporters of the Church of England. The Anglican church effectively disappeared in Rowan County, as did St. Luke's Parish.

In the 1790s three events occurred that would presage the renewal of the Episcopal Church and the organization of St. Luke's Church in 1823. In the early 1790s a colony composed mostly of Episcopalians emigrated from Maryland to western Rowan County. There, they organized Christ Church, which in 1821 became the first Episcopal church within the boundary of present-day Rowan County. In 1794 the Rev. Robert Johnston Miller accepted ordination as an Episcopal priest at the hands of Lutheran clergymen and thereafter ministered to those in a large section of the Piedmont, including Salisbury, and the Appalachian foothills who eventually would organize Episcopal churches. The third event was

The Anglican church effectively disappeared in Rowan County, as did St. Luke's Parish.

actually a series of conventions held in Tarboro between 1790 and 1794 by the state's few Anglican clergy and laymen, that culminated in 1794 with the election of Charles Pettigrew as Bishop of North Carolina. The Rev. Mr. Miller attended the 1794 convention and voted for Mr. Pettigrew. But, alas, Mr. Pettigrew's trip to Philadelphia for his consecration was interrupted, he was never consecrated bishop of North Carolina, and the Episcopal church again lapsed in the state. When the Diocese of North Carolina was established in 1817, the Rev. Robert Johnston Miller was the only surviving clergyman in North Carolina who had attended the 1794 convention and was still serving as an Episcopal priest.

Arguably one of the earliest events of national significance to occur in Salisbury was Elizabeth Maxwell Steele's gift of money to General Nathaniel Greene in the winter of 1781. This portrayal of the event is taken from an engraving published in the four-volume centennial History of the United States of America *co-authored by Jesse Ames Spencer and Benson John Lossing. The engraving was based on a painting by American artist Alonzo Chappell (1828-1887).*

As William S. Powell noted in his bicentennial history of St. Luke's in 1953, the separation of church and state and the abolition of public support for the clergy, prescribed in the state's constitution, may not have had as significant an impact on the church in North Carolina as the end of financial support for priests and missionaries by the Society for the Propagation of the Gospel in Foreign Parts.[1] This was certainly true in

Rowan County, where the matter of a living had been a critical issue for Messrs. Miller, Micklejohn, and Drage. In the state's older, larger cities of Wilmington, New Bern and Edenton, where the Episcopal congregations were sizable, services continued, in a fashion, but in Rowan County they virtually ceased. Occasionally, when a clergyman was passing through town, services might be held and baptisms performed. The Moravian Records document the appearance of a priest in the area in April 1778; however, his name was not cited.

> **10 April: "An English Minister spent last night in the tavern, and today looked about the town."[2]**

> **12 April: "The English Minister attended the preaching service, wearing a black gown. He had told Br. Meyer that he would like to preach here, but Br. Meyer explained that only a few of the people understood English so he did not press the matter, and left during the afternoon."[3]**

After 1778 there is little evidence of Episcopal services in Rowan County until the 1790s, when the colony emigrated from Maryland to western Rowan County and the Rev. Mr. Miller began his missionary work in the area. At this distance it remains unclear why so substantial a group of farmers in Maryland would make the decision to relocate to piedmont North Carolina and how they decided to settle on the lands, watered by

During George Washington's Southern Tour in 1791 he visited Salisbury and was entertained on his overnight stay, 30-31 May. According to long-held local tradition, a ball was held in the president's honor on the evening of May 30 at the Hughes Hotel. Mrs. Lewis Beard was among the guests listed by Dr. Rumple in his History as in attendance. The dress she is said to have worn to the ball descended in the family to her great-granddaughter Miss Mary Locke, and after her death it came to the Rowan Museum and is on display a the Utzman-Chambers House. In 1980 it was modeled in a museum-sponsored fashion show by Cameron Beard Hall, a collateral descendant of Mrs. Beard. John Steele (1765-1815), one of Salisbury's most prominent citizens was apparently away from Salisbury when the president visited, however, he was subsequently appointed Comptroller of the Treasury by the president in 1796 and served in that office until 1802. This watercolor on ivory miniature of John Steele, painted in 1797 by James Peale, is held by the descendant Mary Henderson Messinger, a communicant of St. Luke's, and reproduced with her permission.
Photograph by Charles Goldman

Withrow and Beaverdam creeks, in an area already settled by Scotch-Irish Presbyterians. Prominent in this group were members of the Barber, Chunn, Harrison, Alexander, Lightell, Reeves and Mills families, among others, and the Rev. Hatch Dent, an Episcopal minister ordained by Bishop Seabury in 1785. Following on Mr. Drage, the Rev. Mr. Dent became the second clergyman to establish residence in Rowan County, and like Mr.

Christ Church, Cleveland
Photograph by Jason Williams

Drage, he too soon departed the county and his large farm on Withrow Creek.[4] Tradition establishes the construction of a log church in the community centered between later-day Barber Junction and Cleveland; however, its date of erection is not known. It was in that building that Christ Church is said to have been organized about 1817.

Beginning with his ordination in 1794, the Rev. Robert Johnston Miller (1758-1834) emerges as a most interesting and engaging figure in the history of the Episcopal Church in Rowan County in the years leading up to the admission of Christ Church and St. Luke's into the Diocese of North Carolina. Born in Daldovie, Scotland to George and Margaret Bathier Miller, Mr. Miller was raised in the Episcopal Church of Scotland and attended a classical academy in Dundee. Said in his early years to have anticipated becoming a minister, Robert Miller changed courses in 1774 and immigrated to Boston, where a brother was successfully engaged in trade. During the American Revolution he became a patriot, enlisted, and served in the Continental Army until the surrender at Yorktown. At the end of the war, he apparently remained in Virginia and was to remain there into the mid 1780s. During this period Mr. Miller was attracted to the Methodist Church, and in 1784-85 he was a circuit rider on the Tar River Circuit. He left the Methodist Church after this brief experiment in 1785 and embraced the Episcopal Church.[5]

While his biographers do not explain the reasons prompting his removal to North Carolina, and Lincoln County, in about 1786, a visit to the area and observation of its abundant natural resources may have proved the attraction. When he made an acquaintance with "Gentleman" John Perkins (1733-1804), a wealthy planter then living on the west side of the Catawba River in what is now Catawba County, is not known either. Whatever the case, this friendship was critical to his fortunes as a citizen and minister. In 1752 the young John Perkins had served as a guide for Bishop Spangenberg in his search for lands to establish the Moravian settlement that became Salem. In these travels and others, he gained a wide appreciation for piedmont North Carolina. In subsequent years he would acquire significant tracts of its rich, well-watered and productive lands.

Robert Johnston Miller married John Perkins' eldest daughter, Mary (1762-1827), in 1787 and they first settled on a plantation near Lenoir, a gift from her father that they called Mary's Grove. In about 1792, Mr. Miller and his family relocated to Lincoln County to a community centered on White Haven Church. There he began a ministry that would soon embrace Rowan County. Mr. Miller quickly gained the friendship and respect of Lutheran ministers in the area. Inasmuch as there was no existing Episcopal Church or bishop in North Carolina, Mr. Miller received ordination from his fellow Lutheran brethren. On 20 May 1794, at St. John's Church, Cabarrus County, Mr. Miller was ordained by the Rev. Messrs. Adolph Nussmann, Johann Gottfried Arends, Arnold Roschen, Christopher Bernhardt and Carl August Gottlieb Storch. Robert Miller later recounted the background to his ordination in a letter to the Rev. Francis Lister Hawks.

> Their (the Lutherans) congregations, were at that time in a very declining state, and overrun by imposters assuming the ministerial office without any regular authority whatsoever. To remedy these evils they pressed me with the plea of necessity, to accept ordination from their hands, and mentioned that the Rev. Dr. Pilmour of Philadelphia, had done so in the time of the Revolutionary War. There is now, and was then, a considerable number of Presbyterian clergy in this section and the most of

During St. Luke's "lost years," when neither a parish nor an Episcopal church existed here, the congregations of two churches of German ancestry erected handsome stone buildings in eastern Rowan County which remain today the only two 18th Century stone churches in North Carolina. Members of Zion Lutheran Church (left), also called Organ Church, began their building in about 1792, saw its completion in 1795, and attended its consecration on Easter Sunday 1796. The construction of Grace Reformed Church (right), also called Lower Stone Church, is believed to have occurred simultaneously. A tablet above its south door cites 1795 as its completion date; however, the church was not dedicated until 1811.

Photographs by Jason Williams

Organ

Lower Stone

them with whom I had any intimacy recommended the same course, and the congregation earnestly requested me to accept of it, and that they would be perfectly satisfied with my ministrations. In short, as I thought then, and do think now, contrary to my own better sentiments, I consented to receive the ordination from them, not as a Lutheran minister, but as an Episcopalian.[6]

It was under these circumstances, reflecting the exigencies of the time and place and a unique, enlightened view, that the Rev. Robert Johnston Miller began a ministry and served several congregations until his long-sought ordination as a priest of the Episcopal Church in 1821. Within a day or so of his ordination, he set out for the Episcopal Convention in Tarboro.

The convention held in Tarboro in May 1794 reflected the culmination of the first, ill-fated attempt to organize the remnants of the Anglican Church in the state as the Episcopal Diocese of North Carolina. This effort was led principally by Charles Pettigrew (1744-1807), who had served as rector of St. Paul's Church, Edenton, and the Rev. Nathaniel Blount (ca. 1748-1816). The initiative followed on the first General Convention of the Protestant Episcopal Church in the United States held in New York in 1784; the consecration of the Rev.

Charles Pettigrew, who led the effort to formally organize the remnants of the pre-Revolutionary church in North Carolina into a diocese in the late 18th Century, was elected bishop in May 1794 but he was never consecrated in that office. His likeness was captured in this miniature painted in 1785 by W.J. Williams.
Reproduced by courtesy of the Frick Art Reference Library, New York

Samuel Seabury (1729-1796) as the first Bishop of the United States in the Episcopal Church of Scotland, in Aberdeen, on 14 November 1784; and the General Convention that met in Philadelphia in July 1789 when the constitution and canons of the church were adopted and a Book of Common Prayer was authorized.[7] The first North Carolina convention was held in Tarboro on 5 July 1790 and attended by Mr. Pettigrew, the Rev. James L. Wilson of Halifax, and two laymen. The quartet approved the constitution adopted in Philadelphia and conducted other church business then and at the second meeting in November 1790. Illness prevented Mr. Pettigrew from attending the convention, called for October 1791, that failed to attract a quorum to conduct business. Efforts at the next meeting held on 21 November 1793, were given over to planning a convention to be held in Tarboro in May 1794.[8]

FROM GENERATION TO GENERATION

The Tarboro Convention of 1794 was the largest and last such gathering of Episcopal clergymen and laymen in North Carolina until the convention of 1817 in New Bern, at which the Protestant Episcopal Church in North Carolina was organized. Charles Pettigrew presided over the gathering of seven clergyman and nine laymen, including the Rev. Mr. Miller. The convention accomplished its goal: a constitution was adopted, Charles Pettigrew was elected bishop, and delegates were elected to attend the General Convention in 1795 at which Mr. Pettigrew's consecration was expected to take place. A yellow fever epidemic in Norfolk prevented Mr. Pettigrew's travel to Philadelphia by ship, and none of the delegates from North Carolina attended the convention. Mr. Pettigrew likewise failed to attend the next General Convention; it was scheduled for 1798 in Philadelphia, but an outbreak of yellow fever forced its postponement to 1799. He did not attend that meeting and would remain bishop-elect of North Carolina until his death in 1807. Meanwhile, in the years since 1794 no diocesan convention had been held, enthusiasm spent could not be renewed, and the initiative to formally revive the church in North Carolina failed.[9]

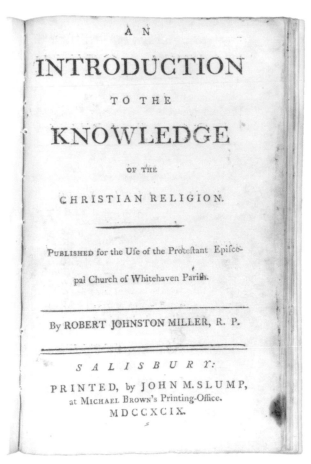

An Introduction to the Knowledge of the Christian Religion, *printed in 1799, is among the earliest works with a Salisbury imprint. Mr. Miller, its author, was the tireless minister to small groups of Episcopalians in the Piedmont, including the small band in Salisbury.*
Courtesy of the North Carolina State Archives

Nevertheless, the Rev. Mr. Miller continued his ministry at White Haven Church and served as a missionary to other small informal congregations of Episcopalians in the area. These included groups later known as St. Peter's and Smyrna churches in Lincoln County and St. Michael's in Iredell County. With the failed effort to formally organize the Protestant Episcopal Church in North Carolina, Mr. Miller could have felt little incentive to organize congregations; however, he preached and administered the rites of baptism, matrimony and burial. Scant evidence exists concerning his efforts in Salisbury; however, the Maryland colony in western Rowan County probably formed the largest single group of Episcopalians living as a community within his purview. The lack of prayer books and other religious publications in Rowan County had been lamented since the Colonial period, and in 1799 Mr. Miller attempted a remedy with a catechism printed in Salisbury, *An Introduction to the Knowledge of the Christian Religion.* [10]

In his essay, "Episcopacy in Rowan County," John Steele Henderson cited St. Michael's, Christ Church and St. Luke's as having "arose in some measure at least from Mr. Miller's labors amongst them for more than thirty years, before either parish was received into regular union with the Diocese."[11] He went on to recount his conversations on the subject with Miss Chrissie Beard "now in her eighty-second year—one of the most highly respected ladies of Salisbury."

Miss Chrissie Beard...says Mr. Miller also preached at a log church, about five miles above town, on the old Wilkesboro Road. This church was built for Mr. Miller by Mrs. Elizabeth Kelly, John Howard, and other neighbors; and Episcopal services were frequently held there. The same lady also says that she remembers perfectly well that her uncle, Lewis Beard, when she was a child, went to Charleston, and brought back with him a number of catechisms, which were eagerly sought for and highly prized by all the Episcopal families, who studied them attentively themselves, and made their children learn them. The introduction of these catechisms must have been some time about the year 1806.[12]

Mrs. Kelly, as will be seen later, would be one of the first thirteen communicants of St. Luke's upon confirmation by Bishop Ravenscroft in 1823.

Throughout his ministry, Mr. Miller never failed to appreciate the importance attached to his status as both the first man ordained in the Lutheran Church in North Carolina and the first English-speaking minister ordained among its clergy.[13] He thus exercised an effectiveness within the Lutheran Church enjoyed by few others until much later, and he particularly appealed to younger members of the German-speaking Lutheran settlements who were beginning to embrace the English language for everyday use. In May 1803 in Salisbury he joined with the Rev. Messrs. Johann Gottfried Arends, Carl A. G. Storch and Paul Henkel, together with several elders and deacons in the church, to form the North Carolina Synod of the Lutheran Church. Mr. Miller served as its first secretary (1803-05) and as president in 1812.[14] In 1811 and 1813 he undertook missionary journeys on behalf of the Lutheran Church into Virginia.[15] This work occurred after his return in 1806 to Mary's Grove in Burke County, where he organized St. Andrews Church and would reside until his death.[16]

In the winter of 1813-14, Mr. Miller began an association with the Rev. Adam Empie (1785-1860), rector of St. James Church, Wilmington, that presaged the organization of the Diocese in 1817. Having come to Wilmington late in 1811, Mr.

The Rev. Robert Johnston Miller died at Mary's Grove, his plantation near Lenoir in Caldwell County, on May 13, 1834. He was buried beside his wife Mary Perkins, the daughter of John Perkins, in the family cemetery on a knoll overlooking the plantation seat.

Photograph by Eliza Frazier Bishop, a descendant of Mr. Miller

FROM GENERATION TO GENERATION

Empie both energized and enlarged the congregation of St. James. He wrote to the Rev. Robert Johnston Miller of his hope for the Episcopal Church in North Carolina.

Wilmington, N.C. Novr. 22nd, 1813

Revd Sir

I have been in this State two years & I have endeavored by enquiry & by travelling about to ascertain what number of Episcopal Clergy this State contains(.) If a sufficient number could be found it is greatly to be wished that the Ch^h could be organized, placed under the superintendance of a *spiritual Head* & accede to the ecclesiastical Union that obtains in the other Sections of the U. States.

As I have lately understood that you are an Episcopalian & that you live somewhere in Burke Co. I take this means of learning whether my information be correct. Be good enough at any event to let me know whether you belong to the Episcopal order And if so whether you are in Priest's or only in Deacon's Orders—as well as the number of your Congregation the place of your residence & the prospects of your Ch^h(.) Inform me also if you know of any Episcopal Clergymen or Congregation in your part of the State & be assured that to hear from you freely & often will always give much pleasure to

Y^r Brother in Christ
A. Empie[17]

Unfortunately, Mr. Miller's response does not survive; it surely would have contained an account of the church in Rowan County. However its tenor can be discerned in a letter Mr. Empie wrote in return.

Wilmington, N.C. March 19th, 1814

Rev^d. & D^r. Sir

Your letter, which came to hand a few days ago, has given me much pleasure not because it brings me very welcome intelligence of an ecclesiastical nature, for from what you say the Ch^h. seems to be at almost its lowest point of declension, but because it speaks a language congenial to my heart, & breathes a spirit of piety of orthodoxy & religious zeal which I had almost despaired & which I greatly rejoice to find in this dark section of the Union. Your desire & solicitude, to see the Episcop. Ch^h. rise again from its ruins, are by me cordially reciprocated & I hope & pray that the period of her resurrection is not far distant.

But I regret that I cant flatter myself with the immediate prospect of effecting a change(.) Ever since my return from the back parts

Having come to Wilmington late in 1811, Mr. Empie both energized and enlarged the congregation of St. James. He wrote to the Rev. Robert Johnston Miller of his hope for the Episcopal Church in North Carolina.

I am rejoiced to hear that this State contains yet some remains of the good old Episcopal Church and am encouraged to hope that Zion here will soon raise up her drooping head.

of this state last fall I have been in such a wretched state of health that I have determined upon leaving this state & returning to my native climate New York. Perhaps however I may return to the Southward after the expiration of two three or four years And should nothing be done before that time I would again renew my exertions.

At present I know of but two Clergymen besides yourself Mr Hatch of Edenton & Mr G. Strebeck of Newbern At the same time I wrote to you I addressed letters also to Mr Micklejohn in Granville Co. Mr Burgess in Halifax Co. & Mr Gurrally of Murfreesburgh; but...I have recd no ansr from either of them,...[18]

As history reflects, Mr. Empie did return to Wilmington, in November 1816, and quickly set about efforts that would lead to the organizational convention of the Protestant Episcopal Church in North Carolina held in Christ Church, New Bern, in April 1817. Within the space of a few months, he was joined in North Carolina by two other Episcopal priests, Bethel Judd, who came first to St. James and on 1 May 1817 took up the pulpit of St. John's Church, Fayetteville; and Jehu Curtis Clay who became rector of Christ Church, New Bern, on 1 January 1817. the Rev. Mr. Clay hosted his Episcopal brethren, an assembly of the three priests and six laymen from the churches in New Bern, Fayetteville, Wilmington and Edenton, and on the 24th of April the Diocese of North Carolina was formed.[19]

At this distance the matter of Mr. Miller's absence from this first gathering of Episcopal clergy since the one he attended in 1794 begs understanding except, perhaps, for reasons of health and distance. Mr. Empie wrote again to his fellow clergyman at Mary's Grove.

Wilmington Jany 26. 1818

Dear Sir

My friend John Winslow Esq of Fayetteville, informs me that he has forwarded to you a copy of the minutes of our convention & one of our Missionary Circulars.—I am rejoiced to hear that this State contains yet some remains of the good old Episcopal Church and am encouraged to hope that Zion here will soon raise up her drooping head. The Lord of the harvest grant it in his own good time.

Our next convention will be held in Fayetteville, on the second thursday after Easter the 2nd. of April. I hope you will deem it expedient to use your influence to obtain contributions for the Missionary fund & to organize the Church in each of the Congregations, where you officiate; that each of them may send a delegate to our next convention; at which, I hope, you yourself will attend.—To be represented in, and in union with the Convention is very desirable on account of the Privileges attending it.—Those who are represented will have the advantage of regular visits from the Bishop of Virginia, who has taken the superintendance of the church in this State;...[20]

Robert Johnston Miller did not attend the diocesan conventions in 1818, 1819 and 1820; however, he had not relaxed his ministry on behalf of the Episcopal Church in Rowan County and the region. He had also followed Mr. Empie's encouragement and organized churches in the congregations where he had been officiating. Christ Church, forming the largest of his congregations, was admitted into union with the Diocese in 1821. In 1822, his White Haven and Smyrna churches in Lincoln County and St. Michael's in Iredell County were admitted into the Diocese. The fifth annual convention in Raleigh opened on Saturday, 28 April 1821, in the Supreme Court Room in the presence of the Rt. Rev. Richard Channing Moore, Bishop of Virginia. On Tuesday, 1 May, Robert Johnson Miller, at the age of 62, achieved his long held ambition when Bishop Moore ordained him deacon; that evening the bishop elevated him to the priesthood of the Episcopal Church. Allmand Hall, a lay delegate from Christ Church, accompanied Mr. Miller to Raleigh and witnessed the ceremonies held in Raleigh's Methodist church.[21]

The sixth diocesan convention was held again in Raleigh in the Supreme Court Room in April 1822. Mr. Miller attended and presented his report as rector of Christ Church, Rowan County. The Diocese's missionary society opened its report with an account of his work.

> The Rev. Mr. Miller, during the last summer and fall and the present spring, has laboured in several of the western counties, particularly those of Iredell, Lincoln and Rowan, in conjunction with Rev. Mr. Davis and the Rev. Mr. Wright. He administered the holy communion in different places, and reports from the several congregations, one hundred and twenty-two communicants. The Rev. Mr. Miller gives it as his opinion, that a favorable opening has been made in the above mentioned section of the state, and recommends the continuance of missionary labours in that field. He states with regret that accidental circumstances prevented any collections in behalf of the missionary fund; but thinks that if the mission can be continued for one or two years, it will then be supported by the contributions of the people. He asserts that the state of society is such in that part of our country, that it is by missionary labours alone that the people can obtain the preaching of the gospel and the administration of ordinances.[22]

Looking back on events of 180 years ago, we see the Diocese's decision to hold its seventh annual convention in Salisbury, the first one held west of Raleigh, was made in recognition of the Rev. Mr. Miller's sustained work on behalf of the Episcopal Church. It also acknowledged the fact that as of the Convention of 1822, five of the 17 churches admitted into union with the Diocese of North Carolina were situated in Rowan, Lincoln and Iredell counties; only two others, St. Jude's and St. Mary's churches in Orange County, were located west of Raleigh. The decision likewise reflected the promise that Mr. Miller and his fellow clergymen saw for an Episcopal church in Salisbury. The promise would be fulfilled.

ENDNOTES

1. SL, 15.

2. RM, III:1227.

3. Ibid, 1228.

4. HRC, 313.

5. John B. Weaver, "Robert Johnston Miller," DNCB, 4, 272-73. See sources cited by Mr. Weaver and *Life Sketches of Lutheran Ministers, North Carolina and Tennessee Synods, 1773-1965* (Columbia, SC, State Printing Company, 1966), 140. See also "The Ministry of the Reverend Robert Johnston Miller in North Carolina," an important unpublished typescript biography, by George MacLaren Brydon, in the Diocese of Virginia Papers, Virginia Historical Society, Richmond, VA. Hereinafter cited as Brydon. Mr. Brydon (1875-1963) was a long-time historiographer of the Diocese of Virginia.

6. Joseph Blount Cheshire, *Sketches of Church History in North Carolina*, North Carolina Collection, Wilson Library, University of North Carolina, Chapel Hill, NC. This volume is a compendium of articles published separately in a church organ. Mr. Brydon copied the text of the letter from a footnote to pages 17-18 of Mr. Cheshire's work; it appears on page 17 of his manuscript.

7. For the reorganization of the American Episcopal Church and the Convention of 1789, see James Thayer Addison, *The Episcopal Church in the United States, 1789-1931* (New York, Charles Scribner's Sons, 1951), 57-73.

8. ECNC, 79-81.

9. Ibid, 82-84.

10. *An Introduction to the Knowledge of the Christian Religion* was printed in Salisbury by John Martin Slump at Michael Brown's printing office. It is one of the earliest surviving Salisbury imprints. See SJLC, 81-82.

11. HRC, 306.

12. Ibid, 307.

13. Brydon, 23.

14. See SJLC, 91-96.

15. For an account of these missionary trips, see Brydon, 24-30.

16. Robert Johnston Miller was buried in the cemetery on his Mary's Grove Plantation where he had buried his wife in 1827. Mr. Miller's house has been lost; however, it was replaced on or near its site by an imposing stone house erected in the 1930s by his great-granddaughter Eleanor Boone Miller Rabb (18__-1949) who continued to call the farm and its new seat Mary's Grove. The house and its residual acreage remain the property of a descendant of Mr. Miller. Unfortunately, the cemetery passed out of family ownership; it is located on a knoll to the north of the house. For further information, see the National Register nomination for Mary's Grove prepared by this author, State Historic Preservation Office, Raleigh, NC.

17. D. L. Corbitt, ed., "The Robert J. Miller Letters, 1813-1831," *North Carolina Historic Review* XXV (October, 1948), p. 487. Hereinafter cited as Miller Letters. For Empie see Alice R. Cotton, "Adam Empie," in DNCB, 2, 157.

18. Miller Letters, 487-88.

19. ECNC, 96-97.

20. Miller Letters, 489.

21. JAC, 1821, 4, 8, 13-14.

22. JAC, 1822, 14-15.

Now located in the baptistry, this imposing window was originally installed above the altar in 1883. It was moved here in 1910 when the present altar and reredos were erected as a memorial to Dr. Murdoch. With the two windows in the side walls of the apse, it formed a suite with the Good Shepherd and the Four Evangelists as its theme. The center lancet, representing the Good Shepherd, is a memorial to the Rt. Rev. Thomas Atkinson (1807-1881), Bishop of North Carolina from 1853 until his death. The left lancet honors the Rt. Rev. Thomas Frederick Davis (1804-1871), a rector of St. Luke's, 1836-1846, who became bishop of South Carolina in 1853 and held the episcopate until his death. John Haywood Parker (1813-1858), who succeeded Mr. Davis at St. Luke's, is memorialized by the figure of St. John in the right lancet. In a departure from design tradition, the attributes of Evangelists are not featured in the windows; however, St. John can be identified as he alone of the group is usually depicted without a beard.   Photograph by Robert Bailey

CHAPTER 3

The Episcopal Church in North Carolina Renewed

St. Luke's Is Organized, a Church Is Built in Salisbury, and the Congregation Establishes Itself 1823–1860

In retrospect, the organization of St. Luke's Church, its admission to the Diocese of North Carolina in 1824, and the consecration of the congregation's brick church by Bishop Ravenscroft in 1828, reflect not simply the renewal of the Episcopal Church in Salisbury, but an important larger role in the flourishing religious life of the county seat in the 1820s and a unique relationship to the history of the Diocese of North Carolina. After a period of just over a half-century, from 1768 when John Lewis Beard conveyed a lot to the "Trustees of the German Lutheran Congregation in the Township of Salisbury" for the erection of a church, until the mid-1820s, Salisbury could boast of but one church building in its growing townscape. Mr. Beard allowed that the church, to be built for the "said German Lutheran congregation," could also accommodate "the High Church of England and...the Reformed Calvin ministers at such time as the said Lutheran minister doth not want to perform divine service in said church."[1] A log church, believed to have been built shortly after the conveyance by Mr. Beard, was replaced ca. 1820 by a frame church on the lot that survives today as the Old Lutheran Cemetery on North Lee Street. Its monuments record the graves of the earliest generations of Salisbury residents. By 1828, Salisbury could boast of three handsome churches, two of which were brick and built between 1826 and 1828, that bespoke its growing sophistication and wealth. Meanwhile, in 1823, the town of Salisbury hosted the seventh annual Convention of the Diocese of North Carolina, a landmark gathering at which the Rev. John Stark Ravenscroft of Mecklenburg County, Virginia, was elected Episcopal Bishop of North Carolina. Near the end of this remarkable decade, on 28 July 1828, Mr. Ravenscroft returned to Salisbury and consecrated the

By 1828, Salisbury could boast of three handsome churches, two of which were brick and built between 1826 and 1828, that bespoke its growing sophistication and wealth.

newly-built Gothic Revival church. In May 1829, the church and its rector, the Rev. Thomas Wright, hosted the Diocese's 13th Annual Convention. In the event, St. Luke's Church was not only the last church in his diocese consecrated by Bishop Ravenscroft, but it was here that he presided over the last gathering of his clergy and the Episcopal laity before his death on 5 March 1830.

The proceedings of the annual conventions of the Diocese of North Carolina were published yearly after each convention. The title page of the Journal of the Proceedings... *for 1823 indicates the meetings were held in "The Church at Salisbury."*
Photograph courtesy of
The North Carolina Collection

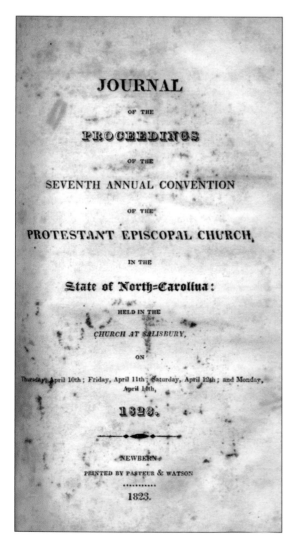

JOURNAL

OF THE

PROCEEDINGS

OF THE

SEVENTH ANNUAL CONVENTION

OF THE

PROTESTANT EPISCOPAL CHURCH,

IN THE

State of North-Carolina:

HELD IN THE

CHURCH AT SALISBURY,

ON

Thursday, April 10th; Friday, April 11th; Saturday, April 12th; and Monday, April 14th,

1823.

NEWBERN:
PRINTED BY PASTEUR & WATSON
·············
1823.

While St. Luke's, its ministers and communicants were destined to occupy important roles in the history of the Diocese in the 19th Century, it was not the first Episcopal church organized within the present boundaries of Rowan County. That place of honor belongs to Christ Church, Cleveland. In the later 19th Century, and as a part of the larger post-Revolutionary War migrations that brought new citizens into North Carolina, a colony of Episcopal families removed from Maryland to lands in western Rowan County. On its admission into the Diocese in 1821, Christ Church comprised the third largest congregation of Episcopalians in North Carolina.[2]

There can be little doubt but that this large community drew the increased attentions of the Rev. Mr. Miller to Rowan County, and that his presence—and theirs—affected the growing presence of Episcopalians in Salisbury. In turn, the existence of Christ Church and the promise of an Episcopal church in the county seat encouraged its designation as the site of the Diocese's seventh convention in 1823. Heretofore, diocesan conventions had been held successively in New Bern, Fayetteville, Wilmington, Edenton and Raleigh. The convention in Salisbury was the first one held west of the capital. The seventh annual convention of the Protestant Episcopal Church in the State of North Carolina was held 10-12 and 14 May in "The Church at Salisbury." By practice the convention was in recess on Sunday, the 13th. Seven of the state's nine Episcopal clergy were present as were 23 leading members of the church laity. This assembly, including wealthy planter Duncan Cameron (1773-1853) of Orange County and the honorable John Louis Taylor (1769-1829), chief justice of the North Carolina Supreme Court, also included John Cowan, Benjamin Lightell (1768-1843), and Samuel Fleming as delegates from Rowan County's Christ Church. The chief item of business at the convention was the election of the first bishop of the newly-organized diocese which had been under the care of Bishop Richard Channing Moore of Virginia. At nine o'clock in the evening of Saturday, 12 April, the convention reconvened after evening worship. Acting for the clergy, the Rev. William Mercer Green (1798-1887), rector of St. John's Church, Williamsboro, placed the name of the Rev. John Stark Ravenscroft (1772-1830), rector of St. James Church, Mecklenburg County, Virginia, before the body. He was unanimously approved by the clergy, and likewise in a subsequent vote by the laity. The matter of raising funds to support the episcopate also moved to resolution during the convention.[3]

On 15 April, Salisbury's *Western Carolinian* quickly reported Mr. Ravenscroft's election to the episcopate. Philo White, the editor, provided readers a fuller account of the convention a week later.

> Divine service was performed every morning and evening during the session of the Convention; and the secular business was transacted in the afternoon of each day.
>
> We generally attended the services each day, and were peculiarly gratified in witnessing the respectful deportment of the several crowded congregations which regularly overflowed the church before the hour of commencement, and the intense interest with which they listened to the many evangelical and excellent discourses which were delivered. To judge from our own limited observation, we think the church is fortunate in its selection of clergymen, who are generally a body of learned, pious, and zealous men, most of whom are in the prime of life; whose perseverance in pastoral labors has been instrumental, under divine Providence, in raising the church, within seven years, from an utterly desolate state, to bright hope and approaching prosperity....
>
> Though of a different persuasion from the Episcopal church, as Christians we cannot withhold our wishes for the success of their labors; for we are more fully convinced, the more we see of the world, that the true glory of a nation, as well as its temporal prosperity, is always promoted by the spread of Christianity and the diffusion of the sublime morality of the Gospel.
>
> Previous to adjournment, the Convention passed the following resolution, expressive of their sentiments towards the citizens of

John Stark Ravenscroft (1772-1830) was elected bishop of North Carolina in Salisbury in the evening of 12 April 1823 and consecrated in St. Paul's Church, Philadelphia, on 22 May of that year. This portrait of Bishop Ravenscroft, commissioned by Charles Peter Mallett of Fayetteville and painted by the distinguished Philadelphia portraitist Jacob Eichholtz (1776-1842) in 1830, was acquired by Aldert Smedes, the founding rector of St. Mary's School for Girls. The painting remains a prized possession of the school and continues to hang in its parlor.
Courtesy of St. Mary's School

Salisbury and its vicinity; to which we add our own testimony that the hospitality and kindly feelings shown to the members of the Convention was never more apparent on any occasion:

Resolved, That the thanks of this Convention be tendered to the citizens of Salisbury and its vicinity, for their kindness in extending to us the use of their Church during the present session, and for their hospitality to the members of the Convention.[4]

After receiving notification of his election from Mr. Green, bishop-elect Ravenscroft proceeded in mid-May to Philadelphia, where the General Convention was sitting, and was consecrated bishop of North Carolina on 22 May 1823 in St. Paul's Church.

Bishop Ravenscroft quickly moved to take up his duties in North Carolina, and in late June he began his visitations to the churches under his care. Within weeks, however, his schedule was interrupted and on 12 July in Raleigh he prepared a "Pastoral Letter" to the clergy and laity of the Diocese. The *Western Carolinian* printed the letter in its issue of 5 August. He concluded his epistle with practical matters.

Bishop Ravenscroft arrived in Salisbury in the late afternoon or early evening of Friday, 5 September 1823. He recounted his experience here in his report to the diocesan convention in May 1824 at Williamsboro.

Western Carolinian   *5 August 1823*

I shall fix myself in this City as early as I can get possession of the house which I have rented, which will be some time in the month of December next.—Direct, for the present, to Boydton, Mecklenburg county, Va. or to Salisbury, N.C. to be left till called for.

Your affectionate friend and pastor,
John S. Ravenscroft[5]

My next appoinment being at Lexington, I proceeded from Mr. Davis's for that place; where, on Friday the 5th, I performed divine service,…In the afternoon went on to Salisbury.

On Saturday evening divine service was performed by desire in the Court House, after which I preached on the subject of confirmation, many of the candidates for that rite being present.

According to previous notice, on Sunday the 7th, divine service was performed in the Church, both forenoon and afternoon, together with a sermon. After divine service in the forenoon, I administered the rite of confirmation to thirteen persons; and after sermon, administered the communion to about forty, of whom one-third were blacks. The Church was crowded with people; but I had no means of ascertaining what proportion considered themselves Episcopalians. To determine this as far as possible, I invited the members and friends of the Church to attend a meeting at Mrs. Beard's, on Monday evening; where I lectured from the 2d chap. of the Acts of the Apostles, and in conclusion, requested those who were disposed to unite in organizing an Episcopal Church in that place, to make themselves known; when twenty-one of the company present rose up, as a declaration of this intention. This number, with those necessarily absent, and others resident in the vicinity, whose sentiments are known, present a very favourable prospect. Hitherto, however, as far as I am informed, no efficient steps have been taken to organize, or provide a clergyman.

Being disappointed in the expectation I had entertained, to be here met by the Rev. Mr. Wright, and the Rev. Mr. Miller, to whom I had committed the arrangement of my official duties west and south of this point, I concluded to proceed, and to visit Christ's Church, in the neighbourhood of Salisbury.—On Wednesday the 10th, accordingly, I left Salisbury, and went on to Capt. Hall's. Here I was joined by the Rev. Mr. Wright, on Thursday morning, and went on with him to meet the congregation of Christ's Church, according to notice;...[6]

Bishop Ravencroft's
First Confirmands
7 September 1823

Mrs. Susannah Beard
Mrs. Eleanor Faust
Mrs. Mary Beard
Miss Christina Beard
Mrs. Elizabeth Kelly
Mrs. Moses Locke
Miss Camilla Torres
Miss Loretta Torres
Miss Margaret Burns
Miss Mary E. Hampton
Miss Anna Maria Kelly
Miss Mary Todd
Mrs. James Martin Jr.[7]

Bishop Ravencroft's five-day visit to Salisbury proved decisive in the effort to re-establish St. Luke's Church. The 13 persons confirmed by his hand at morning service on Sunday, 7 September 1823, would form the heart of the new congregation. All women, these first confirmands shared close ties of kinship and most were members of the Beard, Dunn and Kelly families whose progenitors had come to Rowan County in the colonial period.

Mrs. Susannah Beard (ca. 1760-1840) was the daughter of John Dunn, Esq. (ca. 1725-1783) and the widow of Lewis Beard (1755-1820). Mr. Beard, the son of John Lewis Beard (ca. 1715-1788), was one of Salisbury's wealthiest citizens in the early 19th Century and the builder of the famous toll bridge across the Yadkin River that was designed by Ithiel Town and erected by Samuel Lemly. She occupied a house in the east corner of West Innes and North Church streets, whose site is occupied by the former United States Post Office and Court House.[8] It was here that Bishop Ravenscroft presided over the Monday evening gathering to ascertain prospective members of a new church.

Mrs. Eleanor Faust (1755-1837) was the eldest daughter of John Dunn, Esq., the sister of Mrs. Beard, and the widow of Peter Faust (ca. 1753-ca. 1811). She was also a near neighbor of her sister, living in a house on the northwest side of Church Street that faced across the street onto the side of Mrs. Beard's residence. It stood behind the old Dunn family house that occupied the north corner of West Innes and North Church streets. The site of both is now the location of St. John's Lutheran Church.[9]

Mrs. Mary Faust Beard (1775-1850) was the eldest daughter of Peter and Eleanor Faust and the wife of John Beard Sr. (1767-1845), who was also a son of the patriarch John Lewis Beard. Between 1795 and 1820 she would give birth to a large family of a dozen children.

Miss Christina "Chrissie" Beard (1799-1887), the second daughter of John and Mary (Faust) Beard, was a member of St. Luke's Church for over 60 years. She kept a diary that remains a chief document in the antebellum history of St. Luke's and its parish life. The original diary, said to have been lost in a fire at Archibald Henderson's Chapel Hill residence, was known to many Salisbury residents, including Mr. Murdoch who compiled abstracts from it.

Mrs. Elizabeth Kelly (ca. 1779-1844) was a daughter of William Frohock of Halifax County, North Carolina, and the niece of John

This oil portrait of Mrs. Moses Alexander Locke is the only image of an original communicant of St. Luke's known to survive. The artist is not known.
Courtesy of the Rowan Museum, Incorporated

Frohock, the wealthy planter and miller whose mill, noted on the 1770 Collett map, stood on lands that were later owned by the honorable Spruce McCay (ca. 1755-1808) and in the early-20th Century were developed as Milford Hills. She was the wife of John Kelly (ca. 1750-1812) and the mother of Colonel William Frohock Kelly (1796-1848) of Davie County.

Mrs. Moses Locke was born Mary Beard (1785-1855), the eldest daughter of Lewis and Susannah Beard and the wife of Moses Alexander Locke (1784-1847), merchant and bank director in Salisbury. Mr. Locke was the descendant of prominent 18th Century Rowan County residents, being the son of William Locke (1756-1785) and Jane Alexander, and the grandson of General Matthew Locke (1730-1801), a member of the United States Congress (1793-1799), who is buried at Thyatira Church. Her son William Locke (ca. 1812-1862) was a vestryman at St. Luke's.

Camilla and Loretta Torres, the daughters of Benjamin Torres and Elizabeth Beard, were the granddaughters of Valentine Beard (ca. 1753-1793), the elder brother of Lewis Beard and a soldier in the Continental Army under George Washington, and his wife Margaret Marquedant of Philadelphia. Little is now known of their life after 1823.

Miss Margaret Burns (1808-1879) was the daughter of the late Dr. James Burns (ca. 1773-1818) of Philadelphia and his wife Maria Beard, a daughter of Valentine Beard. In 1828 she was married to her cousin Horace H. Beard (ca. 1807-1858); members of St. Luke's now bearing the Beard surname are descendants of this union.

Miss Mary E. Hampton (1801-1846) was the eldest daughter of John Hampton (ca. 1770-1814) and Leonora Faust (ca. 1785-1856), the granddaughter of Peter Faust, and the great-granddaughter of John Dunn, Esq. In November 1827, as St. Luke's was being built, she was married to Aaron Woolworth (1801-1856), a Massachusetts-born silversmith.

Miss Anna Maria Kelly (1800-1830) was a daughter of John and Elizabeth Kelly and the granddaughter of William Frohock. In December 1820 she married John Beard, junior. Following her death on 6 October 1830, her body was interred in the Lutheran Cemetery.

Miss Mary Todd (ca. 1755-1845) was a daughter of John Todd (ca. 1735-ca. 1798). She died on 31 December 1845; aside from giving her age as 90, her death notice in the *Carolina Watchman* on 2 January 1846 provided no real biographical information.

Mrs. James Martin Jr., was born Sarah Jane Alexander (1794-1864), the daughter of William Lee Alexander and Elizabeth Henderson, the sister of Archibald Henderson. In 1819 she married James Martin (1786-1845), an attorney and Superior Court judge. At the time of her confirmation the Martins were living in the handsome house on West Innes Street built by Lewis Utzman, a grandson of John Lewis Beard. In 1836 they removed to Mobile, Alabama where Judge Martin lost his fortune in a financial panic, died, and is buried. During the Civil War, Mrs. Martin departed Mobile and sought refuge in Charlotte, North Carolina, where she died on 29 April 1864. Her obituary in the *Carolina Watchman* on 9 May 1864 concludes with the paragraph at right.

Bishop Ravenscroft's meeting at Mrs. Beard's with "friends of the church…who were disposed to unite in organizing an Episcopal Church," held on Monday evening, 8 September 1823, marks the organization of St. Luke's Church. "When twenty-one of the company present rose up," and confirmed their commitment to the church, the bishop was reassured.[10] In the months leading up to the convention in 1824 both William Mercer Green and Robert Johnston Miller, who had ministered to Episcopalians in Rowan County for a quarter-century, returned to Salisbury and encouraged the new congregation. On 23 September the *Western Carolinian* advised its readers that Mr. Green, appointed "an agent to make collections for the Episcopal Funds of this Diocese" would preach in Salisbury on the 28th, between his appearance at Christ Church, Rowan, on the 25th, and St. Michael's Church, Iredell County, on the 30th. When making his parochial report at the 1824 Convention Mr. Miller listed the baptism of one adult and one child at St. Luke's and burial of two of its number.[11] Following the parochial reports, the certificates of organization for St. Luke's Church and Union Church, Waynesborough (Wayne County), were presented and the churches admitted into union with the Diocese of North Carolina. Dr. Lueco Mitchell, formerly a surgeon in the United States Navy and living in Salisbury with his wife, Jane C. Henderson, the daughter of Archibald Henderson, represented St. Luke's as a delegate to the convention.

> **Mrs. Martin was long a member of the Episcopal Church in Salisbury, and was one of its most zealous and munificent supporters. Her remains were brought to Salisbury and interred in the Lutheran grave-yard beside her six children. The last rites of sepulture were administered at the altar where she had often knelt in prayer, and after a life of wandering and of harsh vicissitude and much sorrow, she was followed to the grave by a few of the friends of her earlier and prosperous days who deeply lamented her loss.**

Some five months after its union with the Diocese, the congregation of St. Luke's Church was visited again by Bishop Ravenscroft. He departed Raleigh on 4 October 1824 "on a visit to the Churches in the western section of the Diocess (sic)" and reported his visit to the convention of 1825, when Dr. Stephen L. Ferrand was a delegate from St. Luke's Church.

From Lexington I proceeded through Salisbury, for Christ's Church, Rowan County, where I officiated on the 13th and 14th, and, though the weather was very bad, yet to good congregations. Here I was met by the Rev. Mr. Miller, who assisted me on the second day, when I administered the communion to thirty-eight persons.

My next appointment being at Salisbury, I returned thither from Christ's Church, and, after service by the Rev. Mr. Miller, I preached on the 16th; and on the 17th, being Sunday, I performed divine service, confirmed eight persons, preached, and administered the communion to sixteen communicants, assisted by the Rev. Mr. Miller. In the afternoon divine service was again performed; after which I preached a second time. The congregations respectable, both forenoon and afternoon.

On the 18th October I left Salisbury for Burke county, in company with Mr. Miller,...We reached Mr. Miller's hospitable mansion on the 21st;...[12]

Western Carolinian   *8 November 1825*

BISHOP RAVENSCROFT

Will pass thro' this place about the 9th or 10th instant on his way to Christ Church. He will preach here on the 26 & 27th. A meeting of the Vestry of this Church (St. Luke's) will be held on Thursday next, at the house of Doctor Ferrand, where the members and friends of the Church are respectfully requested to attend. *Nov. 5th*, 1825.

During the year the Rev. Thomas Wright, rector of Calvary Church, Wadesborough, also visited St. Luke's and reported the baptism of five persons.[13]

On 8 November 1825 the *Western Carolinian* announced Bishop Ravenscroft's next annual visitation to Salisbury.

The language of the Bishop's report to the 1826 convention reflects the success of the visit and the state of the young church.

On the 7th, I left Milton for Salisbury, where I arrived on the 10th, in time to attend a meeting of the vestry of St. Luke's Church, convened to ascertain the ability and inclination of the congregation to employ a clergyman. For some years past this congregation, together with that of Christ's Church, Rowan, have been altogether dependant on occasional and uncertain services, the injurious consequences of which were beginning to be very visible. As, however, there could be no doubt of their joint ability to maintain a clergyman, and it was hoped the inclination was not wanting, my main object was, to bring them to act with union and effect for this so essential a purpose. Having ascertained that St. Luke's Church was prepared to do their part, I left Salisbury for Christ's Church, where my appointments had previously been made, for the 12th and 13th days of the month; and having been joined by the Rev. Mr. Wright, divine service was performed by him, on the morning of the 12th; after the 2d lesson I baptized two children, and after service confirmed thirteen persons; I then preached a sermon, and afterwards baptised another infant.

After the services of the day were over, the vestry were convened, and readily came to the resolution to unite with St. Luke's Church, Salisbury, in calling and supporting a clergyman, and appointed a committee to arrange and conclude all necessary proceedings with the vestry of St. Luke's.[14]

After a visit to Wadesborough with Mr. Wright, the bishop was again in the county seat encouraging its new church.

Thomas Wright, who became rector of St. Luke's and Christ Church, Rowan County, in January 1826, oversaw the building and consecration of the parish's handsome brick church. He resigned the rectorate of both churches in 1832 and went to Memphis, Tennessee, where he organized Calvary Church and served as its rector until dying of cholera in 1835.
Photograph courtesy of Calvary Episcopal Church

On the 24th, I returned to Salisbury, and to my very great satisfaction found every thing properly arranged betwixt the vestries of Christ's Church and St. Luke's, and a call given to the Rev. Mr. Wright, who readily accepted it.

Nov. 26th, morning prayers were read by the Rev. Mr. Wright, during which I baptized one infant, and afterwards preached to a small congregation of attentive people.

Sunday, the 27th, I baptized two infants, after the service I confirmed one person, preached, and administered the holy communion to ten communicants.

In the evening divine service was performed by Mr. Wright, and a sermon preached by myself in the court-house, being more convenient to the inhabitants generally than the Church, which is situated at the extreme end of the town.

During my visit to this place, an interference in appointments took place, which gave me the opportunity to press upon the members of the Church the necessity, as well as the propriety, of providing a place of worship for themselves. And though the present building has been erected almost entirely at the expense of Episcopalians, yet as the ground was originally given for what is called a Free Church, and each denomination has an equal right

After the sum of $1,291 was subscribed for the new building and its construction commenced, disagreements arose, and some of the subscribers withheld their pledges.

to the use of it. I recommended to surrender it altogether, to submit to the loss, should the other denominations refuse a reasonable reimbursement, and rent some convenient place for present use, until they could provide the means of erecting a suitable building for themselves; and I have reason to believe that this, or such other course as will prevent all collision, will be pursued.

My next appointment being at St. Jude's, in the county of Orange, I took leave of the Rev. Mr. Wright and the brethren in Salisbury and its neighborhood,...[15]

The bishop's published mention of "an interference in appointments," and his statements concerning the construction of the church and the conditions of the gift of land by John Lewis Beard in 1768 prompted a response. In 1827 Philo White printed *A Misstatement in the "Episcopal Journal" of Bishop Ravenscroft Corrected* written by the elders (John Beard Sr. and George Vogler) and deacons (James Brown and Robert Mull) of the Lutheran Church in Salisbury. While the gentlemen did not address the matter of the "interference," they cited the text of the Beard deed granting the property to the "Trustees of the German Lutheran Congregation in the Township of Salisbury"..."for to erect and to build thereon a Church, or meeting-house, for the only proper use and behoof of the said German Lutheran Congregation, forever." And they printed the provision of the deed "that it shall be allowed by the approbation of the Minister, trustees, and elders of said congregation, that any lawful minister of the gospel of our Lord Jesus Christ, shall have liberty to preach in the said Church, if he can and do show a sufficient testimonial, in writing, either from the High Church of England, or from the reformed Calvin Ministers, at such time as the said Lutheran Ministers doth not want to perform divine service in said Church."[16]

The language of the deed is clear; however, the explanation of the circumstances under which funds were raised by subscription, begun ca. 1812-1813, and expended on the construction of a new building on the property reflect misunderstandings which arose at the time. After the sum of $1,291 was subscribed for the new building and its construction commenced, disagreements arose, and some of the subscribers withheld their pledges. The total cost of the building amounted to $1,605.57. "But Messrs. Locke and Allemong, merchants of this place, having, in some manner, become bound to the builders, they met the contract, and asserted a claim on the house for the sum paid by them over and above what the subscription had realized. These gentlemen made repeated efforts to obtain repayment of the sum advanced by them; but circumstances always prevented success. The matter continued unsettled; and, while thus unsettled, a part of the subscribers united with other individuals in forming a Presbyterian congregation in this place." Next Bishop Ravenscroft organized St. Luke's, and the members of the Lutheran Church "revived their ancient congregation." Within the space of a few years, Salisbury boasted three congregations. "This new state of things started the question, Who shall have the new church?"[17]

In retrospect, Bishop Ravenscroft's assertion that "the present building has been erected almost entirely at the expense of Episcopalians" probably derived from the fact that it was the "five persons attached to the Episcopalian church" who met and promptly paid their collective pledge of $350. This left the amount of $1,259.57 being owed to Messrs. Locke and Allemong. Mr. Locke was Moses Locke, whose wife Mary was one of the 13 original communicants of St. Luke's. Mr. Allemong, Henry Allemong, was associated with the Lutheran Church. Over time "other subscribers" paid $319 against that amount with $940.57 remaining outstanding and due to Messrs. Locke and Allemong, some years after the building was completed. The Lutheran congregation paid this sum, prior to printing their "correction" of the bishop's "misstatement."[18]

Meanwhile, the Rev. Thomas Wright (1780-1835) relocated to Salisbury in late December or early January. Taking charge of the Rowan County congregations in January 1826, he began service to St. Luke's as its first rector that would continue until 1832. At the opening of this period he reserved "five Sundays in the year" for the Wadesborough church. Having served as a missionary in western North Carolina, beginning in 1820, Mr. Wright proved to be an excellent advocate for the Episcopal Church in Salisbury during his stay, providing sustained guidance to the small, young congregation in its formative years, and overseeing the construction of its new brick church. Born in New York City, while his parents were there on a visit from Wilmington, he grew to manhood in Wilmington, where the family achieved wealth and respect in business and civic life. He attended the convention of 1820 in Edenton as a lay delegate from St. James Church and was admitted to the order of deacons on 30 April by Richard Channing Moore, bishop of Virginia, who then had oversight of North Carolina clergy. During 1820-1821 Mr. Wright served as a missionary in western North Carolina under the auspices of the Missionary Society and the Diocese. On 28 April 1822, Mr. Wright was ordained priest by Bishop Moore in St. James Church, Wilmington, and returned to Wadesborough where he served as rector of Calvary Church until accepting the invitation of the Rowan County churches. During this period he also ministered to the Rowan churches and others in the region, including St. David's, Cheraw, South Carolina. In 1810 he married Mary Hostler Green (1794-18__), the daughter of William Green and the sister of the Rev. William Mercer Green (1798-1887), who was likewise ordained deacon and priest by Bishop Moore in 1821 and 1823, respectively.[19]

Mr. Wright's kinship with Mr. Green and their close friendship as Episcopal clergymen proved important to the early fortunes of St. Luke's. After his ordination to the priesthood, Mr. Green went as rector to St.

Contract for a Church.

THE members and friends of the Episcopal Church, having determined to erect a Church in the town of Salisbury, and having appointed the undersigned a Committee for the purpose of contracting for and superintending the building of the same, they hereby give notice to all persons disposed to undertake, that they are ready to receive proposals and to enter into a contract for the whole or any part of the work. The walls are to be of brick: other particulars will be made known on application to either of the committee.

JOHN McCLELLAND,
STEPHEN L. FERRAND,
JOHN BEARD, jr.
EDWARD CRESS,
THOMAS CHAMBERS,
Committee.

42
December 20, 1826.

Gentlemen of St. Luke's published notice of a "Contract for a Church" in the Western Carolinian *on 26 December 1826 and in successive weekly issues of the newspaper through February 1827.*

Copy from microfilm courtesy of the North Carolina State Archives

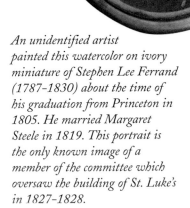

An unidentified artist painted this watercolor on ivory miniature of Stephen Lee Ferrand (1787-1830) about the time of his graduation from Princeton in 1805. He married Margaret Steele in 1819. This portrait is the only known image of a member of the committee which oversaw the building of St. Luke's in 1827-1828.

Courtesy of Mary Henderson Messinger

John's Church, Williamsborough, and assisted other churches in the area, including Emmanuel Church, Warrenton. In this role he organized St. Matthew's Church, Hillsborough, whose certificate of organization he presented to the 1825 convention for union with the Diocese. He resigned charge of St. John's and Emmanuel churches and in 1825 moved to Hillsborough to serve St. Matthew's. There he soon oversaw the building of an imposing Gothic Revival-style brick church erected by Samuel Han(d)cock with the assistance of John Berry (1798-1870), who would soon become Hillsborough's leading contractor/builder. The newly-completed St. Matthew's Church was the site of the 1826 Diocesan Convention and was consecrated on Sunday, 21 May, in the presence of the several clergymen attending the annual gathering.[20] Mr. Wright, who was among that number, had previously reported to his brethren that "Our prospects in the parish of St. Luke's, though not flattering, are as good, perhaps as ought to be expected under existing circumstances."[21]

The "prospects" of the Salisbury church indeed improved in the second half of 1826; grounds for the church were acquired and by the year's end a contractor for the new building was sought. The lot for the church came from an expected source, the Beard family. Although the deed would not be formally executed until 15 September 1827, "Lot number Eleven in the North Square" was set aside for this purpose by the executors of the late Lewis Beard. In 1770, when Claude Joseph Sauthier prepared his map of Salisbury, the lot was the property of George Cathey, enclosed, and probably used for pasture or garden. In 1772 the lot was put up at auction to satisfy Cathey's debts and bid in by William Steele at two pounds and two shillings. Forty years later, in 1812, Mr. Steele's son, John Steele, sold the lot for fifty pounds to Lewis Beard. It lay immediately northwest of lot No. 3 in the North Square, on which stood the Beard mansion and its several outbuildings. Moses Alexander Locke, Charles Fisher (1779-1849), and John Beard Jr., executors of Lewis Beard, conveyed the lot, on payment of $125, to John McClelland, James Martin, Stephen L. Ferrand, Thomas Chambers, Edward Yarborough and Edward Cress who comprised the vestry of St. Luke's.[22]

Meanwhile, on 26 December 1826, the *Western Carolinian* published a paid notice for the proposed church.

Contract for a Church

The members and friends of the Episcopal Church, having determined to erect a Church in the town of Salisbury, and having appointed the undersigned a Committee for the purpose of

contracting for and superintending the building of the same, they hereby give notice to all persons disposed to undertake, that they are ready to receive proposals and to enter into a contract for the whole or any part of the work. The walls are to be of brick; other particulars will be made known on application to either of the committee.

JOHN McCLELLAND,
STEPHEN L. FERRAND,
JOHN BEARD, jr.
EDWARD CRESS,
THOMAS CHAMBERS.

December 20, 1826   Committee.

The second published notice concerning the erection of St. Luke's Church was directed "To Brick Makers" and printed in the Western Carolinian *on 13 March 1827 and in the following successive weekly issues preceding the building committee's meeting to review proposals by 15 April.*
Copy from microfilm courtesy of the North Carolina State Archives

The notice ran in successive weekly issues of the *Western Carolinian* during the following two months, 2, 9, 16, 23, 30 January and 6, 13, 20, 27 February. Response to the advertisement, which was admittedly vague in detail, remains unknown. If the committee received proposals from contractors or builders, they decided against acceptance. Two weeks later, on 13 March, a different paid advertisement appeared in the pages of the *Western Carolinian*, seeking proposals from "Brick Makers, Owners of Saw-Mills, Shingle-Makers, and Mechanicks" to supply brick, lumber, shingles, etc., for "the Episcopal Church in Salisbury." The interested were also advised that "Proposals will likewise be received, for executing the brick-work, and carpenter's work, or for the whole building. Plans will be furnished the undertakers, as soon as the work is contracted for."

The advertisement was published in successive editions of the newspaper on 20 and 27 March and 3 and 10 April leading up to the 15 April committee meeting and the planned awarding of contract(s). Typical of such notices, it was to be printed in the *Greensborough Patriot* and the *Hillsborough Recorder* which would have gained the notice of Piedmont builders. The difference between the two advertisements to build was critical and assured response to the second notice. By 7 March 1827, when the text of the notice was composed, the committee had plans for their new building in hand and a very good understanding of the materials required. Although the omission of the building's dimensions appears curious now, the specific mention of 80,000 bricks was surely indicative of the approximate size of the church to the knowing contractor or mason.

To Brick Makers,

Owners of Saw-Mills, Shingle-Makers, and MECHANICKS.

PROPOSALS will be received by the committee for building the Episcopal Church in Salisbury, for the delivery of eighty thousand *Brick*, 9 inches long, 4½ inches wide, and 3 inches thick. Also, for a large quantity of pine and oak *Lumber*, consisting of scantling, flooring, and other plank of various descriptions. The brick to be all well moulded and well burned; no other will be received. The plank and scantling to be of good timber, sound and clear of knots. A distinct bill of the lumber will be furnished to the lowest bidder, so soon as he gives in his prices for the different kinds of stuff necessary for such a building. A quantity of shingles, 21 inches long and 4 inches wide, will also be contracted for. The proposals will be handed to Edwd. Cress, Esq. who will lay them before the rest of the committee for decision. The proposals will be decided on by the 15th of April next. Therefore, all persons wishing to contract for any of the above materials, must put in their terms before that period.

Proposals will likewise be received, for executing the brick-work, and carpenter's work, or for the whole building. Plans will be furnished the undertaker or undertakers, as soon as the work is contracted for.

JOHN M'CLELLAND,
STEPHEN L. FERRAND,
JOHN BEARD, Jr.
EDWARD CRESS,
THOMAS CHAMBERS,
Committee.

5t57
March 7th, 1827.

☞ The Greensborough Patriot, and Hillsborough Recorder, will publish the above three times, and send their bills to this Office.

Before advancing to its construction, however, some further mention should be made of the men who composed the building committee and vestry of St. Luke's. Four of these gentlemen were members of both bodies: John McClelland, Stephen L. Ferrand, Thomas Chambers and Edward Cress. John McClelland was a man of affairs in Salisbury and a founder of the Salisbury Jockey Club. Dr. Stephen L. Ferrand (1787-1830), a native of Swansboro, North Carolina, married Margaret Steele (____-1824), the daughter of John Steele (1764-1815), the wealthy planter who served as United States Comptroller of the Treasury under Presidents Washington, Adams and Jefferson. Miss Steele was the granddaughter of William Steele and Elizabeth Maxwell, Salisbury's first, now legendary businesswoman. Dr. Ferrand and his family were then occupying John Steele's handsomely finished and furnished plantation seat at Lombardy to the north of Salisbury. According to long-held tradition, the bricks for St. Luke's Church were made on the Lombardy plantation.

In "Episcopacy in Rowan," an essay by John Steele Henderson published in Dr. Rumple's A History of Rowan County, North Carolina, Mr. Henderson wrote "Mrs. Mary N. Steele, widow of Gen. John Steele, gave the ground to make the bricks, and burned them." Mrs. Steele, Mr. Henderson's great-grandmother, lived at Lombardy (pictured above). Photograph courtesy of Edward H. Clement

According to family tradition this watercolor on ivory miniature of Mary Nesfield Steele (1762-1840) was painted in New York about 1791 by an unidentified artist. Mrs. Steele's descendants have remained valued members of St. Luke's to the present. Courtesy of Mary Henderson Messinger

Thomas Chambers (ca. 1796-1826) was a member of the wealthy and influential Chambers family, which is more often associated with the Presbyterian Church. Edward Cress (1804-1838) was a prominent Salisbury merchant and nephew of the very wealthy bachelor merchant Daniel Cress. John Beard Jr. (1797-1876), the fifth member of the building committee, was the youngest son of Lewis and Susannah Beard. He married Anna Marie Kelly (1800-1830) and after her death removed to Florida where he died. The two additional members of the vestry in 1827 were James Martin and Edward Yarborough. Mr. Martin was a judge of Superior Court, Salisbury District, whose wife was among the 13 Salisbury residents confirmed by Bishop Ravenscroft in 1823. Colonel Edward Marshall Yarborough was married in 1823 to Rebecca Long (d. 1827), the daughter of Alexander Long. His father, Captain Edward Yarborough, was host to George Washington when the first president visited Salisbury on 30-31 May 1791. His house stood in the 100 block of North Main Street on the site now occupied by the Washington Building. Colonel Yarborough later moved to Raleigh, where he built and operated the Yarborough House hotel, a landmark in the capital until it burned in 1928.

In May 1827 when the Diocesan Convention met at Christ's Church, New Bern, Mr. Wright reported on his Rowan County parish.

"A commodious building, now ready for consecration, has been erected by the brethren of Christ's Church; and the congregation of St. Luke's, are making arrangements to rear a house of worship in Salisbury, on a lot of ground presented by Major Beard."[23]

Bishop Ravenscroft came to Rowan County two months later and consecrated Christ Church on 29 July 1827, with the assistance of Mr. Wright, Parson Miller and Mr. Green of Hillsborough.

The church building erected in 1827-1828 in Salisbury would bear a remarkable, nearly identical resemblance to St. Matthew's Church in Hillsborough, and the shared appearance of the two buildings was in no way coincidental. St. Matthew's Church is a rectangular gable-front brick building with elevations rising from a fieldstone foundation and laid up in Flemish bond. Attention was focused on the façade, where the central entrance was flanked by tall lancet-arch openings fitted with paired 25-over-25 sash windows below multi-pane transoms. These openings were set in recessed panels, defined by a disappearing stringcourse, and flanked by tall, narrow, blind lancet-arch panels set at the outer edges of the elevation. The symmetrical side elevations were each fitted with corresponding window openings. Through a repetition of motives, symmetry and proportion—and well-executed Flemish-bond brickwork—St. Matthew's Church stood proud and apart in the landscape of the Orange County seat. The church's appearance pleased Mr. Green and his congregation. It also pleased the rector of St. Luke's.[24]

St. Luke's Church, completed in spring 1828 and consecrated on 27 July of that year, is believed to have stood unaltered for some 54 years, until 1882, when Mr. Murdoch's program of improvements added a recessed chancel to the northwest gable end. The earliest known surviving image of St. Luke's Church, dating to ca. 1885-1890, shows the diminutive building enshrouded in English ivy, which covered the upper half of the southwest side. Even so, the similarities to St. Matthew's are

The plan of St. Matthew's Church, Hillsborough, was adopted by the building committee of St. Luke's. This turn-of-the-century view of St. Matthew's, which was consecrated on 21 May 1826, shows the entrance/bell tower that was added to the façade relatively soon after its construction. The lancet-arch brickwork is consistent on the two buildings. Undated, ca. 1900 photograph by an unidentified photographer, courtesy of The North Carolina Collection

obvious. The recessed lancet-arch panels framing the front elevation are in place, repeating the motif seen at St. Matthew's, as do the like window openings, four of which are visible. These contain 20-over-20 sash, of apparently equal height, below a multi-pane transom. The openings are fitted with granite sills, whereas those at St. Matthew's are wood. Handsomely laid Flemish-bond brickwork testifies to the skill of its mason(s). The signal difference in the surviving documentary views of the two churches is that the original frontispiece framing the doorway, itself embellished with blind recessed panels and surely an original feature at St. Matthew's, is visible and intact here at St. Luke's. That image is not recorded at St. Matthew's. In 1829-1830 brickmasons erected a two-stage brick tower, containing a narthex at its base, and a belfry onto the façade of the Hillsborough church. But doing so, they replicated the pair of tall narrow panels flanking the double-leaf doorway, reset it in a recessed rectangular field, and added a third, blind lancet-arch panel in the upper level above the entrance. Moving beyond the façades of the churches, the one important difference in the actual construction of the two buildings, and one which renders St. Luke's the more elegant church, is the use of recessed fields on the side elevations in which the three symmetrical windows are centered.

This key, now in the collection of the Rowan Museum, has long been said to be the key to St. Luke's Church.
Courtesy of the Rowan Museum, Incorporated

In his essay, "Episcopacy in Rowan County," published in 1881 in Dr. Rumple's *A History of Rowan County, North Carolina*, John Steele Henderson (1846-1916) cited the Rev. Francis Lister Hawks as the architect of St. Luke's Church and John Berry as its contractor and builder.[25] Mr. Henderson did not identify the source of these attributions; however, coming just over 50 years after the building was completed and from the pen of a life-long member of St. Luke's, and the descendant and kinsman of several of its earliest members, they can be considered reliable. Mr. Henderson, like Dr. Rumple, had the advantage of a long residency in Salisbury and the opportunity to talk with many of those who figured in the history of the city and Rowan County and who formed the subject of a landmark book that contained "Sketches of Prominent Families and Distinguished Men." While Dr. Rumple (1827-1906) had come to Salisbury in 1860 as pastor of the Presbyterian Church, Mr. Henderson was the son of Archibald and Mary Ferrand Henderson, and the grandson of Archibald Henderson (1768-1822) and Dr. Stephen L. Ferrand, who served on the building committee for the church.

While attributing the design of St. Luke's to Mr. Hawks, Mr. Henderson side-stepped the issue of the church's obvious debt to the earlier-built church in Hillsborough. If, as we believe, Mr. Hawks designed St. Luke's, he was actually the *architect* of St. Matthew's Church,

Hillsborough. When St. Matthew's was built, Mr. Hawks (1798-1866) was a member of the church and its senior warden. Over the course of a much varied life, beginning with his birth in New Bern as the grandson of John Hawks (1731-1790), the supervising architect of Tryon Palace, he had a distinguished career as an Episcopal clergyman, educator and historian. At the time St. Matthew's was built, he was an attorney and a reporter for the North Carolina Supreme Court. In 1826 he gave up law and began study for the ministry, reading theology with Mr. Green, rector of St. Matthew's. Ordained deacon in 1827 and priest soon after, he served churches in Connecticut, Philadelphia, New York, New Orleans and Maryland. Following his death in New York, he was buried from Calvary Church where he had earlier served as rector.[26]

An evident intellectual preciosity was captured in this portrait of Francis Lister Hawks (1798-1866) painted in 1838 by New York artist Henry Inman (1801-1846). Hawks, the designer of St. Luke's, graduated in 1815 from the University of North Carolina, where the Dialectic and Philanthropic Societies Foundation, Inc., holds this painting.
Courtesy of The North Carolina Collection

As built, St. Matthew's Church also enjoyed the attention of William Nichols (ca. 1777-1853), then State Architect of North Carolina. Born in Bath, England, Mr. Nichols came to the United States in 1800, and produced distinguished buildings for clients principally in New Bern and Edenton, including Hayes Plantation, before coming to Raleigh. There he was architect for the remodeling of the State House (1820-1824) and designed the (now lost) Christ Church, Raleigh, among other private and institutional commissions. His association with St. Matthew's came through Duncan Cameron, one of the state's wealthiest planters, whose vast plantation, Fairntosh, was northeast of Hillsborough. On 14 February 1825, Walker Anderson, a nephew of Mr. Cameron, wrote to his uncle from Hillsborough, adding the following postscript:

> **Mr. Nichols has made a farther alteration in the plan of our church, making it 35 x 45 feet, saying that a less width would not be proportionate to the length.**[27]

Existing evidence cannot document the design of St. Matthew's Church entirely to either Mr. Hawks or Mr. Nichols. However, given its appearance and the character of its design relative to the sophisticated work Mr. Nichols was producing elsewhere, together with Mr. Henderson's attribution of St. Luke's to Mr. Hawks, the likely scenario is that Francis Lister Hawks, a talented dilettante, produced a plan for the church that was reviewed and revised by Mr. Nichols as a courtesy. Whatever the case, had William Nichols originally produced the plan for

St. Matthew's, he would not have made so elemental a mistake as faulty proportions in the floor plan of a one-room building.

There is further circumstantial evidence indicating a secondary, advisory role in the design process to Mr. Nichols. In addition to his work as the designer of buildings, William Nichols also produced designs for funerary monuments. Two by his hand stand in Rowan County cemeteries. His memorial to Judge Francis Locke (1766-1823) stands in the cemetery at Thyatira Church. The very handsome Greek Revival-style monument to Archibald Henderson (1768-1822), the most distinguished memorial standing in the Old Lutheran Cemetery, also bears Nichols' signature as designer and was created in 1825 by a Philadelphia marble yard. Archibald Henderson was the grandfather of John Steele Henderson. Given William Nichols' fame and the fact that he had designed the grave marker for the younger Mr. Henderson's grandfather, there is every reason to believe he would have credited him as architect of St Luke's (and St. Matthew's) had that been the fact. Further, on 24 April 1827, as the building committee was considering letting the contract for St. Luke's, the *Western Carolinian* carried a small notice in its pages:

> **Mr. Nichols, late Architect of this state, has been appointed, by the Governor of Alabama, Architect and superintendent of the public buildings of that state.... Mr. Nichols passed through this place last week, on his way to Alabama.**

Had William Nichols had an association with St. Luke's, then about to be built, we believe the editor of the newspaper might well have made some reference to same in print.[28]

Another letter from the hand of Walker Anderson also confirms the builder of St. Matthew's Church, Hillsborough, and the eventual link with John Berry and St. Luke's Church. On a Saturday evening in March 1825 he wrote to Judge Thomas Ruffin, an influential member of St. Matthew's.

> **My dear Sir,**
>
> **Understanding from Mr. Hawks, that you expect to leave town in the morning with the expectation of being absent a fortnight, I must trouble you, tho on the Sabbath, with a little matter of business. Handcock, who contracts for the building of our church, is anxious to know the precise spot, where the building is to be placed, so that in hauling his brick, he may have them laid in the most advantageous situation. I wish that you could be with us in selecting the spot,...[29]**

At present details of the life and career of Samuel Han(d)cock remain obscure. In 1870 when John Berry died, his obituary stated that he was apprenticed to the trade of brickmason. Whether he was formally apprenticed or simply worked in the hire of Samuel Han(d)cock in the 1810s remains unconfirmed, although examined by several scholars. Documents indicate that by about 1821 the two men had a business partnership, and erected the Eagle Lodge in Hillsborough together. Soon, apparently by the mid 1820s, John Berry was contracting for work in his own name. John Berry surely worked with Mr. Hancock on St. Matthew's Church, and carried those skills to his work, documented in Mr. Henderson's statement, at St. Luke's. And those skills as a brickmason are clearly evident in the beautiful Flemish-bond brickwork of this church. John Berry had an important career as a builder, erecting private houses and public buildings in the Piedmont. Among the surviving landmarks he built are the Orange County Court House of 1845, in Hillsborough; and Smith Hall (later Playmakers Theater) at the University of North Carolina, that he erected in 1850-1852 to the designs of Alexander Jackson Davis.[30]

John Berry (1798-1870), the builder of St. Luke's, appears in advanced age with his wife Elizabeth Vincent in this daguerreotype of ca. 1860.
Courtesy of The North Carolina Collection

At the 1828 Diocesan Convention, held at St. John's Church, Fayetteville, Bishop Ravenscroft and Mr. Wright both offered remarks on the circumstances of St. Luke's. In his summary of annual visitations and the state of the church, the bishop gave voice to concerns which affected the church in general.

No change in the condition of the congregations which were visited during the Summer, requiring notice, presented itself. A difficulty was felt, at the period of this visit, as to the ability of St. Luke's Church, Salisbury, and Christ's Church, Rowan, to continue the stipulated salary to their Pastor, under the present pecuniary pressure, which threatened the loss of his valuable services to them, and to the Diocess (sic). This difficulty, however, was happily surmounted for the present, by a new arrangement of the mode of contribution, and by most praiseworthy self denial on the part of the Rev. Mr. Wright, their Pastor. On this always delicate subject to a clergyman, the respective Vestries listened to my representations with attention; and the hope is entertained, that a more close consideration of the serious detriment it will be to all their prospects of religious advancement, and the complete sacrifice it will occasion of the sums expended in erecting their respective places of worship (that in Salisbury being a spacious and handsome brick building,

then covered in, and now nearly finished), together with a more correct and enlarged view of the bounden duty of all Christian people, to provide for the support of religion through its Ministers, will keep the two congregations united, and their present Pastor occupied with, and useful and comfortable in his present charge.[31]

Mr. Wright's parochial report appears colored with the effects of his "most praiseworthy self denial."

> The situation and prospects of the parish have not materially improved since my last report. Little, indeed, of religious concern is apparent, and there is in general a neglect of the holy obligations of the Christian profession. Yet I am not without hope, in some instances, that the God of all grace hath confirmed and strengthened believers in their faith, and that he will ere long add to the number. Our house of prayer will be ready for consecration whenever the Bishop and some other of the Clergy can visit us.
>
> The ladies of the congregation having formed themselves into a Society to procure funds for religious purposes, have made to the Church several valuable presents.
>
> I have relinquished the charge of Christ's Church, and I fear that there is little prospect of obtaining a Minister soon.[32]

The formation of a ladies society at St. Luke's in 1828 followed the pattern seen at other churches in the Diocese and in the Presbyterian denomination as well. Providing charity in the community, these associations were sometimes called "working societies," often held bazaars to raise money, and purchased furnishings that enhanced the comfort and appearance of the church and its worship. One of the final actions at the convention was the decision to hold the 1829 convention at St. Luke's.

The bishop and rector lost no time arranging for the consecration of St. Luke's. Both the *Western Carolinian* and Salisbury's new newspaper, the *Yadkin and Catawba Journal* published by Lemuel Bingham, printed notices in their 22 July 1828 editions announcing the scheduled consecration service on Sunday, 27 July.

Said to date to 1894, this earliest known surviving image of St. Luke's shows the front elevation and the side overlooking Council Street as built. The lancet-arch window openings retain their multi-pane sash like those of St. Matthew's Church.
Courtesy of the Rowan Museum, Incorporated

The notice also informed readers "The pews in the church will be disposed of (at the church) after divine service on Saturday, the 26th, when and where the Vestry will attend and make known the terms." In his manuscript "Episcopal Journal," Bishop Ravenscroft noted "The occasion drew forth a large assemblage of people."[33]

The 13th Annual Convention of the Protestant Episcopal Church in the State of North Carolina opened in Salisbury on Saturday, 23 May 1829. On Sunday, the 24th, the bishop ordained Philip B. Wiley to the priesthood. With the self-described state of his health "greatly impaired," the Salisbury Convention would prove to be the last he would attend in his diocese. John Stark Ravenscroft died on 5 March 1830 in Raleigh, where he was buried in the chancel of Christ Church. His recount of his visitation to St. Luke's in July 1828 appears in the text of his annual address to the convention.

> In Salisbury, the consecration of the building in which we are assembled, and in the performance of which duty I was assisted by the Rev. Mr. Green, Mr. Wiley, Mr. Norment, and the pastor of the congregation, the Rev. Mr. Wright—formed an object of much interest to some and of curiosity to more. The services were consequently well attended, but no visible change appears to have taken place in the congregation. The friends of the church, and of whom we are desirous to hope the best have exerted themselves to erect a house of prayer and sacred offices. But there is not as yet a single male communicant added to the church; and great fear is entertained, that their means of maintaining a clergyman will fail through the unwillingness of the members of Christ's Church, Rowan, to contribute their fair and reasonable proportion of his salary, for an equal portion of his time.
>
> With this last named congregation, the second in number of communicants in the diocese (sic), I spent several days, previous to that of my regular appointment for them, in going from house to house, endeavouring to prevail with them, to continue their union with the congregation in Salisbury, upon its original footing, and thereby secure to themselves and their families, the regular ministrations of the church. My endeavours, however, were fruitless; and this large and important and able congregation, are as sheep without a shepherd—exposed to be scattered and torn by enemies from without, or to melt away, into the indifference and apathy of an uncertain faith, and an unsettled profession.[34]

Despite the fact that there were no male communicants of St. Luke's, four gentlemen of the church appeared as lay delegates to the convention: the Hon. James Martin, Romulus M. Saunders, Edward Yarborough and John Beard Jr.

A like note of pessimism pervaded Mr. Wright's parochial report except for the generous words he lavished on the St. Luke's Female Episcopal Society.

> The present state of the congregation, is by no means flattering, and there is little hope of immediate improvement; as fears are entertained by some of the Vestry, that they cannot maintain a clergyman, even with the aid of Christ's church. Perhaps an unmarried man, who could combine secular with clerical duties, or, who would divide his time between the two churches of Rowan, and the congregation, at Wadesborough, might be supported: and I know not any portion of our country which stands, in greater need of ministerial services. Where there is so little cause of rejoicing, it is gratifying to be able to state, that the few members of the Female Episcopal Society, have wrought diligently, and by the sale of a variety of articles, and from some small donations by liberal gentlemen, they have been enabled to defray the expense of painting the church and procuring cushions, &c. for the pulpit, reading desks, and altar. There is reason to hope, too, that several of this society will soon kneel at the altar which they have contributed outwardly to adorn. By the exertions, chiefly, of one lady, $85 have been presented for the purpose of purchasing a bell.[35]

Despite his earlier announcement that he had given up charge of Christ Church, Rowan, Mr. Wright nevertheless continued to hold services at the county church and also at Calvary Church, Wadesborough, when possible. His frustration with the financial contributions of Christ Church are put in perspective when its reported 70 communicants in 1829 are compared with but 15 at St. Luke's. Mr. Wright also reported six baptisms and two burials for St. Luke's. A year later, in 1830, the situation had not materially changed; the number of communicants at each church remained the same. While resident in Salisbury he continued to hold services at Christ and Calvary churches. Mr. Wright concluded his parochial report, noting that "Societies, auxiliary to the Missionary, Bible, Prayer Book and Tract Society of the Diocess (sic), have been formed in each of my Parishes, and in St. Luke's the Ladies of the Working Society are plying their needles with renewed diligence."[36]

As Blackwell P. Robinson, an Episcopal church historian, has noted, the death of Bishop Ravenscroft on 5 March 1830 "was a deep loss to the Diocese of North Carolina."[37] Held in high esteem by the clergy and laity alike, and a warm personal friend to many throughout the Diocese, he was a figure well-suited to his calling. Bishop Ravenscroft died without surviving issue; in his will he bequeathed personal items and objects employed in his role as clergyman and bishop to friends. "My Spectacles with divided Glasses, my Silver Pencil Case, with my Silver Mounted

Tortoiseshell Snuff Box, I give to the Revd. Thomas Wright, Rector of St. Luke's Church, Salisbury."[38] Bishop Ravenscroft's influence on the fortunes of the Episcopal Church in North Carolina, in the first critical years of its organization and youthful growth, cannot be overestimated nor overstated. The future of the church in North Carolina and the consideration of his possible successor had been principal points of discussion when 10 of the state's Episcopal clergy, including Mr. Wright, convened at St. James Church, Wilmington, in May 1830. It remained at the forefront of conversation through the following year, up to the 15th Annual Convention in Raleigh, when on 21 May 1831 the Rev. Levi Silliman Ives was nominated and elected as the church's second bishop. Mr. Ives (1797-1867), the son-in-law of John Henry Hobart, Bishop of New York, was then serving as rector of St. Luke's Church, New York.

St. Luke's Church also figured in the events surrounding the selection of the Diocese's second bishop, but this time in the person of its rector. In both 1830 and 1831 Mr. Wright was elected a delegate to the General Convention. Following Mr. Ives' election, Mr. Wright and Walker Anderson, a leading Episcopal layman in North Carolina and the nephew of Duncan Cameron, traveled to New York to advise Mr. Ives of his election to the episcopate.

On 13 June 1831 Mr. Wright wrote to his wife in Salisbury.

Mr. Anderson & myself have dined with Mr. Ives and the Profs. of the Theological Seminary…I am more pleased with him than I expected to be. He is very learned, but very modest, or rather very diffident & not morose, as I had been told. He is also very charitable, & several of his fe(male) relatives live with him and are supported by him.…

We have visited the Museum…& traveled the city in every direction, & I often wished to have you all by my side particularly when taking an evening ramble through Broadway. The houses & most of the stores are lighted with gas, in every variety of shape.…

Mrs. Ives is…remarkably plain in person…however I am told intelligent & amicable, & I hope the Sisters of Nʳ. Carᵃ. will make her forget if possible her friends here or rather not lament her separation from them.

The Rt. Rev. Levi Silliman Ives, the second bishop of North Carolina, was painted in 1845 by James Hart in the act of confirming four students of St. Mary's School for Girls in Raleigh. The Raleigh Register *carried an account of the painting in its 2 May 1845 issue.*

"This splendid painting is intended, we learn, to grace the spacious Hall at St. Mary's School—a room well calculated to develop and set off all its beauties and excellencies. It was painted expressly for the esteemed Rector, Mr. Smedes, who desiring in some way to express and perpetuate a sense of his own and the Church's obligation to the Bishop for his constant and unremitted care of this valuable institution, happily thought of this mode."

The Bishop will visit Salisb^y ___ in Novr or Dec^r & probably I may accompany him.

Kiss the children from the least to the largest and may God bless you all. Yr affect Husband. Thos Wright.[39]

Messrs. Wright and Anderson returned to North Carolina. Mr. Ives was consecrated bishop on 22 September 1831 at Trinity Church, Southwark, Philadelphia, and arrived in North Carolina in the autumn. Bishop Ives came to St. Luke's on Saturday, 12 November.

On Thursday, the 10th, I left Pittsborough in company with Mr. Hardin of that place, for Salisbury, by whose kind attentions I was enabled to arrive at the latter place, after a good deal of detention and fatigue, sufficiently early to meet my appointment on Saturday, the 12th.

On that day, I preached to a few persons in St. Luke's, both morning and at night; the Rev. Mr. Wright performing the services. The next day being Sunday, I was gratified to find the Church crowded with an attentive audience; to whom I preached twice, administering the holy Communion in the morning to _____ persons, and Confirmation at night, to 6 persons; the Rev. Mr. Wright assisting me in the services. The faithful and self-denying labors of this Clergyman have, I regret to say, in this Parish, been very inadequately repaid. Recent information, however, from the Congregation, encourages the hope that a better state of things will soon be realised.

On Monday, the 14th, I set out in company with Rev. Mr. Wright, to fulfil my appointment at Christ's Church, Rowan; but remained that night at a Mrs. Hall's on the way, where I performed service, and preached to a number of the neighbors who had assembled to hear the word of life.

The next day I proceeded to Christ's Church, where, after service by the Rev. Mr. Wright, and a sermon by myself, I confirmed 3 persons, and administered the holy Communion to upwards of 60.

This Congregation, as to its spiritual state, seems to be prosperous. It would, however, afford me great pleasure on my next visitation, to find that they had finished their commodious Church, and added a Vestry-room, which, from the secluded situation, is very much needed.[40]

Bishop Ives returned to Salisbury with Mr. Wright, presumably enjoyed his hospitality, and again held services and baptized an adult. He departed the city on the 17th, accompanied by Mr. Wright, for Wadesborough.

Knowing he was about to leave St. Luke's, Salisbury, and North Carolina, Mr. Wright did not attend the diocesan convention in 1832, remaining instead in Salisbury to attend to the business of his expected departure for Tennessee. He did submit, however, a final assessment of the state of St. Luke's.

The care of the Congregations in Rowan, will probably, soon devolve on some other clergyman, and I am happy that I can commit them to my successor in a much better state than I found them. It may with truth be said, that a few years ago, they had a name to live, and were dead, but by the grace and mercy of god, they have revived, arisen from the dust, and been in some measure purified. Some "who were not of us," have gone "out from us;" and now, our principles "the principles of the doctrines of Christ," are better understood and appreciated than at any preceding period. Our services are attended by those who love them, and the blessed Gospel, is in general, honoured by the holy walk of such as profess to believe it. Difficulties must still be encountered by my successor, but they will be of a different character, and by no means as numerous, as, through the goodness of God, have been already surmounted.[41]

While Mr. Wright had baptized two adults and nine children and confirmed six persons at St. Luke's, the total number of communicants had decreased to 11 while Christ Church, Rowan, enjoyed 70 communicants.

Immediately following the convention, Bishop Ives departed Edenton, and traveled west in late May on his way to Tennessee to attend the Diocese of Tennessee's convention.

From Windsor I proceeded directly to Hillsborough, where, on Sunday, the 27th, in St. Matthew's Church, I preached twice, administering the holy communion in the morning, and also confirming two persons, being assisted in the services by the Rector. Thence, on the following day, I started for Salisbury, where I arrived on Wednesday the 30th, and on the Thursday, Friday, and Saturday ensuing, officiated in St. Luke's Church, preaching to unusually serious and attentive congregations— confirming six persons, and administering the holy communion to about twenty. It was a circumstance of peculiar gratification to myself, as it must have been to the worthy and devoted servant of God, who was about leaving this scene of his self-denying labours, to observe among those who, on this occasion, publicly professed their faith, a number of the most deservedly influential gentlemen of the place, and among all, a spirit of increasing solemnity. We trust, in the grace of God, that this may be the dawn of a better day to the parish of St. Luke's.

I was detained in this place longer than I intended, from the loss of one of my horses; which, however, was soon replaced through the kind attention of Judge Martin.

We trust, in the grace of God, that this may be the dawn of a better day to the parish of St. Luke's.

On Sunday, the 3d of June, accompanied by the Rev. Mr. Wright, I visited Christ's Church, Rowan, where I preached; the Rev. Mr. Wright reading prayers, and administered confirmation to eight persons and the holy communion to about fifty.

From this place I proceeded, on the next day, to St. Andrew's Church, Burke County; but having made an appointment here, from the uncertain state of my health, I did not officiate. It was encouraging to find the venerable Rector of that Church so well sustained, under the burdens of age and acute disease, by the blessings of that Gospel, which, with such primitive simplicity and self-sacrifice, he had so long recommended to sinners.[42]

Soon to be transferred by Bishop Ives to the Diocese of Tennessee, and taking leave of him in Rowan County, Mr. Wright set off on horseback and reached Knoxville, Tennessee, on 12 June. He continued on to Nashville where he sat at the fourth convention of the Tennessee diocese, meeting 28-30 June 1832, in the presence of the North Carolina bishop who had been invited to preside over the gathering. Except for Mr. Wright's return to Salisbury late in 1832 to gather his wife, their eight children and possessions for the family's April 1833 removal to Memphis, the story of his life belongs hereafter to the history of Calvary Church, Memphis, which he organized at the home of Thomas Brown Jr. (1784-1839), a long-time friend, on 6 August 1832. Calvary Church, named in honor of his old charge, Calvary Church, Wadesborough, was the second church he founded. The first, organized on 23 July 1832 in Jackson, while en route from Nashville to Memphis, was St. Luke's, the first known

St. Luke's Church, Jackson, Tennessee, was organized on 23 July 1832 by Mr. Wright while en route to Memphis, and became the first namesake of this parish. This photograph shows the church as it stood prior to May 2003 when tornadoes destroyed the façade and roof and effected serious damage to the interior and its furnishings. On 20 February 2005, a groundbreaking ceremony launched the rebuilding of the church.
Photograph courtesy of St. Luke's Church

namesake of this church. the Rev. Thomas Wright served as rector of Calvary Church until his death of cholera on 28 April 1835. His body lies in an unmarked grave in the city of Memphis.[43]

Thomas Wright's departure from St. Luke's was one in a series of removals from the county seat that both reduced the membership of the church and the character of its citizenry. He had concluded his 1832 report writing, "From the Churches in Rowan, several families, and many Communicants, have at different times removed. The number of the latter will soon be increased."[44]

His description of removals from St. Luke's and Salisbury was correct, although the dates for a number of departures cannot be precisely fixed. Mrs. Maria Beard Burns went North, presumably to Philadelphia to live among her mother's people. Her nieces, the Misses Torres, likewise departed Salisbury and are believed to have relocated to Philadelphia. John Beard Jr. left Salisbury after the death of his wife, Anna Maria Kelly, on 6 October 1830. Her burial took place in the Lutheran Cemetery, where he erected a marker to her memory. Judge James Martin and his wife removed to Mobile, Alabama, where he lived until his death. Including the death of Mrs. John Beard Jr., these changes involved five of the 13 women confirmed by Bishop Ravenscroft in 1823.

The pulpit of St. Luke's Church remained vacant from the departure of Mr. Wright in June 1832 until the following November, when the Rev. John Morgan is said to have arrived in Salisbury. Having been responsible, in part, for the departure of Mr. Wright, Bishop Ives surely encouraged Mr. Morgan to leave New York and come south. John Morgan (1803-1877) emigrated from his native London to New London, Connecticut, and graduated from Washington, now Trinity, College. He was ordained a deacon in 1830 and a priest in 1832. Bishop Ives could well have known him personally, or learned of him through his father-in-law, Bishop John Henry Hobart of New York, who dismissed Mr. Morgan to North Carolina.[45] Mr. Morgan did not attend the diocesan convention of 1833 but instead gave his first parochial report at the convention of 1834.

> In addition to the above tabular view of my Parishes, it may be proper to say, that so far as I can learn, the prospects of my field are improving. There has been one third increase in the number of the members of St. Luke's Church. It is also with pleasure I have to inform the Convention that we have ordered an Organ; the Ladies, (as usual,) deserving most, if not all, the credit of it. We hope, ere the next visit of our Diocesan, to have the organ in its place.

> The congregation in Rowan is decidedly improving in regard to the numbers who regularly attend; and I trust in knowledge and grace and zeal. It is anticipated, that at the visit of the Bishop, a considerable number will "subscribe with their right hands to the

Lord." Measures are also in operation to finish the gallery, in order to accommodate the coloured people.[46]

His report illuminates the life of St. Luke's Church on several points. The first, foremost fact is that the church was growing, from 11 communicants reported in 1832 to 20 listed in 1834. For the first time a "colored" individual is numbered among the communicants of St. Luke's. Although his (or her) status is not noted, he was likely a slave, or possibly a free man or woman of color.

During his time in Salisbury, Mr. Morgan had baptized eight adults, 15 infants, and "3 colored," celebrated three marriages, buried three adults, four infants, and one "colored" person. The organ, apparently the first purchased for a church in Salisbury, was a decided improvement. Costing $500, it arrived in the late summer or very early autumn of 1834. On 4 October 1834, the *Western Carolinian* announced a fair to be held by the ladies of St. Luke's, to raise funds for the organ.

A FAIR IN SALISBURY, BY *THE* FAIR!

Mr. Editor: If you will have the goodness to allow me a corner in your paper, I have no doubt you will receive the thanks of all who feel an interest in the information I design to make public.

I understand that the Ladies attached to the Episcopal Church in our Town contemplate holding A FAIR, on Tuesday evening of Court-week, (the 7th instant,) at the Mansion Hotel, for the purpose of disposing of a great variety of useful and curious articles, the effects of their own industry and taste. The Ladies have incurred a considerable debt, by the purchase of an Organ for their Church, and have now to appeal to the public to enable them, by purchasing liberally at their Fair, to meet their responsibilities.

The Organ, which has been partly paid for by the proceeds of a former Fair, has been lately received and erected in St. Luke's Church. I have had the pleasure to see and hear it, and can safely say that its fine and solemn music will add an indescribable charm to the already beautiful and appropriate service of the Episcopal Church.

When I recollect, Mr. Editor, the cause in which these, Ladies are exerting themselves, the fact that the exhibition will be made up of articles wrought by their own delicate hands, and the proverbial gallantry and liberality of the Southern people, I cannot allow myself to think, for a moment, that our fair town women will be disappointed in their praise-worthy endeavors.   M.

Occasional fairs held by the ladies and young women of St. Luke's in the 19th Century are the antecedents of the annual bazaar which has become highly successful. This notice was printed in the Western Carolinian *on 4 October 1834.* Copy from microfilm courtesy of the North Carolina State Archives

The problem of meeting the rector's salary persisted at both St. Luke's, which enjoyed a small but relatively affluent congregation, and at Christ Church, which boasted one of the largest rosters of communicants in the Diocese but continually came up short with cash money to support the clergy. At the beginning of 1835, a trial solution to the problem was undertaken when Mr. Morgan went to Christ Church as rector and the Rev. William Wallace Spear (1812-1895) came as deacon to St. Luke's. The matter is best described by Mr. Spear in his report to the 1835 convention.

The present Minister assumed his responsibilities in this place, with the opening of the year 1835, at the call of the Vestry, with the knowledge and approbation of our Bishop. Previously it had been united with Christ's Church, Rowan, and the connection was dissolved, with the hope that each of these congregations would have their interests more effectually promoted by the more constant attention and regular services of a Minister resident among themselves. The people of St. Luke's made an effort to raise a salary, to the amount which the Bishop had made conditional of my going thither; and for five months past, I have been labouring among them, with an occasional visit to Charlotte and Lincolnton, where some encouragement is held out, for the establishment of Episcopal services.

In Salisbury the experiment has, for the present, succeeded to a degree; though it is not probable that the present plan can long continue. Some peculiar discouragements have attended my ministrations. A large and influential family, with other individual members, have removed to the West; and most of the remainder, who are interested in our cause, are anticipating the same result. One member has been called to her rest; another has been mourned over, as utterly lost to his solemn vows. On the other hand, it is believed by all, that the general attendance on our services has increased; and some tokens for good have attended my labours. One has been added to the communion, with altered views most satisfactory to myself. Two more are candidates on probation, and several are evidently revolving the question of their religious obligation. Over these, and for others, their Minister is anxiously watching, with the prayerful hope,

Ordained a deacon in 1834, William Wallace Spear took charge of St. Luke's early in 1835, but before the year was out he had removed to South Carolina where he was advanced to the priesthood and served as an assistant at St. Michael's Church, Charleston. Photograph reproduced from St. Luke's Episcopal Church (1953)

that the serious impressions may soon issue in decided purpose and open profession.

The Sunday School has recently been re-opened; though that part of the town which is open to us, does not afford more than 20 Scholars.

Besides the usual Sunday services, Junior and Senior Bible Classes are held in the week. They are attended, though not in great numbers, yet I believe with serious feeling.[47]

The experiment failed. Bishop Ives reported to the 1836 convention the dismissal of Mr. Morgan to Maryland and Mr. Spear to South Carolina. Of the two, Mr. Spear would enjoy a more distinguished career as an Episcopal priest. While born in New York City, he grew up in Hillsborough in St. Matthew's Church, and was graduated from the University of North Carolina (1831) and General Theological Seminary (1834) prior to his ordination as deacon by Bishop Ives in St. Matthew's on 20 July 1834. He was advanced to the priesthood in 1836 in South Carolina, where he served as an assistant to the rector of St. Michael's Church from 1836 until 1839, afterward holding the position of rector into 1840. Mr. Spear went to Philadelphia as rector of St. Luke's Church in 1840, but returned to Charleston in 1846, accepting the call as first rector of Grace Church, Wentworth Street. He remained at Grace Church until 1855 when illness forced his resignation. He returned to Philadelphia where he served a number of churches as *locum canons*. Despite illness he lived to advanced age, dying on 29 June 1895.[48]

In 1846 Thomas Frederick Davis followed in the 18th Century footsteps of Mr. Drage and became the second rector of St. Luke's to relocate to Camden, South Carolina, where he had accepted a call to Grace Church. This painting of Bishop Davis is held at Grace Church.

Photograph by Catherine French

Rowan County, having lost both its Episcopal clergymen, was visited by the Rev. Moses Ashley Curtis (1808-1872) who had been assigned as a missionary to the western Piedmont. He reported his efforts to convention.

Since the resignation of Rev. Mr. Spear, I have several times preached to the Churches in Rowan County. I have been unable to procure the requisite information for a report on their present state. It is to be feared, however, that the elements of dissolution are at work, and that without a speedy supply of regular ministerial services they will fast go to decay.[49]

In November 1836 a new Episcopal priest came to St. Luke's and served as rector for just short of a decade. Like Mr. Wright, Thomas Frederick Davis (1804-1871), the son of Thomas F. Davis (1778-1846) and Sarah Isabella Eagles (1784-1829), was a Wilmingtonian, a native of the city, and like Mr. Spear he was a graduate of the University of North Carolina (1822). Following the example of Mr. Wright, he also came to the church and Holy Orders after personal tragedy, which for Mr. Davis was the death of his (first) wife Elizabeth Fleming. He was ordained deacon on 27 November 1831 and priest on 16 December 1832 by Bishop Ives. Mr. Davis was sent as a missionary to the Piedmont, to St. Bartholomew's,

Pittsborough, and Calvary Church, Wadesborough. In December 1833 he accepted a call to St. James Church, Wilmington, and remained in its pulpit until he relinquished the position because of ill health. His health regained, he accepted the call to St. Luke's and Christ Church and came here with his family. In 1840 he purchased the late residence of Judge James Martin, who had departed Salisbury for Mobile, Alabama, occupying the house until leaving Salisbury himself in 1846.[50]

Although Mr. Davis described St. Luke's (and Christ Church) as having "suffered from the want of Religious services, and from the removal of some of their most valuable members," in his first parochial report in 1837, further losses to the congregation were to come, and to be reported to the 1838 convention.

On 19 March 1840 Mr. Davis purchased the Federal-style townhouse built for Lewis Utzman and occupied it while rector of St. Luke's. In 1847, after his removal to Camden, John Bradley Lord, acting as his trustee, sold the property to Maxwell Chambers. This photograph shows the house on its original site, facing onto West Innes Street, prior to the repositioning on its present site at 116 S. Jackson Street.
Photograph courtesy of Frank Goodnight/Diversified Graphics, Inc.

> **This Church has lost, during the past year, by removal to the West, one of the largest families connected with it; among them two of the communicants of the Church. It is expected also that another of the largest and most influential families connected with the Church will certainly remove in the course of the next year. So that our small number has become and is becoming still smaller. The condition of the Church in Salisbury is not encouraging. We still, however, continue to hope for a blessing from that God, who only can give both grace and increase.[51]**

Death and these removals had decreased the number of communicants at St. Luke's to 18, while Christ Church, Rowan, had 78 communicants. On the positive side, he reported 25 in Sunday School at St. Luke's.

Although initially disappointed with the prospects for St. Luke's, the Rev. Mr. Davis applied his energies to the church and his charge, and he soon saw a marked improvement in its spiritual life. A year later his language conveyed the tenor and optimism of the day.

> Although the above tabular view is not very different from that exhibited to the last Convention, it is believed that an important change for the better has taken place in the actual condition of this Church. There has been, generally, a much larger and more interested attendance upon Divine ordinances than heretofore. An increased interest in the Church there certainly is, and, it is hoped, an increased interest in Religion. During the past year, a Tower has been built to the Church and a new Bell purchased for it. Other improvements are also projected, and will, no doubt, be completed. And their Pastor owes it to the people of his charge to say, (which he does with a thankful sense of their kindness,) that, entirely of their own accord, they have almost doubled his salary, and have in every respect exhibited towards him a kind and affectionate regard.—The Ladies' Society has been organized, and are at work for the benefit of the Church.[52]

Renewal also occurred at Christ Church where the number of communicants increased to 91.

The new bell came as a result of a subscription organized by Miss Christina Beard and Mrs. Kerns. It opened on 24 May 1838, with the first gift of $10 from Andre Mathieu. Later, in 1839, Miss Beard recorded the hanging of the bell in the new tower on 7 March. It was rung for the first time on Sunday, the 10th of March.[53] At present, no record survives as to the location of the bell tower, whether it rose from the roof, adjoined the church on one of its elevations, or was free-standing.

When Bishop Ives made his customary visitation in Rowan County in July 1839, he was called upon to preside over the burial of one of St. Luke's leading ladies. In his address to the 1840 convention he reported services at St. Luke's on the 4th of July and three days afterward. He then rode to the Mills settlement in Iredell County.

> From this place we were recalled to Salisbury by the sudden and lamented death of an interesting young lady of that Parish. At the burial I delivered a short address, and at night preached in St. Luke's Church in reference to the melancholy event; —the effects of which event, I pray God, may be as salutary and lasting as the sympathy it excited was deep and pervading.[54]

Miss Christina Beard recorded the death of her friend Mary McNamara on 10 July in greater detail. Miss MacNamara, the daughter of Colonel Robert MacNamara (d. 1843) and Eliza Steele, and the granddaughter of General John Steele, was on her horse, setting off for a

party of friends, when the horse bolted, raced through the grove, and threw her against a tree.

In 1840, when St. Luke's and Salisbury hosted the annual convention of the Diocese of North Carolina for the third time, Mr. Davis welcomed Bishop Ives and six of their 19 fellow Episcopal clergymen to the opening session on Wednesday, 13 May. The lay delegates present included John Bradley Lord, Charles A. Beard and William Chambers of St. Luke's; William Chunn and Thomas Barber of Christ Church. One sure measure of the vitality of the Episcopal Church in Rowan County, and Mr. Davis' efforts, was the presentation of a certification for admission of St. Andrew's Church into union with the Diocese. It was approved quickly, and Rowan County then boasted three Episcopal churches.

The "increased interest in the Church" noted by Mr. Davis in his 1839 parochial report had two notable results that year. In retrospect, the most important of the two was the rector's decision to maintain a parish register. What manner of record keeping had been in place prior to 1839 is not now known; however, the earliest surviving record book at St. Luke's dates to that year and includes a list of communicants as of 1 January 1839. Mr. Davis recorded collections and receipts and the church expenses, including payments to George the sexton, purchases of tallow for candles, and a communion plate acquired at the cost of $9 in February 1845. He maintained separate listings of baptisms, burials, marriages and confirmations. This practice was continued in the same book by his successor John Haywood Parker (1847-1858), and in turn by the Rev.

Built and consecrated in 1840, St. Andrew's Church became the third Episcopal church in Rowan County. Unpainted and little changed, it survives today as a remarkable example of rural antebellum church architecture in North Carolina.
Photograph by Jason Williams

Thomas Goelet Haughton (1858-1866) and by his successor John Huske Tillinghast (1867-1872). (At the end of the book, which ceased to be used with the departure of Mr. Tillinghast in the summer of 1872, is a list of communicants revised on 14 June 1872. The heading "Bona Fide Communicants" includes 67 men and women. A second listing, under the heading "Communicants Who have Lapsed" comprised 26 names, including that of Miss Frances Christine Fisher (the author Christian Reid) who had "joined the Ch. of Rome." The third, final roster, with seven names, was a list of "Persons Confirmed but have never received the Holy Communion.")

At the front of this book, the parish's oldest known register, are the receipts and expenditures of the Ladies Working Society. The first of the receipts are the proceeds of a fair held in September 1839. Miss Beard began recording preparations for the fair in her diary on 4 September, and she continued these notations up to the opening day, Tuesday, 17 September.

> **All met at the fair room again this morning and finished the dressing (;) it makes quite a splendid appearance. The fair room was opened this evening and by 7 o'clock it was crowded. We sold almost everything, had a great deal of fun, the whole affair came off first rate, all appeared delighted, we broke up about 12 o'clock.[55]**

The second day of the fair was equally successful.

> **All met early this morning at the fair room to arrange it and make rum cakes for tonight(,) Mary and Maria Satterwhite baked all day at Horace's and fitted it up as nice as it was last night, the room was filled at an early hour, we sold out early and came home at 11 o'clock. Before we left we counted the money(.) We had $230 clear of expense.[56]**

The disbursement side of the Ladies Working Society account indicates the purpose of their industry. The next month they purchased tallow and wicks for candles and a stove for the church at a cost of $74.58. The stove, apparently purchased by order, was not installed and ready for use until Sunday, 5 January 1840, according to an entry in Miss Beard's diary. The next group of purchases came in April 1840, when ladies prepared the church for the 1840 diocesan convention. Mr. Shives was paid $20 "for painting the church," Mr. Burkhead was paid $12 for "a Chandelier," William Murphy was paid $7.35 "for carpet & covering to cushions," and Mr. Wheeler was paid $13 for a "Box of sperm candles." The final entry in the disbursement side, in August 1840, recorded the purchase of cushions for St. Andrew's Church in the amount of $4.25.

In the usual statistical report of baptisms, confirmations, burials, etc., Mr. Davis reported in 1840 an increase to 25 communicants with four teachers and 28 scholars in Sunday School. He concluded with praise for

We sold almost everything, had a great deal of fun, the whole affair came off first rate, all appeared delighted.

FROM GENERATION TO GENERATION

the good work of his female parishioners. "The Ladies have had a Fair within the past year, from which there was realized about $240." He gave separate reports for his ministry at Christ Church, in the "Mills Settlement" in Iredell County, and St. Andrew's where "A plain country Church, is almost completed,—sufficiently so to be used for worship."[57] Bishop Ives returned to Rowan County in late August 1840, and on the 30th he consecrated St. Andrew's Church.

After hosting the annual diocesan convention in 1840, St. Luke's Church appears to have entered a state that might be described as abeyance. Beginning in 1841 and for most of the period until he left St. Luke's, Mr. Davis's parochial reports lack enthusiasm and detail. The likely reason was financial. In 1841 he reported 92 communicants at Christ Church, 29 at St. Andrew's, and 26 at St. Luke's; this ranking would remain consistent throughout his rectorate here. During these years, St. Luke's membership would not rise above 26 except in 1846, when he reported a dramatic increase to 38 communicants. Nevertheless, funds were consistently low during the early 1840s and the ministry at Rowan churches, including St. Luke's for a period, was supported by missionary funds. Early in this period, on 15 January 1842, a daughter born to Mr. Davis and his wife on 28 October 1841, died; after the funeral at St. Luke's, her body became the first to be buried in the churchyard. [58]

On 9 May 1841, during the convention at St. James's Church, Wilmington, Charles Bruce Walker (18__-1875) was ordained deacon and subsequently came to Rowan County, where he assisted Mr. Davis at the Rowan County churches and the missions in adjoining counties. On 24 August 1844, Bishop Ives elevated Mr. Walker to the priesthood at Christ Church, and he was thereafter identified as Mr. Davis's "assistant." In 1845 Mr. Walker was dismissed to the Diocese of South Carolina, having accepted a call to Trinity Church, Edgefield, where he remained until 1849. He also was rector of Zion Church, Eastover, from 1860 to 1862, but otherwise appears to have served largely as an assistant, missionary or priest in charge of churches in South Carolina. His last position, as rector of St. Mark's Church, Pinewood, began when he succeeded the Rev. Frederick Bruce Davis (18__-1873), a son of Thomas Frederick Davis, in 1873.[59]

During the 1840s Mr. Davis usually held services on Sunday morning at St. Luke's unless he was preaching at Christ Church, and often in the evening. When absent from Salisbury, his place was filled by Mr. Walker during his tenure here, or on some few occasions by other clergy who might be in town, including Joseph Blount Cheshire, T. S. W. Mott and A. F. Olmsted. On his visitations the bishop would preach several times through the course of his stay in Salisbury. Funerals and weddings were also held in the church. As now, Easter and Christmas drew larger than usual congregations. On 21 December 1844, Miss Beard helped dress the church for Christmas, and on Christmas day she noted "it looked very beautiful;" however, she gave no clue as to what constituted St. Luke's Christmas "dress" in 1844.

Late in May 1846 Thomas F. Davis departed Salisbury for the diocesan convention held at Christ Church, Raleigh, and made his final, perfunctory report as rector of St. Luke's, Christ Church and St. Andrew's; and missionary to churches in Iredell, Davie, Davidson and Surry counties. As chairman of the Committee on the Application of New Congregations, he presented the applications of the Church of the Holy Cross, Valle Crucis, and St. Paul's Church, Louisburg, for union with the Diocese.[60] Before the year was out, he was dismissed to the Diocese of South Carolina by Bishop Ives, who lamented the loss.

> **That such priests as the Rev. Thomas F. Davis and the Rev. Moses A. Curtis should be allowed, with the most heartfelt reluctance, to leave the Diocese, and for no other reason than the want of necessaries of life, is to my mind, a problem, on all Christian grounds beyond the possibility of solution. No circumstances, during the fifteen years of my Episcopate, have tended so much as this to fill me with sadness and apprehension.[61]**

Mr. Curtis went to Trinity Church, Society Hill, where he remained until 1856 and his return to St. Matthew's, Hillsborough, whose pulpit he occupied until his death in 1872. Mr. Davis accepted a call to Grace Church, Camden. Miss Beard recorded Mr. Davis' departure with his family from Salisbury on 18 November 1846. Thomas Frederick Davis was elected Bishop of South Carolina on 6 May 1853, and five months later, on 17 October, he was consecrated in New York together with Thomas Atkinson, the successor to Bishop Ives and the Third Bishop of North Carolina. Bishop Davis remained rector of Grace Church until 1867, having his son, the Rev. Thomas Frederick Davis Jr. (1828-1865), as his assistant rector from 1855 until his death.

Bishop Davis died at his Camden residence on 2 December 1871, and his body was buried in the Quaker Cemetery, Camden, near that of his son and namesake.[62] On 8 May 1847, Mr. Davis had sold his Salisbury residence on West Innes Street and its grounds of four lots (#33-34, 41-42), in the West Square to Maxwell Chambers.[63] Mr. Chambers (1780-1855), in turn, offered it to the Presbyterian Church for use as a manse, and it was first occupied by the Rev. Archibald Baker.[64]

John Haywood Parker (1813-1858), a widower who succeeded Mr. Davis as rector of St. Luke's in 1846, was a native of Tarboro, the son of Theophilus Parker, and a graduate of the University of North Carolina (1832). On 31 May 1846, he was ordained deacon at Christ Church, Raleigh, and advanced to the priesthood in May 1847 at Christ Church, New Bern.[65] Through a realignment of responsibilities in 1848, Mr. Parker served as rector of St. Luke's and as a missionary of The Church of Redemption, Lexington, among others. Christ Church, St. Andrew's and

St. Philip's Church, Mocksville, were placed under the charge of the Rev. Oliver Sherman Prescott, deacon, who came as a missionary to Rowan and the adjoining counties.[66] Mr. Prescott's assignment here by the diocesan missionary committee was a first step in the separation of St. Luke's and Christ Church/St. Andrew's as spheres of pastoral responsibility. That said, however, Mr. Prescott apparently served in this post for less than one year, and by the time of the 1849 convention, Mr. Parker was again giving his attention to Christ Church, St. Andrew's and the region's other missions. the Rev. James Gilbert Jacocks, who had come to Christ Church as a deacon and missionary, gave the parochial report to convention in 1850. He remained at Christ and St. Andrew's churches until 1855, during which time the relationship between St. Luke's and the other Rowan County churches was effectively ended. This separation continued when Mr. Jacocks was succeeded by the Rev. George Badger Wetmore (1821-1888), who served these churches until 1887. John Haywood Parker's ties to Salisbury were strengthened on 25 January 1854, when he was married to Mrs. Ann Ferrand Lord, the widow of John Bradley Lord (d. 1851), the daughter of Dr. Stephen L. Ferrand, and the granddaughter of John Steele. the Rev. Joseph Blount Cheshire, who was married to Mr. Parker's sister, Elizabeth Toole Parker, performed the marriage ceremony. Mr. Parker had officiated at Mr. Lord's funeral on 10 June 1851, and the next year he presided over the burial of an infant son and daughter, apparently twins, born to the widow Mrs. Lord.

In 1849 John Haywood Parker and St. Luke's were hosts to the first of two diocesan conventions held during his rectorate here. Although the church elected four delegates to the convention, only John Bradley Lord and William Locke took their seats. The second convention was held in 1857. During the eight years between these two conventions, important events occurred in the life of the Diocese of North Carolina and St. Luke's Church. Through the course of the later 1840s, concerns about the bishop's high churchmanship had been given voice and questions raised about certain "Romish" practices at Valle Crucis, the mission school and theological seminary that Bishop Ives had established in 1842 in Ashe (now Watauga) County. Absent from the 1848 convention because of ill health and confinement by fever in Edenton, Bishop Ives responded in his address to the clergy assembled in Salisbury in 1849.

> **For the quieting of some minds disturbed by unfounded rumors, I beg the Diocese to be assured that, at this religious house, no doctrine will be taught or practice allowed which is not in accordance with the principles and usages of our branch of the Holy Catholic Church, contained in the Book of Common Prayer. And furthermore, that the property of the establishment has been secured to the Church, for the use of the mission on the above specified condition.[67]**

At this religious house, no doctrine will be taught or practice allowed which is not in accordance with the principles and usages of our branch of the Holy Catholic Church, contained in the Book of Common Prayer.

The Rowan County Court House, erected 1855-1856, epitomized the rising fortunes of Salisbury in the antebellum period. This view of the Court House was published as a post card and sold by Buerbaum's Bookstore. It was inscribed by Theodore Buerbaum for his nephew Karl Buerbaum, "One of the prettiest buildings in NC, except for the barbaric tower on top, put there by the ignorance of our county commissioners."
Courtesy of Susan Goodman Sides

Criticism and controversy continued nevertheless, and it was exacerbated when Episcopalians in North Carolina received *A Pastoral Letter to the Clergy and Laity of His Diocese*, an 80-page epistle written at Valle Crucis and dated 8 August 1849. Reaction was fierce within the Diocese and from afar, and it took the form of letters, pamphlets, and publications including *Auricular Confession in the Protestant Episcopal Church; Considered in a Series of Letters Addressed to a Friend in North Carolina* written by the Rev. Francis Lister Hawks and published in 1851. Bishop Ives' views, questions of theology, and Valle Crucis occupied the clergy in North Carolina at the conventions of 1850 and 1851, and up to the convention of 1852, when the fever pitch of discussion appeared to abate.[68]

But it was simply the calm before the final storm. A number of influential people in the Diocese had come to blame illness for the bishop's distress and the extremity of his views. Thus it was not surprising that the diocesan Standing Committee approved his request of 27 September for a six-month leave from the Diocese, effective 1 November, to undertake a travel cure in Europe and a request for a $1,000 advance on his salary. On 22 December 1852, Bishop Ives wrote from Rome to his brethren in the Diocese of North Carolina, resigning his position as their bishop and stating his determination "to make my submission to the Catholic Church."[69] Bishop Ives' apostasy to Rome became the most dramatic event of the American Episcopal Church's infatuation with the Oxford Movement.[70] When the clergy gathered in Raleigh at Christ Church in May 1853, they elected the Rev. Thomas Atkinson (1807-1881), rector of Grace Church, Baltimore, as the Third Bishop of North Carolina.

In Salisbury the events of the late 1840s and 1850s were altogether more fortuitous. The opening salvo for a decade of prosperity came on 14 June 1849, when a convention was held in Salisbury to promote and raise subscription capital for the newly-chartered Central Railroad of North Carolina. Over 200 business and political leaders in North Carolina gathered in the Lutheran Church, the same building where John Stark Ravenscroft was elected bishop in 1823, and elected former North Carolina Governor John Motley Morehead president of the new company.[71] Two months later, Salisbury's *Carolina Watchman* announced efforts under way for the construction of a new Lutheran Church. The completion and the consecration of the building were delayed until 25 May 1857, when St. John's Church, standing in the north corner of Main and Liberty Streets, joined St. Luke's and the Presbyterian church as the third brick church in the county seat. Ironically, the railroad tracks linking eastern North Carolina with Charlotte in the west were completed in shorter time. The first train passed through Salisbury on 29 January 1856. Meanwhile, a second series of meetings in 1855 began raising capital for the construction of the Western North Carolina Railroad that would link Salisbury with Asheville. The opening of the North Carolina Railroad through Salisbury brought a degree of growth, enterprise and public spirit heretofore unseen in Salisbury. Prosperity was made visible in many forms. Rising incomes enabled the construction of many houses, stores and other buildings, including the Rowan County Court House of 1855 immediately in front of St. Luke's, and refurbishments and improvements to others. Civic improvements, likewise, took yet other forms. In 1855 the city commissioners voted $100 to the cost of the granite wall erected by Robert Hendry around the English Cemetery to the northwest of St. Luke's, and $300 for an enclosure, whether granite, brick or iron fence, to protect the Old Lutheran Cemetery.[72] In March 1859 gas lights were turned on in Salisbury. The *Western Carolinian* reported the illumination to its readers.

> **Our town was lighted with gas for the first time on Thursday evening last. Nearly all our Stores and quite a number of private homes were fairly flooded with the rich light, in some cases almost equal to noon-day splendor. The Messrs. Myers outshone all the rest. Their splendid store, as lighted up on that evening, surpassed anything of the kind ever seen here before; and equal, it is said by some, to the brilliant displays of New York or Philadelphia.**

In 1860 Salisbury had a population of 2,420 persons, white and slave, which represented an increase of nearly 1,000 from 1850.

St. Luke's also saw a dramatic increase in membership in this period. Although Bishop Ravenscroft had confirmed 13 persons at the church's organizational meeting in 1823, the first reported number of communicants following its admission into the Diocese in 1825, was six. The number did not rise to 20 until 1834, and it remained below 30 for a dozen years, until 38 communicants were reported in 1846. Mr. Davis

Few aspects of the history of St. Luke's have aroused as much interest as the species of the great evergreen tree which grew for over a century in the churchyard. The tree, said to have been a gift of Wade Hampton III of Columbia to Miss Julia E. Long, was planted at St. Luke's in 1857, the year she was married by Mr. Parker to James C. Smythe. Mr. Hampton (1818-1902) was a friend of the Long family and later served as governor of South Carolina (1876-1879). The tree had acquired such acclaim by the turn of the century that postal views, including this one, were published by Buerbaum's Bookstore. The tree was then believed to be a Thuya orientalis; however, in 1984 it was identified as a Libocedrus decurrens, commonly called an incense cedar. The tree died and was taken down in 1999.

St. Luke's Archives

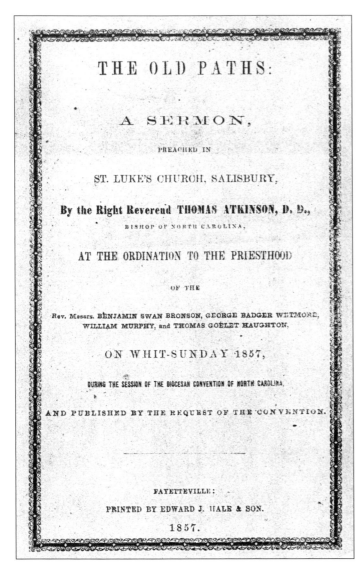

THE OLD PATHS:

A SERMON,

PREACHED IN

ST. LUKE'S CHURCH, SALISBURY,

By the Right Reverend THOMAS ATKINSON, D. D.,

BISHOP OF NORTH CAROLINA,

AT THE ORDINATION TO THE PRIESTHOOD

OF THE

Rev. Messrs. BENJAMIN SWAN BRONSON, GEORGE BADGER WETMORE, WILLIAM MURPHY, and THOMAS GOELET HAUGHTON,

ON WHIT-SUNDAY 1857,

DURING THE SESSION OF THE DIOCESAN CONVENTION OF NORTH CAROLINA,

AND PUBLISHED BY THE REQUEST OF THE CONVENTION.

FAYETTEVILLE:

PRINTED BY EDWARD J. HALE & SON.

1857.

The sermon preached by Bishop Atkinson at the ordination of Messrs. Bronson, Wetmore, Murphy and Haughton at St. Luke's on Sunday, 31 May 1857, was printed for the Diocese by Edward J. Hale & Son, one of North Carolina's major antebellum printers.

reported 39 (38 white, one "colored") communicants in 1852, 1853 and 1854.

In 1856 he reported, but did not comment on a near 20 percent increase to 49 communicants of which 48 were white and one was "colored." Neither did he provide insight into the sudden increase in contributions from $131.36 in 1855 to $445.95 in 1856; however, the total included a contribution of $76 to the erection of St. James's Church in the Mills settlement of Iredell County.[73] Mr. Parker made his final parochial report in 1858; the number of communicants rose, in the space of one year, by just over 50 percent to 74, of whom 71 were white and three were "colored." Two years later, in 1860, the reported membership rose to 80 for the first time. By comparison, the Presbyterian church had 90 members that year.[74]

Mr. Parker could take satisfaction ever so briefly in the strong, growing church. On 15 September 1858, John Haywood Parker died and was interred in the yard of St. Luke's. the Rev. Joseph Blount Cheshire, who had officiated at his brother-in-law's wedding here in 1854, returned and officiated at his funeral and burial. A white marble obelisk marks his grave. Bishop Atkinson, on his annual visitation to the churches in the western part of his diocese, came to Salisbury on 12 October, and described his reaction.

I found this Church draped in black, because of the recent death of the Rector of the Parish, the Rev. John Haywood Parker, and never perhaps was that mark of grief more properly worn. He had spent his early youth in secular pursuits honorably and usefully, but had been led by the grace of God to consecrate his superior talents and energy to the service of Christ and his Church. In that service he labored with great disinterestedness and zeal, and with marked success until called to his reward. He was peculiarly qualified to be useful as a Minister, not only by piety and intelligence, but by warm and tender affections, by great suavity and cordiality of manner, and by a rare combination of zeal and discretion. It was said by one who well knew the town in which he lived, that his loss would be more deeply felt than that of any other man who could be taken from it. I have cause to regret him not only as an efficient fellow-laborer and wise counsellor, but an attached friend, whose hospitality I often enjoyed, and whose thoughtful kindness greatly facilitated my labors in the part of the Diocese in which he lived.[75]

Illness had visited itself on Mr. Parker in the winter of 1856-1857 when he was assisted at St. Luke's by Dr. J. T. Wheat, a professor at the University of North Carolina, and by the Rev. Thomas Goelet Haughton, beginning in January 1857.[76] Mr. Haughton had impressed many members of St. Luke's during his service here, but he had not gained the high regard of all. Mrs. Archibald Henderson put the matter plainly in a diary entry for 17 October 1858, recounting a meeting that day at St. Luke's to elect the vestry.

> Mr. Henderson and I were the only ones who knew that ladies were permitted to vote. I think the voters ought to inform themselves a little better. We elected 5—Messrs. Fisher, Locke, Blackmer, J. Murphy and S. Harrison. They are to decide upon the clergyman. I feel confident Mr. Haughton will be called but shall ever regret the decision and did not hesitate to express my opposition. I wanted Mr. Snowden called. I believe that Sister Jane and myself were the only opposition. We were nearly 2 hours at the church.[77]

The vestry, comprising Charles Frederick Fisher, William Locke, Luke Blackmer, James Murphy and Samuel R. Harrison, called Mr. Haughton, then serving as rector of Christ Church, New Bern. He returned to St. Luke's in November 1858. On 20 February 1860 he was married by the Rev. George Badger Wetmore to Ann (Ferrand) Lord Parker, the widow of the late rector. Mr. Haughton (ca. 1813-1880), who is believed to have been a native of Chowan County, graduated from the University of North Carolina in 1834. Except for his practice of law, little is known of his life during the two decades preceding his ordination as deacon in 1856 and as priest in 1857. He would serve as rector of St. Luke's through the long, difficult years of the Civil War.

JOHN HAYWOOD PARKER.
BORN JANUARY 21, 1813.
DIED SEPTEMBER 15, 1858.

The death of John Haywood Parker was widely mourned in Salisbury. After preaching his funeral sermon, Joseph Blount Cheshire officiated at Mr. Parker's interment in the churchyard. A white marble obelisk was later erected over his grave.
Photograph by Jason Williams

ENDNOTES

1. RCD, 7/13.

2. St. James Church, Wilmington, with 156 communicants listed in its 1821 parochial report was the largest in the Diocese; 17 of that number were described as "Africans." Richard S. Mason, rector of Christ Church, New Bern, reported 64 communicants (JAC, 1821, 8-9).

3. JAC, 1823, 3, 21-23; ECNC, 115-116.

4. *Western Carolinian*, 22 April 1823.

5. The house occupied by Bishop Ravenscroft in Raleigh is lost; however, the plantation seat he built on Burwell family lands on the north side of the Meherrin River in Lunenburg County, Virginia, following his marriage in 1792 to Anne Spottswood Burwell, still stands and is known as Ravenscroft. His residence near Boydton, which he acquired after becoming rector of St. James, is lost.

6. JAC, 1824, 8-9.

7. This list of 13 confirmands was recorded in Miss Chrissie Beard's diary which has been lost. In the late 19th Century, Mr. Murdoch copied the names into a book of records he was compiling on the history of St. Luke's. Eleven names in the listing were first published in "Episcopacy in Rowan" in HRC, 309. For now unknown reasons, Mr. Henderson omitted the names of Anna Maria Kelly and Mrs. James Martin, junior.

8. HRC, 310.

9. Ibid, 157.

10. JAC, 1824, 9.

11. Ibid, 21.

12. JAC, 1825, 7-8.

13. Ibid, 13.

14. JAC, 1826, 11.

15. Ibid, 12.

16. John Beard and others, *A Misstatement in the "Episcopal Journal" of Bishop Ravenscroft, Corrected* (Salisbury, Philo White, 1827), 2-3.

17. Ibid, 4-5.

18. Ibid, 6.

19. The most complete account of the life of Thomas Wright appears in Ellen Davies-Rodgers, *The Great Book, Calvary Protestant Episcopal Church, 1832-1972, Memphis, Shelby County, Tennessee* (Memphis, The Plantation Press, 1973), 716-26, hereinafter cited as Davies-Rodgers. Mr. Wright's cousin Ann Eliza Wright (1798-1843), the daughter of Judge Joshua Grainger Wright, was the wife of the Rev. Adam Empie.

20. For Green see DNCB, 2, 362-363, and the genealogical information on the Green family appearing in Appendix A of Davies-Rodgers.

21. JAC, 1826, 27.

22. RCD, 30/8-9. James Carter and Hugh Forster, Trustees for the Town Lots, conveyed ownership of lot #11 in the North Square twice: first in 1756 to George Cathey (RCD, 3/66) and in 1761 to Mrs. Elizabeth Gillespie (RCD, 4/763). After Steele acquired the lot (RCD, 8/11) it remained in his family for 40 years until General John Steele sold it in 1812 (RCD, 20/307).

23. JAC, 1827, 24.

24. My understanding of the construction history of St. Matthew's Church was greatly aided by the Rev. N. Brooks Graebner, rector, through telephone conversations and a visit to the church on 13 February 2003. He also provided to me a photocopy of his "St. Matthew's Architectural History Timeline" that he has revised and updated through continued research.

25. HRC, 315.

26. See Gertrude S. Carroway, "Francis Lister Hawks," in DNCB, 3, 76-77.

27. Cameron Family Papers, Southern Historical Collection, Wilson Library, University of North Carolina, Chapel Hill, NC. N. Brooks Graebner provided a photocopy of the letter to me.

28. For a further account of Mr. Nichols and his work, see John L. Sanders, "William Nichols" in DNCB, 4, 369-71. See also C. Ford Peatross and Robert O. Mellown, *William Nichols, Architect* (Tuscaloosa, ALA, The University of Alabama Art Gallery, 1979).

29. Ruffin Papers, Southern Historical Collection, Wilson Library, University of North Carolina, Chapel Hill, NC. N. Brooks Graebner provided a copy of this letter to me.

30. Mary Claire Engstrom, "John Berry," in DNCB, 1, 146-47. See also Eva Ingersoll Gatling, "John Berry of Hillsboro," *Journal of the Society of Architectural Historians* 10 (1951).

31. JAC, 1828, 12-13.

32. Ibid, 23-24.

33. Microfilm Copy in the North Carolina Collection, Wilson Library, University of North Carolina, Chapel Hill, NC.

34. JAC, 1829, 8.

35. Ibid, 18.

36. JAC, 1830, 11.

37. ECNC, 171.

38. Wake County Wills, 21/385-89, Office of the Clerk of Court, Wake County Court House, Raleigh, NC.

39. Thomas Wright to Mary Wright, 13 June 1831, Wright/Cotton/Douglass Family Papers. The W. S. Hoole Special Collections Library, The University of Alabama.

40. JAC, 1832, 26.

41. Ibid, 15.

42. JAC, 1833, 8-9.

43. Davies-Rodgers, 112-13, 122-25, 128, 132, 134-35, 155-58.

44. JAC, 1832, 15.

45. SL, 57.

46. JAC, 1834, 24. In a short sketch, "The First Organ in Salisbury," printed on 20 April 1969 in "St. Luke's Messenger," James Shober Brawley identified Henry Erben of New York as the organ's maker. He did not cite the source of this attribution.

47. JAC, 1835, 18.

48. SL, 59-60. William Way and Virginia Kirkland Donehue, *By Grace, Through Faith: A History of Grace Church, Charleston, 1846-1999* (Columbia, SC, R. L. Bryan Company, 2000), 7-9, 20-28. Also see George W. Williams, *St. Michael's, Charleston, 1751-1951* (Columbia, SC, University of South Carolina Press, 1951), 56, 58-59, 315.

49. JAC, 1836, 35.

50. See SL 49-50. See also Thomas Frederick Davis, *A Genealogical Record of the Davis, Swann and Cabell Families* (N.p., privately published, 1934), 9-10, 26.

51. JAC, 1838, 21.

52. JAC, 1839, 19.

53. Entry in abstract of Miss Christine Beard's diary.

54. JAC, 1840, 8.

55. Entry in abstract of Miss Christine Beard's diary.

56. Ibid.

57. JAC, 1840, 15-16.

58. Entry in abstract of Miss Christine Beard's Diary. The grave of the Davis infant is not marked.

59. SL, 61. Albert Sidney Thomas, *A Historical Account of the Protestant Episcopal Church in South Carolina, 1820-1957* (Columbia, SC, R. L. Bryan Company, 1957), 393, 540, 548, 550, 602, 648, hereinafter cited as Thomas.

60. JAC, 1846, 22-23, 34.

61. JAC, 1847, 31.

62. For Mr. Davis in South Carolina see Thomas, "Episcopate of Bishop Davis," 49-82, and 508.

63. RCD, 38/80.

64. FPC, 402-03.

65. SL, 58-59.

66. JAC, 1848, 33-34.

67. JAC, 1849, 10.

68. For a larger discussion of these events see ECNC, 199-216.

69. JAC, 1853, 15-16.

70. For reactions to his apostasy see ECNC, 217-19.

71. RS, 166.

72. Board of City Commissioners Minutes, Vol. 1, 126, 151 cited in FPC, 43.

73. JAC, 1856, 35, 54.

74. FPC, 45.

75. JAC, 1859, 18.

76. JAC, 1857, 51-52.

77. Diary of Mrs. Archibald Henderson, Henderson Family Papers, Southern Historical Collection, the University of North Carolina, Chapel Hill, NC.

The view of St. Luke's from the Old English Cemetery is a moment of beauty in the townscape of Salisbury and one that recalls the many published photographs of English churchyards.
Photograph by Robert Bailey

This pair of windows in the side walls of the chancel were designed as part of the suite of three windows on the theme of The Good Shepherd and the Four Evangelists and installed in the church in 1883. The figures in these windows, like those flanking The Good Shepherd in the window relocated from the chancel to the baptistry, appear without their usual attributes. However, their role as the authors of the four Gospels of the New Testament is reflected in the quill and book held by each figure. According to an account of the windows published in the Carolina Watchman *on 19 July 1883, the Macay memorial window on the left contains the image of St. Matthew while that of St. Mark (right), is a memorial of Archibald Henderson and members of his family.*

Photographs by Robert Bailey

CHAPTER 4

St. Luke's and Salisbury

The Civil War and Reconstruction 1861–1872

The Civil War diminished the lives of virtually everyone in the South. Southern institutions, including the church, did not go unscathed.

The promise seen in the town and at St. Luke's in the closing years of the antebellum period, with prosperity visible at nearly every turn, would prove short-lived. The Civil War diminished the lives of virtually everyone in the South. Southern institutions, including the church, did not go unscathed. The North Carolina Railroad, whose cars had transported a wide range of goods into Salisbury and its stores and carried away the produce of Rowan County's fields, quickly brought the war into the lives of those living in the county seat. On 2 November 1861 the Confederate States of America purchased the three-story antebellum brick cotton factory standing beside the railroad tracks and within a month, in early December, it became the first Confederate prison in North Carolina. The prison and its operation exerted a powerful presence in the lives of Salisbury residents and remained the most visible, ever-present symbol of a war fought on distant battlefields. Through the course of the next three years and three months, thousands of prisoners were incarcerated here in a prison camp that came to comprise some 16 acres and numerous buildings. As the war neared its end in February 1865, the prison was abandoned, and some 5,149 prisoners either walked away from the prison or were removed in railroad cars.[1]

The notoriety of the Salisbury Prison and the Confederate munitions, distillery, warehouse and depot facilities located here along the North Carolina Railroad drew General George Stoneman to Salisbury in April 1865. Over the course of two days, 12 and 13 April, General Stoneman and his troops laid waste to the prison, its facilities and the Confederate stores in warehouses along the rail lines. The fires were still smoldering on 17 April when Jefferson Davis, his Cabinet, and their entourage arrived in Salisbury on their flight south. The president of the Confederate States of America spent the night in the home of the rector and his family. Within weeks, Federal troops occupied Salisbury and made it headquarters for the Western District of North Carolina. Under orders of the provisional governor, William Wood Holden (1818-1892), new officers were appointed to the courts and other positions in the city government. Thus began the process of reconstruction.[2]

At St. Luke's, the Rev. Thomas Goelet Haughton, who came back to the church in 1858 as a bachelor priest and was married to the widow of his predecessor in 1860, presided over the fortunes of the church and its service to the community throughout the war. In the first years of his rectorate, a wardrobe was purchased for church vestments, decorations were bought for Christmas and material acquired for an "Epiphany Star," communion wine was purchased from Miss Christine Beard, and the sexton and others paid for their work on the church, its grounds and repairs to the organ, together with the expected expenses of the church. However, in the years of 1861 through 1865, as the times became leaner and life increasingly impoverished, the disbursements listed in the parish register were limited to wood, payments to the sexton and to others who prepared fires in the church, charity and the Confederate States of America Bible Society. The dollar amounts of collections increased as the war continued and Confederate currency increasingly lost its value. In May 1865 the communion offering, the last collected in Confederate currency, was $187 and designated for the "Poor in Town." The communion offering in June, for church expenses, was $10.03 in U.S. currency."

The Rev. Mr. Haughton resigned on 16 July 1866, and was succeeded in March 1867 by the Rev. John Huske Tillinghast (1835-1933). In retrospect, his rectorate appears to have been somewhat uneventful, but that would be a misleading view of the steady guidance and leadership he provided St. Luke's and the larger Salisbury community coming to terms with a new political and civic order. Mr. Tillinghast served as rector of St. Luke's until 10 June 1872, departing Salisbury after serving as host of the 56th Annual Convention of the Diocese of North Carolina that opened on Wednesday, 29 May, at St. Luke's. One important footnote to his role as an Episcopal priest in Salisbury dates to 17 September 1868, when he presented Francis Johnstone Murdoch as a candidate for deacon's orders to Bishop Atkinson on his annual visitation to St. Luke's. Mr. Murdoch was made deacon here, and four years later he returned to Salisbury to undertake the longest rectorate in the history of St. Luke's Church.[3]

FROM GENERATION TO GENERATION

In the time of antebellum plenty, omens foretold the future. Few books in the history of modern publishing enjoyed a title more prescient than Hinton Rowan Helper's *The Impending Crisis of the South: How to Meet It*. Helper (1829-1909), born in that part of Rowan County that was set apart as Davie County in 1836, spent a part of the 1850s in Salisbury and is said to have written portions of his powerful abolitionist tome in the town. Published in New York in 1857 by Burdick Brothers, *The Impending Crisis of the South* captured the imagination of many and shaped the fervor of political thought leading up to the selection of Abraham Lincoln as president in 1860.[4] Fiery debate continued from the streets of the county seat to the halls of Congress. Salisbury resident Francis Burton Craige (1811-1875), a member of the United States Congress since his first election to the body in 1853, championed state's rights and favored secession.

Another son of Rowan County, John Willis Ellis (1820-1861), born in the part of Rowan County that became Davidson County in 1822, and confirmed at St. Luke's in 1858, also stood at the center of political debate. Elected to the North Carolina House of Commons in 1844, and serving as a judge of the Superior Court of North Carolina since his election in 1848, John Willis Ellis was elected governor of North Carolina in 1858 and inaugurated on New Year's Day, 1859. He was reelected and sworn in for his second term on 1 January 1861. Soon thereafter, the matter of secession came to occupy much of his official life.[5] The seizure of Fort Sumter on 13 April 1861 was followed by President Lincoln's call for troops two days later. In response, Governor Ellis informed the President, with words whose sting can be felt to the present, that "You can get no troops from North Carolina." The press toward secession increased, and at a special convention held in Raleigh on 20 May 1861, the ordinance of secession was passed unanimously. Mr. Ellis's role as a Confederate governor was short, as his health failed in the throes of crisis; he died on 7 July. First interred in a family cemetery in Davidson County, his body was brought to Salisbury in the spring of 1866 and laid to rest beside that of his first wife Mary White in the Old English Cemetery, within sight of the church in which he had been confirmed on 28 March 1858.[6]

Henry Toole Clark (1808-1874), a wealthy Edgecombe County planter, succeeded Mr. Ellis as governor. Governor Clark also had connections to St. Luke's. In 1852 he married Mary Weeks (Parker) Hargrave, a widow, whose brother John Haywood Parker was then rector. He responded to Confederate Secretary of War Leroy P. Walker's request for prison facilities by informing him of the availability of the former cotton mill here

John Willis Ellis, a native of Rowan County, was confirmed in St. Luke's Church on 28 March 1858 by the Right Rev. Thomas Atkinson, Bishop of North Carolina. Just over four months later, on 5 August, he was elected governor of North Carolina. Engraving by E. G. Williams & Bro., New York, published in the *Biographical History of North Carolina, Volume VII*, 1908

Little of the misery of imprisonment in the Confederate Prison is visible in this picturesque bird's eye view of the prison drawn by Charles A. Kraus and issued as a lithograph in 1886 by J. H. Bufford's Sons of Boston, New York, and Chicago. Mr. Kraus was in Salisbury in 1864 when he was married by Dr. Rumple to Sara Krimminger.

The image was reproduced as a postal by Buerbaum's Bookstore

at a price of $15,000. Although Mr. Walker authorized the purchase in July 1861, the deed for the property was not executed until 2 November. Just over a month later, on 9 December, 120 prisoners arrived at the building newly fitted up as a prison. Prisoners of war were confined at the Confederate States Military Prison into July 1862, when the provisions of the Dix-Hill Cartel were put into operation and prisoners exchanged between the Union and Confederate governments. Then, until autumn 1864, the prison was used for both military and civilian incarcerations. As the Confederate position deteriorated in the last months of 1864, thousands of prisoners were shipped by rail to the Salisbury prison and on 6 November 1864 it is said to have housed the largest number ever, a total of 8,740 men.[7] Two communicants of St. Luke's had particular roles at the Confederate States Military Prison throughout its existence. Dr. Josephus Wells Hall (1805-1873) was named surgeon to the prison hospital in late December 1861 and was surgeon-in-charge at its closing in the spring of 1865. Samuel R. Harrison, a furniture maker, provided many hundreds, and perhaps thousands, of coffins for those who died at the prison.

The prospect of war fostered apprehension in Salisbury, and a sense of uncertainty was felt at St. Luke's even before the fall of Fort Sumter. Raising funds for the rector's salary was not always easy, even in the best of times, and with political unrest brewing in the spring of 1861, the task was even more difficult. Mrs. Archibald (Mary Ferrand) Henderson, the sister of Mrs. Haughton, described the vestry's resolution in a letter to her son written on 2 April 1861.

> The vestry of our Church held their usual meeting yesterday, Easter Monday. As they failed to raise $800 for Mr. Haughton by subscription, they determined to rent the pews. They charge us $60 for ours. Mr. Boyden is charged the same. The four front pews are free to be given to Mr. Love's family, the Beards and Howards, Mr. Locke's. Your Aunt also as the clergyman's wife has a pew rent free. I have no idea it will work well here. Judge Caldwell gets his seat for $40, Richard and Julius, his sons, subscribe and bring the pew up to $75. There are but three that rent for $60—all others are cheaper.[8]

The Civil War intruded quickly into the life of St. Luke's and its effects were experienced in many ways, large and small, throughout the parish. On 13 June 1861, *The Church Intelligencer* published two prayers authorized by Bishop Atkinson for use in the Diocese. A copy of one, "A Prayer for Those Who Have Gone Forth to War in the Defense of Their State and Country," survives in the papers of Mrs. Archibald Henderson with the notation that it was used at St. Luke's during the war.[9]

> Oh! Most Gracious Lord God, our Heavenly Father, we commend to Thy care and protection, Thy servants, who in behalf of their families and their country, have gone forth to meet the dangers of

The home of Josephus Wells Hall was one of Salisbury's most fashionable antebellum residences. Dr. Hall and his family occupied the house while he served as chief surgeon at the Confederate Prison hospital and a vestryman at St. Luke's, and his descendants lived here until 1972, when it was acquired by the Historic Salisbury Foundation. In this photograph of ca. 1865 Dr. Hall, his wife, and a servant are standing on the first story of their ornate two-tier verandah, while their daughter Henrietta stands above them. Miss Hall and Julius D. McNeely were married in St. Luke's on 22 May 1866 by Mr. Haughton.
Photograph courtesy of the Historic Salisbury Foundation

war. Direct and lead them in safety; bless them in their efforts to protect and defend this land, preserve them from the violence of the sword and from sickness, from injurious accidents, from treachery, and from surprise; from carelessness of duty, from confusion and fear; from mutiny and disorder; from evil living and from forgetfulness of Thee. Enable them to return in safety and honor, that we, being defended from all who would do us hurt, may rejoice in Thy mercies, and Thy Church give Thee thanks in Peace and Truth, through Jesus Christ, our Lord. Amen.

However devoutly offered, prayers did not stop bullets and soon a scion of St. Luke's was among the town's first casualties of the war. Colonel Charles Frederick Fisher (1816-1861), the son of Congressman Charles F. Fisher and Christiana Beard, a daughter of Lewis Beard, had served as president of the North Carolina Railroad since 1855. He resigned the position in the late spring and raised a regiment, the Sixth, which he

The death of Colonel Charles Frederick Fisher, an early casualty of the Civil War, was mourned in the parish, the city and throughout North Carolina. He was a grandson of Lewis Beard, whose heirs conveyed the land on which St. Luke's stands, and the father of Frances Christine (Fisher) Tiernan (1846-1920), who achieved fame as the novelist Christian Reid and saw the name of her 1876 novel, The Land of the Sky, become the sobriquet of the Asheville region.

This engraving is reproduced from that published in Dr. Rumple's *A History of Rowan County*

led into war. He died in the first Battle of Manassas, Virginia, on 21 July 1861, and his body was brought back to Salisbury. Mr. Haughton recorded his burial in the Lutheran Cemetery in the church register, describing him as a "vestryman of this church, who died a Martyr to Southern Rights."[10] Meeting on 26 July, the vestry adopted a resolution honoring Colonel Fisher that was published on 9 August in *The Church Intelligencer*. Remembering him as "our worthy brother and efficient co-laborer in the cause of the Church, to which he was ardently attached, and to which he was a munificent benefactor," the vestry resolved "That, in his death, the State has lost a distinguished citizen—and society, a valuable member— the Church, and ardent friend—and the Vestry, an able co-adjutor."[11]

The roster of losses continued through the war. A year later, on 30 July 1862, Mr. Haughton buried Lieutenant James H. Kerr (184_-1862), the eldest son of Major James E. and Catharine (Huie) Kerr and the grandson of General William Kerr, who died of "Camp Fever—a Martyr for the Rights of the South." His body was also buried in the Lutheran Cemetery; however, it lies unmarked. On 20 May 1863 another scion of Salisbury and St. Luke's followed Colonel Fisher and Lieutenant Kerr in death. William Campbell Lord (1838-1863), the son of Ann (Ferrand) Lord Parker Haughton and the late John Bradley Lord, was the stepson of two rectors of St. Luke's, the grandson of Stephen L. Ferrand who had served on the building committee for the church, and the great-grandson of John Steele. A graduate of the University of North Carolina in 1858, he had just taken up the practice of law when the war began; he served as captain of the 57th Regiment, North Carolina Troops. On 1 June the *Carolina Watchman* published news of his death "near Hamilton's Crossing, Va., from the effects of a wound through the left lung received in the storming of Marye's Hill," and continued with a long glowing account of his final days, his character and the promise of manhood cut short once again.

> **Tenderly borne from the field by some of his men, to all of whom he had already endeared himself, he was placed in quarters where he received every comfort and attention which his desperate condition required. Soon the loved ones from home were near him with sweet and tender ministerings. For days his life hung in the balance, and then came hopeful words to anxious friends. But alas! the sad end could not be averted. Gradually sinking under his terrible wound, after sixteen days of suffering, he calmly fell asleep in his mother's arms.**

> **His remains arrived at home on the following Sunday, and, in the evening of the same day, were borne to their last resting place, followed by the whole sorrowing community.**

Mr. Haughton officiated at the burial of other Confederate soldiers who either died in Salisbury or whose bodies were brought here for burial. Among this number were William Palmer (d. 1862) of the South Carolina State Troops, Lieutenant Colonel F. M. Kent (d. 1864) of the Louisiana Light Infantry and commandant of the Confederate States Military Prison at Salisbury, and Gideon McRory (d. 1864) of the Tennessee Calvary. These burials during the war were listed along with others performed by Mr. Haughton, which included William Locke (d. 1862), a vestryman at St. Luke's, and his (second) wife Jane (d. 1862), Chambers McConnaughey (d. 1863), "a Gentleman highly respected," in the Thyatira burying ground, and a number of infants, children, and slaves.

Mr. Haughton also presided at happier occasions, marrying church members and their slaves, as well as two officers of the Confederate States Army in October 1864 in the church: Lieutenant Charles H. Snead and Sarah Williams on the fifth, and Colonel F. C. Singeltary and H. E. Williams on 19 October. Baptisms and confirmations also continued through the war. One baptism merits mention, in part because Mr. Haughton also made particular reference to it in his parochial report to the annual convention of 1864. After listing the various statistics for the church, he offered a one-sentence addendum. "Visited, baptized, and (we trust) prepared for death, 1 criminal in prison under sentence of death."[12] A longer description appears in a roster of baptisms in the parish register under the date of 9 December 1863. "Jacob Wilson Murph, in Jail, under sentence of Death, who was hung on 11th Decr. 1863, but Repented, Believed, & Trusted in his Merciful, Pardoning Saviour to wash away his Sin, & receive him into His Ever^g King^m." The *Carolina Watchman* carried a short notice of the execution in its 14 December edition.

By themselves, the parochial reports published in the journals of the Diocese's annual conventions through the course of the war provide little insight into the character of church life during the early 1860s. The report submitted by Mr. Haughton in the spring of 1861, probably before the fall of Fort Sumter, gives no clue of the "impending crisis." In 1862 Mr. Haughton added two sentences to his submission of statistical data.

> **I deem it due to the energy and zeal of the Ladies of the Parish to state, that for one year past they have had in successful operation a "Ladies Church Society," the profits from which have been encouraging (notwithstanding the dreadful war that is upon us,) and have greatly benefitted the Church.**

> **Since the last Convention the Church has been deprived, by death, of two of its valued members, Col. Charles F. Fisher and Mrs. Jane A. Locke.**[13]

He also reported $40, provided to the "Sick and wounded soldiers from N. C.," among the church's total contributions of $242 to good causes and the bishop's salary ($40). For reasons now unknown Mr. Haughton apparently submitted no account of the church to the 1863 convention or, if so, it was lost and not published. In 1864 a total of $1,953.95 contributed by the church to missions, the bishop's salary ($40), and a series of church causes reflects the depreciated Confederate currency. Just under one-half of this amount was contributed to the Confederate States Bible Society ($770) and the Confederate States hospitals ($121). Mr. Haughton reported 31 funerals (28 white, three colored) in 1864, a number which cannot be reconciled with the listing of burials in the church register; however, the twenty funerals reported in 1865 precisely match his entries in the church register. His possible role in conducting services for some of the dead at the Confederate States Military Prison has yet to be resolved.[14]

The monies raised for charity, relief and other good works at St. Luke's during the war were supplemented by communicants' private donations. While the Confederate States Military Prison at Salisbury has remained strong in the public conscience to the present, less is known about the medical and hospital facilities located in Salisbury. One such was the Salisbury Way-Side Hospital that was opened here in July 1862. The Hospital Committee, including vestrymen Luke Blackmer and Moses W. Jarvis, mounted "An Appeal for the Sick and Wounded Soldiers" that was issued as a broadside and printed in the *Carolina Watchman* on Monday, 11 May 1863.

AN APPEAL
For the Sick and Wounded Soldiers
Salisbury, May 7th, 1863

The brave soldiers of our Army on the Rappahannock have again met the enemy on the field of battle and scattered them "Like leaves of the forest when autumn hath blown." The flag of our young Republic floats gloriously over another field of blood. But victory is obtained at a fearful cost. The best blood of our nation has been shed freely on the Rappahannock, and in addition to those who have fallen in death, there are thousands of others who are wounded and disabled from present service. These will seek their own quiet homes as soon as their wounds will admit of their removal; some, whose wounds are not so serious, will come at once; others as soon as they are able. While on their way home they need places where they can obtain rest and refreshment without charge. Such a place is the Salisbury Way-Side Hospital, where more than twelve hundred of our sick and wounded soldiers have been fed and lodged, and clothed, and nursed since July last, and where all who come in the future shall be carefully provided for. But we need provisions, medicines, delicacies for the sick, and money. Will you help us now to take care of your own, or your neighbor's sons and brothers and fathers, who have so bravely fought and bled for us on the terrible fields of the Rappahannock? It is not the Hospital Committee that calls on you, it is the voice of the poor maimed and bleeding soldier that asks of you to give him "food and fire" in exchange for the blood he has shed for you. A word to the patriotic is sufficient.

JAMES C. SMYTH,
L. BLACKMER,
J. J. BRUNER,
J. D. BROWN,
WM. OVERMAN
M. W. JARVIS,
F. M. Y McNEELY.
Hospital Committee

The Civil War continued on its relentless course through 1864, coming to its bitter end the following spring. In April 1865 Salisbury was visited by two of its most famous figures, within a week of each other. This might not have been unusual except that the men represented the opposing sides of the war. General Robert E. Lee surrendered the Army of Northern Virginia to General Ulysses S. Grant on Palm Sunday, 9 April 1865, but the news had not reached General George Stoneman, who was approaching Salisbury in his infamous sweep of the Piedmont and western North Carolina. At daybreak on Wednesday, 12 April, General Stoneman and some 4,000 of his troops entered Salisbury, from the west and northwest, and quickly went about the destruction of the prison and the Confederate stores in warehouses lining the North

Carolina Railroad tracks. His work done, the general and his troops left Salisbury the next day. The devastation was horrific; however, General Stoneman is said to have shown a real degree of deference to personal property. Margaret Beall Ramsay (d. 1941) recounted the visit in "Reminiscences of Harrowing Days in Salisbury," published in the *Salisbury Sunday Post* on 25 September 1932. She concluded her memoir by writing "Salisbury…may well afford to hold Stoneman's name in grateful remembrance."

Her remembrance and those of others, including Abner Marcellus Rice (1856-1945), who had witnessed Stoneman's passage through Unity Township, are well known. Another account, that of Captain John Keais Hoyt, has not been published. John Keais Hoyt (1840-1912), a native of Washington, Beaufort County, North Carolina, was in Mobile, Alabama, when the war broke out and he immediately joined the Mobile Guards, organized in Montgomery as the 3rd Alabama Infantry Regiment. The regiment was dispatched to Virginia, where it was mustered into Confederate service at Lynchburg in May 1861, and in 1862 it was assigned to the Army of Northern Virginia. Mr. Hoyt was elected captain of his company in May 1862.

Captain Hoyt came to Salisbury in autumn 1863, apparently in connection with duties at the Confederate military depot, and remained here through the end of the war. On the morning of the 12th, when General Stoneman entered Salisbury, Captain Hoyt was in a scouting party near Salem, where he heard the "artillery fire…that heralded the fall of Salisbury to Stoneman's forces." It was nearly five months later that Captain Hoyt penned his account of events in a letter to his sister Clara. In the interim he had been in Chatham County attending to the family's investments in mining operations, and had returned to Salisbury to gather personal belongings.[15] Here, on 10 September, he wrote a much delayed letter to his sister.

> I was not at Salisbury at the time of its capture. Five of us had left the afternoon previous on a scout, Col. Thos. Ruffin being one of the number. We were within five miles of Salem next morning at daylight (the enemy were expected to come from that direction) when we heard the artillery firing at Salisbury. We instantly wheeled our horses, and started back in full gallop. We reached the railroad bridge over the Yadkin just at 12 o'clock M. You probably remember this bridge. It is about seven miles from S. Earthworks had been thrown up on the north side of the river about a week previous. In these we found about five hundred men & six pieces of artillery. Simultaneously with our entering these works the Yankee skirmishers emerged from the woods on the opposite side of the river. We then first knew that Salisbury had fallen. We fought the Yankees at this point until nine oclock that

night. We saved the bridge, whipped off their artillery, and drove back thrice our numbers, in great confusion. By this time the entire sky was red with the light of the conflagration at S. Tongues of flame, bright & scorching, shot far up in the still night and seemed to threaten the very heavens, while ever and anon, some scarcely perceptible breath of air brought to our ears the low moan of the roaring flames that told of their fierce ragings. My anxiety for my friends at S. became so great, the idea of their being surrounded by such dangers & horrors became so intolerable, that anything was preferrable to uncertainty. So I determined to go into town that night. But the bridges had all been destroyed, the ferry boat sunk. So I had to ride thirty miles down the river to effect a crossing. My horse was a good one & the night was not dark. So off I started at a slapping pace, and by noon the next day had made my sixty miles. As I rode up on the crest of a high hill the Yankees were setting fire to the last of some govt. buildings, a few hundred yards distant. I hid my horse in the bushes, and stood there watching the flames, & waiting for night. After dark, I borrowed a long greatcoat from a countryman & throwing it over my uniform & saber went across the fields and entered the town. Never have I witnessed such a scene of desolation. And as I stole along through the ruins of the still burning buildings, a sense of loneliness came upon me. I felt as if I was alone in the world. This feeling was increased when I entered the town proper. The houses all closed & dark, not even a ray of light penetrated through the chinks of any of the closed shutters. Streets deserted. Not a soul to be seen. My own footsteps gave back a hollow echo that was ghostlike. But presently I came upon figures standing in groups dark & motionless. While in another direction, a shadowy column turning a corner gave back a muffled tramp-tramp as it rapidly disappeared. Cautiously entering the dwelling of a friend, I ascertained that the Yankees had hurriedly left since dark. They had heard that Gen. Beauregard was near at hand with a large force. Thus ended my last adventures during the war.

This scene of devastation greeted Salisbury's second important visitor at the end of the Civil War. Jefferson Davis (1808-1889), President of the Confederate States of America, had stopped briefly in Salisbury while

Jefferson Davis (1808-1889) visited Salisbury twice as President of the Confederate States of America.

This portrait was painted in 1863 by John Robertson and is reproduced courtesy of The Museum of the Confederacy, Richmond, Virginia.

As the former president of the ill-fated Confederate States of America, Jefferson Davis suffered a certain notoriety during the last 24 years of his life. Following his death on 5 December 1889, the Illustrated London News *published an account of his life on 14 December under the heading "The Late Mr. Jefferson Davis." Two of its four illustrations were half-page engravings of events during his flight at the end of the war. This engraving, carrying the caption "Mr. Jefferson Davis and his party retreating across the Pe-Dee River, North Carolina, at the fall of the Southern Confederacy, 1865," shows the presidential party crossing the Yadkin River into Rowan County on 17 April 1865. Signed "P Naumann," it is based on the sketches made by the artist/ correspondent of the News who was traveling with Mr. Davis and what remained of the Confederate government.*
Reproduction courtesy of The North Carolina Collection

traveling by train in September 1864. That visit had also been recounted in anecdotal fashion by John Keais Hoyt in a letter to his sister dated 29 September of that year. Davis's circumstances, and those of the South in general, had taken a radical turn during the months leading up to his overnight visit in Salisbury on 17-18 April 1865 in the home of the rector of St. Luke's.

On 2 April, a week before his surrender at Appomattox, General Lee advised Mr. Davis that Richmond, the capital of the Confederate States, could not be held. The message urging Jefferson Davis to make immediate preparations to depart Richmond was delivered to him on Sunday morning while he sat in his pew at St. Paul's Episcopal Church. He left the church and spent the remainder of the day overseeing the efforts leading up to the evacuation of the Confederate government to Danville. The train carrying President Davis, members of the Confederate cabinet, and others, departed Richmond that evening about eleven o'clock. The Davis party arrived in Danville in the afternoon of 3 April; the city just above the Virginia/North Carolina line would serve as the capital of the Confederacy for a week. On 10 April Jefferson Davis received preliminary reports of both General Lee's surrender and the approach of General Stoneman from the west. Burton Norvell Harrison (1834-1904), the president's secretary, organized the departure later that day by train for Greensboro.

Thus began a month-long flight south through North Carolina, South Carolina and Georgia, that ended with Jefferson Davis' capture

near Irwinville, Georgia, on 10 May. The events of this period have been retold time and again; however, the accounts of two men who made the entire journey with the Confederate president bear on the stay in Salisbury.[16] John Taylor Wood (1830-1904), a grandson of President Zachary Taylor, a nephew of Jefferson Davis' first wife, and a captain in the Confederate States Navy, kept a diary that opened with the evacuation from Richmond. Burton Harrison recounted the harrowing days in "The Capture of Jefferson Davis," which was published in *Century Magazine* in October 1883 and reprinted in *The Harrisons of Skimino* in 1910.

Jefferson Davis, his Cabinet and their traveling party remained in Greensboro from the 11th of April until the 15th, when they set out on horseback and in ambulances and wagons. They spent the evening in Jamestown and continued on the next day, Easter Sunday, toward Lexington, camping some four miles east of the county seat. Captain Wood recorded the event in simple terms. "People along the road afraid to take the P. in. Benjamin, Davis & others camping out for the first time."[17] On Monday, 17 April, the party traveled from Davidson County into Salisbury. Captain Wood's record is again brief. "22 miles to Rev. Mr. Orton's Salisbury. Crossing the Yadkin by the R. R. bridge. Stoneman a few days ago destroyed the depots, arsenal & all public property, the fires yet smouldering. Met Col. Cary & other friends. Write home every day."[18]

Burton Harrison treated the experience in greater detail in his memoir.

In Lexington and in Salisbury we experienced the same cold indifference on the part of the people, first encountered at Greensboro', except that at Salisbury Mr. Davis was invited to the house of a clergyman, where he slept. Salisbury had been entered a few days before by a column of the enemy's calvary (said to be Stoneman's), and the streets showed many evidences of the havoc they had wrought. With one or two others, I passed the night on the clergyman's front piazza as a guard for the President.

During all this march Mr. Davis was singularly equable and cheerful; he seemed to have had a great load taken from his mind, to feel relieved of responsibilities, and his conversation was bright and agreeable.[19]

At the close of the Civil War, when many in the South became increasingly hesitant to extend hospitality to Jefferson Davis, the rector of St. Luke's and Mrs. Haughton welcomed Mr. Davis and members of his party at their East Innes Street home on Monday, 17 April 1865. Jefferson Davis spent the night with the Haughtons and continued on toward Charlotte the following day. Their house, located in the west corner of Innes and Lee Streets and facing northeast, later passed into the ownership of Dr. Julius Andrew Caldwell, an assistant surgeon in Colonel Fisher's Sixth Regiment.
This photograph of Dr. Caldwell's residence, dated July 1906, probably represents the appearance of the house in 1865; however, the porch possibly dates to Dr. Caldwell's ownership.
Courtesy of the Rowan Museum

After breakfast with the Haughtons, President Davis and his party departed Salisbury, traveled through Cabarrus County where they spent the night of the 18th, and arrived in Charlotte on 19 April.[20] There, at the onset of a week's stay at the home of Lewis F. Bates, the head of the Southern Express Company, Jefferson Davis learned of the assassination of Abraham Lincoln.[21]

Because of "the disturbed state of public affairs," the annual convention of the Diocese of North Carolina, usually held in late April or early May, was postponed until 13-15 September 1865 in Raleigh. Matters of church finance and the question of reunion with the Protestant Episcopal Church in the United States dominated discussion at the convention. Since 1861 the North Carolina diocese had been a part of the short-lived Protestant Episcopal Church in the Confederate States of America. In June 1865 the presiding bishop of the national church, John Henry Hopkins, had written to the Southern bishops inviting them to return to the church and join their fellow bishops in Philadelphia in October. Bishop Atkinson was disposed to attend the meeting, and the diocesan convention passed a resolution supporting reunion on agreeable terms. Bishop Atkinson and Bishop Lay of Alabama were the only two southern bishops to attend the General Convention that opened on 4 October in Philadelphia. There Bishop Atkinson exercised critical influence on the language of a resolution concerning the reunification of the national church.[22]

Thomas Atkinson (1807-1881) was ordained a priest in 1837 by Bishop Moore of Virginia and served successively as rector of St. Paul's Church, Norfolk; St. Paul's Church, Lynchburg; St. Peter's Church, Baltimore; and Grace Church, Baltimore, up to his election as Bishop of North Carolina on 17 October 1853.

This engraving by George E. Perine of New York was made from a photograph by Van Orsdell of Wilmington, where Bishop Atkinson resided. It was published in 1876 by A. R. Elliott of Hertford, North Carolina.

The plight of churches in the Diocese was widespread but unevenly felt. Those in the eastern part of the state, where most of the North Carolina fighting had occurred, suffered to a greater extent than those in the inland, western section of North Carolina, including Salisbury, where St. Luke's came through Stoneman's two-day occupation unscathed. Although the building stood firm and handsome, the fortunes of its communicants were impoverished by the increasing depreciation of Confederate currency. From the outbreak of the war until December 1864, when $251 was collected as a Christmas offering for the poor, the monthly offerings had not totaled $100 or more except in three months of the later year. In March 1864, $121 was collected at the Easter communion for the sick and wounded in hospitals, in May $720 was given for the Confederate States Bible Society, and in August $100 was collected "for chaplains in army." In April 1865, with the war at near-end, communicants at St. Luke's contributed $1,400 for "Fayetteville sufferers." The last collection at the church in Confederate currency, $187, occurred in May 1865. In June 1865 the collection of $10.03 was in United States currency. Individual collections for the remainder of 1865 did not rise above ten dollars on any occasion except for the bishop's visit on 27 August and at Christmas, when $24.70 and $28.04 were contributed, respectively. In 1865 Mr. Haughton reported a total of $3,451.64 in contributions by St. Luke's communicants in both currencies; contributions reported in 1866, all in United States currency, totaled $594.50.[23]

Another impact of the war at St. Luke's Church was the presence of refugees who became communicants here and left at or near the war's end. Five of this number are identified in a roster of communicants as "Refugee" and their later status as "Removed": Mrs. Williams, Mrs. Benbury, Miss Sarah Williams, Harriet Williams and Mrs. Wood. Sarah and Harriet Williams, possibly sisters and daughters of Mrs. Williams, were married in St. Luke's. Two officers of the Confederate States Army, Captain Hugh Cole and Captain Hoyt, probably joined when stationed in Salisbury. "Left" is written beside their names in the roster, as it is for an additional five communicants: Mrs. Shepperson, Mary Love, Betty Love, Croswell Morris and Mrs. Morris.

One feature of the immediate post-war occupation period in Salisbury was the appearance of a new newspaper, *The Daily Union Banner*, which succeeded the *Salisbury Banner* and began publication on 14 May 1865, with J. J. Stewart as editor. In its issue of Saturday, 7 October 1865, it published an editorial account of an incident that had recently occurred at St. Luke's under the heading "Sacrilege and Disloyalty."

Sacrilege and Disloyalty

We learn that on last Sunday at the Episcopal Church, in this city, while the Pastor was reading the prayer in the liturgy, for the President of the United States—a female threw up above her head a small Confederate flag. It is not in our line, and we do not propose to comment upon this conduct in its irreligious aspect, but to enter our protest against such actions being construed as evidence of any general sentiment of the good people of this community and to warn the offender, whoever she may be, and all others of her notions, against a repetition of the scene. Such conduct is not only disloyal, but impolite—every one has an implied invitation to church and those who attend, should by every rule of politeness do nothing there which they would not do in their own house in the presence of an invited guest.

So far from this being regarded as any indication of the popular sentiment, we think that it is a rare, and perhaps individual exception. We know, and we express what we know when we say that the feeling expressed in the scene in church, is not felt or entertained by one man in five hundred.

We earnestly trust that it will not be repeated, but that hereafter, young ladies will attend church for legitimate purposes and those only.[24]

The Rev. Thomas Goelet Haughton resigned as rector of St. Luke's on 16 July 1866. The reason for his resignation remains unconfirmed, and an air of mystery surrounds the later years of his life leading up to his death in Salisbury in October 1880. Bishop Atkinson expressed his own uncertainty in his address to the 1867 diocesan convention. "The Rev. Thomas G. Haughton has resigned the Parish of St. Luke's, Salisbury, and has, I understand, taken charge of one on the Eastern Shore of Virginia, but he has not applied for letters dismissory, nor do I certainly know his present residence.[25]

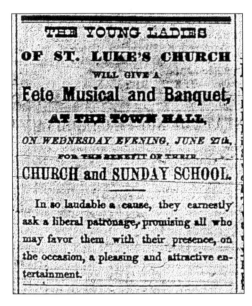

This notice for an entertainment sponsored by the young ladies of St. Luke's was published in The Old North State *on Thursday, 21 June 1866.*

Mr. Haughton, his wife and their son Thomas Ferrand Haughton were living in Salisbury in October 1869 when she died on the 15th and was buried in the English Cemetery near her first husband. The Rev. George Badger Wetmore, who had officiated at her marriage to Mr. Haughton, presided over her funeral. Mr. Haughton took up the practice of law, served as mayor of Salisbury in the early 1870s, and died here. The notice of his death, published in the *Carolina Watchman* on 14 October 1880, under the heading "Death of T. G. Haughton, Esq.," was brief. "This sad event occurred this morning about 10 o'clock, after an illness of eight or ten days." Another account of the circumstances of his death was recorded by Mr. Murdoch in an entry for 14 October 1880 in a roster of funerals in his parish record book. "Thomas Goelet Haughton (with an impoverished service) Sometime rector of St. Luke's Church but at the time of his death deposed from the ministry and living under sentence of Greater Excommunication pronounced by the Bishop—and therefore buried without the service of the Church in the English Burying Ground." His grave, presumably near his wife's, lies unmarked to this day. Mr. Haughton's personal possessions were put up for sale at two auctions held on 27 November 1880 and 12 February 1881. Books from his library, including religious and historical works, were bought by several gentlemen including the Rev. James Alston Ramsay, J. A. Hedrick, J. O. Crosby and the Rev. Mr. Murdoch who also acquired "1 Lot Sermons" for thirty cents.[26]

St. Luke's Church was without a resident priest from 16 July 1866 until March 1867, when the Rev. John Huske Tillinghast (1835-1933) came to the parish. At the age of 31 when he arrived in Salisbury, Mr. Tillinghast had enjoyed a varied life. Born in Fayetteville on 19 September 1835 to Samuel Willard and Jane Burgess (Norwood) Tillinghast, he enjoyed much of his childhood in Hillsborough with his grandparents, Judge William Norwood (1767-1842) and Mrs. Norwood. He attended the University of North Carolina in 1853-54 and studied for the ministry at the Episcopal Theological Seminary, Alexandria, Virginia. His obituaries identify him as a graduate of the College of William and Mary while other sources, including *Stowe's Clerical Directory*, cite Hampden-Sydney College as his alma mater, with graduation there in

1857. Whatever the case, he served as a teacher after graduation, but he returned to the family fold in Fayetteville and was living there with his parents and ten siblings in 1860. Ordained deacon in 1861, he served as a priest at St. John's Church, Rutherfordton, for a period before enlisting in the 44th Regiment, North Carolina Troops, in April 1862. Mr. Tillinghast was appointed chaplain to the regiment on 8 October 1862 and served for a year, resigning in October 1863 to accept a call as assistant to the rector of Trinity Church, Mobile, Alabama. He returned to North Carolina in the fall of 1864 to serve as rector of St. Paul's Church, Clinton. In 1865 he was advanced to the priesthood and was married to Sarah Jane Wilkins (ca. 1838-1923) of Rutherfordton.[27]

Mr. Tillinghast had given voice to both the rewards and frustrations of his pastoral duties in Clinton in an account of the parish published in *The Church Intelligencer* on 12 July 1866. He lamented "A church build-

When John Huske Tillinghast came to Salisbury as rector of St. Luke's in spring 1867, he was a young man in his 32nd year, not the distinguished patriarch of this photograph made in later life in South Carolina.
St. Luke's Archives

ing unpainted, and so daily suffering; unplastered, and so uncomfortable for worship, save in pleasant weather; the want of a bell, a serious want in a village that has no standard of time." Thus, little surprise attended an announcement eight months later, published on 7 March 1867, under the heading "Clerical Change" in the last issue of *The Church Intelligencer*, "The Rev. Mr. Tillinghast, of Clinton, N.C. has accepted a call to the rectorship of St. Luke's church, Salisbury, and wishes his letters and papers directed accordingly."

Mr. Tillinghast would have found immediate comfort in his first view of St. Luke's Church. His maternal grandfather, Judge William Norwood (1767-1842), was a member of the vestry that reorganized St. Matthew's Church in 1824 and undertook the erection of a new church in 1825.[28] When staying with his beloved grandparents in Hillsborough, John Huske Tillinghast attended services at St. Matthew's, and on coming to Salisbury he would have recognized similarities in the two buildings if he were not already acquainted with their kinship. the Rev. Mr. Tillinghast began his rectorate here on 15 March, and

he remained at St. Luke's for just over five years, departing Salisbury in mid-June 1872. He gave his first parochial account as rector to the 1867 convention and was "gratified to report the Parish in a hopeful and apparently flourishing condition.[29]

His first important act as rector was the preparation of a pastoral letter by which means he ended the practice of pew rental in St. Luke's and admonished his parishioners to practice the stewardship required of all Christians. Mr. Tillinghast's "Pastoral Letter" was printed on the front page of *The Old North State* on Saturday, 26 April 1867.

To the Parishioners of St. Luke's Church, Salisbury, N.C., Greetings:

Grace, mercy and peace, from God the Father, and our Lord Jesus Christ, be with you, amen.

The purpose of this communication is to say; that as the sittings in our parish church are hence forth to be, and to be held, FREE, it therefore becomes necessary to consider some other plan of raising the necessary pecuniary means for carrying on the work of the church, than as before by renting the pews—It has been determined, to adopt the Primitive and Scriptural plan, of making the church to depend for her pecuniary support on the voluntary offerings of the Faithful. You are therefore, my Brethren, requested and expected, "to lay by in store, according as the Lord has prospered you" an offering, to be laid, "the first day of the week" on God's holy table. That is to say, let each one determine how much,—what proportion of his income he ought to give to Christ's church and poor, and deposit it with the Sunday collection, by weekly installments.... If therefore at any time, yourself and family are detained from church, *send in*, your contribution, and if you can not present your prayers, defer not to send your "alms." ... It is well for us to remember, that it is as much the duty of a christian, to give to Christ, that is, to his church and his poor, as it is a duty to pray, in fact "prayers and alms" have always, and ever should go up together, like those of Cornelius "for a memorial" before God.

The rule should be that none of us should "go before the Lord *empty*," but let each one make it a matter of *conscience* to bring or send to God's House a weekly offering. If you are particularly prospered in your business, or met with any stroke of unlooked for prosperity, acknowledge your gratitude to the Giver of all, by a special and liberal "thank-offering. "Honor the Lord with thy substance and with the *first fruit* of all thine increase."—Take out, then, *God's* portion *first*, and accommodate your expenses to the remainder of your income. As the *proportion* which you should give—consider that, God *required* of the *Jew* one-tenth (1-10) of his income, ... so it would seem that a christian, should be ashamed to offer to God, *less* than a tenth (1-10)—and indeed, it is but reasonable, that a sincere and zealous christian would esteem it a great privilege to be thus a co-operator with God, and would desire to give *as much as he could*—... Let every one feel that he is personally responsible for the support and growth of this Church, and let *each one* do according to his ability, denying himself, using daily economy, that he may have somewhat, in any wise, "to cast into the treasury of God." ...

I have dwelt at some length on this subject, and resorted to this printed pastoral, above and beyond the teaching from the pulpit, to call your attention fully, to this *great and greatly neglected duty*. It is my purpose, God helping me, to see to it, that you shall not be ignorant of your duty for want of faithful and plain dealing publicly, and from house to house. I trust, also, by the grace of God to be enabled to practice what I preach. In conclusion, then, my brethren, let us remember, that as we "*sow*," we shall "reap." When we come to make up the final "reckoning" with "Our Lord," we shall find, that "what we've spent, we've wasted." "what we've left, we've lost," but, "what we *gave*, we HAVE." Yours, faithfully,

JOHN HUSKE TILLINGHAST
Rector

His letter and ministry proved effectual, and in 1868 he gave a positive account of parish life.

> **The Rector is gratified to be able to say that his hopes of progress expressed last year, with reference to this Parish, have been in a good degree realized, and he hopes for yet more decided progress hereafter. The congregation in addition to the money raised as reported, which does not in fact cover the whole amount (since the assessment of year before last, $130 ought to be added), have provided their pastor with a furnished house and done much for him outside, in the way of presents of clothing and gifts in kind. We have resorted to no equivocal method of raising money, depending entirely on the offertory and direct appeals.[30]**

The identity of the "furnished house" remains unknown. In the 1870 Census Mr. Tillinghast is listed with his household between the Mansion House hotel and the Rev. Jethro Rumple, pastor of the Presbyterian church, who was then living in the two-story Federal house, since known as the Utzman-Chambers House, at its original location in the west corner of Innes and Jackson streets. His family included Mrs. Tillinghast, their first-born child, John W. Tillinghast, a second son William Norwood Tillinghast, who was born in Salisbury on 19 August 1869, and the rector's sister Emily R. Tillinghast. A third child, Mildred Lewis, was born to the couple in 1871.

Soon after his arrival in Salisbury, Mr. Tillinghast undertook the compilation of a list of communicants at St. Luke's. The first of two lists compiled during his rectorate is dated 1867. Sixty-one persons, including Mrs. Tillinghast, are listed before an additional eight members were "Added by 1st Communion, July 1867." By 1869 he had amended this list, reducing the number of communicants to 55, 17 fewer than he had reported in 1868. He described the reasoning for this action in his parochial report.

> **There are a good many persons connected with this Parish as communicants whose connection is nominal. They are *dead* branches, they do not attend public worship or receive the Communion, *such are not reported*, having practically "excommunicated" themselves.[31]**

The number of communicants rose in 1870 by three, to 58, two of whom were faithful "colored" members of the church.[32] The number remained the same in 1871, but decreased to 55 in his report of 1872. However, these figures do not coincide with a "List of Communicants 1871" in the church register that includes 89 names. Apparently, an unidentified one-third of those on that list were, to use Mr. Tillinghast's language, "dead branches." In his last year as rector he was paid $646.05 toward a promised salary of $672.40. This was not only a reduction from

The Rector is gratified to be able to say that his hopes of progress expressed last year, with reference to this Parish, have been in a good degree realized, and he hopes for yet more decided progress hereafter.

1871, but the second year in a row that payments to him did not equal the vestry's promise.[33]

Whether the matter of salary entered into his consideration is not known; however, in the late spring, as he was laying plans to receive Bishop Atkinson and his fellow Episcopal clergymen at St. Luke's for the 56th Annual Convention, he had resolved to leave Salisbury and to accept a call from Zion Church, Eastover, South Carolina. In a letter to the vestry submitted on 1 May, he resigned the rectorship of St. Luke's, effective 10 June 1872. His last official act as rector was to preside at the burial of Scotia Campbell Beard, the infant daughter of John and Ellen (Bryce) Beard, on the tenth of June in the Lutheran Cemetery.

When Mr. Tillinghast departed Salisbury in mid June 1872, the greater part of his long life lay before him. He acquired a house in the country outside Eastover, southeast of Columbia in lower Richland County, where he lived until his death on 10 January 1933. From 1872 to 1882 Mr. Tillinghast was rector of Zion Church, Eastover, and St. John's Church, Congaree. He was next priest of St. John's Church, Charleston, from 1882 to 1884, and then served as rector of Epiphany Church, Eutawville, from 1884 to New Year's Day 1886. He was called back to Zion Church, Eastover, and served as rector until 1920, when he resigned and was named rector emeritus. In his obituary published in *The State* on 11 January 1933, Mr. Tillinghast was "said to have been the oldest Episcopal minister in the United States, the oldest alumnus of William and Mary college and the oldest surviving chaplain of the Confederate army." His body was interred beside that of his wife in the cemetery at Zion Church, Eastover.[34]

ENDNOTES

1. For the history of the Confederate States Prison at Salisbury see Louis A. Brown, *The Salisbury Prison: A Case Study of Confederate Military Prisons, 1861-1865* (Wilmington, Broadfoot Publishing Company, 1992). This is a revised and enlarged edition of the work first published in 1980. Hereinafter cited as *The Salisbury Prison*.

2. Of the numerous accounts of General Stoneman's visit to Salisbury, a good concise example appears in John G. Barrett, *The Civil War In North Carolina* (Chapel Hill: The University of North Carolina Press, 1963), 356-59.

3. JAC, 1869, 19.

4. See James W. Wall, "Hinton Rowan Helper," DNCB, 3: 97-98.

5. See Noble J. Tolbert, "John Willis Ellis," DNCB, 2: 151-52.

6. Ibid. "Gov. Ellis' Remains," *Carolina Watchman*, 7 May 1866. Mary White (1824-1844) was the first-born, only surviving child of Philo White (1796-1883), a founder and editor of the *Western Carolinian* (1820-1830), who later was involved in newspaper publishing in Raleigh and Racine, Wisconsin, and served as a diplomat in Germany and South America from 1849 to 1859. See D. A. Yanchisin, "Philo White," DNCB, 6: 182.

7. *The Salisbury Prison*, 8, 17-19, 35, 77, 140.

8. Quoted in *SL*, 28.

9. See *SL*, 28. The question of when the prayer was first used at St. Luke's cannot now be answered; however, it was probably in 1861, soon after it was issued by the bishop, rather than in 1862 as Mrs. Henderson wrote. The obvious variance in text between the prayer published in *The Church Intelligencer* in 1861 and that appearing in Mr. Powell's St. Luke's in 1953 is the use of "Gracious" in the opening sentence of the first and "precious" in the Powell text. *The Church Intelligencer* republished both prayers in its 28 November 1862 edition. The first of the two occasional prayers was titled "A Prayer for the People of the Confederate States."

10. *HRC*, 232-35, 363-69.

11. The members of the vestry were William Murphy, Luke Blackmer, Moses W. Jarvis, Samuel R. Harrison, William Locke and John M. Coffin. Mr. Jarvis came to Salisbury as cashier of the Salisbury Branch of the Bank of North Carolina.

12. JAC, 1864, 42.

13. JAC, 1862, 44.

14. JAC, 1864, 42; JAC, 1865, 57.

15. I am grateful to George Stevenson, private manuscripts archivist, North Carolina State Archives, for drawing my attention to the John Keais Hoyt Letters, P. C. 1842, in the State Archives. This biographical account of Captain Hoyt is abstracted from his description of the collection.

16. One recently-published account of the collapse of the Confederacy is Burke Davis' *The Long Surrender* (1985).

17. Diary of John Taylor Wood, Volume 3 (2 April-16 July 1865), 16 April 1865, John Taylor Wood Papers, Southern Historical Collection, University of North Carolina Library, Chapel Hill. Hereinafter cited as Wood Diary. Judah P. Benjamin was the Confederate Secretary of State.

18. Wood Diary, 17 April 1865. "Mr. Orton" is a phonetic misspelling of the rector's name.

19. Fairfax Harrison, ed., (*Aris Sonis Focisque*) *The Harrisons of Skimino* (N. p.: De Vinne Press, 1910), 240.

20. In *Jefferson Davis, A Memoir*, 2 volumes. (New York: Belford Company, 1890), 2: 627-628, Varina Howell Davis reprinted an extract of a letter written by someone who attended the breakfast at the Haughton house. The writer of the letter, who is not identified, recounted a conversation involving a young girl, who was described as the rector's daughter and who is said to have expressed her fear of death at the hands of President Lincoln to her father and Mr. Davis. Jefferson Davis is said to have responded, "Oh, no, my little lady, you need not fear that. Mr. Lincoln is not such a bad man, he does not want to kill anybody, and certainly not a little girl like you." Whether such an incident occurred is unclear; however, no one in the Haughton family conforms to the description of the girl as "a child of only seven or eight years." Burke Davis repeated the anecdote in *The Long Surrender*.

21. A short account of the travel from Greensboro to Charlotte appears in Haskell M. Monroe Jr., Lynda Lasswell Crist et al, eds., *The Papers of Jefferson Davis*, 11 vols. (Baton Rouge: Louisiana State University Press, 1971-2003), 11: 549.

22. ECNC, 247, 252-53.

23. JAC, 1865, 57; JAC, 1866, 38.

24. The identity of this female churchgoer is not known. Notwithstanding Mr. Stewart's reference to young ladies, the "offender" might well have been one of four women, all of whom attended St. Luke's, mentioned in an article on Hinton Rowan Helper written by Walter "Pete" Murphy and published in *The State Magazine* on 7 November 1942. "In my boyhood days it was my good fortune to accompany an aunt of mine, Mrs. Julia Smythe, on frequent visits to her close friends, Mrs. Jane Boyden (mother of "Baldy" Boyden), Mrs. Giles Pearson (sister of Governor John W. Ellis), and Miss Christine Fisher (sister of Col. Charles Fisher and aunt of Christian Reid), all of whom were unreconstructed rebels. From their conversation I learned much of the War Between the States and of events which preceded it and of the reconstruction period. They all knew Helper and his name was frequently mentioned in their conversations, all were agreed upon two things in connection with him, that he was a thoroughly despicable scoundrel and an exceedingly handsome man."

25. JAC, 1867, 21.

26. Rowan County Estates Papers, North Carolina Division of Archives and History, Raleigh, North Carolina.

27. "Death Claims Aged Minister," *The Columbia Record* (Columbia, SC), 10 January 1933. "J. H. Tillinghast Dies at His Home," The State (Columbia, SC), 11 January 1933. *Stowe's Clerical Directory of the American Church, 1932-33* (Northfield, Minnesota: G. Stowe Fish, 1932), 330. Weymouth T. Jordan Jr., compiler, *North Carolina Troops, 1861-1865, A Roster*, Vol. X (Raleigh, North Carolina Division of Archives and History, 1985), 397. *Alumni History of the University of North Carolina* (Chapel Hill, General Alumni Association, 1924), 623.

28. Mary Claire Engstrom, "William Norwood," DNCB: 4, 379-80.

29. JAC, 1867, 74.

30. JAC, 1868, 112.

31. JAC, 1869, 77.

32. JAC, 1870, 67.

33. JAC, 1871, 75; JAC, 1872, 81.

34. Albert Sidney Thomas, *A Historical Account of the Protestant Episcopal Church in South Carolina, 1820-1957* (Columbia, SC: The R. L. Bryan Company, 1957), 223, 302, 314, 378, 544, 548.

The program of renovations and interior decoration, initiated during Mr. Pike's rectorate and completed during that of Mr. Morris,
enriched the setting for worship at St. Luke's. Photograph by Robert Bailey

The figures of St. William of York and St. Wulstan in this window are memorials, respectively, to William and James Murphy. They and their brother Andrew, who built the Greek Revival-style house at 229 West Bank Street, were the sons of John Murphy (1779-1848) and his wife Mary Furr (1793-1867), a daughter of Tobias Furr. William Murphy (1812-1867) was married (first) to Eleanor J. Hampton (1815-1844). Mary, their eldest daughter, was married to Samuel R. Harrison and resided at Chestnut Hill until her death in 1883. James Murphy's wife Elizabeth was the elder sister of Susan Wainwright Chunn, his brother William's second wife. The Chunn sisters were the daughters of William Chunn, a prominent member of Christ Church, Rowan County. St. William of York (d. 1154), seen in his bishop's robes, was elected and consecrated Archbishop of York in 1140; however, ecclesiastical intrigues frustrated his effective exercise of the office until 1154. Soon after being restored to his see, he died suddenly, possibly of poisoning. St. Wulstan (ca. 1008-1095), seen also in his bishop's robes and holding a crosier, was a Benedictine monk who became Bishop of Worcester and an able administrator. He is seen standing over the tomb of Edward the Confessor who approved his election. St. Wulstan was an ardent church builder and, no doubt, a favorite of Dr. Murdoch.
Photograph by Robert Bailey

FROM GENERATION TO GENERATION

CHAPTER 5

The Murdoch Rectorate

St. Luke's and Its Missions in Town and Country 1872–1909

B efore the month of June 1872 was out, the Rev. John Huske Tillinghast was succeeded at St. Luke's Church by a priest who would serve St. Luke's longer than anyone in its history. Francis Johnstone Murdoch (1846-1909), ordained deacon in this church in 1868 and ordained priest at St. Paul's Church, Edenton, in 1870 by Bishop Atkinson, accepted the call to St. Luke's on the 28th of June. He remained rector of the church until his death on 21 June 1909. The length of his rectorate, however, was but one of many factors that distinguished his career as a minister, educator, businessman and citizen of his city and state. Soon after coming to St. Luke's, he set about organizing mission chapels in both Salisbury and Rowan County, as well as the neighboring counties; today St. Paul's and St. Matthew's churches and the Church of the Good Shepherd, Cooleemee, honor his foresight. In his own parish he enjoyed seeing the congregation double in size to nearly 150 communicants, while he proudly supported the organization of the St. Luke's Chapter of the Brotherhood of St. Andrew in 1887, and the Bishop Lyman Chapter of the Daughters of the King in 1892. Mr. Murdoch also oversaw the enlargement and refitting of the small Gothic Revival church in two building programs that essentially created the church we know today. As an educator he was valiant in his efforts to establish a boys' school in Salisbury, but failing that, he tutored some dozen men for the ministry and long served as a trustee of both St. Mary's College and the University of the South at Sewanee. No doubt inspired by his fellow, senior clergyman, the Rev. Dr. Jethro Rumple, the revered, long-time minister of First Presbyterian Church and author of *A History of Rowan County, North Carolina*, he gathered up the history of the church in

The length of his rectorate, however, was but one of many factors that distinguished his career as a minister, educator, businessman and citizen of his city and state.

Rowan County and planned to see it into print. He amassed what became arguably the largest private library of his day in Salisbury, and was a frequent contributor to *The Church Messenger* in the 1870s and 1880s. In 1890 the University of the South conferred an honorary doctorate on Mr. Murdoch and he was thereafter known as Dr. Murdoch.

Outside the parish, Mr. Murdoch became as well known as a founder of the textile industry in Salisbury in the 1880s, as a director and officer of several companies in which he made investments. These and other business interests prompted a degree of contention within the parish and criticism by the vestry to which he is said to have responded, "Gentlemen, if I end my business interests in this town you'll all grow poor and if I resign as rector of this parish you'll go to hell. Therefore I choose neither…next order of business."[1] Whether his utterance of those sentiments is fact or fiction remains uncertain; however, the substantial profits from these investments, among others, provided Mr. Murdoch a real degree of financial independence. This, in turn, enabled him to pursue a ministry to the parish, its missions and the Episcopal Church that has remained unrivaled by his successors.

Francis Johnstone Murdoch's family was of Scotch-Irish ancestry and among the last of that group to make their way to western North Carolina, following, years later, in the wake of the great emigration of the Scotch-Irish to the Piedmont in the third quarter of the 18th Century. Henry Murdoch (1710-1771), the rector's great-grandfather, is said to have resided at Glasslough, Ireland, and he is the first member of the family about whom much is known. His son Robert Murdoch (1751-1838) married Mary Johnstone and their eldest son, William, was born in Glasslough in 1795. William Murdoch married Margaret Nixon (1807-1883) in 1829 and resided with her at Anaroe, County Tyrone, Ireland, where the first eight of their dozen (known) children were born between 1830 and 1841. In about 1843 Mr. Murdoch, his wife and their seven surviving children left Ireland and came to America, settling briefly at Perryville (now Milroy), Pennsylvania. There, Henry Murdoch (1843-1844), the ninth of their offspring, was born on 9 October 1843. He and his youngest sister Mary Elizabeth (1841-1844) both died in July 1844 and were buried at Perryville in the Presbyterian churchyard. Probably soon thereafter, the family, including six children, left Pennsylvania and made their way to Buncombe County, North Carolina. There, at Swannanoa, Francis Johnstone Murdoch was born on 17 March 1846. Two other sons, John Hamilton (1848-1898) and Rollo George (1853-

1885), were also born in Buncombe County, but spent their adult lives in Charleston, South Carolina, where several members of the family relocated.[2]

Mr. Murdoch's formative years were spent in Asheville or the surrounding area. He was educated at Colonel Stephen Lee's school at Asheville. Precocious from youth, he enlisted in Company E, the Bethel Regiment, at the age of 15 on 27 April 1861 and was mustered out, under-age, on 12 November 1861. He was then sent to The Citadel, Charleston, South Carolina, where he was a member of the Citadel Cadets. On 18 September 1864, he was confirmed in the Episcopal Church in Asheville by Bishop Atkinson. Presumably this event occurred in Trinity Church, which the Rev. Jarvis Barry Buxton Jr., had organized in 1851 and where he served as rector until 1891. Mr. Murdoch is believed to have studied for the ministry with Mr. Buxton (1820-1902), who was also the first principal of the Diocese's Ravenscroft School for boys that opened in Asheville in 1856. Mr. Murdoch was licensed as a lay reader on 8 November 1867, and he was admitted to the diaconate by Bishop Atkinson on 17 September 1868 in St. Luke's Church.[3]

The period from September 1868 to June 1872, when he came to St. Luke's, was one of service to missions and churches in western North Carolina. Bishop Atkinson dispatched Mr. Murdoch to serve as deacon-in-charge at St. John's Church, High Shoals, a small industrial community in northern Gaston County. Mr. Murdoch made his first report to the convention of 1869 when St. John's seven communicants comprised three "White" and four "colored" members.

Francis Johnstone Murdoch (1846-1909) was rector of St. Luke's for well over half his life, from June 1872 until his death on 21 June 1909. He appears here, in his later years, wearing a white linen surplice and stole.
St. Luke's Church Archives

I entered upon my duties in this Parish in October last. During the winter I have held occasional services at Long Creek Furnace, and Dallas, in this County, and also at Rehoboth Furnace, in Lincoln County. At the latter point there is a Sunday School kept up by a zealous Communicant. Rev. W. Wetmore has services at Rehoboth also. At Dallas we have one Communicant. Though our number of laborers is small yet all the Communicants who can teach, work zealously. It is my happiness to labor among those who earnestly strive to do what they can. We believe that Almighty God will, in his own good time, give us a blessing, and therefore we think the prospect here to be as bright as the promises of God.[4]

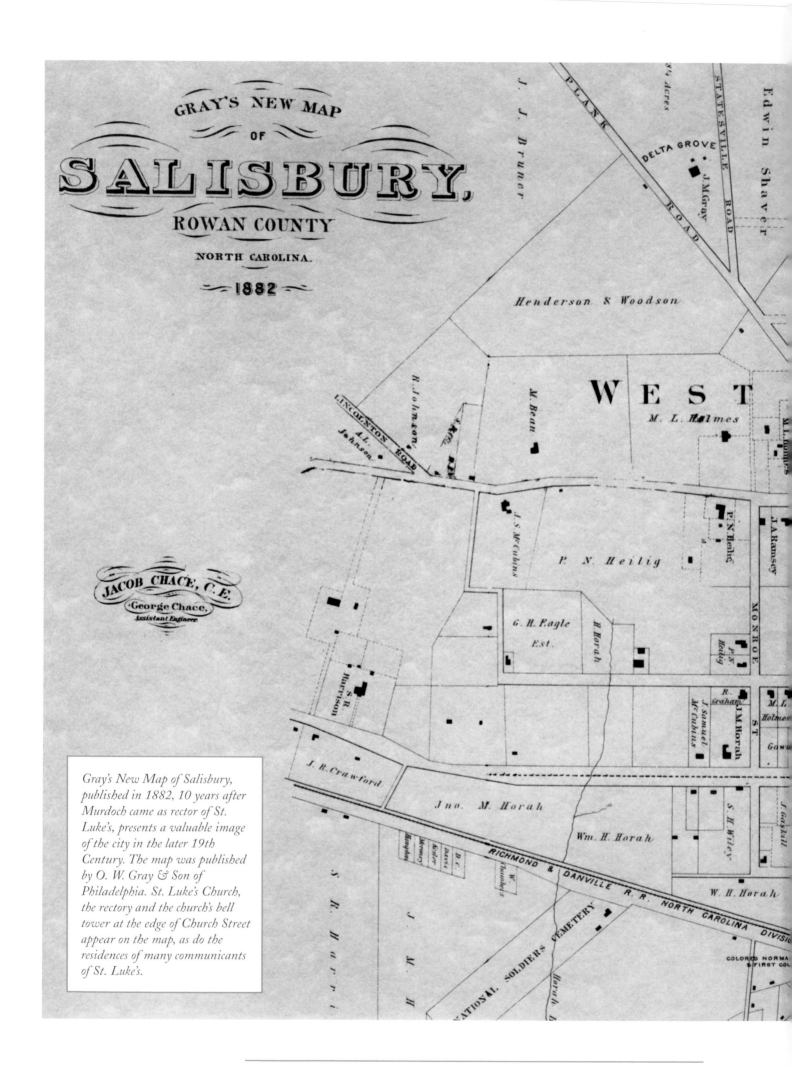

Gray's New Map of Salisbury, published in 1882, 10 years after Murdoch came as rector of St. Luke's, presents a valuable image of the city in the later 19th Century. The map was published by O. W. Gray & Son of Philadelphia. St. Luke's Church, the rectory and the church's bell tower at the edge of Church Street appear on the map, as do the residences of many communicants of St. Luke's.

A year later, in 1870, he reported 26 communicants of whom 11 were white and 15 were "colored." His reports for baptisms, catechumens, confirmation and funerals clearly indicate St. John's biracial, largely working class character."[5]

The report in 1870 was made to the convention assembled in St. Paul's Church, Edenton, and there on 8 May he was ordained priest by Bishop Atkinson. The bishop ordered Mr. Murdoch to Asheville, where

One of the few times Dr. Murdoch was photographed in the pulpit of St. Luke's occurred in autumn 1894 when the altar and chancel were lavishly decorated for a diocesan convention of the Daughters of the King. The inventiveness in the choice and arrangement of flowers and plants gave way to convention in the 20th Century.

St. Luke's Church Archives

he was to take charge of a series of missions in Buncombe County, Waynesville and Hendersonville, together with St. John's Church, Rutherfordton. In addition to those duties, he returned to St. John's Church, High Shoals, where he baptized 22 persons, and also held services at other points in Asheville and Buncombe County.[6] During this period in Asheville, Mr. Murdoch succeeded George T. Wilmer as principal of the Ravenscroft School, which had been reorganized as a theological institution in Asheville.[7] When Mr. Murdoch gave up his work in Asheville to accept the call to St. Luke's, his role as an educator did not pass entirely into memory. Instead, it would be revived in his hope for the parochial school at Chestnut Hill.

During the 1872 annual convention in Salisbury, the vestry of St. Luke's met with Bishop Atkinson concerning a successor to Mr. Tillinghast. He is said to have recommended Mr. Murdoch to them. Mr. Tillinghast endorsed the recommendation. The vestry made the call to him by letter, dated 1 June, in which they offered a salary of $650 "with the prospect of a handsome increase, as our Parish improves in church life." Four weeks later, on 28 June, Mr. Murdoch formally accepted the call to St. Luke's, and officially began his rectorate on the 29th.

In *This Was Home*, Hope Summerell Chamberlain recalled two anecdotes from Mr. Murdoch's first years in Salisbury.

> There were two sorts of mild bigotry rife in Salisbury: that of the Puritans and that of the predetermined never to allow themselves to be so classed. A new Episcopal rector had come in about this time, one who was to give good account of himself in the town, but very zealous at first with a youthful fervor, which was going to turn everything over at once. I could tell stories of what the Presbyterians and Methodists sincerely thought of him at first!

He was Anglican in his devotion to ritual, and a man of genuine piety. He tightened up the slackness which had long been allowed in his parish, and he once gave Mrs. Boyden to understand that he expected her to be in her place for morning worship, at the appointed moment, and that the latch of the church door would be drawn against all late comers.

"Then I will have to enter through the vestry," said Mrs. Boyden placidly.

I am afraid the "Dissenters" laughed derisively at first, and then became annoyed over the things he thought important, for the Rev. Frank Murdoch was as Scotch as his name, and brought a truly John-Knoxian fervor into his Anglican convictions.[8]

Indeed, Mrs. Boyden, a leading figure in St. Luke's, was not one to receive marching orders easily. Born in 1805, Jane Caroline Henderson was the daughter of Congressman Archibald Henderson (1768-1822) and the sister of Archibald Henderson (1811-1880) who was married to Mary Steele Ferrand, the late Mrs. Haughton's sister. She was first married to Dr. Luceo Mitchell and next to the Honorable Nathaniel Boyden (1796-1873), who had served two terms in the United States Congress and was a judge on the North Carolina Supreme Court. They were the parents of Archibald Henderson Boyden (1847-1929), who enjoyed a high reputation in Salisbury and for whom Boyden High School was named.

The second episode recounted by Mrs. Chamberlain in her memoir occurred in 1877 and centered on a third Archibald Henderson, a grand-nephew of Mrs. Boyden, the son of her nephew John Steele Henderson. This young Archibald was born on 17 July 1877 in the house built by John Steele, his great-great-grandfather.

When a first heir to the Hendersons was born, the young rector and his leading parishioner put their heads together to think of a distinctive way to dedicate him in baptism. Why not administer the rite by the triune immersion, on the eighth day, as was practiced in England before 1700? The child's mother besought the two young enthusiasts to be careful with her precious baby, and the family doctor was asked to be present to see that they did not injure it in their zeal. So a font was improvised, the water warmed to the proper temperature, and the Doctor gave the young Priest

John Steele Henderson (1846-1916), a life-long member of St. Luke's, had a long and distinguished career as a jurist, civic leader, member of the North Carolina General Assembly, and United States Congressman. His congressional tenure, from 1885 to 1895, coincided with his long service on the vestry of St. Luke's as its senior warden. His "Episcopacy in Rowan County," an account of the Episcopal Church published in Dr. Rumple's A History of Rowan County *in 1881, remains a standard text.* Engraving by E. G. Williams & Bro., New York, published in Biographical History of North Carolina, *Volume I, 1905*

lessons in how to hold the tender infant, how to close its mouth and nose effectively as he immersed it the three times.

At first all went well. "In the name of the Father," "In the name of the Son"—but the third time the Rector's technique failed him. Somehow he allowed the baby to swallow water, and it was choked on the name of the Third Person in the Trinity. The mother cried out from her bedroom, the doctor, seizing the heir of the Hendersons, administered first aid, while the prayers worked on to a conclusion.

After that, when the rest of the Hendersons came along rather regularly, it was a joke when the Doctor would solemnly inquire, "John, is this child going to be christened by the old English Triune Immersion?"[9]

Among Dr. Murdoch's first initiatives on becoming rector was to compile a roster of the communicants of St. Luke's. He described their status as "Bona Fide," "Lapsed," or those "Persons Confirmed but have never received the Holy Communion," in his listing dated to 14 June 1872.

St. Luke's Parish Register

John Steele Henderson (1846-1916), a long-serving vestryman at St. Luke's who would also serve as a United States Congressman (1885-1895), remained a close friend and supporter of Mr. Murdoch.

With an engaging manner Mr. Murdoch quickly settled himself in his church and community. He soon drew a number of fair-weather members back to St. Luke's. In 1873 he had reported 68 communicants, but in 1874 he reported 36 "added by 1st communion and lapsed persons restored" which, with offsets by death (three), removal (two), and one who either remained lapsed or was "lost" anew, plus two newcomers to St. Luke's, comprised a total of 100 communicants.[10] During these first years he had also been busy with improvements to the church. In December 1872 the vestry approved the purchase of a "steel composition bell" from a Cincinnati foundry. On its arrival in spring 1873, the decision was made against hanging it in the existing church tower whose appearance and location, presumably atop the roof ridge, is now unknown. Instead, Philip P. Meroney was engaged to erect "an independent belfry, very plain and at moderate cost." Later that spring, at the congregational meeting on 14 April, Mr. Murdoch appealed for "a decent alms basin" stating "that he was unwilling to use the present tin plate much longer." The "tin plate" was apparently replaced, and during the summer of 1873 Luke Blackmer placed an "elegant chancel railing" in the church.

In late autumn of 1873 St. Luke's suffered the death of two of its most highly esteemed communicants, both of whom were members of the vestry at their demise. Judge Nathaniel Boyden (1796-1873), a native of Massachusetts and a resident of North Carolina since 1822, had relocated to Salisbury in 1842. Here, in 1845, Mr. Boyden married Jane (Henderson) Mitchell. He quickly gained wide respect and was elected to both the North Carolina Senate and the United States Congress. In 1871 he was appointed to the North Carolina Supreme Court. The children of his first marriage, John A. Boyden, Mrs. Dr. A. M. (Ruth) Nesbit and Nathaniel Boyden Jr., came to Salisbury with their father, and likewise figured in the life of St. Luke's. Judge Boyden died on 20 November 1873 and was buried in the Old Lutheran Cemetery.[11]

Two weeks later, on 6 December 1873, Dr. Josephus Wells Hall (1805-1873) died suddenly at his residence on South Jackson Street. Mr. Murdoch officiated at his funeral service at St. Luke's and preceded the coffin a short distance to the Old English Cemetery where his body was buried. Dr. Hall was long survived by his widow Mary Cowan Hall (1823-1902), the daughter of Thomas Lincoln Cowan, a granddaughter of Captain Thomas Cowan who built Wood Grove, and a great-granddaughter of pioneer Michael Braun Brown who built the pre-Revolutionary stone house in eastern Rowan County that bears his name.[12]

In 1874, having weathered some now unknown disagreement with church worthies and having submitted a letter of resignation on 6 February that the vestry would not accept, Mr. Murdoch turned to the cause of Episcopal missions in Rowan County. St. Mary's Chapel became the first of a group of some dozen churches and chapels in Rowan and neighboring counties that engaged his attention and talents until his death. St. Paul's and St. Matthew's churches prospered and survive today as does St. George's, at Woodleaf, and its parent St. Andrew's, which are associated with Christ Church, Cleveland. The buildings that housed St. Jude's, St. Peter's and St. Philip's churches survive; however, their congregations have all long since ceased to exist. St. Mary's, St. Mark's, St. Joseph's and St. John's churches have all been lost.

Mr. Murdoch established St. Mary's Chapel in an existing frame church, standing about mid-way between Salisbury and China Grove and near the residence of Charles H. McKenzie. Members of the McKenzie and related families were among its first, most faithful communicants. In the spring of 1875 when a furnace was installed at St. Luke's, the vestry voted to give the old stove and pipe to the infant mission. In his parochial report, Mr. Murdoch reported the receipt of "$136 in answer to his appeal to help to build a Chapel to be known as St. Mary's Memorial Chapel."[13]

On 25 November 1875 Charles H. McKenzie (1834-1901) and his wife Ellen Sumner (1841-1912) conveyed a tract of two and one-half acres as the site of the proposed church.[14]

By 1876 Mr. Murdoch could give a more promising account of the mission.

> **Since my last report, St. Mary's Memorial Chapel, in the Southern portion of my Parish, has been completed. Forty-three of the Sunday School Pupils reported, belong to the Sunday School at St. Mary's.[15]**

Later that year, on Monday, 20 November, Bishop Atkinson paid his first (known) visit to St. Mary's where he "preached, confirmed four persons, addressed them and administered the Holy Communion."[16] Mr. Murdoch held regular services at St. Mary's Chapel "on alternate Sunday afternoons" and a Sunday School was under the charge of Charles H. McKenzie.[17] Despite the promise of local interest and the donation of the church grounds by Mr. McKenzie, efforts to raise money for a new chapel moved slowly, and it was not until 1883 that the new church was completed and consecrated. Mr. Murdoch noted the accomplishment in his annual report.

One of the few surviving images of St. Mary's Chapel is this pastel by Miss Margaret Bell (1907-1969), a granddaughter of Dr. and Mrs. Murdoch.
St. Luke's Church Archives

SAINT MARY'S CHAPEL
ROWAN COUNTY

The old St. Mary's chapel has been pulled down and a new one built, almost entirely at the expense of Mr. Thomas Sumner. The cost of the new chapel is not known to the Rector but is estimated in this report at $800. The church was closed for several months for repairs, and for many months no services were held at St. Mary's while the new chapel was being erected.[18]

Bishop Atkinson came to Salisbury in November 1883, and on the 14th he consecrated St. Mary's Church and confirmed four new members. In his episcopal address at the next diocesan convention he noted, "This new Church is a great gain to the neighborhood, and reflects much credit upon the liberality and zeal by which so satisfactory a result has been accomplished." Although St. Mary's was set apart in its own parish in 1888, and flourished for some time, it failed in the early 20th Century and the building was lost. Today only the cemetery marks its location.[20]

Meanwhile, Mr. Murdoch had fostered important developments at St. Luke's that met with success. As a bachelor priest, he had not required the provision of a residence that the vestry had made available to Mr. Tillinghast and his family. He apparently kept rooms in the Boyden House or another of the city's hotels after coming to Salisbury, and may also have taken quarters in a private residence. In late 1875 or early 1876, conversation arose among the vestry concerning the availability of the two-story brick house standing in the south corner of Council and Church streets and its potential as a parish rectory. The house had been erected in 1867 for John I. Shaver (1810-1873), and in January 1875 his widow Mary and son Edwin sold the property to W. C. Coughenour for $2,275.[21] The purchase of the house was apparently a foregone conclusion when the vestry met on 3 April 1876, voting to acquire the house as a rectory. The deed conveying the property for $2,525 to the vestry, comprising John Steele Henderson, Stephen Ferrand Lord, Archibald Henderson Boyden, Peter A. Frercks, John R. Ide, Aquilla J. Mock and B. Frank Rogers, was dated 31 March 1876.[22] Mr. Murdoch now had a handsome residence, befitting his status, which he would occupy alone for eight years until his marriage to Eliza Jane Marsh.

The two-story brick house erected by John I. Shaver in 1867 served as the parish rectory from 1876 to 1961. It was named the Canterbury House in 1962.
Photograph by Robert Bailey

His short service as head of Ravenscroft School in Asheville encouraged Mr. Murdoch's ambition to establish a parochial boys' school in Salisbury, and by 1878 the first of two such institutions affiliated with St. Luke's had opened. The first notice of it in his parochial report of 1878 read simply: "Since the Parochial School was begun I have not been able to minister anywhere outside my own parish."[23] The next year he reported the school employed two teachers and had 30 male scholars.[24] The parish Sunday School had eight teachers and 58 students. By 1880 the number of students in the parochial school had decreased to 14, and by 1881 the school had apparently closed, as no mention of it was made in Mr. Murdoch's annual report.[25] While the rector was handsomely housed by the parish, he might have been a little remiss, to the thinking of the ladies of St. Luke's, in his dress. Early in 1881 Miss Mary Ferrand Henderson was instrumental in raising $56 which her brother, as secretary of the vestry, reported was given to Mr. Murdoch "to purchase him a suit of new clothes."

With their rector dressed and well housed, the leaders of St. Luke's turned to improvements to the church. An instance of simple maintenance occurred first, in November 1880, when the vestry decided to replace the deteriorated fence enclosing the churchyard with a new one to be six inches lower than the old one. Whether the fence was built later in 1880 or early in 1881 is unclear; however, it was not until 6 June 1881 that the churchyard committee reported the expenditure of $26.15 for painting it.

Attention was next directed to the interior and the condition of the plasterwork. During the second half of 1881 the vestry discussed the matter, debated the cost of installing a new coat of plaster on the church walls for $125, raised some $150 by subscription for the work, and finally, on 7 November, advised the committee to use their discretion as to when to begin the plastering. With the walls repaired the vestry looked upward. On 13 March 1882 the committee on church repairs "was authorized to ceil the Ch. overhead if deemed expedient." The work was done and the following month the vestry authorized the ceiling to be painted. These piecemeal efforts were the prelude to a larger action.

Except for the addition of the chancel railing installed in 1873, through the generosity of Luke Blackmer, the interior of the rectangular brick building consecrated in 1828 had seen little change until 1881-1882, when the plaster was replaced and the ceiling installed. In late spring of 1882 discussion arose concerning a more critical improvement to the fabric of St. Luke's. Through travel to annual diocesan conventions held at churches throughout the state, Mr. Murdoch and leading members of the church, serving as delegates to the conventions, had become aware of improvements in church design through the course of the 1870s and early 1880s. This path toward more churchly buildings had actually begun in the antebellum period with the construction of the Chapel of the Cross, Chapel Hill, in 1842-1848, to the design of Thomas U. Walter; St. Paul's Church, Wilkesboro, in 1848-1849, to the design of William Grier; and Christ Church, Raleigh, in 1848-1852, to the design of Richard Upjohn. Christ Church, alone, was built on a cross-plan that would be adopted subsequently for costlier buildings in the Diocese. The Chapel of the Cross and St. Paul's Church were designed with recessed chancels in apse extensions to their rectangular naves.

Discussion at St. Luke's fixed on the erection of an apse addition to the northwest gable end of the church, thereby providing a spacious recessed chancel. At a vestry meeting on 3 July 1882, Stephen Ferrand Lord moved "that the present Ch. building be enlarged by the addition of a recess chancel, & that the matter will be agitated until the work is accomplished." The motion carried and the work advanced through the summer and fall of 1882 under the direction of the building committee, comprised of the rector and Messrs. Samuel R. Harrison, Joseph O. White and Luke Blackmer. Beginning in the mid-19th Century, stained glass windows had come into use as decorative enhancements for American church interiors, and the vestry of St. Luke's considered them for the windows on the three sides of the apse. The large opening above the altar in the northwest end of the apse was set aside on 17 July as a memorial to the Rt. Rev. Thomas Frederick Davis, a former rector of St. Luke's and later Bishop of South Carolina; the Rt. Rev. Thomas Atkinson, Bishop of North Carolina; and the Rev. John Haywood Parker, also a rector of St. Luke's. In September the vestry considered the application of Mrs. William G. McNeely for a

Elaborate decorations were the order of the day when the ladies of St. Luke's dressed the church for the diocesan convention of the Daughters of the King in autumn 1894. This is one of the few photographs that show the appearance of the chancel before its remodeling in 1909-1910. Visible on the left is a part of the organ case. Its date is uncertain; however, the pews are later 19th Century.
St. Luke's Archives

memorial window and assigned the southwest side window in the chancel to her. The window in the pendant northeast wall was assigned later to John Steele Henderson.

Although no architect has been identified for the apse addition to St. Luke's, the maker of the stained glass windows installed in the chancel is known. These three windows, the oldest surviving decorative features in St. Luke's celebrated Gothic Revival-style interior, are the work of Edward Colgate of New York. On 23 October the vestry requested John Steele Henderson "to correspond with Edward Colegate (sic), architect, about stained glass windows."

In the closing decades of the 19th Century, Edward Colgate was one of the most prominent suppliers of stained glass windows in the United States. Little is known about him and his firm, the Colgate Art Glass Company. He first appears as a member of the firm Sharp, Son and Colgate, the successor firm to Sharp and Son which, by 1867, had succeeded the firm of Sharp and Steel established in 1851 in New York City by Henry Sharp. These firms had supplied windows to a number of Episcopal churches in the Northeast, as well as for the Bowdoin College Chapel.[26] How the vestry came to know of Mr. Colgate is not known; however, Mr. Murdoch, among others, might have seen windows produced by the firm(s) and Mr. Colgate in their travels. In 1883 when Mr. Henderson contacted Edward Colgate, his firm had offices at 318 West 13th Street in New York City, with its factory at 8 Gansevoort Street.[27]

Work on the addition progressed in late October and early November. At the vestry's meeting on 13 November,

> **The building comm. reported the plastering, white washing & painting as all nearly finished—and that they had contracted to purchase new seats from Marsh & Kern at a price of $91.75. The seats to be furnished as soon as possible. The vestry resolved to tender the old seats to the Concord Congregation.**

The vestry's next meeting, on 4 December 1882, was taken up entirely with matters concerning the improvements. Mr. Murdoch reported on progress with the work, his hope "the church would be open in a very short time," and that the Concord church had accepted the old seats. Mr. Blackmer, for the building committee, reported receipts of $730.75 and disbursements of $631.93. On a motion of Mr. Henderson, the rector was authorized "to suit his own tastes" about gas fixtures for the chancel. The vestry next considered and approved the proposal submitted by Mr. Colgate for the windows. The large triplicate window would cost $400, while the smaller side windows would be produced at $112.50 each, for a total cost of $625. Mr. Murdoch scotched consideration of a lesser quality triplicate window costing $300 by pledging $50 to the costlier memorial for his fellow clergymen. Except for the windows, which arrived in June, the chancel addition was completed in the late winter or spring of 1883 and services renewed in the church.

On 19 July 1883, the *Carolina Watchman* provided its readers with an account of the newly installed memorial windows.

> The Episcopal Church.—New and handsome stained glass windows have just been put in the chancel of St. Luke's church in this place. The window in the end of the chancel is a triple window. In the centre bay there is the figure of Christ as the Good Sheppard with a lamb in his arms. In the bay on His right is a figure of St. Luke after whom the Church was named. While on His left is a figure of St. John the beloved disciple. Above the three bays in the tracery, there is a cross on one side, and a crown on the other, with a dove above. The centre bay of this window is a memorial to Bishop Atkinson, who, for more than twenty-seven years governed the Church in North Carolina. Another bay is a memorial to Bishop Davis, of South Carolina, who was a Rector of this Church from 1836 to 1846. The third is a memorial to the Rev. John H. Parker who followed Mr. Davis and ministered in the Church for about a year as a Deacon, and becoming Rector, when ordained to the priesthood, continued so for eleven years until his death.
>
> There are also two smaller windows in the sides of the Chancel. One containing a figure of St. Matthew, is a memorial of Mr. Wm. Macay, and the deceased children and grand-child of Mrs. Wm. McNeely. The other contains a figure of St. Mark, and is a memorial of Mr. Archibald Henderson and his deceased children and grand-child. We believe the windows are handsome as any in the State. They have to be seen to be appreciated.

Mr. Murdoch recounted the improvements at St. Luke's in his parochial report to the annual convention in 1883 with remarkable understatement: "During the year St. Luke's Church has been greatly changed and repaired and a recess chancel added to it." His report focused on the aforementioned completion of St. Mary's and noted "A parish paper has been published during the year." He offered a separate report for All Saints Mission in Concord which had gratefully received the old, perhaps original seating from St. Luke's.[28] The first issue of "The Register" apparently appeared in July 1882. In June 1883 Mr. Murdoch and Mr. Henderson were reelected editors of the parish quarterly and its price fixed by the vestry at ten cents per annum.

The principal event in Mr. Murdoch's life in the mid-1880s and one with no little import to St. Luke's was his marriage on 14 May 1884 to Eliza Jane Marsh. Having reached the age of 38, Mr. Murdoch was nearly a confirmed bachelor when his courtship of Miss Marsh, a communicant of St. Luke's, led to nuptials.

With St. Mary's Church established, and having preached at various points in the county through the years, Mr.

Eliza Jane Marsh as she appeared at about the time of her marriage to Dr. Murdoch on 14 May 1884. Courtesy of Harriett (Lang) Hornthal, a great-granddaughter of the couple

Murdoch turned his attention to the organization of a second mission in Rowan County in 1885. This was an ambitious undertaking, given the financial condition of the parish which had been in arrears for the rector's salary since 1884. Had Mr. Murdoch not had private means and a great affection for Salisbury and St. Luke's, he no doubt would have sought a more remunerative position elsewhere. At the end of December 1885 the

St. Jude's was the second rural chapel organized by Dr. Murdoch in Rowan County. The small gable-front building has been remodeled and greatly expanded by the successive congregations which have held services here.
Photograph by Jason Williams

church was in arrears to Mr. Murdoch in the amount of $170.37, and he described "the financial condition of the parish to be deplorable." This amount appears insubstantial today; however, it represented a high percentage of the sum of $492.47, which he reported in spring 1886 as having been paid as salary during the previous year. He also reported an indebtedness of $2,000 on church property that had a total value of $7,000.[29]

The first mention of the mission that would become St. Jude's appears in the vestry minutes for a meeting of 5 October 1885, when "Two old pews were placed at the disposal of the Rector for a proposed new chapel on the Sherrill's Ford Road." On 16 March 1886 Hugh H. Dobbins of Watauga County conveyed a lot on the south side of the Sherrill's Ford Road to Bishop Lyman and trustees of the Diocese of North Carolina, "for the use of a Congregation to be gathered in the neighborhood under the name of Saint Jude's Church."[30] This property included the grave of Joseph N. Dobbin (1856-1884), and was a part of the lands of a family that had been in Rowan County since the mid-18th Century and intermarried with the Graham family. A year later, in his parochial report for 1887, Mr. Murdoch wrote "During the year a new Church, called St. Jude's, has been erected at a cost of about $200."[31]

Concurrent with his efforts to establish St. Jude's, Mr. Murdoch was moving forward with plans for a third mission in Rowan County. St. Matthew's would become the first of the group to survive to the present as a viable institution. On 22 December 1886, William G. and Ann McNeely conveyed to Bishop Lyman and the trustees of the Diocese of North Carolina a tract of some five acres on the Statesville Road for a congregation which "shall worship in a church to be designated and called 'Saint

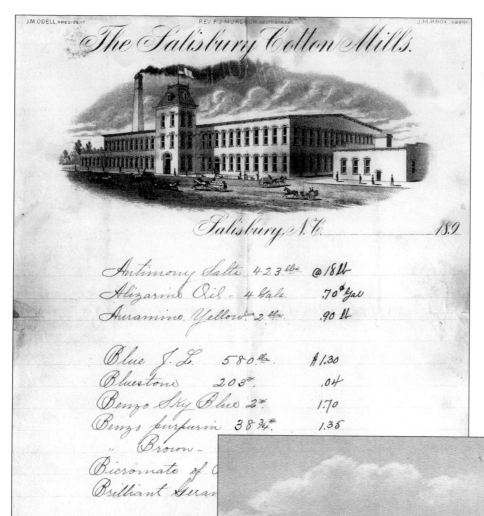

The Salisbury Cotton Mills were the first of a group of important textile mills erected in Salisbury during the great Piedmont textile boom of the late-19th Century. The company letterhead, bearing the name of Dr. Murdoch as secretary/treasurer, included an engraving of the proposed mill building that was more impressive than the complex of buildings seen in a contemporary post card published by Mr. Buerbaum. The small frame building on the left side of the postal, with a cupola above the center entrance, is either a school or possibly a chapel.
Courtesy of the Rowan Museum

Matthews Church,' to be built on said above described land: said Church building to be a memorial to the late William McCay and his daughter Annie McCay Lord...."[32] Following on the donation of the southwest chancel window in 1883, this gift was the second memorial that Mildred Ann (Hunt) McCay McNeely (1835-1887) donated to honor her first husband, William Spruce McCay (1808-1856), and first-born daughter Anne (1854-1879). According to church tradition, a frame church was erected on the property in 1887, possibly through the support of Mrs. McNeely; however, there is no mention of the building in the St. Luke's vestry minutes, which suffer a gap after 31 December 1885 to 2 May 1887, nor does Mr. Murdoch report it in either his 1888 or 1889 parochial reports.

Other events of a secular nature in 1887 also came to have importance in the life of Mr. Murdoch and St. Luke's Church. In December 1887

Mr. Murdoch became an investor and officer in the first of four textile mills organized in Salisbury in the years up to 1895, and he would subsequently establish Episcopal missions to serve the community of workers that developed around each. Beginning in April 1887, the *Salisbury North Carolina Herald* advocated the construction of cotton mills in the county seat as a spur to development using the slogans "Cotton Mills for Salisbury" and "Lets all Pull Together and Our Factory Will be Assured." Despite the newspaper's continued advocacy for mills, the idea failed to gain momentum until the closing months of the year. On 9 November the Rev. R. G. Pearson, described as a Presbyterian evangelist, held a revival service in the Farmer's Warehouse, and exhorted community leaders to erect cotton factories as a means of providing employment to the increasing poor, stating that "Next to the Grace of God, Salisbury needs a cotton mill." A meeting of city fathers held the next morning, chaired by Mr. Murdoch, spawned a series of meetings that culminated in mid December with the organization of the Salisbury Cotton Mills and the subscription of $30,500 in capital. John Milton Odell (1831-1910), a great pioneer of the textile industry in Concord, was elected president and Mr. Murdoch was elected secretary-treasurer of the company which opened its plant in 1888. The rector became the third president of the concern, succeeding Samuel H. Wiley, and held that office at his death in 1909. In October 1888 Mr. Murdoch next became an investor in the Rowan Knitting Company that erected a factory at the corner of Clay and Horah streets. Later, when the Vance Cotton Mill was organized in 1891, Mr. Murdoch became president of the company, serving in that capacity until his death. St. Luke's rector was likewise involved in the organization of the Kesler Manufacturing Company on 27 July 1895, and served as both a director and later president of the company.[33]

Today these mills, which made Salisbury an important center of textile production in late-19th Century North Carolina, are little remembered. Nevertheless, they and others that followed quickly in their wake, including the Patterson Manufacturing Company in China Grove, were critical to the economic development of Rowan County and Salisbury. Mr. Murdoch's decision to invest in the textile industry was no doubt critical to his remaining in Salisbury and at St. Luke's when other opportunities came his way. One such incident had occurred in November 1887, during the course of Mr. Pearson's revival. The *Carolina Watchman* printed an account in its pages on 17 November 1887.

> **We are pleased to learn that the action of the congregational meeting held in the Episcopal church last week, resulted in the determination of the pastor, Rev. F. J. Murdoch, to remain in his present position. He has declined the invitation to a pastorate in**

Mississippi, and will continue to labor in this field, where his services are most highly appreciated, and his popularity extending far beyond the circle of his own communion.

On a more personal level, the handsome income that Mr. Murdoch derived from his investments essentially freed him from any real dependence on his salary as rector. It afforded him and his family a very comfortable life, enabling them to leave the brick rectory in December 1900 for a large, handsome, newly-completed house on West Horah Street.

But, this financial freedom was years away from conditions in 1887 and 1888, when some $1,900 was still due Mr. Coughenour for the rectory, and the parish was in arrears about $275 on the rector's salary. Nevertheless, further improvements were made at St. Luke's. Apparently an unidentified donor had contributed a new pulpit to the church, and in October 1887 the vestry decided "that the old Pulpit & Recording desk be given to two of the Country churches. Mr. Murdoch said he wanted one for St. Jude's & other for St. Andrew's." Then, at the annual congregational meeting in April 1888, church members voted "to purchase a Pipe Organ to cost not less than $1,000." On 28 May the vestry considered other items. A proposal to alter the chancel railing was tabled; however, the vestry "ordered that a door be placed on the first landing on the stairway leading to the Gallery and that the Rector be requested to supervise the work." The vestry also accepted the hymn board presented by Mrs. Charles Price, and asked the rector "to place it in the church." The mention of the gallery is one of the few known references to this feature of St. Luke's and confirms both its existence and its survival in 1888.

Meanwhile, Mr. Murdoch and St. Luke's were host to the 72nd Annual Convention of the Diocese of North

The Rev. John Thomas Wheat had a long and distinguished career as an Episcopal clergyman and educator in the South following his ordination in 1826. In 1849 he took up the chair of Rhetoric and Logic at the University of North Carolina, holding the post for a decade. In 1867 he accepted a call as rector of St. Lazarus Church, Memphis; the newly-organized congregation included Jefferson Davis and his wife. In the sketch of his ancestor's life published in the Dictionary of North Carolina Biography *James Shober Brawley, related the explanation of the church's name in which Jefferson Davis is said to have exclaimed that "We, like Lazarus, were licked by dogs." Mr. Wheat resigned at St. Lazarus in 1873 and eventually came to Salisbury to live with his daughter Josephine May Wheat, who was married to Francis E. Shober. He died at the home of his granddaughter, Mrs. Boyden, in 1888 and was buried from St. Luke's.* St. Luke's Archives

Carolina that opened its four-day gathering in the church on Wednesday, 23 May 1888. The convention had last met in Salisbury in May 1872, when Mr. Tillinghast was host. On its second day, the delegates approved the organization and establishment of St. Mary's Church as a separate parish comprising Rowan County's Locke, Litaker and China Grove townships.[34] The convention also remembered one of its oldest priests by approving a memorial for the Rev. John Thomas Wheat (1801-1888), who died in Salisbury on 2 February at the home of his granddaughter Mrs. Archibald Henderson (May Wheat Shober) Boyden.[35] His funeral was held from St. Luke's with interment in the Old English Cemetery.

The organization of St. Mary's Church as a parish in 1888 represented one milestone in the long ministry of Mr. Murdoch; another occurred the following year with the ordination of Benjamin Sumner McKenzie as deacon. Mr. Murdoch's experience as a missionary priest in western North Carolina had convinced him of the need for clergymen to serve the many small congregations of Episcopalians in the region. As rector of St. Luke's he set about to improve the situation by encouraging promising young men to pursue the ministry. The first of those who responded to Mr. Murdoch's persuasion was Francis Emanuel Shober (1860-1919), the son of Francis Edwin and Josephine May (Wheat) Shober and the grandson of the Rev. Dr. Wheat. No doubt supported by his grandfather, Mr. Shober was ordained to the diaconate by Bishop Lyman in St. Luke's on 1 June 1884. He served as a priest at St. John's Church, Barrytown, New York, until 1891, when he gave up holy orders and took up journalism as a profession.[36]

Mr. Murdoch's next protégé, Benjamin Sumner McKenzie, was the first of a small but effective group of ministers who came to be called affectionately "Mr. Murdoch's boys." The son of Charles Harris and Ellen (Sumner) McKenzie, he grew up in the area that became St. Mary's parish. On 26 February 1889, Bishop Lyman ordained him to the diaconate at St. Mary's Church and reported to the next convention that "He will minister in this Church, and in other neighboring Missions, in connection with Rev. Mr. Murdoch, under whose supervision and guidance he will still continue."[37] The following year Mr. McKenzie was listed as assistant to Mr. Murdoch at St. Mary's, and minister in charge of All Saints Mission, Concord, and the Church of the Redeemer, Lexington. Meanwhile, the St. Jude's mission had passed into the care of the Rev. Edward P. Green, who had succeeded George Badger Wetmore (1823-1888) at Christ Church, Cleveland, and at St. Andrew's Church.[38]

In retrospect, the initiatives Mr. Murdoch and St. Luke's undertook in the 1880s represented a prelude to a larger series of projects in the 1890s. Although his proposal to further remodel and enhance St. Luke's failed early in the last decade of the 19th Century, only to come to splendid fruition at the end of his life, he realized the ambition to

In retrospect, the initiatives Mr. Murdoch and St. Luke's undertook in the 1880s represented a prelude to a larger series of projects in the 1890s.

FROM GENERATION TO GENERATION

provide a series of mission chapels for the several distinct neighborhoods that comprised Salisbury's rapidly growing cityscape. He also revived his dream of a boys' parochial school in Salisbury, with the opening of a school in September 1891 in the old Harrison mansion known as Chestnut Hill. This occurred in a period when Mr. Murdoch continued in his ventures well beyond the pulpit of St. Luke's, increasing his investment in the town's burgeoning textile industry and serving as an officer in the companies. Little wonder attends his failure to compose parochial reports in 1890 and 1891: he was busy with good works on every front. He could also take pleasure in a certain new status among his fellow Salisbury and North Carolina clergymen. In 1890 the University of the South awarded him an honorary degree, Doctor of Sacred Theology, in recognition of his contributions to the Episcopal Church and its ministry. Thereafter (and hereinafter) he would be known as Dr. Murdoch.

At its first meeting in 1890, on 12 January, the vestry had two important matters at hand. The death of the Rev. Dr. John Thomas Wheat on 2 February 1888 had occasioned mourning among both his family and the communicants of St. Luke's, where he worshiped in his last years. It also prompted strong feelings of affection among his former parishioners in Memphis, Tennessee, where he had served as rector of St. Lazarus Church. Dr. Wheat, who had been ordained priest in 1826, enjoyed a distinguished career as a minister and educator, including a decade at the University of North Carolina and the Chapel of the Cross. In 1867 he accepted a call to Memphis to become rector of St. Lazarus, a church newly-established by members of the old Confederate order. Prominent among its founders was Jefferson Davis. He is said to have explained the name for the church by exclaiming that, "We, like Lazarus, were licked by dogs." Dr. Wheat lamented the lack of suitable communion silver to Mrs. Davis, who quickly took the matter into hand. The next Sunday she and other women in the church received the alms basins and left them "heaped high with brooches, rings, bracelets, chains and gifts from loved ones." As James Brawley, Dr. Wheat's great-great-grandson recounted, "Enough precious metal was given to make a communion service consisting of a chalice, a paten and a flagon." After Dr. Wheat's retirement as rector of St. Lazarus, a yellow fever epidemic hit Memphis in 1873. It and subsequent outbreaks of disease took a heavy toll; St. Lazarus failed, and its small surviving congregation was merged with Grace Church in 1877. When word of Dr. Wheat's death reached Memphis and Mrs. Davis, she orchestrated the gift of the communion ware to St. Luke's as a memorial to Dr. Wheat. The vestry resolved to thank the Memphis donors, a list headed by Varina Howell Davis (1826-1905). Although Dr. Murdoch had replaced the "tin plate" shortly after his arrival here, the Memphis silver was the first important communion service at St.

Varina Howell Davis, who spent the final forty years of her life as the wife and widow of the president of the failed Confederacy, held Mr. Wheat in high regard for his service at St. Lazarus. Having been instrumental in the creation of the communion ware for St. Lazarus, she oversaw its gift to St. Luke's as a memorial to Mr. Wheat. The gift was accompanied by the following statement: "The Parishioners of Saint Lazarus Church, of Memphis, Tennessee, raised a subscription to purchase a Communion Service for their use. As it pleased Almighty God, to permit the beloved Parish to be blotted out, these humble worshippers to be scattered, and the Church to be used for other purposes, those who raised the fund desire to present to St. Luke's, Salisbury, N. C., this service in memorial of our tender, gentle, learned and eloquent Pastor, the Rev. Dr. John Thomas Wheat, so long connected with Saint Lazarus Church, and bound to those of his scattered flock who remain alive, by the tenderest ties of sympathy, affection, and profound respect. Varina Howell Davis and others."

Carte-de-visite by Mathew Brady, ca. 1860, reproduced courtesy of The Museum of the Confederacy, Richmond, Virginia

Photograph of the communion silver, believed to be by James Torrence, is in the St. Luke's Archives.

Luke's, and it remains in use today.[39] With no little irony, the gift nearly coincided with the death of President Jefferson Davis on 6 December 1889.

The second important action by the vestry at their January 1890 meeting was to approve the organization of missions to be called St. Peter's and St. Paul's. St. Peter's had been in the planning for over a year. On 6 October 1888, Dr. and Mrs. Murdoch deeded a lot in the northeast corner of Clay and Horah streets, measuring 100 by 150 feet, to Stephen Ferrand Lord, Theodore Buerbaum and Cathew A. Rice, trustees of St.

Peter's Chapel, giving them the right to mortgage the entire lot to raise money "to erect a Chapel to be known as St. Peter's Chapel on the half of the lot nearest Clay street." When the chapel was completed and free of debt, the trustees were to convey the property to the Diocese of North Carolina.[40] A frame chapel costing $900 and serving the Brooklyn neighborhood was standing at the corner by 1892.

Whether construction of the two mission chapels was undertaken concurrently is unclear, but likely. St. Paul's Chapel was apparently completed first, on its original site adjoining the Salisbury Cotton Mills. On Sunday afternoon, 10 May 1891, Bishop Lyman held services there and recorded the service in his episcopal diary.

> At 3 P.M. in St. Paul's Chapel, a very neat and churchly edifice in the immediate suburbs of Salisbury and near a large cotton factory, I preached and confirmed eight persons. This mission is a very interesting and encouraging one. It was established and is carried on by Dr. Murdoch, and the good work is going on in a most successful way. The building was crowded with a very attentive congregation, most of whom had never before been present at a Confirmation service.[41]

The small rectangular lot on which the church was erected, measuring 60 by 67 feet, had been conveyed by the company to Dr. Murdoch. He and Mrs. Murdoch, in turn, deeded the property to Bishop Cheshire and the trustees of the Diocese of North Carolina on 14 February 1894. Two provisions of the transaction bear restating.

> 1st that the Church built thereon shall be known as St. Pauls Church because that S. Pauls Cathedral London is the Mother Church from which the Church in North Carolina sprang and because Dr. Theophilus Draige the first Rector of St. Lukes Parish Rowan County was sent here by Richard Ferrick Bishop of London whose cathedral was St. Pauls.

> 2nd that said S. Pauls Church be a memorial to Robert Murdoch and Rollo Murdoch, deceased brothers of F. J. Murdoch, the grantor.[42]

Robert Murdoch (1833-1884) and Rollo George Murdoch (1853-1885) both died in Charleston within five months of each other, and were buried from St. Phillip's Church in Magnolia Cemetery.

Even as St. Peter's and St. Paul's chapels were advancing to completion, Dr. Murdoch was laying plans for the third Episcopal mission in the town of Salisbury. The deed for the church lot, executed by Mary Steele (Ferrand) Henderson on 18 April 1892, was but a month old when the rector reported on St. Luke's parish and its buildings to the convention that opened on 18 May at St. Barnabas' Church, Greensboro.[43]

...Mrs. Mary S. Henderson has deeded to Trustees a parcel of land near the Vance Cotton Mills, on which St. John's Chapel is now being built. The Trustees are to reserve a lot each for the chapel, a rectory and a school-house, and hold the funds arising from the sale of the remainder as an endowment for St. John's Chapel. The Trustees hope to realize eventually $1,500 or $2,000 for the endowment fund.[44]

When initiating the gift with Mrs. Henderson, Mr. Murdoch had taken care of a critical need for the parish: a residence for an assistant priest. By May 1894, a chapel valued at $500 and a rectory costing $1,000 had been erected on the lots donated by Mrs. Henderson.[45] With the completion of St. John's Chapel, Salisbury boasted St. Luke's, the mother church, and three missions. This arrangement continued through the remainder of the century, except that a fire in 1897 destroyed St. Paul's Chapel, and the new church was rebuilt on the present South Main Street site in 1898.

While building this series of mission chapels and providing pastoral care to the communicants of St. Luke's, the Salisbury and Rowan missions, and, at times, the congregations of Christ Church, Cleveland, and St. Andrew's, Mr. Murdoch was pressed at every turn. Having seen Mr. McKenzie and Mr. Green advance to priesthood, Mr. Murdoch took on other assistants and guided their early ministerial studies as they provided a much-needed ministry in the parish and the county. Sidney Stuart Bost (1871-1935) was the son of Henry Connor Bost (1841-1887), a vestryman at St. Andrew's Church. He grew up in the family residence on today's Potneck Road. In 1892, Mr. Murdoch listed him and Robert Bruce Owens as lay readers, assisting him with services at Christ and St. Andrew's churches and St. Matthew's and St. Jude's chapels, stating "Valuable services have been rendered in this field by the two lay readers whose names have been put at the head of this report."[46] On 20 May 1892, at the close of the Diocese's 77th convention held in Greensboro, Mr. Bost was admitted to the diaconate at St. Barnabas' Church. Six months later, on 17 November, Bishop Lyman added Robert Bruce Owens (1871-1954) to the order of deacons in St. Luke's. Having gained these two deacons as assistants, Mr. Murdoch simultaneously lost the good services of the Rev. Benjamin Sumner McKenzie, who resigned his work at St. Mary's Church, Rowan, and All Saints in Concord to accept a call to St. Matthew's Church, Hillsborough, and Orange County's St. Mary's Chapel. Although removed from Rowan County, Mr. McKenzie did not forget his mentor and the parish in whose churches he gained stature. He returned to St. Luke's on 18 February 1894, when Bishop Cheshire ordained him priest.[47]

Sidney Stuart Bost, who grew up in St. Andrew's Church, was one of the young clergymen whose progress to the priesthood was encouraged by Dr. Murdoch.
Photograph reproduced from *St. Andrew's Episcopal Church: The Sesquicentennial, 1840-1990*

The ordination of Mr. McKenzie was followed two years later at St. Luke's by that of both Messrs. Bost and Owens. On 31 May 1896 Dr. Murdoch presented Sidney Stuart Bost and Robert Bruce Owens to Bishop Cheshire, who ordained both to the priesthood.[48] Mr. Bost then became rector of Christ Church, Cleveland, and St. Andrew's Church. He also took charge of St. Jude's and St. Matthew's chapels as well

as St. George's Chapel, which had been erected in about 1893 in Woodleaf as a memorial to the Rev. George Badger Wetmore. Mr. Owens assumed the rectorate of St. Paul's Church and served as an assistant minister at both St. Peter's and St. John's missions, where Dr. Murdoch was minister-in-charge. Presumably, he occupied the rectory at St. John's. Dr. Murdoch remained in the pulpit of St. Luke's while also ministering to the communicants of St. Mary's church. This arrangement also proved to be temporary.

Dr. Murdoch soon lost these capable priests while gaining others. In 1898 Bishop Cheshire reported the removal of Mr. Owens to Oxford, where he became rector of St. Stephen's Church; and Mr. Bost to Durham, where he assumed the rectorate of St. Philip's Church. On 7 November 1897 Bishop Cheshire made Simeon Jeremiah Michael Brown, a descendant of pioneer Michael Brown, a

deacon in St. Luke's Church. Mr. Brown assisted Dr. Murdoch at both St. Peter's and St. John's missions through the remainder of the 19th Century. In 1899 Dr. Murdoch gained a new assistant, Thomas Lee Trott (1876-1941), who was admitted to the diaconate at St. Luke's Church on 26 February. Mr. Trott then served under the rector, assisting him at St. Andrew's, St. George's, St. Jude's and St. Matthew's. Dr. Murdoch presented another of his protégés, John Linker Saunders, as a candidate for the diaconate to Bishop Cheshire at St. Luke's on 10 June 1900. Having been made deacon, Mr. Saunders then served as minister in charge at St. Jude's and St. Matthew's under Dr. Murdoch.

During the 1890s, when the Rev. Dr. Murdoch was occupied with his investments in the textile industry, with nurturing his several missions in town and country, and with tutoring young men for the ministry, he was

In the late 19th Century, Woodleaf grew into a sizable village. A new Episcopal chapel, named St. George's in memory of George Badger Wetmore (d. 1888), was built about 1893. It replaced St. Andrew's Church as the site of regular services in the community.
Photograph by Jason Williams

The Rev. Simeon Jeremiah Michael Brown (above), another protégé of Dr. Murdoch's, served as a priest at St. George's, and he instituted the annual homecoming at St. Andrew's in 1907.
Photograph reproduced from *St. Andrew's Church*

busily engaged with other efforts important to St. Luke's: the Convocation of Charlotte's Church School for Boys, and improvements to the fabric of St. Luke's Church. Dr. Murdoch long hoped to bring his interest in parochial education and training young men for the ministry to fruition in a school in Salisbury. Financial reverses in the late 1880s forced Samuel R. Harrison to give up his handsome estate, Chestnut Hill, which fronted on the Charlotte Road (South Main Street) and stretched west to Fulton Street. The greater part of this acreage was acquired by the Dixie Land Company and platted into 103 lots. The southern end of Church Street was extended through the development, and crossed by newly-built Chestnut, Harrison, Johnson and Cemetery streets. Mr. Harrison's handsome two-story brick Italianate mansion and outbuildings were set apart on lot #3 in the center of a block bounded by Chestnut, Main, Harrison and Church streets. On 6 July 1891 Dr. Murdoch, trustee for the Convocation of Charlotte's

For a brief period in the late-19th Century, Samuel R. Harrison's handsome Italianate-style house, built in 1869 and known as Chestnut Hill, served as the premises of a short-lived Episcopal school for boys. Dedicated on 28 October 1912 as Murdoch Memorial Mission Hall, in memory of Dr. Murdoch, the house was home to Episcopal clergymen including William Hill Hardin and others who served St. Paul's and the area missions. In 1942 it was renovated and set aside for use as a parish house for St. Paul's Church.

Photograph of ca. 1942 courtesy of the *Salisbury Post*

Church School for Boys, made the first of three purchases, acquiring lot #1 in the west corner of Main and Chestnut Streets for $500 from Patrick H. Thompson. Six months later he purchased the adjoining lot to the northwest (#53) for $200 from W. F. Purvis. On 2 May 1892 Dr. Murdoch acquired the Harrison mansion, outbuildings and immediate grounds, comprising lots #2-4, 51, and 52 from James S. McCubbins Jr., for $4,300.[49] He thus gained control of the entire block bound by South Main, Chestnut, South Church and Harrison streets.

Dr. Murdoch, in the role of school treasurer, provided a useful precise of the school in his report to the diocesan convention two weeks later.

SALISBURY, CHURCH SCHOOL FOR BOYS

A Board of Trustees, appointed by the Convocation of Charlotte, consisting of Rev. R. Wetmore, Rev. F. J. Murdoch, D.D., and Rev. J. B. Cheshire Jr., D.D., has control of the Church School for Boys. During the past 18 months, about $2,500 has been paid on this property, and there is a debt on it of $3,000. The property is worth about $6,000. A school for boys, with an average attendance of nearly 30, has been kept up there since Sept. 1st, 1891, by Mr. J. M. Hill. It is hoped that next fall a boarding department can be opened, and that the original idea of an inexpensive school for boys can be carried out. Liberal subscriptions towards paying for this property have been paid by two persons in Charlotte, one in Ansonville, one in Winston and one in Morganton. Nothing else has been paid by any other than residents of Salisbury. The notices of this school, which have appeared in Church papers, have elicited quite a number of inquiries from a distance as to whether salaries could be given to relatives who wanted to teach, or whether education could be given to others at less than cost. If the number and interest of those who want to help the school was equal to that of those who want to be helped by it, it would be very prosperous.[50]

It would appear that Dr. Murdoch, flush with enthusiasm, was given to overstatement in this instance. At the next diocesan convention, in 1893, William Robards Wetmore (1834-1904), rector of St. Luke's Church, Lincolnton, and dean of the Charlotte Convocation, gave a much less optimistic report.

I am sorry to have to report that, so far, we have been unable to put in operation the inexpensive school for boys in Salisbury. This school, as a means of supplying ministers, would be of great help to the missionary work of the Diocese.[51]

In 1894 Dr. Murdoch noted some improvement.

The Church School for Boys at Salisbury has been kept up, with an attendance of over forty pupils. The property belonging to this institution is worth about $7,000, and encumbered with a debt of $3,000. We are unable as yet to open a boarding department.[52]

The seeming conflict in these reports reflects the frustrating reality of the school operation to which Bishop Cheshire gave voice in his address to the convention of 1895. "…I would call the attention of our Clergy and people to Dr. Murdoch's school for boys at Salisbury. That is as yet only a day-school, but a little co-operation with him might develop it into the so much needed economical boarding school for boys."[53]

But support and success would elude Dr. Murdoch in this endeavor. In 1896 the property was tendered to the Diocese of North Carolina and accepted at convention. A year later, 21 May 1897, Dr. Murdoch, trustee for the Charlotte Convocation, conveyed the entire property to Bishop Cheshire and trustees of the Diocese, subject to a mortgage of $3,000.[54] The school operated in strained circumstances for another two years. Finally, in his report to the convention of 1900, Dr. Murdoch admitted defeat.

The Board of Trustees respectfully report that the Executive Committee had to close the School in the fall of 1899 for lack of patronage caused by the great improvement in the free public schools of Salisbury. We deem it best that the School should not be opened during the coming school year, and that the buildings be rented out.

The debts on the property are...$124.06.

The Treasurer has on hand $40, received for rent. The rents will soon pay off the debts and will afford a revenue for the education of young men for the ministry. We have here a very valuable property, and it will no doubt be handled for the advantage of the Church.[55]

As the school neared its demise, another calamity struck the neighborhood. The nearby frame church erected for the St. Paul's mission and then serving as the school chapel was destroyed by fire in April 1897. The diocesan trustees decided against rebuilding on the original site, sold the lot to Mrs. L. J. Surratt, and applied the proceeds to a larger lot which they conveyed on 11 May 1898 to C. A. McKethan, Samuel R. Harrison and T. W. File, trustees for St. Paul's parish. This new lot, in the north corner of Main and Harrison streets and measuring 75 by 125 feet, became the site on which the present brick church of St. Paul's was erected in 1898.[56]

At St. Luke's Church improvements were made in the 1890s to both the physical plant and the worship program. The recessed chancel addition had been in place for some seven years when discussion arose concerning further improvements to the church. The extent and character of these improvements appeared to change through the course of time, without necessarily being refined, until 21 January 1894 when the congregation "worshipped in the improved Ch. for the first time." Subsequent to these initial improvements, a series of stained glass windows was added in the side walls of the church and a new organ purchased. In 1895 a second building, the chapter house for the Bishop Lyman Chapter, Daughters of the King, was erected. Comprising 15 members, this group was the first of a series of modern women's organizations that have continued to augment church life to the present.

St. Paul's Church, a small appealing brick church, was built in 1898 and consecrated on 28 October 1912 by Bishop Cheshire.
Photograph by Jason Williams

The first extended discussion concerning new improvements to the church appears to have occurred in the late winter of 1890-1891. At a meeting on 16 March 1891, the vestry reached a general agreement "to remodel the church by cutting down the walls & make a gothic roof. It was also recommended that the ladies wait till we could change the church before purchasing a new organ." Dr. Murdoch and John Steele Henderson were made a committee to develop the new plans. The two men went about the task, and a special meeting of the vestry was held on 6 June, at which "Mr. Henderson explained Mr. McBee's plan." A congregational meeting on the subject was proposed for the following Sunday.

On 18 June 1891 the *Carolina Watchman* printed a notice for the meeting.

> **There will be a meeting of St. Luke's congregation on Sunday morning next. The Episcopalians will determine whether they will build a new church or enlarge the old building. The rector and vestry hope that a large congregation will be present. No one will be asked to make a subscription at the meeting.**

Discussion continued through the summer and plans refined by McBee for improvements, expected to cost between $2,000 and $3,000, were considered at a vestry meeting on 28 September. The matter was continued through fall 1891. Finally on 28 December, on a motion by Stephen Ferrand Lord, the vestry adopted the McBee plans and determined to "go to work to make the improvements as soon as possible." The church's St. Cecilia Society, named for the patron saint of music, was to be granted any part of the work the rector thought proper. In February 1892 the society was raising funds for "the little window in the chancel" whose location is now unknown.

Although no known copy of Silas McBee's plan for the church renovation survives, certain coincidences suggest that it may well have been along the lines implemented in the 1907-1909 expansion. Silas McBee (1853-1924), a native of Lincolnton and a son of its St. Luke's Church, graduated from the University of the South in 1876 and went on to have a distinguished career in the Episcopal Church as an architect, educator and editor. He served on the university's board of trustees for two extended periods, 1878 to 1886 and 1887 to 1907. The years from 1884 to 1907 coincided with Dr. Murdoch's tenure as trustee from 1884 until his death. Both men were sitting on the board in 1886 when Convocation Hall, an imposing Victorian Gothic brick building designed by Halsey Wood, was completed. The principal architectural feature of the hall is its Breslin Tower, modeled on the tower of Magdalen College, Oxford, which was often copied on ecclesiastical buildings in the United States in the later 19th and early 20th centuries, including St. Luke's.[57]

In the event, "as soon as possible" expanded to occupy all of 1892 and 1893, and in the process the scope and scale of work appear to have been much reduced. Discussion of a new furnace costing "$165.00, which Mr. Neave guaranteed to heat the enlarged Church," suggests that an expansion of the floor plan, beyond the 1828 building and the 1883 chancel addition, was being contemplated. The purchase of the furnace was delayed; the church was heated by a single stove in the winter of 1892-1893. By the 6th of March 1893, the scope of work was reduced. "Mr. Murdoch volunteered to get prices for the inside work of the present building which we decided to commence & do this year" was the conclusion recorded by Mr. Lord, the vestry secretary. A month later he wrote, "The Rector submitted plans for church improvements to cost $600.00 which were adopted" at both the congregational and vestry meetings on 3 April. Dr. Murdoch, John Steele Henderson and Archibald Henderson Boyden were appointed to a building committee to execute the work. The minutes of the subsequent vestry meetings indicate further delay in undertaking the work, and it was not until fall 1893 that the vestry contracted for improvements. The sum of $694.28 was expended on apparently modest changes to the fabric of the church. Except for the addition of new stained glass windows and the organ, the interior of St. Luke's was apparently unchanged until the addition of electric lights in 1900. The vestry accepted the offer of the ladies of the church to pay for the wiring, and on 22 April "the rector was instructed to have 30 lights placed in the church."

For a dozen years, from the construction of the recessed chancel and the installation of its memorial windows in 1883 until 1895, the character of lighting in the church was marked by contrast. Dim, colored light illuminated the chancel, while natural sunlight streamed through the many-paned sash windows in the nave. In April 1893 Messrs. Boyden and Overman were each given permission to erect memorial windows in pendant halves of the lancet-arch openings on the northeast and southwest sides, respectively, of the church, nearest the chancel. Apparently, they failed to follow through with their intentions. Next, in January 1894, the window on the northeast side of the church was offered to Messrs. Boyden and Trantham "if they want it," and the opposite opening in the southwest side, overlooking Council Street was granted to the Daughters of the King. The matter languished for a year and was taken up earnestly in the winter of 1895. After considering the work of several stained glass manufacturers and decorators, the vestry again settled on Edward Colgate at their April meeting.

Although the account of the deliberations concerning the stained glass windows does not specify the number of windows being ordered from Mr. Colgate, in all likelihood the three memorial windows in the original southwest elevation of St. Luke's Church were installed at the same time in 1895. All appear in place in turn-of-the-century documentary views of the church. The Bishop Lyman Chapter, Daughters of the King, were the donors of the paired panels in the opening nearest the chancel that honor Bishop Theodore Lyman and the Rev. Theodorus Swaine Drage, the first resident rector of St. Luke's Parish. John Allen Holt (1830-1902) and his wife Augusta M. Carncross (ca. 1832-1918), who were married in 1852 by Mr. Parker, were the donors of the paired windows in the (then) center bay honoring Mrs. Holt's mother and sisters and two of their seven children.[58]

The paired panels in the bay nearest the south front corner of the old church were installed as memorials to brothers in the Murphy family. The memorial panel honoring James Murphy (1821-1874) and his wife Elizabeth C. Chunn (1823-1892) was installed in 1895; its wording, and a lack of reference in the church records, leaves unnamed the identity of the donor. The pendant panel, given in memory of William Murphy (1812-1867) by his wife Susan

Wainwright Chunn (1825-1900) and children, is either the original 1895 window installed by Mrs. Murphy, or one installed after her death by their son, Clarence Wainwright Murphy, who received permission to do so in May 1901.

The final pair of windows known to have been installed in the church before the remodeling and expansion program of 1907-1909 are those in the northeast side of the sanctuary, and both probably date to 1902. No known record of their designer survives; however, Mr. Colgate is the likely source. On 12 May 1901 Clarence Wainwright Murphy was granted permission to erect a memorial to his mother Susan Wainwright (Chunn) Murphy and to replace the earlier memorial to his father. Seven months later, 7 January 1902, the vestry approved the installation of a panel as a memorial here to Laura (Murphy) Overman (1849-1875), the daughter of William and Susan Murphy and wife of William H. Overman (1846-1901), that was erected by the church. The opening in the adjoining center bay was assigned by the vestry to Mrs. Winburn and Mr. and Mrs. Peter Frercks. Mrs. William A. (Annie Cole Smith) Winburn erected a panel to her deceased son Francis Nelms Winburn (1891-1895); Peter Augustus (ca. 1825-1909) and Fanny (Kelly) Frercks remembered their only child Francis MacRae Frercks (1887-1899) in the panel bearing his name.

Worship services at St. Luke's in the 1890s were enhanced also with the purchase of a new organ. Surviving parish records provide little infor-

This photograph of ca. 1900 shows St. Luke's as it appeared after the installation of three stained glass windows on the Council Street side of the church in the mid 1890s. The openings flanking the entrance retained their original multi-pane sash windows below a lancet-arch transom.
Courtesy of the Rowan Museum. An almost identical view of the church was published as a postal by Buerbaum's Bookstore.

1. The twin lancet-arch panels of the Holt window are based on events of the Old and New Testaments. The left lancet, entitled "Samuel and Eli," is based on the Lord's calling to Samuel which appears in I Samuel, the third chapter. In the window Samuel appears before his teacher Eli, thinking it was his voice he heard in his sleep, and answers "Here am I." After the third call, Eli realizes it is the Lord calling Samuel and he instructs his pupil to answer the next call saying, "Speak, Lord, for thy servant heareth." The right lancet takes as its theme the instruction of Timothy by his mother Eunice. In Acts, chapter 16, verse one, Timothy is described as "the son of a certain woman, which was a Jewess, and believed; but his father was a Greek." Timothy became a disciple of Paul, and the relationship of the two ministers is celebrated in Paul's first and second letters to Timothy, which appear as books of the New Testament.

2. Two children of the parish who died young were remembered by their families in this window. The figure of the young David playing his harp is a memorial to Francis McRae Frercks (1887-1899). It was originally installed while the young boy was living; however, the inscription was changed after his death on 19 May 1899. The figure of the Madonna holding the Christ Child is a metaphorically-charged memorial erected by a mother, Mrs. Winburn, for her son Francis Nelms Winburn (1891-1895).

3. The choice of St. Alphege and Saint Hilda on the memorial windows to Laura Murphy Overman and her mother, respectively, does not reflect the degree of associative symbolism seen in the Frercks and Winburn window. Saint Alphege (ca. 953-1012) became bishop of Winchester in 984, and in 1005 he was consecrated Archbishop of Canterbury. In 1011, when the Danes took possession of southern England, the archbishop was imprisoned with others and the payment of £3,000 was demanded for his release. Alphege refused to make the payment or to allow others to do so on his behalf. In 1012 he was killed by the Danes in a drunken fury; his body was buried in St. Paul's Cathedral. The example of Saint Hilda (614-680), the well-regarded Abbess of Whitby, however, may well have appealed to the three surviving children of Susan Wainwright (Chunn) Murphy (1825-1900). As the Oxford Dictionary of Saints notes, "She was an excellent example of how in the Anglo-Saxon Church an able woman could attain to great influence and authority without, however, there ever being question of her being ordained."

Photographs by Robert Bailey

mation on the music program at St. Luke's until this period, although the church had acquired an organ in 1834 and it and its successor(s) no doubt figured prominently in services. In March 1883 Mr. Henderson was directed by the vestry to order music requested by the organist, Miss Lena Shober: four volumes of "Cantata Domino," one book "Voluntary," and six copies of Goodrich's hymnals. At the annual congregational meeting held on 2 April 1888, the assembled members voted "to purchase a Pipe Organ to cost not less than $1,000." Approval to purchase a new organ came in September 1894, when the vestry decided to add $300 to the amount raised by the St. Cecelia Society to that end. The matter languished until spring 1895, when in April the vestry authorized the rector to contract for a new organ and in May they agreed to allow the construction of the organ which would "…obstruct one of the windows." This new organ did not arrive at St. Luke's until late summer or early autumn of 1896. The old organ was to be removed to the chapter house. A final 19th Century reference to the church's musical instrument occurs in December of that year when the vestry secretary recounted, "Permission was given Lizzie Bingham to practice on the organ provided she wishes to learn for the purpose of assisting in the service of the church & provided she practices alone."

These mentions of the Bishop Lyman Chapter, Daughters of the King, the St. Cecilia Society and the chapter house provide evidence of the growing presence of women and associations in the life of the church. In truth, women were critical to the organization of St. Luke's in 1823 and every stage of its growth thereafter. Ladies working societies had existed at St. Luke's in its earliest years, and they raised funds for various projects and improvements through the antebellum period. The St. Cecilia Society was composed of those who sought to improve the church's musical program. Another society, a chapter of the Daughters of the King, was organized at St. Luke's in November 1892. It was the first chapter in North Carolina, and named itself the Bishop Lyman Chapter, in honor of the long-serving bishop, Theodore Benedict Lyman, who would die a year later, on 11 December 1893. The society was organized by Mrs. Murdoch who, in turn, was elected president. Mrs. Joseph O. White was elected vice-president, with Miss Mary McNeely serving as secretary and treasurer. The other dozen original members were: Mrs. J. W. (Ann Eliza Bernhardt) Neave, Mrs. Thomas B. Marsh, Mrs. Julius D. (Henrietta M. Hall) McNeely, Mrs. Bessie Walker, Mrs. Archibald Henderson (May Wheat Shober) Boyden, Mrs. William S. (Clara A.) Blackmer, Mrs. Charles Price, Mrs. James P. (Beulah Stewart) Moore, Miss Nannie Craige, Miss Mary Smith, Miss Addie White and Mrs. Francis E. Shober.

The frustration suffered by Dr. Murdoch and others in the failed effort to enlarge and improve St. Luke's in the early 1890s was mitigated in part by the construction of a separate building on the grounds for

church purposes. A chapter house became the first successful project undertaken by the Bishop Lyman Chapter. At a meeting on 4 September 1893 the vestry unanimously approved a motion "that the Daughters of the King be allowed to build a large room to the side & rear of the Church for their meetings & other church purposes." The building remained in planning for a year, until September 1894 when the vestry agreed to borrow any necessary amount above $200 to be raised by the chapter. The small rectangular freestanding building, now serving as the chapel, was completed in 1895. Of plain, workmanlike brick masonry, it was fitted with lancet-arch windows and a doorway in its southwest side that now opens into the hallway off the library. The current appearance of the former Chapter House owes to 20th Century refittings.

St. Luke's Bishop Lyman Chapter, Daughters of the King, erected a small brick chapter house for meetings and parish activities. It stood separate from the church until the addition of the cloister, and was refitted later as a chapel. Visible on the left side of the photograph is the board-and-batten covered base of the 19th Century bell tower that was taken down in the 1940s.
St. Luke's Archives

Organized in 1892, the chapter was named in honor of Theodore Benedict Lyman (1815-1893), who was consecrated Assistant Bishop of North Carolina in 1873 and in 1881 succeeded Bishop Atkinson on his death.
Photography courtesy of the Diocese of North Carolina

Whether the turn of the 19th Century was celebrated in any particular way in Salisbury and at St. Luke's is not known; however, the life of the church continued in its well-established course through the first decade of the 20th Century. Early in 1902 Dr. Murdoch renewed his efforts to enlarge and improve the church, but that effort also failed. Five years later Frank Pierce Milburn was hired to enlarge and remodel the church. Although Milburn's proposals were adopted and the work was undertaken in 1908, Dr. Murdoch did not live to savor the accomplishment. While on a family visit in Charleston, he died unexpectedly, on 21 June 1909. The congregation's memorial took the form of a new altar and reredos which remains the chief decorative feature of the chancel. As the

FROM GENERATION TO GENERATION

church improvements proceeded, Dr. Murdoch continued with his usual ministry to the St. Luke's parish and gave a large measure of attention to its mission chapels. Between 1900 and his death in 1909, Dr. Murdoch extended his mission work with the organization of new chapels bearing the names of St. Mark and St. Joseph. He also continued to tutor young men for the ministry to assist him at the older, established missions and those dating to the final decade of his life.

Electric lights appear to have been installed in spring 1900, in time for the 84th Annual Convention of the Diocese of North Carolina that gathered for the eighth time in Salisbury, and the seventh time in this present church. Dr. Murdoch welcomed his fellow clergyman and lay delegates to the opening session on Wednesday morning, 16 May 1900. The organization of a new mission in the county, known as St. Mark's, occupied some part of Dr. Murdoch's energies in the second half of the year. He gave his first official account of the mission in his report to convention in 1902.

> In that part of Rowan County lying between the Wilkesboro and new Mocksville roads on the west and east, and between Second and Deal's Creeks on the north and south (a territory in which there was no place of worship of any denomination), there has been built since last Convention a chapel, to be known as St. Mark's Church, 18x36 feet. The Rev. Mr. Trott has kept up serv-

The immediate neighborhood of St. Luke's has changed dramatically through the course of the 20th Century. St. Luke's bell tower is visible in the background, behind the brick gable end of the chapter house. None of the other buildings seen in this handsome turn-of-the-century photography of the Rowan County Jail survive. The jail was demolished and the Rowan County Court House, designed by Frank Milburn, was completed on the site in 1912.
Courtesy of the Rowan Museum

ices semi-monthly, and has conducted a Bible class. The land for the church was given, and the entire cost of the lot and building has been about $200, all of which is paid. Communicants from St. George's who will attend this church have not yet been transferred.[59]

The mission evolved from a Sunday school operated at nearby Gheen's School House by Mr. Trott and William Thomas Bost, a prospective candidate for the diaconate. Michael Beaver, a leading citizen of the area, donated the site for the church in which services were first held on 16 December 1900. In July 1901, during his annual visitation to Salisbury and Rowan County churches, Bishop Cheshire held services at St. Mark's, baptized Michael Beaver and confirmed seven members of the mission, including Mr. Beaver.[60] Bishop Cheshire visited the mission a second time, on 10 November 1902, when he baptized Gertrude Coggins and Rebecca Redwine and confirmed them, together with Gertrude Winecoff, Bessie Weant and William Edgar Cozart.[61] Apparently his final visit came on 10 November 1903, when he confirmed Thomas Cozart, the last of only 13 persons known to have been confirmed at St. Mark's Chapel.[62]

With only 13 communicants at its height, St. Mark's remained the smallest of the Rowan County missions and would eventually become one of the shortest-lived. In 1902 Mr. Trott, who would remain minister in charge until 1905, reported, "This church has never been ceiled, and we need help."[63] After Mr. Trott went to St. Philip's, Durham, Dr. Murdoch took the church under his wing for a year. It was next under the charge of the Rev. Simeon Jeremiah Michael Brown. The church was last under the care of the Rev. Walter L. Loflin, who made his final report as minister in charge in 1914, reporting two families, six baptized people in the mission, five communicants and six services during the year on Sundays. He concluded "It is impracticable to hold services in this Mission except during the summer months."[64] Whether St. Mark's Chapel was ever finished is not known, but, whatever its state, it was the last rural mission church erected under Dr. Murdoch's care. No record of its appearance is known to exist.

Concurrent with his efforts to organize the mission of St. Mark's out of a Sunday School, Dr. Murdoch also applied himself to the organization of a mission at the recently built cotton mill at Cooleemee, just across the South Yadkin River in Davie County. This mission, soon named the Church of the Good Shepherd, Cooleemee, was a natural extension of his efforts to establish Episcopal chapels for workers at the Salisbury mills. A chapel had been completed in the spring of 1901.[65]

Dr. Murdoch surely had some involvement with the proposed St. Stephen's Church on the Sherrill's Ford Road. On 24 October 1905 John A. Boyden, his wife Mary L. Cole Boyden and her sister Sue Cole Smith conveyed a one-acre tract on the north side of the road to Bishop Cheshire and trustees of the Diocese "for a congregation of the Episcopal Church to be gathered in a Chapel to be built on said lot to be known as St. Stephen's Chapel."[66] The chapel, which would have been the second Episcopal mission on the Sherrill's Ford Road, was never built.

Dr. Murdoch's next and final mission in Salisbury was eventually more successful. Although

The small frame chapel erected for the Church of the Good Shepherd at Cooleemee was replaced in 1925-1926 by this more substantial late-Gothic Revival church.
Photograph by Jason Williams

he had voiced some concern for a church for the black residents of Salisbury in 1883, nothing came of the idea until 1901. On 7 March of that year, he and Mrs. Murdoch conveyed a lot in the south corner of Marsh and Caldwell streets to Bishop Cheshire and the diocesan trustees for a congregation "to be of colored persons."[67] Fronting on West Marsh Street, the lot measured 46⅓ feet in width and 100 feet in depth, along Caldwell Street. The absence of a proposed name for the congregation is a possible indication that plans for the mission were as yet unsettled. Whatever the case, a chapel known as St. Philip's does not appear in the diocesan roster of "Unorganized missions and other congregations" until 1917, when it was under the care of the Rev. Dr. Henry Beard Delaney (1858-1928), who in 1918 was elected Suffragan Bishop of North Carolina with responsibility for the "colored" congregations.

St. Joseph's Chapel in Spencer was the last in the series of missions organized over a space of about 30 years by Dr. Murdoch. A site for the church, lot #3, block 16, in the plat of Spencer, was donated on 5 December 1903 by Alexander B. Andrews Jr., to Bishop Cheshire and the trustees of the Diocese of North Carolina and reported at the convention of 1904.[68] Under the conditions of the deed, requiring a church to be built within one year, a chapel valued at $800 and facing onto Rowan Avenue was erected quickly, and Dr. Murdoch made his first report as minister in charge of the mission to the convention in 1905.[69] He remained minister in charge of St. Joseph's until his death.

Dr. Murdoch required assistance with both his earlier missions and those established after the turn of the century, and to that end he continued to encourage men for the priesthood. John Linker Saunders, who had been made a deacon in St. Luke's on 10 June 1900, was followed in that path by Richard Louis Bame. Mr. Bame, formerly a Lutheran minister, came under the influence of Dr. Murdoch, and with the support of St. Luke's vestry was added to the diaconate at St. Luke's on 22 September 1901. After a short period in Raleigh working under Dr. Marshall at Christ Church's St. Saviour's mission, he returned to Rowan County and assisted Dr. Murdoch at St. Matthew's. Mr. Bame was never ordained priest in the Episcopal Church, and exactly when he gave up the ministry is uncertain; however, on 21 September 1910 he was officially deposed as a deacon.[70]

Locke Winfield Blackwelder was the next protégé of Dr. Murdoch's to take up holy orders and serve churches in Salisbury and Rowan County. He was made deacon at Christ Church, Cleveland, on 7 August 1904, and he worked under Dr. Murdoch at St. Jude's, St. Matthew's and St. John's Chapel in Salisbury. In 1907 Thomas Lee Trott, who had ministered to various churches under Dr. Murdoch since his admission to the diaconate, and then relocated to Durham as assistant to the Rev. Mr. Bost at St. Philip's Church, was ordained priest. In retrospect, a certain appropriateness attended Dr. Murdoch's last Sunday service at St. Luke's on 13 June 1909. Having received Bishop Cheshire as a guest on Saturday, he presented Locke Winfield Blackwelder and Francis Wellington Ross Arthurs to the bishop at the 11:00 a.m. Sunday service as candidates for the priesthood.[71] Some days afterward Dr. Murdoch departed Salisbury for a family visit in Charleston, South Carolina.

Dr. Murdoch obviously took some pleasure in the modest improvements to the church in the 1890s, the addition of handsome stained glass memorial windows, the purchase of a new organ, and electric lights in the nave, all in place for the 1900 diocesan convention. But having seen one after another of his fellow Salisbury ministers oversee the building of new churches for their congregations, he was determined to see St. Luke's enlarged and enhanced. In the 1880s he had watched as the town's Lutheran congregation erected a large Gothic Revival-style church, completed in 1885 on the site of their earlier church, facing onto North Main Street.[72] Then in 1891-1892, he must have looked with a certain priestly envy on the efforts of Dr. Rumple and his congregation at First Presbyterian Church, as they constructed their great Romanesque Revival-style brick church. Designed by Charles Webber Bolton, it immediately became one of the most important buildings ever erected— and ever destroyed—in the county seat.[73] Its imposing tower, preserved from destruction, is a landmark to the present. Then, a few yards to the west, in the north corner of Council and Church streets, the town's Baptist congregation erected a large, imposing late-Victorian Gothic church just after the turn of the century.

For a time Dr. Murdoch's urge to build was sated by the construction of a house for his family on Horah Street. By the later 1890s, his investments in real estate and the town's mills provided him and his family a very comfortable life. In December 1900, the rector and his family moved into the just-completed two-story house in the 200 block of West Horah Street. Today the site of the house, sold out of the family and demolished, is marked by the extensive boxwood plantings of Mrs. Murdoch's garden, in what is now the side lawn of the First United Church of Christ. The church occupies the site of the residence of Luke Blackmer, a long-time communicant of St. Luke's.

In the spring of 1902, Dr. Murdoch renewed his efforts to enlarge St. Luke's; the matter was discussed by the vestry but came to naught. As with other church projects, the death of a communicant and

Dr. Murdoch's residence, completed in 1900, was one of the city's most imposing houses of its period. Barely visible through the branches is a balustraded widow's walk which crowned its hip roof.
Courtesy of Harriett (Lang) Hornthal

his or her legacy eventually came to be a deciding factor in the ability to move forward. The deaths of Susan (Chunn) Murphy in 1900 and her son-in-law, William H. Overman (1846-1901), and the legacy bequeathed as a memorial to her long-deceased daughter, Laura (Murphy) Overman, amounted to nearly $2,000 in 1907. It would enable Dr. Murdoch to achieve his dream for the parish. He agitated once again for church improvements in June 1903, telling the vestry that he would like to see the work accomplished in 1904 by the 75th anniversary of the building's consecration on 27 July 1829. At its meeting on 10 August 1903, the vestry passed motions to the effect that "The Church (is) to be enlarged according to Mr. McBee's plan & that the enlargement be three bays instead of two." In addition to using $222.10 in the church improvement fund and $705.89 in the Overman legacy, the vestry resolved to ask the congregation to subscribe $1,250 for the project. Messrs. Lord and L. F. Young were appointed to the committee to raise the subscription.

Inertia set in again, and the project languished until spring 1904, when Dr. Murdoch prodded the vestry to action. At a meeting on 16 May

Theodore Buerbaum (1861–1926), a native of Prussia, came to Salisbury in 1876 and in 1879 opened his celebrated bookstore which published dozens of postal views of Rowan County buildings and scenery. His business at 106 South Main Street survives, as does his house at 414 South Main Street. Mr. Buerbaum was a member of St. Luke's and, like Dr. Murdoch, an investor in the city's textile enterprises.

Courtesy of the Rowan Museum

Theodore Buerbaum moved the appointment of a committee of three to formulate plans for the church improvement. The motion carried and the rector, John Steele Henderson and Stephen Ferrand Lord were named to the committee. Another near-year passed until 24 April 1905, when the secretary of the vestry recorded, "The vestry was asked to discharge the Com. on Ch. improvement as they could not agree on a plan." The matter rested for another year, until another annual congregational meeting on Monday, 16 April 1906, when "Mrs. A. H. Boyden spoke very feelingly & well of the great need of Ch. improvement" but, alas, to little avail.

The improvement effort that at last proved successful appears to have owed as much to the general building boom that occurred in Salisbury in the opening years of the 20th Century as initiative within the church. A general air of prosperity was felt throughout the town, a feeling not unlike that of the 1850s when the arrival of the North Carolina Railroad ushered in a similar but short-lived expansion. The railroad was again a major impetus to growth and income, together with the warehousing and related facilities in Salisbury and the establishment of the railroad shops complex at the heart of the new town of Spencer to the north. Now, a half-century later, the half-dozen or so cotton mills and other successful manufacturers contributed to the town's wealth. New buildings, or lesser improvements, appeared to be rising on virtually every block. In short, the appearance of Salisbury changed greatly in the first decade of the 20th Century.

Beginning in 1900, an important series of commercial, domestic, public and institutional buildings were erected. The Washington Building, with its granite façade, was built in 1900 and followed in quick order by buildings that have become landmarks in the city: the Egbert Barry Cornwall Hambley mansion, the Southern Railway Passenger Station, the Grubb Building, the Empire Hotel, a new Peoples National Bank, the now lost Salisbury High School on North Ellis Street, and a host of residences including those of Colonel Franklin Fletcher Smith, David Cannon and our own Dr. Murdoch.[74] The town's thirst for new buildings reached a climax in 1912, when both the Rowan County Court House and the United States Post Office and Court House were dedicated and the five-story Yadkin Hotel opened for business.

As clients, designers and builders, a large number of people and concerns were responsible for the new architectural fabric of Salisbury; however, one man, Frank Pierce Milburn (1868-1926), exercised a larger influence than anyone. After opening his architectural office in Kenova, West Virginia, in 1890, and soon relocating it to Columbia, South Carolina, Mr. Milburn became one of the most prolific and best known architects in the American South. Central to this success was a remarkable talent; skill in self-promotion through a series of appealing monographs of his and his firm's work from 1901 to 1922; appointment as architect for the Southern Railway Company in about 1902; his role as the unofficial house architect for the University of North Carolina (Chapel Hill), where his work includes the President's House; and numerous commissions for county court houses. He was also the architect of the first high-rise office building in North Carolina, the Charlotte National Bank (Independence) Building, completed in 1909, and would soon be responsible for others.

In Salisbury Milburn and his firm designed the Southern Railway Passenger Station and Railway Express Office; People's National Bank; the Empire Hotel; the now-lost Rowan County Jail, adjacent to St. Luke's on Church Street; the Grubb Building; as well as the Sanders Hotel and the Snider Memorial Hospital that were not built. The Mission Revival-style residence of Franklin Fletcher Smith is attributed to him. Mr. Milburn was also the architect for the Southern Railway Y.M.C.A. in Spencer. The work here was so substantial that the *Salisbury Evening Post* carried a front-page story in its 4 February 1907 issue, indicating that Mr. Milburn would soon open a branch office here. That did not come to pass. Among all his work in Salisbury, including four buildings that survive today as major landmarks in the city, his least known commission was the enlargement of St. Luke's Church in 1907-1909.[75]

Frank Pierce Milburn (1868-1926), the architect of St. Luke's expansion, designed many important buildings throughout North Carolina that remain landmarks to the present.
Courtesy of the North Carolina State Archives

After episodic frustrations over the course of some 15 years, the matter of improvements to St. Luke's moved quickly in 1907. In April Dr. Murdoch and Richard Henderson were appointed a committee to secure plans for the church enlargement. An overture to Mr. Milburn met with quick success. "Milburn's outline plan for the improvement of the Ch. was generally approved…" at a vestry meeting on 20 May, and a decision made to place the proposal before the congregation. The next day the *Salisbury Evening Post* ran a short article on its front page with the caption "Church Plans Drawn: Architect Milburn Makes Plans for Episcopal Church."

> **Architect Frank P. Milburn has made plans for a more commodious edifice for the congregation of St. Luke's Episcopal church. There is no certainty that the plans will be accepted nor even that the church will be enlarged but the matter is under consideration.**

The vestry reconvened two weeks later, and the secretary recorded the deliberations.

> **Plans for ch. improvements as changed were shown the Vestry & approved. Organ on the floor not elevated. The Present Cellar to**

be razed. Extra room to be used as a Baptistry. The roof to be slate & buttresses on side. The plans with the changes as agreed upon were sent back to Architect Milburn to finish & perfect.

As there is no record of any further significant discussion of the plans, Mr. Milburn must have incorporated the vestry suggestions into the final set of construction drawings prepared for the church. At their next meeting the vestry members decided to raise an additional $5,000 for the project through subscription due 1 July 1908. They also began other related discussions. The great window centered in the southeast end of the church had attracted donors. Five of its seven panels were assigned at this meeting to Mr. Boyden, Dr. Henry Truesdale Trantham, Thomas Benjamin Marsh and to Walter Steele Blackmer (two). Archibald Henderson Boyden remembered his mother Jane (Henderson) Boyden (1805-1884), Dr. Trantham (1852-1929) raised a window in memory of his wife Mary (Henderson) Trantham (1858-1886), and Thomas Benjamin Marsh honored the memory of his wife Agnes (Neave) Marsh (1872-1902). Walter Steele Blackmer (1861-1922) donated four of the seven panels in the Ascension window; one honored his father Luke Blackmer and another his late mother Judia (Cole) Blackmer (1832-1903); and two others were erected in memory of his brothers, William Cole (1857-1903) and Stephen Shelton (1870-1906) Blackmer. Another important memorial dating to this period, a brass eagle lectern, was given in memory of Frances Wheat Shober Haviland (1867-1905) by the Misses Haviland and placed in the church during spring 1908.

The process of raising funds for the building project took up most of a year. It was not until May 1908 that the vestry gave permission to contract for building the extension to the church, although the necessary $5,000 had not been fully subscribed. Meanwhile, work had already begun on the smaller organ chamber addition. By December 1908, most of the work had been completed, and $5,061.49 paid out against receipts of $5,159.35. Of this last amount $2,012.96 was from the Laura Murphy Overman fund, $2,807.50 from subscriptions and the remainder from other sources. Work continued into early 1909, apparently on something of an ad hoc basis, with the decision to install a new floor on top of the existing one made in March. The proposed installation of a rose window in the baptistry prompted much discussion over at least two different designs. Finally, on 12 April 1909, "It was decided to finish up the church in as far as possible at once so as to occupy the addition & then see what next could be done." A few weeks later the building committee asked the vestry "to say what color the kalsoming should be. It was decided to make the whole Church the same color only a shade lighter." Although Dr. Murdoch would attend two further meetings of the vestry, on 9 May and 7 June, the issue of color was the last important matter in regard to the physical improvements to St. Luke's in which he exercised his voice.

Frank Pierce Milburn's renovation of St. Luke's, one of his several important building projects in Salisbury, is one of at least seven (presently) known ecclesiastical projects in a prolific career that spanned the years from 1889 until his death in 1926. Three, including St. Luke's, were for North Carolina clients, and three were commissions for churches in South Carolina. Mr. Milburn's office had one church commission in Georgia. Each appears to have come as a result of earlier projects in their respective cities. Mr. Milburn's work in Winston-Salem, where he designed a now-lost Forsyth County Court House and the Wachovia Bank Building, dates to the 1890s. The commission to design a new church for the First Baptist congregation there followed on the heels of those successful buildings. Milburn's Victorian Gothic church was replaced by the large imposing Classical Revival-style building, designed by Dougherty and Gardner of Nashville, Tennessee, and dedicated in 1925, which continues to house the congregation.

The Gothic Revival-style enlargement and remodeling of St. Luke's 1828 building essentially produced the church in which we worship today.

A growing membership similarly influenced the congregation of the First Presbyterian Church in Durham to replace its existing church in 1914. Milburn, who designed the Durham County Court House and many other buildings in the city, was chosen as the architect. George Washington Watts, the wealthy industrialist and philanthropist, agreed to contribute three-fourths of the estimated $80,000 cost. Construction began in April 1915 and quickly advanced for a year to its completion in April 1916 and the dedicatory services on 14 May 1916. The imposing red brick Gothic Revival church, embellished with stone dressings, stands at 305 East Main Street, Durham, and continues to serve its congregation.

Mr. Milburn's ecclesiastical design work in South Carolina and Georgia is generally contemporary with his North Carolina commissions and likewise reflect continued patronage in towns where he also designed other buildings. He had prepared a preliminary plan for the Associate Reformed Presbyterian Church in Newberry, South Carolina, by 1901; however, the brick church at the corner of Main and Calhoun streets was not completed until 1908. Designed in a free Gothic Revival style, it features a corner entrance tower with flanking gable-framed facades overlooking the two streets. St. Mary's Catholic Church in Greenville was completed in 1904, and dedicated on 4 November of that year. It, too, is a free interpretation of the Gothic Revival and has a dominant four-stage entrance tower beside the corbelled gable-front overlooking West Washington Street. In Columbia, St. Peter's Catholic Church stands but a few blocks from the State Capitol which Mr. Milburn remodeled and enlarged. Begun in 1906 and dedicated on 17 January 1909, St. Peter's Gothic Revival detailing is also inventive. The form of the church, with a multi-stage entrance tower centered on the façade overlooking Assembly Street, recalls that of the parish's original church designed by Robert Mills. Milburn's design for a Methodist Church in Washington, Georgia, also followed on his design of the

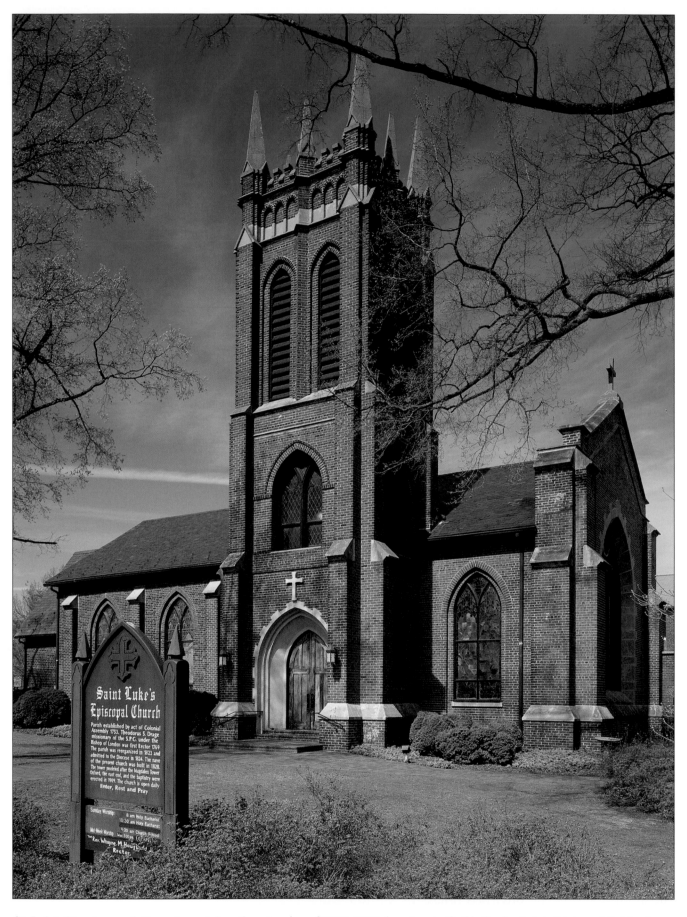

St. Luke's Church, essentially unchanged since the expansion of 1908–1909, incorporates Gothic Revival-style fabric and finishes from three distinct periods: the Gothic "survival" of the early 19th Century, the late-Victorian Gothic Revival, and the early-20th Century Gothic Revival which reached its apogee in North Carolina with the construction of Duke Chapel. Photograph by Robert Bailey

Wilkes County Court House, which was completed there in 1904. The church building committee decided to accept an alternative design submitted by George C. Thompson instead of Mr. Milburn's design, and construction began on the new church in 1907.

The Gothic Revival-style enlargement and remodeling of St. Luke's 1828 building essentially produced the church in which we worship today. The brick façade of the old church, facing southeast, was taken down and the rectangular building extended by two bays to the southeast. Milburn enlarged its plan to a cruciform by the addition of an imposing three-stage tower on the Council Street elevation and a pendant baptistry on the northeast side. The tower, containing the narthex and belfry, was modeled on the Breslin Tower at the University of the South, Sewanee, reflecting Dr. Murdoch's long tenure (1884-1909) as a clerical trustee at the school and his affection for the institution. Whether it also reflects an association with the earlier McBee plans for St. Luke's remains a tantalizing but unconfirmed possibility. Milburn and the builders replicated the brickwork of the original building, which was enhanced with shallow buttresses on its side walls, and enlivened the tower, buttresses and openings with cast-stone dressings. The relocation of the entrance allowed for the great memorial window in the church's new southeast gable end; it became a principal feature of both the exterior of the building and the interior, where late morning light filtering through its colored panes has welcomed members to Sunday services for some 95 years. Milburn added two principal decorative features to the nave, the Ascension Window and the openwork ceiling. Dr. Murdoch's death in 1909, as the work was nearing completion, occasioned the erection of the reredos and altar in his memory.

A sad irony attended the approaching completion of the St. Luke's Church improvements in the summer of 1909. The enlarged and refitted church, so long advocated by Dr. Murdoch, became a reality in the 37th year of his rectorate. In the closing days of June, just before he might have celebrated his 37th anniversary as rector of St. Luke's on 29 June, the handsome building became the site of his funeral. Dr. Murdoch held his last meeting with the vestry on Monday, 7 June, and probably spent the following days preparing for the Sunday service, when two of his protégés would be ordained priests by Bishop Cheshire, and for a much anticipated visit with his family in Charleston. The service on Sunday, the 13th, went as expected; however, the day's joy was tempered in the afternoon by the death of Peter Frercks (1825-1909), an aged, wealthy member of St. Luke's. Dr. Murdoch officiated at his funeral in St. Luke's and the interment in Chestnut Hill Cemetery on the 14th. At some point in the next few days, he and Mrs. Murdoch departed for Charleston. His last days were spent in the company of Mrs. Murdoch, his sisters Margaret (1838-1917) and Henrietta Anne (1840-1917) Murdoch, and the family of their late brother John Hamilton Murdoch (1848-1898), who were then occupying the family residence at 69 Meeting Street. There, in the imposing Federal-style mansion built by Dr. John Ernest Poyas and acquired in 1884 by brothers James Savage, John Hamilton and Rollo George Murdoch, he died unexpectedly, shortly before midnight on 21 June 1909.

Dr. Murdoch is seen facing the altar in this view of the church photographed in autumn 1894, on the occasion of the diocesan convention of the Daughters of the King. The organ case is visible on the left.
St. Luke's Archives

Dr. Murdoch's death elicited a widespread outpouring of grief, remembrances and memorials. The *Salisbury Post* published a long obituary in its afternoon edition on the 22nd, under the headline "A City in Sorrow." Its account of his life opened with rhythmic, heartfelt phrasing.

> **Dr. Murdoch is dead. Early this morning as the people of Salisbury rose from their nights rest they learned of the death of Dr. Murdoch. Stunning, unexpected, almost unbelievable, few could realize the terrible meaning of these words: Dr. Murdoch is dead.**
>
> **In low whispers, in awe stricken tones it is spoken of, the mouths of strong men quiver, tears dim their vision.**
>
> **Dr. Murdoch is dead.**

Mrs. Murdoch, the rector's sister Margaret, Francis Johnstone Murdoch Jr. (1886-1961), and Captain Richard Henderson accompanied Dr. Murdoch's body back to Salisbury, arriving here just before noon on Wednesday, the 23rd. Mr. Murdoch and Captain Henderson had traveled to Charleston, on learning of the rector's death, for the sorrowful purpose. Bishop Cheshire, who had been a guest of the Murdochs a week previous, returned to Salisbury and officiated at the funeral of the rector at five o'clock on Wednesday afternoon. Clergy throughout the Piedmont attended the funeral and accompanied the body of Dr. Murdoch to his grave in Chestnut Hill Cemetery. Newspaper editors in Asheville, Charlotte and Durham, among other cities, offered tributes praising his leadership as a priest, educator, businessman and citizen; memorials were prepared and published on behalf of the Minister's Association of Salisbury, the Salisbury Perpetual Building and Loan Association, Vance Cotton Mills and St. Luke's Chapter of the Brotherhood of St. Andrew. The vestry members, who served as pallbearers, also issued a memorial.[76] Liberal quotations could be cited from any or all of the group; however, two reflect the general tenor of a widely-held appreciation for a man who served the congregation of St. Luke's longer than any of its priests. The *Charleston News and Courier* published one of the earliest on the 23rd of June.

To

Francis J. Murdock, D. D.
Rector of Saint Luke's Church, Salisbury, North Carolina
This is affectionately dedicated

HYMN 216.

CONFIRMATION.   C. W. MURPHEY.

Thine for - ev - er, God of love, Hear us from thy throne a - bove;

Thine for - ev - er may we be, Here and in e - ter - ni - ty. A - men.

Dr. Murdoch received many accolades during his lifetime and at his death. One such was a short confirmation hymn composed by Clarence Wainwright Murphy (1865-1926) and dedicated to the rector.
St. Luke's Archives

The Rev. Francis Johnstone Murdoch, D.D., died at the Murdoch homestead in this city, Monday night, and was taken away yesterday afternoon to his old home in Salisbury, N.C., to be buried in the soil he loved so well and among the people he had served so faithfully. His summons came with shocking suddenness, but in death as in life he was ready for whatever call the good God made upon him. He was a living epistle of the things in this world that are worth while. Nor only was Dr. Murdoch a devoted and able minister, but he was a thorough-going businessman, and to his initiative and wise management is the town of Salisbury indebted for many of its most prosperous industries. Everyone believed in him, and followed him, and his neighbors will bury him with honor and sorrow that they shall not see his like again.

When the clergy and delegates to the 94th Annual Convention of the Diocese of North Carolina convened in St. Paul's Church, Winston-Salem, in May 1910, they heard Bishop Cheshire offer his reflection on the life of a man he had known as a personal friend and fellow clergyman for some 40 years.

Of the Rev. Dr. Murdoch I do not know how to speak adequately; and however restrained I might be in my language concerning him, were I to say all I think, I should fear to be counted extravagant. He was a man of extraordinary intellectual force, and of rare discrimination of judgment and lucidity of thought. His capacious and vigorous mind seemed not to feel the burden or difficulty of the most intricate and stubborn problems; and his ability to set forth in clear exposition his own views was a constant surprise even to those who knew him best. This clearness of view and precision of statement made him a wonderfully attractive and successful teacher, as many of our brethren of the Clergy can testify. And yet all which has been said does not touch the best and the greatest of that which he was. He was a little child in humility and reverence and submission to the teaching and to the discipline of his Heavenly Father and to his Saviour and Lord. It was a privilege to sit and learn of him in his public preaching and exhortation; it was a greater privilege now and again in the revelations of personal intercourse and of private discourse to catch brief glimpses of the gentle and trustful soul, and of the tender and loving heart, which too often was unsuspected by those who came in contact only with his masterful will and intellect in the routine of daily conventional and practical life. His heart was fixed on God, and the Church of God commanded the full loyalty of his life service. Many of us feel that we shall never find another who can supply his place to us.[77]

1. This statement is cited by George Raynor, late editor of *The Salisbury Post*, in his article, "Murdoch: successful with ministry to the soul and to the pocketbook," published in the *Post* on 18 June 1988. The first installment of the two-part sketch of Dr. Murdoch appeared in the pages of the newspaper on 11 June 1988.

2. The principal source on the genealogy of the Murdoch family is the records compiled by Eliza Marsh (Murdoch) Lang (1911-1997), a granddaughter of Dr. Murdoch's, and her daughter Harriet (Lang) Hornthal (b. 1938). Copies of this material were made available to the author by Mrs. Lang's brother, William Speight Murdoch (b. 1920), a member of St. Luke's.

3. See Lawrence F. London, "Frances Johnstone Murdoch," DNCB, 4, 343-44. Also see Claiborne T. Smith Jr., "Jarvis Buxton," DNCB, 1, 292-93.

4. JAC, 1869, 71-72.

5. JAC, 1870, 61.

6. JAC, 1871, 67-68.

7. Established as the Ravenscroft School for Boys in 1856, it was closed in 1864, reorganized by Bishop Atkinson, and reopened in 1868 under the Rev. Mr. Wilmer to train young men for the ministry.

8. Hope Summerell Chamberlain, *This was Home* (Chapel Hill: University of North Carolina Press, 1938), 201.

9. Ibid, 201-02. Archibald Henderson (1877-1963), a distinguished mathematician and professor at the University of North Carolina, Chapel Hill, achieved fame as a literary critic and the biographer of George Bernard Shaw. He also would succeed his father, the author of "Episcopacy in Rowan County," published in 1881 in Rumple's *A History of Rowan County, North Carolina*, by writing a centennial history of St. Luke's in 1923.

10. JAC, 1874, 105.

11. See Max R. Williams, "Nathaniel Boyden," DNCB, 1, 204-05.

12. See Sarah Aull and Mary Brandon, *Dr. Josephus Wells Hall: A Man of Energy and Enterprise, Salisbury, North Carolina* (Salisbury: Salisbury Printing Company, 1994). Dr. Hall's remains and his gravestone were later removed to Chestnut Hill Cemetery.

13. JAC, 1875, 103.

14. RCD, 51/182-84. The deed was made to Mr. Murdoch, John Steele Henderson and Stephen Ferrand Lord, trustees, for $5.00 and gave them permission to mortgage the property to raise funds to erect the church. When built and paid for, the church property was to be conveyed to the Diocese of North Carolina. The property was mortgaged in December 1875 for the sum of $200 to the Salisbury Savings and Loan Association (RCD, 51/185-87). The mortgage was paid by Ellen S. McKenzie on 1 November 1877. The trustees, in turn, conveyed the St. Mary's Chapel property to Bishop Lyman and the diocesan trustees on 14 November 1883 (RCD, 65/74-75.

15. JAC, 1876, 124.

16. JAC, 1877, 55.

17. Ibid, 162. Mr. Murdoch also reported holding "occasional services at Franklin, and two other points in Rowan County. Arrangements have just been made for regular Sunday services in Franklin. Large congregations assemble to hear sermons at any point in the country where a minister will go to have services. It is a very great shame that there is not a minister stationed at Salisbury, whose sole duty it would be to act as Missionary in Rowan."

18. JAC, 1883, 118.

19. JAC, 1884, 54.

20. Some insight into the early-20th Century history of St. Mary's can be gleaned from a report on the Charlotte Convocation prepared by the Rev. William Hill Hardin, archdeacon of the convocation, and published in *The Carolina Churchman* in November 1919.

    "October 5th, a memorial service was held in St. Mary's Church, Rowan County, six miles from Salisbury, on the Charlotte road. Years ago, St. Mary's was quite a prosperous Parish, but gradually the congregation removed to other sections of the country, and because of the fact that there was no material left in the immediate neighborhood from which to draw, it was necessary to discontinue regular services; however, a memorial service is to be held each year, as is the case at old St. Andrew's near Woodleaf, followed by a dinner on the grounds. On the occasion above referred to, the weather conditions were ideal, and long before the hour set for the service, every seat was taken. The Archdeacon preached the sermon, and administered the Holy Communion, more than forty people receiving. At the conclusion of the service, a bountiful dinner was served on the grounds adjoining the Church, which was greatly enjoyed by all present."

21. RCD, 52/194. On 16 September 1867 the *Carolina Watchman* informed its readers that "Mr. John I. Shaver has just finished a two story brick dwelling on the corner of Church and Council;...." Whether Mr. Shaver occupied the house is uncertain; in April 1870 when he the placed the property with Luke Blackmer, trustee, the house was occupied by a Major Robbins (RCD, 45/5).

22. RCD, 52/479.

23. JAC, 1878, 91.

24. JAC, 1879, 171.

25. JAC, 1880, 149.

26. Robert O. Jones, compiler, *Biographical Index of Historic American Stained Glass Makers* (Raytown, Missouri: Stained Glass Association of America, 2002), 25, 113.

27. See Trow's *New York City Directory*, Vol. XCVI, For the Year Ending May 1, 1883. (New York: Trow City Directory Company, 1882), 75, 300. The entry in the 1883-1884 directory is the same except that Mr. Colgate had moved his residence from Manhattan to 660 Greene Avenue, Brooklyn, where he lived until his death.

28. JAC, 1883, 118.

29. JAC, 1886, 76-77.

30. RCD, 69/213-15

31. JAC, 1887, 97.

32. RCD, 69/359-60.

33. Dr. Murdoch's role in the textile industry in late-19th Century Salisbury is noted in an account of the early textile mills established here written by Mrs. F. J. Murdoch Jr., and published on 12 April 1953 in the *Salisbury Sunday Post*. See also James Shober Brawley's coverage of the textile development in RS, 220-222 and Paul D. Escott, *Many Excellent People: Power and Privilege in North Carolina, 1850-1900* (Chapel Hill: University of North Carolina Press, 1985), 203, 213-15. Three of

these mills were later acquired and merged with major Piedmont textile concerns: the Kesler mills were acquired and incorporated into the Cannon Company in 1928; the Vance mill was purchased in 1931 by Carl A. Rudisill, who operated a series of mills in Gaston County, and renamed Cartex; in 1952 the Salisbury Cotton Mills were merged into the Cone system. The Rowan Knitting Company factory was described as "long ago torn away" by Mrs. Murdoch in 1953.

34. JAC, 1888, 34.

35. Ibid, 11.

36. See James Shober Brawley, "Francis Emanuel Shober," DNCB, 5, 339.

37. JAC, 1889, 9.

38. JAC, 1889, 87-89, and 1890, 90-92, 100. In 1890 Mr. Green reported that, at St. Jude's, "New seats have been put in this little house of worship. We hope to have it ceiled and a nice chancel soon." Mr. Green also had charge of St. James, Iredell County.

39. See James Shober Brawley, "John Thomas Wheat," DNCB, 6, 164-65, "Death of Dr. Wheat," *Carolina Watchman*, 9 February 1888. Helen Cheney, "St. Luke's Communion Set Created of Abiding Love," *Salisbury Sunday Post*, 29 September 1957.

40. RCD, 70/374-75.

41. JAC, 1891, 81-82.

42. RCD, 79/102.

43. RCD, 74/420-21.

44. JAC, 1892, 124.

45. JAC, 1894, 132.

46. JAC, 1892, 122.

47. JAC, 1894, 82.

48. JAC, 1897, 61.

49. RCD, 74/432-37. Mr. Harrison's imposing two-story brick residence was completed in 1869 (*Old North State*, 20 August 1869). Samuel R. Harrison died on 28 June 1908. His obituary in the *Carolina Watchman* (1 July 1908) provides useful insight. "At one time he was quite wealthy, but unfortunate investments and other accidents took from him nearly all of his estate. He was confirmed in St. Luke's Episcopal church 64 years ago, and has been a worthy and honored member of the church since that time. Since the establishment of St. Paul's church on Chestnut Hill, Mr. Harrison has been closely identified with that, the locality of the church making his attendance more convenient." Dr. Murdoch officiated at the funeral of this long-time communicant of St. Luke's held at St. Paul's.

50. JAC, 1892, 125.

51. JAC, 1893, 145.

52. JAC, 1894, 141.

53. JAC, 1895, n.p.

54. JAC, 1896, 45. RCD, 80/265.

55. JAC, 1900, 44.

56. RCD, 82/408-09, 586-87.

57. See Allen H. Stokes Jr., "Silas McBee," DNCB, 4, 119-20.

58. The Holt family is little known today; however, the house they occupied at 324 South Fulton Street survives, although since refitted for apartments, and the box-

wood lining their front walk has long since grown together forming a handsome mass planting. Mr. Holt was a conductor for the North Carolina Rail Road and was on the first train to depart Salisbury in 1854. Charlotte A. Carncross died in 1877, Mary Elizabeth (Carncross) Ritter died in 1889; the date of Adelia E. (Carncross) Slater's death has not been confirmed. The left panel is in memory of Henry Allen (1855-1868) and Blanche Elvira (1865-1871) Holt.

59. JAC, 1901, 110.

60. JAC, 1902, 54. The names of those baptized, confirmed, married and buried as members of St. Mark's are recorded in a record book maintained by Mr. Trott from 1900 into 1908 when Simeon Jeremiah Michael Brown made the last entry.

61. JAC, 1903, 56.

62. JAC, 1904, 55.

63. JAC, 1902, 102-03.

64. JAC, 1914, 113-14.

65. JAC, 1901, 68.

66. RCD, 105/214-15. Two years later, on 19 September 1907, C. B. Miller, Mc. L. Ritchie and their wives conveyed a lot at the corner of Patterson Street and Central Avenue, China Grove, to Bishop Cheshire and the diocesan trustees for a congregation "to be organized in the town of China Grove and to be known as St. Philips Church" (RCD, 114/466-67). That congregation was not organized. In 1916 the Church of the Ascension was built on Ross Street, China Grove, largely through the generosity of William Joshua Swink (1853-1939), and consecrated on 8 October of that year (RCD, 142/79). After the death of Mr. Swink's widow, Anna Swift (Hearne) Swink, in 1946 the Diocese of North Carolina closed the church and sold the property to Cannon Mills Company in 1947 (RCD, 296/503-04).

67. RCD, 90/370-71.

68. RCD, 99/64-65.

69. JAC, 1905, 112.

70. JAC, 1911, 70.

71. A short article under the title, "Ordination Service," appeared in the *Salisbury Evening Post* on 14 June 1909.

72. See SJLC, 171-74.

73. See FPC, 72-87. Charles Webber Bolton became one of the leading and most prolific ecclesiastic architects in Philadelphia, with an especially large practice in the Presbyterian Church. Born in Zelienople, Pennsylvania, and educated at Lafayette College, he was first a company architect with the Southwest Virginia Mining and Development Company, Pocahontas, Virginia, but by 1884 he had established himself in Philadelphia where he maintained a practice until his death. For a part of this long period he worked in association with his father, Charles L. Bolton, also an architect. At his death he was credited with the design of over 500 churches.

74. The Washington Building stands at 118 North Main Street. The Hambley mansion is now known as the Hambley-Wallace house, and occupying the spacious grounds at 508 South Fulton Street. The Southern Passenger Station stands on the east side of Depot Street, at the head of Liberty Street. The Grubb Building, long known as the Wallace Building, continues to tower over downtown Salisbury at the north corner of Main and Innes streets. The Empire Hotel stands on the west side of the 200 block of South Main Street. The Peoples National Bank occupies the south corner of Main and Fisher streets. Franklin Fletcher Smith's house stands at 201 South Fulton Street, opposite Mr. Cannon's house at 202 South Fulton Street. Dr. Murdoch's house stood on the south side of the 200 block of West Horah Street.

75. The remarkable career of the prolific Mr. Milburn has drawn few scholars as yet. The principal biographical work remains Lawrence Wodehouse, "Frank Pierce Milburn (1868-1926), A Major Southern Architect," *North Carolina Historical Review L* (July 1973), pp. 289-303. Mr. Milburn and his firm, Milburn, Heister & Co., published an important series of illustrated promotional monographs including: *Examples from the Work of Frank P. Milburn and Company, Architects, Washington, D.C.; Selections from the Latest Work of Milburn, Heister & Co., Architects, Washington, D.C.* (ca. 1913); *Selections from the Latest Work of Milburn, Heister & Co., Architects, Washington, D.C.* (ca. 1920); and a third volume of the same title published in 1922. The only ecclesiastical building published in any of the works is the First Presbyterian Church, Durham, North Carolina.

76. See *Salisbury Evening Post*, "City in Sorrow," 22 June 1909; "Dr. Murdoch's Funeral," and "Resolutions of Respect," 23 June 1909; "Tribute of Respect," 3 July 1909; "Resolutions of Respect," 5 July 1909; and "In Memoriam," 9 July 1909.

77. JAC, 1910, 59-60.

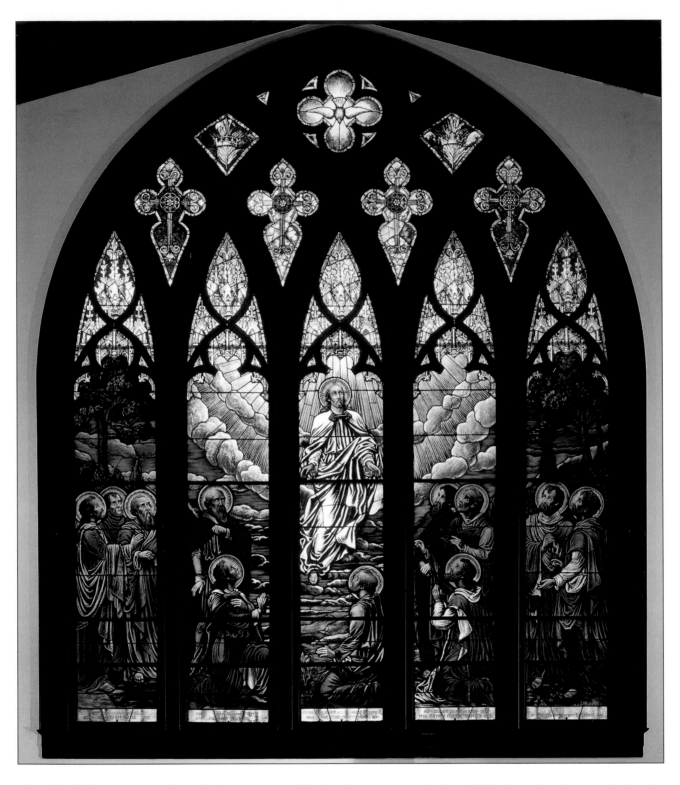

Once Mr. Milburn's general scheme for the expansion of the church was approved in June 1907, donors for the great window in the southeast end of the church quickly came forward and were approved at the July vestry meeting. Individual panels in the five-part window were assigned to Archibald Henderson Boyden, Henry Truesdale Trantham (1852-1929) and Thomas Benjamin Marsh (1863-1933), and two panels were designated as the gift of Walter Steele Blackmer (1861-1922). However, it was not until November 1909 that the design for the window submitted by the Montague Castle Company was approved. In November 1910, Mr. Cheatham reported that a part of the window had been shipped from the works in New York. The complete window was in place in 1911. The center panel is the gift of Mr. Boyden in memory of his mother, Jane Henderson Boyden (1805-1884). It, in turn, is flanked by panels given by Mr. Blackmer in memory of his parents, Luke Blackmer (1824-1889) and Judia Ann Cole (1832-1903), and his two brothers, William Cole Blackmer (1857-1903) and Stephen Shelton Blackmer (1870-1906). The right panel was the gift of Mr. Marsh in memory of his wife, Agnes (Neave) Marsh (1872-1902). The left panel was erected by Dr. Trantham in memory of his wife Mary Ferrand (Henderson) Trantham (1858-1886).
Photograph by Robert Bailey

CHAPTER 6

A Church Evolves

Continuity, Growth, Tradition
and Celebration at St. Luke's
1910–1957

The death of the Rev. Dr. Francis Johnstone Murdoch on 21 June 1909, after nearly 37 years as rector of St. Luke's Church, left a pronounced vacuum in the life of the church and the community. For much of that long period, and particularly during the last decades of his rectorate, his identity was inseparable from his church; his death effectively removed the figure of a learned, wise, caring father from his flock. Those who came to St. Luke's in his wake met quickly with the difficulty of succeeding a legend. the Rev. Thaddeus Ainsley Cheatham served as rector for about a year, followed in turn by Frank James Mallett and Warren Wade Way, who each stayed about four years. In 1918, another senior figure entered the chancel of St. Luke's in the person of the Rev. Mark Hemingway Milne; his rectorate, continuing up to his death in 1938, would become the second longest in the history of St. Luke's. While World War I had some effect on the life of the church, which saw service by 47 members of the parish, the effects of World War II were widespread and pronounced. At least 74 members of St. Luke's served during World War II and the Rev. Edward Brailsford Guerry, who succeeded Mr. Milne in 1939, resigned as rector in 1943 to serve as an army chaplain. William Moultrie Moore Jr., came to St. Luke's in 1944 and remained here until 1952. The 200th anniversary of St. Luke's Parish was celebrated during the rectorate (1952-1957) of his successor, the Rev. Thom Williamson Blair. William S. Powell's bicentennial history of St. Luke's, published in 1953, which has well served the parish to the present, also came to have the honor of being among the first in his distinguished series of historical works, including the six-volume *Dictionary of North Carolina Biography*, and *The North Carolina Gazette*.

While World War I had some effect on the life of the church, which saw service by 47 members of the parish, the effects of World War II were widespread and pronounced.

The near half-century from 1909 to 1957 was marked by important growth in the parish family and an increase in communicants, from 160 in the last year of Dr. Murdoch's rectorate, to 419 in 1957. The number of parish organizations increased in like fashion, with circles for women, men's organizations and the Young People's Service League. Attempts to organize a Boy Scout troop also proved successful. Among the lasting accomplishments of this period was the growth in the parish's Sunday School; an untiring effort to provide classrooms came to fruition with the erection of the Parish Hall in 1938. Later expanded by a new kitchen and additional Sunday School rooms, this facility was the first major construction project following the erection of the new altar and reredos in Dr. Murdoch's memory, and the cloister linking the chapter house with the church, both accomplished in Mr. Cheatham's short tenure. The cloister, flanked by a vestry and small Sunday School rooms, was enclosed and this linkage enlarged in the early 1950s.

The death of Dr. Murdoch was followed by the deaths of a number of his parishioners and long-time communicants. Among the first was that of John Steele Henderson (1846-1916), who served as senior warden at St. Luke's for some 40 years and was the parish's first historian, having written "Episcopacy in Rowan County" for Dr. Rumple's *History*.

The fruits of Dr. Murdoch's long labor are illustrated by this map of the Episcopal churches in Rowan County and the mission at Cooleemee (opposite). All except the Church of the Ascension, China Grove, and St. Phillip's Church, Salisbury, existed at the time of his death. Through the generosity of Dr. Murdoch's widow and his sister Miss Margaret Murdoch (1838-1917) the frame chapel at St. Matthew's was replaced by this brick church as a memorial to Dr. Murdoch in 1912.

Map drawn by Donnie Moose
Photograph of St. Matthew's by Jason Williams

Another faithful vestryman, Stephen Ferrand Lord, died in 1920. Frances Kelly Frercks, a long-time benefactor of St. Luke's and Episcopal causes, died in 1931, leaving the parish two bequests providing funds for a new organ and a sum that effectively enabled the church to undertake, at long last, the erection of the Parish Hall. Other deaths in the congregation also changed its character. At mid-century, the doors on the past closed with the death of Dr. Murdoch's widow Eliza Marsh Murdoch (1861-1951), at the age of 89. Some years before her death, on the sixth of February, she had overseen the removal of boxwoods from her garden to St. Luke's where they continue to enhance the grounds.

Episcopal Churches of Rowan County
(and Cooleemee)

Prepared by Donnie Moose

1. Saint Luke's
2. Christ Church
3. Saint Andrew's
4. Saint Mary's
5. Saint Jude's
6. Saint Matthew's
7. Saint George's
8. Saint Mark's
9. Church of the Good Shepherd
10. Saint Joseph's
11. Ascension
12. Saint Paul's
13. Saint Peter's
14. Saint John's
15. Saint Phillip's

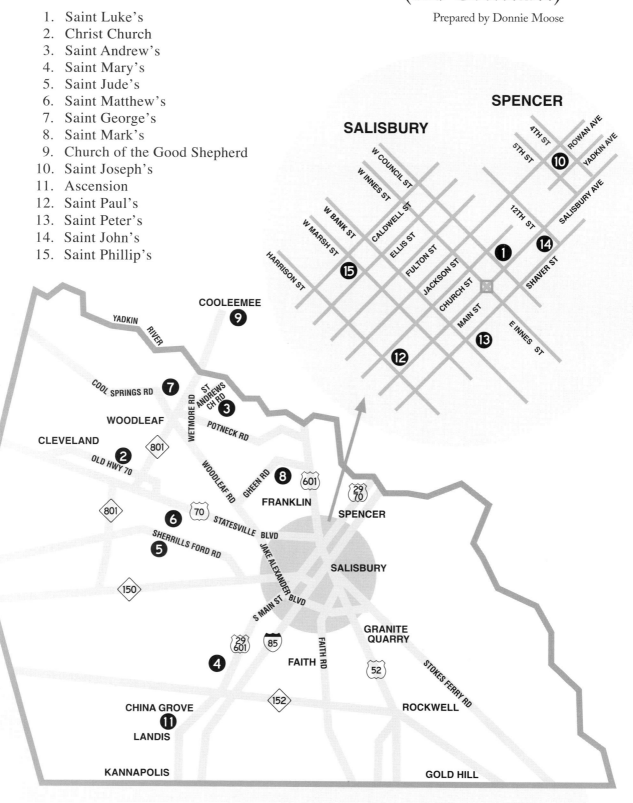

At Dr. Murdoch's death the planned improvements to St. Luke's were largely complete except for the new stained glass windows in the addition to the nave. His demise occasioned both the search for a new rector and a means of honoring his memory. The two efforts proceeded hand-in-hand through the summer and autumn of 1909; however, the first-named task proved more difficult to accomplish. Today's studied process of choosing a rector and issuing a call, which was perfected through the 20th Century, was not in place in 1909. The vestry was frustrated not just once but twice, and hindsight suggests the matter of responsibility for the numerous missions established by Dr. Murdoch

Thaddeus Ainsley Cheatham came to St. Luke's in autumn 1909 as a supply minister following the death of Dr. Murdoch. He accepted the parish's call as rector, but resigned in 1910 to return to Pinehurst where he had a long career as priest at the Village Chapel.
St. Luke's Archives

may have figured in the considerations of those sought as rector. The vestry's first choice was the Rev. Alfred Rives Berkeley, then priest-in-charge of missions at Madison, Mayodan, etc., under Edwin A. Osborne, Archdeacon of the Convocation of Charlotte; who declined the vestry's offer and remained at his posting. Bishop Cheshire encouraged the selection of the Rev. McNeely DuBose (1859-1911), a former rector of St. Mary's School then serving as rector of Grace Church, Morganton. The vestry, however, decided to issue a call to Francis Moore Osborne, then in charge of several missions in Charlotte. He too declined the call.

The vestry next agreed to accept the bishop's offer to provide a supply minister for the remainder of 1909, and looked forward to the arrival of the Rev. Thaddeus Ainsley Cheatham, then in charge of the Village Chapel in Pinehurst. Mr. Cheatham (1877-1956), a native of Granville County and a graduate of the University of North Carolina in 1900, received his bachelor of divinity degree from the University of the South in 1903. He was ordained deacon that year by Bishop Cheshire, who advanced him to the priesthood in 1904. After brief tenures at St. Bartholomew's Church, Pittsboro, and Christ Church, Tyler, Texas, he served as rector of St. Timothy's Church, Wilson, beginning in 1906. Mr. Cheatham's short stay at St. Luke's is remembered chiefly for his role in further improvements to the church fabric. In 1953 Mr. Cheatham recalled these efforts in a letter to William S. Powell.

FROM GENERATION TO GENERATION

It was in 1909 after Dr. Murdock's (sic) death that I was invited to supply at St. Luke's Church Salisbury. They called me to be Rector and I accepted with the understanding that I might not be able to stay, because of my wife's precarious heath. I stayed a little more than a year when it seemed right that I should come back to Pinehurst. When I arrived at St. Lukes the Vestry had decided to place a beautiful Altar to the memory of the late beloved Rector, Dr. Murdock. In the Chancel above the old Altar was the memorial window to Bishop Atkinson. I felt that this window should be moved and a reredos put in its place. Hon. John S. Henderson was the Senior Warden and of very great influence. He was Salisbury's first citizen and my good friend but he did not agree with me that the Atkinson window should be moved. I did not press the matter but at the next Vestry meeting I said, "Gentlemen of the Vestry, this is your Parish. We ministers are birds of passage, we go on but you remain. My only desire is to help you build a beautiful Chancel in this hallowed shrine. I have therefore prepared two drawings, one shows the memorial Altar as it will be placed under the Atkinson window, the other shows the same memorial Altar with the reredos and a rose window above. The decision is entirely in your hands."

In October 1909 members of the Daughters of the King proposed to the vestry that a memorial to the late Dr. Murdoch be in the form of a new altar. Under the guiding hand of Mr. Cheatham, the memorial was enlarged to include both an altar and a reredos. Plans for the improvements were sought and in December 1909, those of the American Seating Company were accepted. In this photograph, dating to ca. 1943–1945, the eternal flame candle, which burned through World War II, stands on the altar. The candle was a gift of Frances Hardin in summer 1943.
St. Luke's Archives

A cloister linking the chancel with the chapter house was part of an addition in 1910 that provided much-needed Sunday School and vestry rooms. The screen of lancet-arch openings overlooking Church Street is visible in this photograph of ca. 1950, which includes Jane Norvell Wagoner (Gamewell) sitting on the steps with "Tammie," her pet cocker spaniel. St. Luke's Archives

Mr. Henderson, Grand old gentleman that he was, looked at the drawings and said, "I vote that we move the Atkinson window." There was no more to be said and every one was happy over the results. As Rector it was my responsibility and privilege to remodel the Chancel and Sanctuary, to build the cloister leading to the "Chapter House" and to add additional Sunday School rooms.[1]

The episode involving John Steele Henderson and the relocation of the Bishop Atkinson memorial appears to have occurred at the vestry meeting of 14 December 1909. In meetings before and after that date, other important decisions were made. On 22 November the vestry approved the designs submitted by the Montague Castle Company of New York for the Ascension Window and the two windows in the side walls of the nave addition. Donors for the great Ascension Window had been identified in 1908, and others came forward to erect the two smaller windows. The Henderson family, presumably in the person of John Steele Henderson, erected the window in the southwest side as a memorial to (his parents) Archibald Henderson (1811-1880) and Mary Ferrand Henderson (1819-1899). The death of Peter Augustus Frercks on 13 June 1909 occasioned another instance of Mrs. Frercks' generosity, when she donated the pendant window on the northeast side as a memorial to her husband.[2]

Meanwhile, in 1909-1910 decisions were reached also on the design of new chancel furniture, including the pulpit, with attention paid to making the detailing of all the fittings harmonious. In the summer of 1910 the vestry also agreed to replace the congregational seating; however, it remains unclear whether the pews, new then to St. Luke's, were bought direct from the manufacturer (or, less likely, comprised a lot of pews, noted in the vestry minutes, that were put up for sale by a Greenwich, Connecticut, church). The minutes also record occasional discussion concerning the disposition of the "old organ;" however, the purchase of a new organ and its donor is curiously absent from mention. Stephen Ferrand Lord donated the pulpit as a memorial to his parents, John Bradley and Ann (Ferrand) Lord. The seven-branched altar candelabras were given in memory of Archibald Boyden Brawley (1909) and attorney Charles Price (1846-1905). The Nicolson family donated the flanking Eucharistic candlesticks in memory of William Samuel Nicolson (1900) and Jane Hannah Nicolson (1903-1909).[3]

The second architectural project dating to Mr. Cheatham's rectorate was the erection of an addition linking the church with the then free-standing chapter house built in 1895 by the Daughters of the King. The need felt for some time was made more pressing by the growth of the church's Sunday School program and an increasing number of church societies that needed meeting space. At the vestry meeting on 2 August, "Mr. Cheatham reported that all the details in regard to the new building & vault have been drawn & all arrangements made." The "new building" enclosed the area between the two existing blocks and provided a passage linking the church and chapter house, a vestry, Sunday School rooms and the church safe. A cloister carried across the northwest front of the addition facing onto Church Street. Expansions to this addition in later years have both removed the cloister and altered the 1910 plan of this area; however, the vault has remained stationary.

In 1910, before the addition of the cloister, the Men's Bible Class posed for this photograph with the Baptist Church in the background. Standing on the steps, left to right: Mr. Cheatham, minister; John Steele Henderson, teacher; Gus Price, Frank Chunn. Front Row, Left to Right: A. P. Kelly, Louis H. Clement, Sam Wiley, Robert Nicolson, B. W. McKenzie, Ike Lyerly, _____. Second Row: John R. Ide, Mr. Adams, Pete Murphy, Walter Blackmer Sr., Max Gregg, Hayden Clement, Mr. McKenzie, Arthur Frazer, Capt. Smith, Mr. Kepler, Mr. Doub, Lee Mock, Capt. Coughenour. _____, _____. Third Row: Stephen Ferrand Lord, A. P. Buerbaum, Gilbert Hambley, _____, Mr. Dorsett, Dr. Whitehead McKenzie, Waverly B. Strachan, H. M. Armstead, Dr. Henry Truesdale Trantham, _____. L. H. Clement, _____, _____, Albert H. Graf, _____, _____. Back Row: Donald Clement, Leon Henderson, Locke McKenzie, Capt. Henderson, Jack Robinson, Henry Hobson, Burton Craige, _____, John Henderson, _____, Dr. Vance Brawley, J. H. White, _____, _____, _____, _____, _____, _____.   St. Luke's Archives

As construction on the cloister addition was proceeding and enhancements in the church were finding their place, Mr. Cheatham submitted his resignation. When he came to St. Luke's in fall 1909, he also had responsibilities to the Village Chapel in Pinehurst. Whether he gave up that service on accepting the rectorate at St. Luke's is uncertain; however, for both ministerial and personal reasons (the health of his wife), Mr. Cheatham decided to return to Pinehurst in a full-time capacity. This decision proved to be the making of a long, distinguished service to the Village Chapel and the resort community of Pinehurst. There he oversaw the building of a handsome Colonial Revival church designed by Hobart Brown Upjohn; it was completed in 1924 at the south end of the Village Green. Beginning in the 1910s, when Pinehurst was still a part-year resort with a season from mid-autumn to late spring, Mr. Cheatham also served as a supply minister at Calvary Episcopal Church, Pittsburgh, Pennsylvania. Mr. Cheatham retired in 1951, died in Pinehurst on 4 November 1956, and was buried at Mount Hope Cemetery in Southern Pines. His wife survived him. Mr. Cheatham concluded the afore-quoted letter to Mr. Powell with an appreciation.

My short Rectorship at St. Luke's Salisbury was a period of opportunity and happiness and I look back upon it with a sense of deep appreciation that I was called there at a particular time when I could serve the parish and the Kingdom of God.

The choice of a successor to Mr. Cheatham in 1910 proved an altogether easier, less frustrating task than that experienced by the vestry on Dr. Murdoch's death. By early November, it decided to call the Rev. Frank James Mallett, rector of St. John's Church, Sharon, Pennsylvania, who promptly accepted the call. In 1910 in his only report to convention as rector, Mr. Cheatham noted "The Rectory has been made comfortable and attractive."[4] This owed in part to his own efforts. The vestry decided to purchase the furnishings acquired by Mr. Cheatham so that the rectory would be in good order when Mr. Mallett and his family arrived.

The decisions by those who have served as rectors of St. Luke's Church are no doubt made for many reasons, including both personal and professional considerations. In retrospect, Mr. Mallett's decision to come as rector eludes easy explanation except for the fact that it was another step in his return to his first parish. Mr. Mallett (1858-1944) was the first Englishman to serve St. Luke's Parish since the Colonial period and, as events prove, the last. He was born in King's Lynn, Norfolk, England, the son of John and Elizabeth (Brown) Mallett. In 1882 he was married to Mary Emily Long. Their first child, Mabel Mallett (1883-1968), was followed by a second daughter, and in the mid 1880s the family of four left England to locate in New Albany, Indiana. Whether he had undertaken ministerial studies in England is uncertain; however, he was ordained deacon and priest in 1888 and 1889, respectively, and served in those years as rector of St. Paul's Church, New Albany. In the 1890s he was rector for brief periods at a succession of four churches in Ohio and Michigan, and dean of St. Matthew's Cathedral, Laramie, Wyoming, before going to St. John's Church, Sharon, Pennsylvania. In 1893 a son, Reginald Mallett (1893-1965), was born to the couple; he too would become a priest and serve as the Third Bishop of Northern Indiana (1944-1963).[5]

The Rev. Mr. Mallett, Mrs. Mallett, and their three children arrived in Salisbury in December 1910, and quickly settled into the rectory, the church and the community. Mr. Mallett's rectorate, which extended through September 1914, was marked by the usual events in church life. In September 1911 the vestry decided to insert a floor in the belfry, thereby creating a small space above the narthex "to use for a store room." A steep flight of stairs provided access. In mid-winter 1912 the rector gained permission to build a fence around the rectory grounds and saw the work completed in March. The ladies of the parish supplied a church supper in January 1913. Filling persistently rising vacancies for the positions of organist and

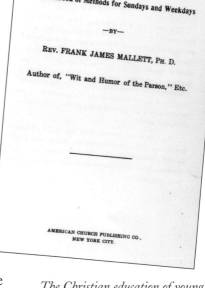

Frank James Mallett (1858-1944), the first English-born priest to serve St. Luke's since the colonial period, was rector from December 1910 through September 1914.
St. Luke's Archives

Helping Boys
A Handbook of Methods for Sundays and Weekdays
—BY—

REV. FRANK JAMES MALLETT, PH. D.

Author of, "Wit and Humor of the Parson," Etc.

———

AMERICAN CHURCH PUBLISHING CO.,
NEW YORK CITY.

choir leader occupied discussion through 1913, and that autumn the sum of $375 was expended to renovate the organ. The facilities added in 1910 failed to meet the needs for the church Sunday School program, and in February 1914 a group of ladies representing the several guilds met with the vestry. Their spokesman, Mrs. Emma Lewis (Speight) Morris, pressed the case for Sunday School rooms. The matter of facilities was enlarged upon and the vestry endorsed the concept of erecting a parish hall and necessary classrooms. Alas, this initiative came to naught, despite the fact that several churches in the Diocese were adding such parish halls and educational wings to their church plants. St. Luke's would wait another 24 years, until 1938, to build the long-awaited parish hall and Sunday School rooms.

The religious life of the parish and its organizations likewise continued in its pattern. When Dr. Mallett came in 1910, St. Luke's had one organization for men, the Brotherhood of St. Andrew; and four for women: the Woman's Auxiliary, Daughters of the King, St. Luke's Guild

The Christian education of young people was a particular interest of Mr. Mallet's throughout his ministry. His Helping Boys: A Handbook of Methods for Sundays and Weekdays, *published in 1911, reflected his long pastoral experience.*
Courtesy of The North Carolina Collection

St. Luke's Church
SALISBURY, N. C.

The Rev. F. J. Mallett, Ph. D., Rector

ASH WEDNESDAY

Penitential Service, Holy Communion and Sermon
at ....10 a. m.
Evening Prayer and Address at............ ....5 p. m.

SUNDAYS

Holy Communion at 8 a. m. every Sunday, except
the first in the month, then at.................11 a. m.
Morning Prayer with Sermon at...... .... 11 a. m.
Evening Prayer with Sermon at.................7:30 p. m.

WEEK DAYS

Service daily at 5 p. m. except on Thursday when
service with sermon, will be held at .....7:30 p. m.
(Address each day except Monday and Saturday)

HOLY WEEK

Every day at 9 a. m. and 5 p. m. and in addition
Holy Communion on Maunday Thursday at......9 a. m.

GOOD FRIDAY

Service at 9 a. m.
The Three Hours Service, with addresses on the 7
last words from the Cross......... 12 noon, to 3 p. m.

EASTER DAY

Holy Communion at.................... ....7 a. m.
Morning Prayer with Holy Communion and Ser-
mon at................... .... 11 a. m.
Evensong and Sermon at.............................7:30 p. m.

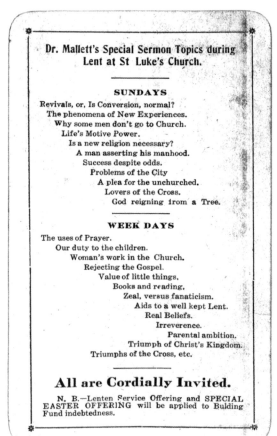

Dr. Mallett's Special Sermon Topics during Lent at St Luke's Church.

SUNDAYS

Revivals, or, Is Conversion, normal?
The phenomena of New Experiences.
Why some men don't go to Church.
Life's Motive Power.
Is a new religion necessary?
A man asserting his manhood.
Success despite odds.
Problems of the City
A plea for the unchurched.
Lovers of the Cross.
God reigning from a Tree.

WEEK DAYS

The uses of Prayer.
Our duty to the children.
Woman's work in the Church.
Rejecting the Gospel.
Value of little things.
Books and reading.
Zeal, versus fanaticism.
Aids to a well kept Lent.
Real Beliefs.
Irreverence.
Parental ambition.
Triumph of Christ's Kingdom.
Triumphs of the Cross, etc.

All are Cordially Invited.

N. B.—Lenten Service Offering and SPECIAL
EASTER OFFERING will be applied to Bulding
Fund indebtedness.

This double-sided Lenten card is one of the few printed materials that survive from Mr. Mallett's rectorate.
Courtesy of the Rowan Museum

and St. Agnes Guild. Within a year Dr. Mallett's strong commitment to the upbringing of boys and young men saw its result in the publication of his *Helping Boys: A Handbook of Methods for Sundays and Weekdays*, published in 1911 by the American Church Publishing Company; and the formation of a Boy Scout Troop at St. Luke's.[6] By 1912 Miss Mabel Mallett, the rector's daughter, had organized a Junior Auxiliary for the young people in the parish that flourished for a while but proved short-lived, as did the scout troop.[7] The year 1912 also saw the organization of the Altar Guild, the oldest single organization in the history of the parish that continues in service with its original name, and has proven to be a permanent part of parochial life. During his rectorate, Dr. Mallett appears to have confined his services in the parish to St. Luke's. In both 1911 and 1912, he reported holding no services at St. John's and St. Joseph's, although he was listed as priest in charge of both missions. Dr. Murdoch's other missions, either organized or unorganized, enjoyed other associations with some under the Convocation of Charlotte. When the Rev. William Hill Hardin was made Archdeacon of the Convocation these gained his attention, and he reopened both on 15 June 1912 with Walter L. Loflin as priest-in-charge.[8]

During the summer of 1914, Dr. Mallett resolved to depart Salisbury and on 27 August, while on vacation in Fletcher, he tendered his resignation effective 1 October 1914. He had accepted a call to his first parish, St. Paul's Church, New Albany, and he returned to serve that church until 1928. After a brief association with Trinity Church, Florence, Alabama, in the early 1930s, he relocated to White Plains, New York, where his son was rector of Grace Church. He spent some part of his retirement in North Carolina, probably including the years after Mrs. Mallett's death in 1938; however, he died in Baltimore on 27 May 1944, while Reginald Mallett was rector of Grace and St. Peter's Church. His body was buried in the Old Chapel Hill Cemetery.

The nearly four-year rectorate of the Rev. Mr. Mallett was succeeded at St. Luke's by another of similar duration. Two months after his departure, the Rev. Warren Wade Way arrived in Salisbury and assumed charge of the parish on 10 December 1914. Mr. Way (1869-1943), born in Irvington, Illinois, to Newton Edward and Lizzie Heaton (Erwin) Way, graduated from Hobart College in 1897. Having been ordained a deacon in 1892, he attended General Theological Seminary in the late 1890s and was ordained priest in 1899. He served briefly as a missionary in the Diocese of Springfield, Illinois, before accepting a call in 1901 as rector of Grace Church, Cortland, New York, whence he came to Salisbury. Mr. Way arrived with his wife and a family of three children.[9]

The patterns of worship and parish life continued largely unchanged during Mr. Way's rectorate. The number of communicants in the parish, which rose from 178 in 1911 to 211 in 1914, increased to 237 in 1918 when Mr. Way submitted his last parochial report.[10] Sunday School attendance fluctuated around 100. Church receipts and disbursements changed little during the period, and the number and character of parish societies remained stable. Mr. Way reported holding monthly services at St. Joseph's, Spencer, in 1916 and 1917, and these appear to have continued into 1918.

During this period of routine church life, two events of note occurred in the parish. Members of the Steele-Henderson family had long been prominent members of St. Luke's, and perhaps none more so than John Steele Henderson (1846-1916). Throughout a long and distinguished career as a member of both the North Carolina General Assembly and the United States House of Representatives (1885-1895), an attorney, businessman and civic leader in Salisbury, he had also served for some 40 years as senior warden at St. Luke's. He was elected for his final term on 24 April 1916, and attended his last meeting with the vestry on the 3rd of July. He died three months later on 9 October. His funeral the next day, held from St. Luke's, was conducted by Mr. Way, the Rev. Edwin A. Osborne of Charlotte and the Rev. William Hill Hardin, who had succeeded Mr. Osborne as Archdeacon of the Convocation of Charlotte. The *Salisbury Evening Post* carried an account of the funeral on 11 October.

Warren Wade Way (1869-1943) succeeded Mr. Mallett as rector in December 1914, and served the parish into summer 1918, when he relocated to Raleigh to become rector of St. Mary's School.
St. Luke's Archives

> **There was a large attendance of townspeople, a number from Rowan, and quite a number of out-of-town people were present to pay their last respects to the memory of this splendid man. The church was taxed to its capacity and many were unable to gain admittance. People of every walk and calling and standing in the community were present, and there were a number of colored people present. A section of the funeral procession was composed of colored people, servants and others connected with the Henderson household, and to whom the deceased was a strong friend.**

Attending in a body were a number of Confederate veterans headed by Mr. A. Parker. Colonel Henderson was one of the best friends of the old soldiers and his comrades were deeply affected by his death.

A final paragraph concluded the account.

The floral offerings were among the most numerous and beautiful ever seen at a funeral in Salisbury and came not only from friends in this city but from many other points.

Mr. Henderson's daughter Elizabeth acknowledged his fellow vestrymen's floral offering, "a wonderful cross of roses and chrysanthemums."

The vestry adopted a resolution honoring their long-time senior warden and decided that the addresses at the upcoming annual parish meeting, to be held in the Community Building on St. Luke's Day, would be "in the nature of memorials to the late senior warden." Mr. Henderson's long, exceptional service as a layman had been unprecedented at St. Luke's.

A second event of importance that occurred at St. Luke's during Mr. Way's tenure was one of larger significance in the Diocese of North Carolina and the Episcopal Church. In 1823, Salisbury was host to the annual diocesan convention, at which the Rev. John Stark Ravenscroft was elected the first Episcopal Bishop of North Carolina. That meeting was held in the Lutheran church, standing in what is known today as the Old Lutheran Cemetery on North Lee Street. In May 1918, St. Luke's Parish hosted the 102nd Annual Convention and history was made again in Salisbury—and within the walls of this church. On 15 May, the second day of the convention, the Rev. Dr. Henry Beard Delany was elected Suffragan Bishop of the Diocese of North Carolina. He was both the first black man to be elected a bishop in the state, and only the second African-American bishop in the United States.

This landmark event was appreciated at the time with a front-page article appearing in the *Salisbury Evening Post* the following day under the heading "Henry B. Delaney (*sic*) Suffragan Bishop."

The convention met at 3 o'clock on Wednesday afternoon, after an hour and a half noon recess, and at once went into the election of Suffragan Bishop for colored work. The Rev. Henry Beard Delaney, D. D., of Raleigh, was elected to this office without opposition or a dissenting vote. As previously stated he will have charge of the work among colored Episcopalians in East Carolina, North Carolina, and South Carolina dioceses, and is the first colored man to be elected to this office in a Southern state east of the Mississippi river. The South Carolina diocese has

From 1912, when the Rev. William Hill Hardin (1868-1934) came to Salisbury as the resident archdeacon of the Convocation of Charlotte, he was an imposing figure, both physically and spiritually, in the city and the region. Archdeacon Hardin followed in the footsteps of Dr. Murdoch, giving a large part of his time to the area missions. Following his death on 23 June 1934, the Salisbury Post *lamented his passing in an editorial in the next day's newspaper.*

"No man in Rowan was more widely known or more universally beloved than Rev. William H. Hardin, who passed away at his home in this city Friday night. He literally lived and loved himself into the hearts of the people, the people he served so unsparingly.... Jovial he was, kind, good-natured, a man among men. He appealed to men and drew them, and remaining they were influenced by him to a higher living."

Courtesy of Elizabeth Hardin Taylor

signified its willingness to accept the man chosen by the North Carolina diocese. This is regarded as a most important and progressive step by the North Carolina diocese.

This accolade came after a long service to black Episcopalians in North Carolina. Mr. Delany (1858-1928) was born in Georgia, raised in Florida and educated there at a school operated by the Freedman's Bureau, before enrolling at St. Augustine's School (now College) in Raleigh, where he graduated in 1885. He remained at St. Augustine's until 1908, serving as a teacher, administrator and chaplain. During this period he was ordained a deacon in 1889 at Raleigh's St. Ambrose Church, and ordained priest there in 1892. Having served on the diocesan Commission for Work among Colored People from 1889 to 1904, he was named Archdeacon for Negro work in the Diocese in 1908. On 21 November 1918, he was consecrated bishop in St. Augustine's Chapel, a building whose erection he had supervised in 1896.[11]

Bishop Delany's attendance at the 1918 convention here was not his first visit to Salisbury. About 1916 he had become involved in the effort to establish an Episcopal church for blacks in Salisbury. On 7 March 1901, Dr. and Mrs. Murdoch had conveyed a small rectangular lot in the south corner of Marsh and Caldwell streets to the trustees of the Diocese "for the use and benefit of a congregation of said Church in said Diocese to be of colored persons whose church Building shall be in the city of Salisbury, N.C."[12] Nothing came of Dr. Murdoch's intention for 15 years, until the summer of 1916, when a storm damaged the small frame church serving the St. Peter's mission at the corner of Clay and Horah Streets. The decision was made to erect a brick church for St. Peter's on a new lot some two blocks away, in the northeast corner of Bank and Shaver streets. In 1917 Archdeacon Hardin explained the fate of the damaged building in his parochial report for St. Peter's. "The old chapel was dismantled and removed to a lot given by the late Dr. Murdoch for a colored mission, near Livingston (sic) College, and is now known as St. Philip's Chapel."[13]

Having been the site of the election of John Stark Ravenscroft as Bishop of North Carolina in 1823, Salisbury was also the site of the 102nd Annual Convention of the Diocese, at which the Rev. Henry Beard Delany (1858-1928), above, was elected suffragan bishop of North Carolina for colored work.

Courtesy of the Episcopal Diocese of North Carolina. The May 1918 issue of *The Carolina Churchman* carried a photograph of St. Luke's on its cover.

THE CAROLINA CHURCHMAN

Organ of the Diocese of North Carolina and the Thompson Orphanage

ST. LUKE'S CHURCH, SALISBURY—WHERE THE CONVENTION OF THE DIOCESE MET, MAY 14, 15 AND 16, 1918.

Diocesan Convention Number

Vol. IX. No. 7.   May, 1918

During his visitation to Salisbury in February 1917, Bishop Cheshire consecrated St. Peter's Church (top) during the 11:00 morning service on 18 February and that afternoon consecrated St. Phillip's Church.

Photographs by Jason Williams

Archdeacon Delany preached the sermon on Sunday, 18 February 1917, when Bishop Cheshire consecrated both St. Phillip's and the new St. Peter's churches.

On 26 June 1918, some six weeks after hosting his fellow clergymen at St. Luke's, Mr. Way submitted his resignation as rector, effective 1 September. He was departing Salisbury for Raleigh to succeed his friend, the Rev. George William Lay, as the rector of St. Mary's School. Mr. Lay was a cousin of Mrs. Way, nee Louisa Atkinson Smith, and they were the grandnephew and grandniece, respectively, of Bishop Atkinson. During his 14-year tenure, Mr. Way oversaw St. Mary's transformation to a junior college, which received accreditation in 1927, and made advances towards its operation as a four-year college. During a financial crisis in 1931, Mr. Way submitted his resignation as rector, and it was accepted in the winter of 1932. That same year he was awarded an honorary degree, LL.D., by Hobart College, and he accepted a call as rector of St. James Church, Atlantic City, New Jersey. After a decade in this final post, he retired in 1942 to Tryon, North Carolina, and died there on 11 June 1943. He is buried in Tryon.[14]

The choice of a successor to Mr. Way apparently came easily and quickly. By the end of July, the vestry had decided to issue a call to the Rev. Mark Hemingway Milne, then rector of Christ Church, Delavan, Wisconsin. The circumstances surrounding the vestry's selection of Mr. Milne are obscure, and it remains unclear how the leaders of St. Luke's would have learned of a priest in a small town some 60 miles southwest of Milwaukee. Likewise, we have no insight into why Mr. Milne, at the age of 47, determined to come south to St. Luke's. Whatever the case, the choice proved good for both Mr. Milne and St. Luke's, where he served as rector for 20 years.

The Rt. Rev. Joseph Blount Cheshire Jr., Fifth Bishop of North Carolina, came to Salisbury on many occasions during his long episcopate that began in 1893 and ended with his death on 27 December 1932.

Horton photograph, Christ Church Archives

The rectorate of Mark Hemingway Milne (1871-1938), lasting from 1918 until his death, was the second longest in the history of the parish. This photograph by Alexander's Studio was published in the 1934 parish yearbook.

St. Luke's Archives

Mark Hemingway Milne (1871-1938), the son of David and Catherine (McDougall) Milne, was born in Corning, New York. He graduated from Hobart College in 1896 and from the General Theological Seminary, New York, in 1899. The Rev. William D. Walker, Bishop of the Diocese of Western New York, ordained Mr. Milne deacon and priest in 1899 and 1900, respectively. Having served as rector of St. Philip's Church, Buffalo, and Trinity Church, Hamburg, New York, from 1899 to 1902, he was curate at St. Paul's Church, Buffalo in 1902 to 1904. In 1904 he left his native New York State to accept a call to St. Peter's Church, Butler, Pennsylvania, where he remained until 1910. In that year he relocated to Delavan, Wisconsin, whence he came to Salisbury. In 1905 Mr. Milne married Alma Tuttle (1873-1925), and they were the parents of a son, David Tuttle Milne. The Milnes arrived in Salisbury on the 10th of October 1918.[15]

Mr. Milne's rectorate at St. Luke's, beginning at the close of World War I and ending with his retirement and death in 1938, at the outset of World War II, was one of normalcy with little interruption to the conventions of parish life. His arrival, however, coincided with an outbreak

---

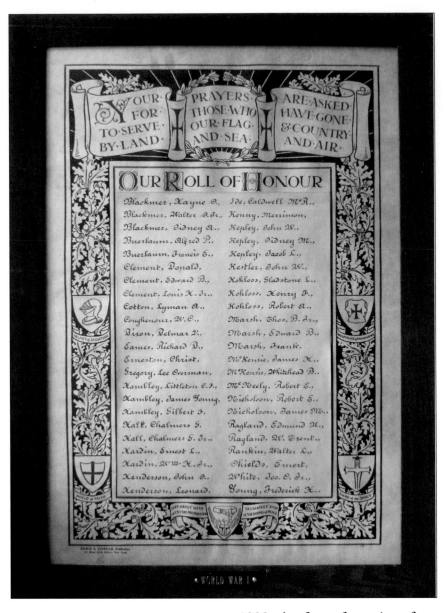

OUR ROLL OF HONOUR

Blackmer, Wayne E.,
Blackmer, Walter E. Jr.,
Blackmer, Sidney A.,
Buerbaum, Alfred P.,
Buerbaum, Francis E.,
Clement, Donald,
Clement, Edward B.,
Clement, Louis X. Jr.,
Cotton, Lyman A.,
Coughenour, W. C.,
Dixon, Delmar V.,
Eames, Richard D.,
Erneston, Christ,
Gregory, Lee Overman,
Hambley, Littleton C.J.,
Hambley, James Young,
Hambley, Gilbert J.,
Hall, Chalmers G.,
Hall, Chalmers G. Jr.,
Hardin, Ernest L.,
Hardin, Wm. H. Jr.,
Henderson, John D.,
Henderson, Leonard.

Ide, Caldwell McR.,
Kenny, Merrimon,
Kepley, John W.,
Kepley, Sidney M.,
Kepley, Jacob L.,
Kestler, John W.,
Kohloss, Gladstone L.,
Kohloss, Henry J.,
Kohloss, Robert A.,
Marsh, Thos. B. Jr.,
Marsh, Edward B.,
Marsh, Frank,
McKenzie, James X.,
McKenzie, Whitehead B.,
McNeely, Robert E.,
Nicholson, Robert E.,
Nicholson, James Mc.,
Ragland, Edmund H.,
Ragland, W. Trent.,
Rankin, Walter L.,
Shields, Ernest,
White, Jos. O. Jr.,
Young, Frederick X..

• WORLD WAR I •

The World War I Roll of Honor lists the names of 46 communicants of St. Luke's who served during the war. Some among the group are little remembered in the parish today; however, Sidney Alderman Blackmer (1895-1973) went on to success as an actor on the New York stage and in movies. Photograph by Charles Goldman, St. Luke's Archives

of Spanish Influenza that occasioned the cancellation of public services for a period. Mary Nicolson recalled that during this period, the Milnes allowed the rectory to be used as a "soup kitchen" to feed flu victims temporarily housed in the Community Building that served as a makeshift hospital in the fall of 1918. Life soon returned to its rhythms, and in December vestry elections were held and the annual Every Member Canvass was undertaken. Stephen Ferrand Lord, the senior member of the vestry, was appointed senior warden, and was re-appointed to the position after the vestry elections in December 1919. He would serve the church for but half of this final term. His death on 6 July 1920 brought to a close a long, distinguished service to St. Luke's as a vestryman for 50 years, and the loss of one of its oldest communicants.[16]

The need for Sunday School rooms, voiced through the 1910s, continued into the first years of Mr. Milne's rectorate. Although there would be no enlargement of the church plant until 1938, the first of a series of committees to undertake such a project was formed in March 1922. A committee composed of Albert H. Graf, Ross Minish Sigmon (1892-1942), Peter Ambrose Wallenborn, Mrs. Claudius Stedman (Emma) Morris (1881-1972) and Miss Ellen Fletcher was given the charge to investigate the matter and report back to the vestry. The idea advanced through the spring, and in June the vestry asked Mr. Milne "to obtain plans for improvements and for a parish house if some could be secured on approval and without cost." That approach, verging on parsimony, reflected something of the financial thinness of the time and a lack of will that would doom any prospects for another 15 years. Nevertheless, plans were secured by the end of the summer and displayed in the vestibule for inspection. In January 1923 the committee, in the person of Mrs. Morris, Miss Mary Henderson and Mr. Wallenborn, reported pledges of $8,000 in hand, $4,000 in legacies available for the purpose, and the need to raise a total of $30,000 for the project. Fund-raising continued through 1923 and into 1924, when Ernest L. Hardin reported in May that pledges on the parish house totaled just over $17,000, exclusive of the legacies.

At present, with the plans unavailable, nothing is known of the proposed facility beyond the name of its designer. Hobart Brown Upjohn (1876-1949), the grandson of Richard Upjohn, the great 19th Century church architect and the designer of Raleigh's Christ Church, was then a leading American church architect in his own right. He had been working in North Carolina, principally for Episcopal congregations, since the early 20th Century, when he designed the Church of the Holy Comforter, Burlington, and the parish house addition to his grandfather's Raleigh church. The circumstances of St. Luke's approach to him are not known; however, they may have been associated with his contemporary commission for an addition to the parish house for St. James Church, Wilmington. Mr. Upjohn enjoyed a wide patronage in North Carolina in the 1920s and before the decade was out, a series of distinguished churches would be erected to his designs: Chapel of the Cross, Chapel Hill; First Presbyterian Church, Concord; the Village Chapel, Pinehurst; and First Presbyterian Church, Wilmington, together with other institutional buildings.[17] But, alas, history did not decree the construction of the parish house Mr. Upjohn proposed for St. Luke's. Despite the pressing need, the funds could not be raised for the project.

Nevertheless, the congregation simultaneously laid plans for another project that it brought off with great success. The 100th anniversary of St. Luke's organization as a modern parish and admission into union with the Diocese of North Carolina would occur on 7 May 1924; church leaders decided to celebrate the centennial on St. Luke's Day, 18 October 1924. The celebration swelled to fit the occasion and was held over two days, Saturday and Sunday, in the presence of both Bishop Cheshire and Mr. Penick, Bishop Coadjutor; together with Mr. Way, who returned to the parish, and Mr. Hardin, Archdeacon of the Charlotte Convocation. James W. Fletcher, a member of the vestry, and Mrs. Clarence

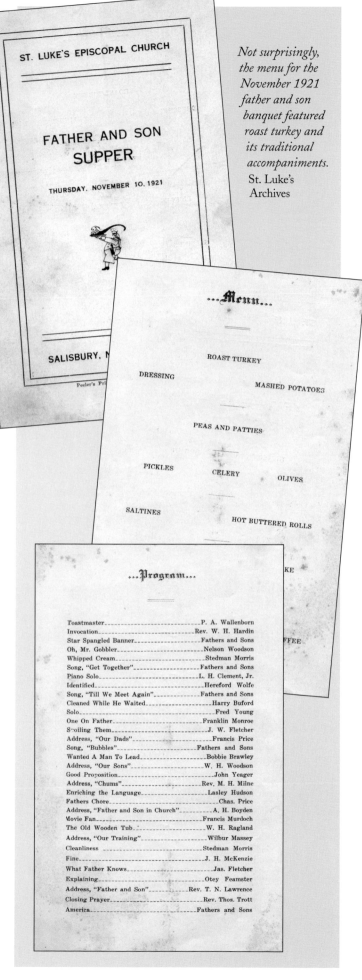

Not surprisingly, the menu for the November 1921 father and son banquet featured roast turkey and its traditional accompaniments.
St. Luke's Archives

Dated to 1924, this photograph is believed to represent a Sunday School class taught at St. Phillip's Church by Miss Howe. Back row, left to right: Fats Massey, _____. Essie Mae Ratz, Julian Noble, Liddell Gaither, Frances Clark, Alta Clarke (Meeks), Louise Gaither (Jackson), Joe Duncan. Front row: John Lash, Calvin Kirkland, Gerroy Fisher, Elizabeth Fitzgerald, Leroy Kelsey, Louise Jacobs (?), Dorothy Fisher, Mary Milton Dalton, Helen Leazer (Wood), and Elizabeth Duncan (Koontz). Mrs. Koontz (1919-1989) went on to have a distinguished career in education and public service, both in Raleigh and Washington, D.C. She made the identifications of her classmates in 1976.
St. Luke's Archives

(Josephine Branch Craige) Kluttz, the president of the St. Agnes Guild, were co-chairmen of the centennial. On St. Luke's Day, a special loan exhibition of historical artifacts was mounted in the Chapter House and available for view from four o'clock until six o'clock, when supper was served on the church grounds. Mrs. Robert Linn Bernhardt, president of the Altar Guild, and Mrs. Robert Vance Brawley, president of the Woman's Auxiliary, organized the exhibition, while Miss Caledonia "Callie" Beard (1872-1945), Mrs. Claude S. Morris, Mrs. Paul Bernhardt, Mrs. Charles Franklin (Penelope Skinner) Massey and Miss Louise Neave (1878-1966) had charge of other exhibits honoring the parish and its associations. The *Salisbury Evening Post* carried an account of the events on St. Luke's Day in its issue of 20 October, under the heading "Interesting and Valuable Loan Exhibit."

> The loan exhibit held Saturday afternoon in the chapter house at St. Luke's Episcopal church in celebration of the one hundredth anniversary of the union of St. Luke's parish with the Diocese of North Carolina contained many articles and groups of articles of

interest, not only to the congregation but to the community as well. On entering the large room one was reminded that the chapter house was built by the Daughters of the King, who raised six hundred dollars to defray the cost. A brilliant leafed vine, a Virginia creeper, has grown luxuriantly since it was planted near the door by Mrs. F. J. Murdoch many years ago.

Within the room were displayed records of historic value and interest too numerous to permit of careful examination. One of many which attracted the attention was the carefully penned Apostolic Succession, written by the late Rev. Francis J. Murdoch, rector of St. Luke's from 1872 to 1909. At a table was the special exhibit arranged by the Woman's Auxiliary, where were seen personal articles belonging to Dr. Murdoch, his infant cap, his christening robe, worn also by his son and grandson at their christening, photographs of him at the time he went to war, his soldier cap, and records of his work as a builder of the church.… Articles brought from Liberia by Miss Mary Wood McKenzie, collected during her mission work there included articles of wearing apparel, household articles, and a mask called a devil's head, worn by natives to terrify insubordinates.

Dr. Murdoch left to the church a "Book of Rememberance" in which are sketches written in his own handwriting, of eminent persons, who have passed on…. Dr. Murdoch left also a book of the history of the church in the county.

A valuable book in the exhibit contained the files from 1826 and 1827 of the Western Carolinian, a Salisbury newspaper antedating the Carolina Watchman, edited by the late J. J. Brunner. In a copy of this paper, dated March 27, 1827, was noticed a quaintly worded advertisement calling attention to "Mechaniks" that proposals would be considered by the building committee of St. Luke's congregation for material for a church. Eighty thousand bricks, perfectly moulded and of uniform size, and good walnut and hickory lumber, well seasoned, were among the articles to be supplied.…

The records of the Sunday school show the present splendid church school has grown from a total enrollment of twenty scholars in 1835, with Mrs. Shober as superintendent and teacher. In those early days the classes were named, some of them on record

Mary Wood McKenzie (1891-1964), a life-long member of St. Luke's, went to Liberia in 1922 and had a long career there in the mission field, first as a teacher at the House of Bethany and as its principal beginning in 1932. In 1943 she married the Rt. Rev. Leopold Kroll, Bishop of Liberia, and in 1945 they retired to Salisbury, where he died in 1946. She last served as librarian at St. Andrew's School in Tennessee. Here she appears in a rickshaw in Liberia, probably in the 1930s.
St. Luke's Archives

being "Buds of Promise," "Heirs of the Kingdom," and "Children of Christ." Following Mrs. Shober came T. F. Young and Mr. Stephen F. Lord.…

The choir exhibit included the first vestments used and photographs of the early members of the choir. The handsome collection of altar furnishings was displayed, each article bearing the name of the person who had used, made or given it to the church.

The beautiful communion set, it was seen, was presented to St. Luke's church as a memorial to "our tender, gentle, learned and eloquent pastor, Rev. Dr. John Thomas Wheat," by members of St. Lazarus congregation, Memphis, Tenn., after that church had gone out of existence following the war. The chalic (*sic*) and patten were made of jewels and silver plate dropped in the alms plates by women of the congregation of which President Jefferson Davis was senior warden. Mrs. Davis was a devout member of the church and much interested in procuring the communion set, which in the gray days in 1869 it was impossible for the impoverished southerners to purchase. The treasured memorial came to St. Luke's in 1888 (sic).

The church organ was bought by the ladies of the church with money made by the sale of Mr. John S. Henderson's "Episcopacy in Rowan." All of the memorials in the church, Sunday school, chapter house and cloister were marked with dates and facts concerning them.

The exhibit continued until six o'clock, when supper was served on the lawn, from a long table decorated with red and white dahlias, the same brilliant flowers, which were effectively used in the church and chapter house. In the center of the table was the St. Luke's birthday cake, elaborately iced and ornamented, and with one hundred tiny red candles on it, the topmost decoration being the cross outlined with candles. At one end of the table was another cake which held lighted pink candles. Just before supper, Mrs. P. H. Bernhardt made the following remarks: "This is a day of anniversary. In the center of the table is St. Luke's birthday cake with its one hundred candles. It is only fitting that our beloved Bishop Cheshire, representing the Diocese of North Carolina should cut the first slice. This is Mrs. Murdoch's birthday also. She has been an inspiration to all who come in contact with her and St. Agnes Guild wishes to honor her. On behalf of St. Agnes Guild, I have the privilege of presenting this cake." Every one present joined in singing greetings for St. Luke's birthday and Mrs. Murdoch's birthday.

The ladies of the church are to be congratulated upon the success of this excellently arranged and managed exhibit…. The beautiful birthday cakes were the work of Mr. James A. C. Wren and Miss Mary Wren.

On Sunday morning, Bishop Cheshire presided at the Holy Eucharist at 7:30 a.m. and the 11:00 a.m. confirmation, when Dr. Archibald Henderson presented his historical address. Although the church was having difficulty raising the funds to pay for the Upjohn drawings for the parish house, the vestry voted to support the publication of Dr. Henderson's centennial address, and it was issued in paper covers in 1925.[18]

In the history of St. Luke's the failure to build the parish house was but one casualty of 1925. Another was the death of Mrs. Milne, at the age of 53 years, on Tuesday, 8 April 1925. In its long history as a parish, Alma (Tuttle) Milne (1873-1925) was the first and only wife of a rector known to die while her husband was priest at St. Luke's. Mr. Way came from Raleigh to join the Rev. John C. Seagle, of St. Paul's Church, to conduct her funeral on Wednesday morning. Her body, accompanied by Mr. Milne, their son David, and James McKenzie, was taken then by train to Hornell, New York, for burial. The closing paragraph of her obituary, published in the *Salisbury Evening Post* on the afternoon of the ninth, conveys the affection and respect she had gained here.

Although she had been a resident of Salisbury only about seven years Mrs. Milne was one of the most beloved women of the city, having endeared herself at once to all whom she came in contact. She was a woman of culture and rare attainments, a literary woman of high rank, and these with her cheerful disposition and helpful characteristics made her a valuable aid to her husband in his labors as rector of St. Luke's church. She was a woman of sympathetic nature and believed in and practiced the principle of charity in its broadest sense. To the needy and the suffering she was ever ready to lend a helping hand, and for all she had a kindly word, a pleasant smile and a godspeed wish. Not only did she

On Saturday, 18 October 1924, St. Luke's Day, the parish celebrated the 100th anniversary of its admission into union with the Diocese of North Carolina in the presence of Bishop Cheshire. On Sunday Dr. Archibald Henderson (1877-1963) delivered an address on the history of St. Luke's parish, drawing on his personal research and that of his father, John Steele Henderson.

St. Luke's Archives. The address was published later in paper covers.

Photograph of Dr. Henderson in 1945 courtesy of Rowan County Public Library

love people but people loved her for her gentleness, her goodness and her sweet and friendly disposition, and this love was manifest in the beautiful flowers that crowded her sick room and the numerous callers upon her during her confinement and until her condition became so critical as to preclude visitors. In her death this city has lost one of its most beautiful and lovely characters; the church one of its most zealous and conscientious workers.

Surprisingly, the affluence of the 1920s was little seen at St. Luke's; however, a block away, on West Innes Street, the congregation of St. John's Church erected a handsome modern Gothic Revival-style edifice to replace its 19th Century North Main Street building. The vestry, having realized the church could not raise funds for the parish house, shelved the idea for the remainder of the decade. Smaller projects engaged the congregation's attention, which was next focused on the church interior. In June 1926, after discussion over the course of months, Bate Toms and Edward Clement were made a committee and charged with both making final decisions on whitening the walls and implementing the work. By early September, the "interior of the church had been

The parish archives contain many photographs of children and Sunday School classes. This one, made in the early 1920s, is of a group posed in front of the cloister. Front row, left to right, Mary Jane Pugh, Peter Wallenborn, Dick Coughenour, Charlie Woodson, Virginia Yeager; second row Margaret Wain, Buck Woodson, Lorraine Wallenborn, Nancy Coughenour, Locke McKenzie Jr., Margaret Woodson, Clarence Kluttz, Billy Coughenour, Henry Fairley Jr.; third row, Boyden Brawley, Caroline Neave, Elsie May Wain, Annie Wain, William Overton, Jim Woodson, William Hunter, Miss Susie Whitehead (Mrs. John Osborne), and Tom Overton.

St. Luke's Church

Salisbury, North Carolina

LITANY FOR CHILDREN

368   (TUNE 473-2)

Jesu, from Thy throne on high
Far above the bright blue sky,
Look on us with loving eye:
Hear us, Holy Jesu.

2 Little children need not fear,
When they know that Thou art near:
Thou dost love us, Saviour dear:
Hear us, Holy Jesu.

3 Little hearts may love Thee well,
Little lips Thy love may tell,
Little hymns Thy praises swell:
Hear us, Holy Jesu.

4 Little lives may be divine,
Little deeds of love may shine,
Little ones be wholly Thine:
Hear us, Holy Jesu.

5 Jesu, once an infant small,
Cradled in the oxen's stall,
Though the God and Lord of all:
Hear us, Holy Jesu.

6 Once a child so good and fair,
Feeling want, and toil, and care,
All that we may have to bear:
Hear us, Holy Jesu.

7 Jesu, Thou dost love us still,
And it is Thy holy will
That we should be safe from ill:
Hear us, Holy Jesu.

8 Be Thou with us every day,
In our work and in our play,
When we learn and when we pray:
Hear us, Holy Jesu.

9 When we lie asleep at night,
Ever may Thy angels bright
Keep us safe till morning light:
Hear us, Holy Jesu.

10 Make us brave without a fear,
Make us happy, full of cheer,
Sure that Thou art always near:
Hear us, Holy Jesu.

11 May we prize our Christian name,
May we guard it free from blame,
Fearing all that causes shame:
Hear us, Holy Jesu.

12 May we grow from day to day,
Glad to learn each holy way,
Ever ready to obey:
Hear us, Holy Jesu.

13 May we ever try to be
From all sinful tempers free,
Pure and gentle, Lord, like Thee:
Hear us, Holy Jesu.

14 May our thoughts be undefiled,
May our words be true and mild,
Make us each a holy child:
Hear us, Holy Jesu.

15 Jesu, Son of God most high,
Who didst in a manner lie,
Who upon the cross didst die:
Hear us, Holy Jesu.

16 Jesu, from Thy heavenly throne,
Watching o'er each little one,
Till our life on earth is done:
Hear us, Holy Jesu.

17 Jesu, Whom we hope to see
Calling us in heaven to be
Happy evermore with Thee:
Hear us, Holy Jesu. Amen.

51

Lord, dismiss us with Thy blessing;
Fill our hearts with joy and peace;
Let us each, Thy love possessing,
Triumph in redeeming grace:
Oh, refresh us,
Travelling through this wilderness.

2 Thanks we give and adoration
For Thy Gospel's joyful sound:

May the fruits of Thy salvation
In our hearts and lives abound:
May Thy presence
With us evermore be found;

3 So that when Thy love shall call us,
Saviour, from the world away,
Fear of death shall not appall us,
Glad Thy summons to obey.
May we ever
Reign with Thee in endless day. Amen.

Lorraine Wallenborn recently recalled "Each year during Lent Mr. Milne had a children's service on Friday afternoon. If a child had perfect attendance, he received a silver cross pin. In subsequent years, for perfect attendance, the year was engraved on the cross." A regular feature of these services was the "Litany for Children." Elizabeth Hardin Taylor recalls "We all sang first and last verses together and alternated sides for the other verses, kneeling and joining in on 'Hear us, Holy Jesu'." St. Luke's Archives

scraped & painted white and was greatly improved," at a cost of $175. Another part of the improvements were new light fixtures that were donated and installed by the Southern Power Company. In April 1927 the redecorated church was the setting for the diocesan convention of the Woman's Auxiliary.

Having been quiet for some time, the voices of those committed to expanded facilities at St. Luke's were raised anew in the 1930s. In April 1931, a new committee was appointed to study the matter; it consisted of Ross M. Sigmon, Mrs. Claudius S. (Emma) Morris, the superintendent of the Sunday School, and Peter A. Wallenborn. In this instance, the prospect under consideration was additions to the chapter house rather than a major new building. To this end the committee approached Thomas Hooper Yoe Sr. (1902-1955), a skilled Salisbury draftsman, for the work, and he submitted tentative plans later that spring when Mrs. Lyman Cotten was named a fourth member of the building committee. Mr. Yoe refined the plans during the summer of 1931, and they were put out to bid. Whether the bids for the additions came in above budget is not clear, but again, in November 1931, the project was postponed.

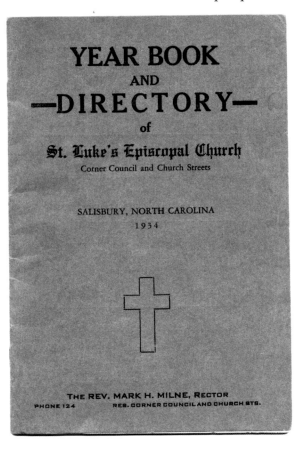

The publication of the first parish directory in 1934 was another initiative during Mr. Milne's rectorate.
St. Luke's Archives

The deaths of two communicants and their legacies to St. Luke's proved to be the factor that would enable the church to finally erect the much needed facilities in 1937-1938: Anna May Shober Boyden, the widow of Major Archibald Henderson Boyden, died on 13 January 1930, and Frances Kelly Frercks, the widow of Peter A. Frercks, died on 15 May 1931. Meanwhile, other needs were addressed and the life of the church continued in its patterns, even if in the straitened circumstances of the Depression. In the fall of 1930, when St. Luke's hired J. Francis Griffith as choir director and Mrs. Griffith as church organist, the prospects for the parish music program greatly improved; however, the optimism was short-lived. By fall 1931, financial difficulties forced the Griffiths to halt construction on the grand house they were building to the west of Salisbury, and they gave up their positions at St. Luke's as well.

In the settlement of both the Frercks and Boyden estates, the financial exigencies of the day forced some adjustment and occasioned delays until the mid 1930s.[19] In 1934, St. Luke's received the compromise sum of $7,500 from the Boyden estate, and at year's end a small portion of it was used to purchase "table silver for the Chapter House," which was being used as a parish hall. In January 1936, the Frercks estate neared settlement. St. Luke's learned that $5,334.51 would be paid on Mrs. Frercks' bequest of $7,000 to the parish house fund, and $7,620.72 would be paid on her bequest for a new organ.[20] After years of difficulty in meeting the annual budgets, the financial condition of the parish looked up and plans were set in motion.

The acquisition of a new organ was accomplished first, in part because Mrs. Frercks' bequest was sufficient to the purpose and, secondly, organ-makers were anxious for the commission after years of reduced patronage in the 1930s. In April 1936, the organ committee's unanimous choice of an Aeolian-Skinner Company organ was reported to the vestry and accepted. The organ could be installed for $7,620. The old organ was then sold to the West End Methodist Church, Gastonia, for $450 through Heckman & Newcomer. The new organ was installed in 1936-1937 and accepted in June 1937, when payment was authorized.

The installation of this new, larger, and more valuable organ at St. Luke's provided yet another opportunity to redecorate the church interior. In May 1936 Francis J. Murdoch Jr., and Lee Overman Gregory were appointed a committee to arrange for painting "the walls of the church and staining the pilasters, beams an (*sic*) ceiling to make them match the church seats and other woodwork." The project occupied the better part of a year as it expanded to include repairs to, and replacement of plaster, and the replacement of the wood foundation under the church floor which was found to be damaged by termites. A. R. Lazenby undertook the work and also enlarged the church basement; across Council Street his carpenters enclosed the second-story veranda of the rectory.

Mrs. Frances Kelly Frercks, the widow of Peter A. Frercks, was a generous supporter of St. Luke's Church. At her death on 15 May 1931, she bequeathed funds to the church for the purchase of a pipe organ. The organ was built and installed in St. Luke's by the Aeolian-Skinner Organ Company in 1936-1937 at a cost of $7,620.
St. Luke's Archives

As renovation of the interior progressed in 1936 and 1937, attention was simultaneously paid to the exterior of the church and its grounds. Copper gutters were installed on the church by Karl Wallace Arthur in the autumn of 1936. Damaged and unwanted trees in the churchyard were removed, and the Davey Tree Company was engaged to attend to the parish's prize incense cedar (*Libocedrus decurrens*). Boxwoods, donated by Irvin Oestreicher and planted in 1933, were supplemented in the churchyard by the gift of others by Mrs. F. J. Murdoch Jr., that fall. In January 1937 a flagstone walk was laid from the church's Council Street door to Church Street, where an opening was cut in the hedge encircling the church grounds. In mid-year W. W. Clark submitted a request to erect a ledger stone over the grave of the Rev. John T. Clark, the Virginia-born Episcopal clergyman who had died in Salisbury on 25 October 1886, and was interred in the churchyard. His became the second marked grave on St. Luke's grounds.

The major accomplishment of the 1930s at St. Luke's, the realization of a long-felt need, was the erection of a parish house and Sunday School rooms. After decades in which committees were appointed, their members approached the work with enthusiasm, and they then saw their efforts fail,

In this view of St. Luke's, believed to date to the early 1920s, the churchyard is enclosed with a privet hedge, streetcar tracks can be seen on Council Street, and the twin towers of St. John's Church, then standing on North Main Street, are visible.

St. Luke's Archives

the committee appointed in January 1937 saw their work to fruition. The initial five-member committee, enlarged to seven in March, was chaired by Ernest Lauriston Hardin (1896-1978), the younger son of the Rev. William Hill Hardin and a stockbroker. Serving on the committee were Hearne Swink (1900-1975), an executive with Cannon Mills Company; William Frederick Robertson Jr. (1905-1983), an executive with the North Carolina Finishing Company; Francis Johnstone Murdoch Jr.; and Mrs. Emma Lewis (Speight) Morris, the long-time head of the parish Sunday School program. This group was soon joined by Dr. Frank Baker Marsh (1896-1991) and Donald Clement (1886-1975).

Mr. Hardin, and perhaps others on the committee, had seen the parish house erected in 1930 at St. Paul's Church, Greenville, North Carolina, which was designed by Leslie Norwood Boney Sr. (1880-1964), a Wilmington architect. In April 1937, Mr. Hardin wrote to Mr. Boney indicating the church's interest in erecting a parish house and the use of the Greenville building as a model. The architect responded quickly, and taking into account certain requirements requested by Mr. Hardin, he produced preliminary plans replicating the Greenville building in part, and submitted them to the committee in mid-May.[21] With further committee input, these were further refined through the summer. The final plans were reviewed by the vestry, approved at its meeting in October 1937, and immediately put out to bid. The contract was awarded to Edward Walter Wagoner of Salisbury in the amount of $19,050, and signed in October. Mr. Wagoner's company was to substantially complete the building by 16 February 1938. With a tight schedule calling for the essential erection of the building in the space of four months, the

Wagoner firm began work almost immediately and submitted their first monthly report on 3 November. Detailed monthly reports were thereafter submitted on the first of each month, with a final accounting made on 26 February 1938.[22]

As the parish house neared completion, plans were developed for the laying of its cornerstone on 30 January 1938. The Rt. Rev. Edwin Anderson Penick, Bishop of North Carolina, presided over the ceremonies with the assistance of Mr. Milne. In its next-day account of the event the *Salisbury Evening Post* published a full listing of the items placed in the cornerstone.[23] In fall 1938 a bronze tablet, executed by The Payne-Spiers Studios of New York, was installed on the parish hall wall beside the front door. The seven donors whose legacies supported its construction were listed: Stephen Ferrand Lord, Henrietta Hall McNeely, Clarence Wainwright Murphey, Anna May Shober Boyden, Frances Kelly Frercks, Frank Lee Norvell and Sallie Coffin Taylor. A certain equanimity attended this listing but, in fact, the Frercks and Boyden bequests accounted for about one-half of the costs of the building. Through the course of 1938, the parish hall and Sunday School rooms were furnished and quickly became the scene of church activities.

The Rt. Rev. Edwin Anderson Penick presided at the dedication of the newly-completed parish house, and the ceremonial laying of its cornerstone, on 30 January 1938. He is seen in the center of this picture, flanked on the left by Ernest Lauriston Hardin, chairman of the building committee, and on the right by Mr. Milne.
Courtesy of the *Salisbury Post*

Seen in this photograph of 25 September 1945, the parish house and adjoining Sunday School rooms answered long-felt needs. St. Luke's Archives

The erection of the new building was the crowning achievement of Mr. Milne's rectorate, and on 10 October 1938 he celebrated his 20th anniversary as rector of St. Luke's. Having reached the age of 67, and having spent the last 13 years as a widower, he was looking to retirement in the closing days of 1938. At the end of October he effectively announced his retirement to the vestry. Although many in the parish and community knew of concerns he held for his health, his sudden death on the evening of 28 December was a shock and surprise. It came as the result of a heart attack he suffered in the lobby of the Rowan Memorial Hospital, where he was paying a visit. Bishop Penick, who had visited the parish earlier in December, returned to officiate at Mr. Milne's funeral, after which his body was taken to Hornell, New York, for burial beside Mrs. Milne's.

In addition to his death notice, the *Salisbury Evening Post* honored the late rector on 29 December with an editorial tribute, describing him as "a man of liberal conceptions and generous social impulses" and concluding with these paragraphs.

> **He was modest, as becomes a man of God, quiet, humble, and devout. His wealthy parishioners and the impoverished among them were alike to him the creatures of his concern and of his solicitude.**
>
> **Faithful in the performance of all of his duties and alert to opportunities for extending his helpfulness in any quarter where need appeared, Mr. Milne is mourned today among Salisbury's more prominent citizenry and its humbler inhabitants as well.**
>
> **He was a noble and useful man.**

During Mr. Milne's 20-year tenure at St. Luke's, the life of the parish and its organizations had continued in their usual fashion, meeting the needs of the church family and providing Christian service, assistance and charity in the community, the region and beyond through the organizations of the Diocese and the national church. Mr. Milne reported 240 communicants in his first parochial report in 1919, with receipts and disbursements of $5,986.14 each. Ten teachers instructed the 45 students in Sunday School. The church organizations consisted of the Woman's Auxiliary, the St. Luke's Guild, the Altar Guild and the Brotherhood of St. Andrew.[24] The number of women's societies increased with the organization of the St. Agnes Guild, the Mary and Martha Guild, and later, the May Brawley Guild. The Boy Scout Troop was reorganized in the parish in 1927, and by 1929 it had 16 members; the parish's Young Peoples Service League had 20 members that year. The surprising statistic for 1929, however, was that for the parish Sunday School which included 17 teachers and 93 pupils; even with allowances for some of that number being in the Sunday School at St. John's Chapel (reported with St. Luke's), it is difficult to imagine how the classes were accommodated each Sunday.[25]

FROM GENERATION TO GENERATION

These parish organizations continued through the 1930s, when the May Brawley and St. Agnes Guilds became branches of the Woman's Auxiliary. The records of the societies survive largely in the annual reports distributed at the annual parish meetings and entered into the vestry minutes. They reflect a high level of activity and a wide range of programs and undertakings. Funds for special projects were raised through both the usual and unusual means. Chicken salad suppers were a staple of parish life in both the 1920s and 1930s. The St. Agnes Guild raised $90.25 at their "Chicken Salad Supper & Coke Sale" in October 1924. In 1930 the guild held both a "tacky party" and a "vanishing tea." Three years later, in 1933, the Mary and Martha Guild held a chicken salad supper on 4 March and a "Heinz spaghetti supper" in December that netted the guild $66.06, while the May Brawley Guild earned $90.82 from plant sales that year. Rummage sales and bazaars were held through the years, and various guilds also raised funds by preparing meals for other church organizations or special parish events. For some years the Mary and Martha Guild mounted plays at the Capitol Theatre. Its performance of "Jack and the Bean Stalk" was well attended in 1934. The Mary and Martha Guild also compiled the parish's first cookbook, appropriately titled *The Mary and Martha Guild Cook Book.*[26]

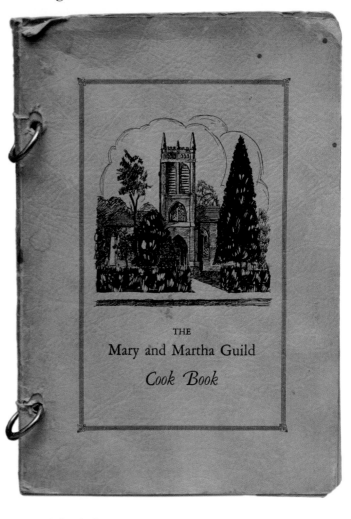

THE
Mary and Martha Guild
Cook Book

The ladies of the Mary and Martha Guild compiled and published the parish's first cookbook. Mrs. William A. Hennessee's recipes for devil's food cake, beaten biscuits and white fruit cake were included as was Will Blackmer's recipe for "Cherry Bounce."
St. Luke's Archives

The speed with which Mr. Milne's successor was chosen in the month following his death suggests the vestry had begun the process once he had confirmed his intention to retire. On 9 January the vestry resolved to issue a call to the Rev. Edward Brailsford Guerry, and within three weeks the call was issued and his letter of acceptance was received. Mr. Guerry (1902-1992) was a native of Atlanta, Georgia, and the son of the Rev. William Alexander and Anne (McBee) Guerry. His mother was a daughter of Vardry Alexander McBee of Lincolnton and the younger sister of the well-known Episcopal Churchman Silas McBee, who had designed the unbuilt 19th Century addition to St. Luke's for Dr. Murdoch. Mr. Guerry's father, also a priest and of Huguenot descent, was consecrated Bishop Coadjutor of South Carolina in 1907, became bishop in 1908 and held the office until his death in 1928. Having received his bachelor's degree from the University of the South in 1923, he studied law and received an LL.B. degree from the University of Pennsylvania. After practicing law he entered the Virginia Theological Seminary and was graduated cum laude in 1932. Ordained deacon in 1932 and priest in 1933 by the Rt. Rev. Albert Sidney Thomas, his

Edward Brailsford Guerry (1902-1992), succeeded the much-beloved Mr. Milne as rector in 1939. He was instrumental in the church's decision to sponsor a Sea Scout troop, and he is seen in this photograph accepting the charter for the troop, Sea Scout Ship #40, on 31 May 1939 from Bunn Hackney, a regional director of the Boy Scouts. On the front row, left, is R. J. Everest, an official with Duke Power, who made High Rock Lake available for scout activities, and on the right are Ernest Hardin and Donald Clement, troop sponsors. The Salisbury members of the troop, in white uniforms, are, clockwise: Milton Shoaf, Larry Hardin, Bill Stanback, Julian McKenzie, Jimmy Davis, Ed McKenzie, _____, Jennings Hill, and Dick Coughenour.

Courtesy of Donald Clement Jr.

father's successor as Bishop of South Carolina, he was the third of the bishop's four male children to enter the priesthood. In October 1932 he assumed charge of Trinity Church, Pinopolis, South Carolina, and the Barrows Mission at Moncks Corner, where he remained into 1935. In that year he became rector of South Farnham Parish and chaplain of St. Margaret's School, Tappahannock, Virginia. He came to St. Luke's from Tappahannock.[27]

Mr. Guerry's rectorate figures among the shortest in the history of the parish. He had served at St. Luke's for about three years when he announced in February 1942 that he had applied for a reserve commission in the army, and active duty as a chaplain. The commission came in September 1942, and he resigned effective 28 September to take up the commission as a First Lieutenant in the U.S. Army. The vestry accepted his resignation, but then reconsidered and offered Mr. Guerry leave while serving in World War II, reserving the rectorate for his return. In January 1943, four years after accepting the call to St. Luke's, he made his resignation permanent.

During his tenure here, Mr. Guerry and his wife occupied rented residences. Although the vestry decided to purchase the "Starnes house" on Maupin Avenue as a rectory in January 1939, they did not. Whether the Guerrys lived in it is uncertain; however, beginning in September 1939 they resided in the Frank Link house at 602 Maupin Avenue, a

large frame bungalow at the corner of Maupin Avenue and Stanley Street, and remained there until Mr. Guerry entered the army. The parish's two-story brick rectory, which had last been updated and redecorated for the Milnes on their arrival in 1918, had received little attention since then, particularly in the period following Mrs. Milne's death in 1925, after which Mr. Milne resided there alone for 13 years. Nevertheless, the rectory was rented out and the income applied toward the rent of the Guerrys' residence.

Following Mr. Milne's death, his son offered the parish the rector's library, which was accepted; however, more than a year passed until the church seriously took up the matter of a memorial to the late rector. Initially, two possibilities were considered: new lights for the church, or a memorial window. Eventually the vestry decided on a memorial window. The firm of R. Geissler, Inc., of New York, a church furnishings house, was approached for the design of a window to be placed in the opening in the northwest side of the bapistry. The firm's proposal, "Our Lord With the Children," was accepted by the vestry in May 1941 at a cost of $500.[28] A short article in the *Salisbury Sunday Post* on 1 June, announcing the memorial, informed readers that the sketch for the window was on display under the designated opening, and that a special collection was to be taken that day. Funds were raised, the window ordered, and it arrived in Salisbury in early autumn. Bishop Penick came to Salisbury and presided at the dedication service on Sunday afternoon, 9 November 1941. The *Post*, on 10 November, opened its account of the service with the bishop's words of tribute.

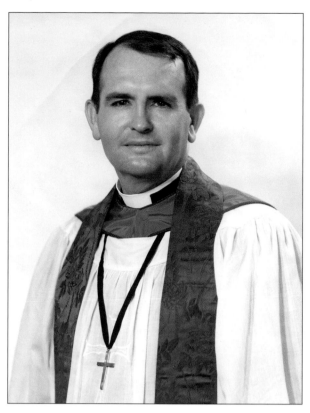

The Rev. Edward Brailsford Guerry
Photograph by Ronald Allen Reilly of Charleston

> **Mark Hemingway Milne had the royal gift, the golden gift, the true pastor's instinct—a love of people. He knew, and loved, the human heart. He was more than a pastor looking after his congregation—he was a shepherd, caring for his flock, one by one.**

In May 1941, as the Milne memorial was advancing, St. Luke's received an offer from Mrs. Burton Craige to install new lights in the church as a memorial to her older sister, May Wheat Boyden Brawley. Mrs. Brawley (1881-1929), and Mrs. Craige, nee Jane Caroline Henderson Boyden (1884-1970), were daughters of Colonel Archibald Henderson Boyden (1847-1929), a mayor of Salisbury for whom the new high school completed in 1926 was named. The Geissler firm's Gothic-style design for the lighting, made at the request of Mrs. Craige, was accepted on 30 May. The new hanging lights arrived about the same time as the Milne window, and were installed in December 1941. The old lights, apparently the fixtures donated by the Southern Power

In 1941 and 1942 three stained glass windows designed and produced by the New York firm of R. Geissler, Inc., were erected in St. Luke's Church. The Milne memorial window (left), designed on the theme "Our Lord With the Children," reflected Mr. Milne's long pastoral care of the parish and his ministry to its youth. The two windows installed in the side walls of the vestibule in 1942 reflected events in the life of Jesus Christ. The "Baptism of Christ" (center) was erected as a memorial to Louis Henry Clement (1854–1926) and his wife Mary Caroline (1857–1913) by their sons. The complementing window, "The Last Supper," is a memorial to Pauline Bernhardt Woodson (1879–1942). Photographs by Robert Bailey

Company, were given to the Rev. Gerhard Charles Stutzer for use in St. Paul's and St. Peter's churches. When first installed, the new lights represented a distinct contrast and were criticized for being "too bright;" the wattage of their lamps was reduced. Although Mrs. Craige was known then as the donor of the new lights, she declined the suggestion of a memorial plaque or any notice of her gift. For many years this remembrance of her sister, through lanterns that continue to illuminate services at St. Luke's, was forgotten.

The Milne window was the first of three designed by the Geissler firm and installed in St. Luke's Church during Mr. Guerry's rectorate. The second and third windows were a pair destined for corresponding openings in the side walls of the vestibule. Pauline Bernhardt Woodson (1879-1942), the daughter of Paul Mathias Bernhardt and wife of Walter H. Woodson Sr., died on 15 January 1942; her grief-stricken husband and their four sons, Walter Jr., Paul, Nelson and James, immediately decided to erect a window to her memory. At the same time, Louis Henry Clement (1854-

1926) and Mary Caroline Buehler Clement (1857-1913), who erected the grand Queen Anne-style house at 302 S. Ellis Street, were remembered by their four sons, Louis H. Jr., Hayden, Edward Buehler and Donald. The Geissler firm prepared designs for both windows, which were approved separately in the spring. Both were erected by early September 1942. When these windows were installed a small stairway, situated against the vestibule's northwest wall and linking it with the middle level of the tower (apparently used by bell ringers), was removed.

Worship services at St. Luke's were further enhanced by two additional, coordinated memorials in 1942. The Altar Guild donated a brass alms basin in memory of Mrs. Woodson, a long-time member of the guild. Pauline Bernhardt Woodson's siblings, Lily Bernhardt Toms and her brother Paul Leake Bernhardt Sr., then donated a basin in memory of their mother, Mary Jane Leake Bernhardt (1853-1929). This pair of basins was supplemented later by a second pair donated, respectively, to the memory of Ann Eliza Bernhardt Neave (1878-1945) by her children, and in honor of Lily Bernhardt Toms by her husband. The four alms basins have remained in use at St. Luke's to the present.

Although the attack on Pearl Harbor on 7 December 1941, did not interrupt the annual parish meeting on the 8th when a "delicious turkey supper" was served, it and World War II affected the life of St. Luke's in many other ways in the years to come. Less than two months later, Mr. Guerry announced his application for a reserve commission in the U.S. Army. In mid 1942, both James Hampton McKenzie and Julian Hart Robertson resigned from the vestry for war service; Mr. Robertson was then junior warden and president of the North Carolina Finishing Company. On 6 September, Sunday afternoon services were renewed at St. John's Chapel, which had been renovated and newly painted through the generosity of Cartex Mills and its officers, Thomas W. Borland and William Harden. The responsibility for these twice-monthly services was shared with Mr. Stutzer, priest in charge of St. Paul's. Now, otherwise lacking a clear explanation, the revival of the mission chapel appears to have been occasioned by the need to minister in the St. John's neighborhood, to the families of factory workers who had entered service. In spring 1943, the open land around St. John's was tilled for use as a Victory Garden by mill employees.

Through the course of 1942, men of St. Luke's Parish joined the war effort as both enlisted men and officers. Mr. Guerry wrote to each of these men in newsletters, offering Christian counsel and short accounts of church and community life. St. Luke's archives contains letters written in reply by several of these servicemen to Mr. Guerry, including those of Nelson Woodson, Frank L. Shields, William S. Murdoch, Charles Collier and David A. Bunch. The most poignant of the group is one written on 19 June 1942 by young Robert Marion Wingate, a member of Boyden High School class of 1942, and then a Seaman 2nd Class in the United States Navy.

June 19, 1942

Dear Mr. Guerry,

I got your letter yesterday and I certainly did appreciate it. I am sure that all the men in the services, as well as myself, feel honored that you folks at home are thinking of us. Letters do not come so often and we really are glad to get them.

I am also glad to hear that the church is very active and I hope that the good work will keep on going steady. The commanding chaplain of the air station just recently granted our school a chapel of its own and we attend services every Sunday morning. Attendance is not required but we always have a large group attending. Because we are sailors we have not lost our faith in God or our eagerness to participate in church services. The civilian population in Virginia does not think very highly of service men but I believe that they would change their minds if they were to attend some of our church services.

I haven't as yet been able to locate an Episcopal chaplain but I am sure that there is one on the base somewhere. At the present we have Chaplain Williams who is Methodist and he really is a swell man. The chaplains take more interest in the enlisted men than the other officers and any enlisted man who attends church services would give his right arm for any of them.

I have passed all the requirements to go to flight school for training as a commissioned officer and I will be leaving sometime in the near future. I will send you my address when I am transferred and I would appreciate it if you would send me a church bulletin once in a while. I like to know what the church is doing and I am especially interested in the Young People's Service League. Would you tell all the members hello for me because I have not forgotten the swell times that I had at the meetings.

I would like to thank you for the prayer book that was given me when I left Salisbury. When I enlisted I brought my prayer book with me but the smaller one is handier and easier to use. I realize that I am a bit young to be giving advice but I wish that you would pass on an axiom that I have learned from my experience in the Navy. My mother passed it on to me but I only recently came to appreciate it. It is: "He who lives in faith lives in victory." If all the people believed in it we would have no trouble in winning this war.

Sincerely yours,
Robert M. Wingate

Mr. Wingate had joined the Naval Air Corps before graduating from Boyden. He was in service less than a year when he was killed in a practice flight on 23 February 1943. Altogether, 74 men and women of St. Luke's served during World War II.

That same month, the St. Luke's vestry honored Bishop Penick's recommendation to accept Mr. Guerry's resignation. It also acceded to his request to relocate the diocesan convention, scheduled for May 1943 in Salisbury, to a more central point in the Diocese because of gasoline rationing; the convention was held at St. Philip's Church, Durham. The search for a new rector occupied the congregation and its vestry for the remainder of the year, even as further memorials were enriching the fabric of the church. The first, unanimous choice for rector was the Rev. David Watt Yates, rector of St. Philip's Church Durham, who declined the call. A few weeks later a call was issued to the Rev. William Stephen Turner, rector of St. Paul's Church, Winston-Salem, but he too declined

"The Boyden High Yellow Jacket," edited by Robert Marion Wingate before he joined the Naval Air Corps, published his photograph on the front page of its 28 May 1943 edition.

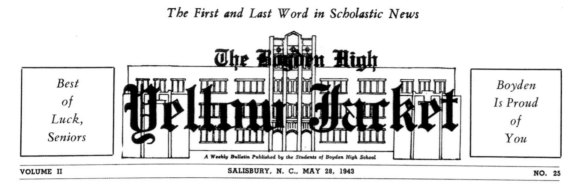

The First and Last Word in Scholastic News

The Boyden High Yellow Jacket

A Weekly Bulletin Published by the Students of Boyden High School

Best of Luck, Seniors

Boyden Is Proud of You

| VOLUME II | SALISBURY, N. C., MAY 28, 1943 | NO. 25 |

COLONEL BOYDEN COMMENTS
By THE STAFF

It's been a year packed full of changes, thrills and varied activities, but nevertheless one with a great deal of fun, for this, Boyden's first graduating class to feel the full effects of a nation engaged in total war.

If, perhaps years from now, just one member of this memorable class reads this column and is reminded of a few of these little happenings and minute incidents, then yours truly will have done a good job.

Do you remember: The surprise registered on students' faces when they first saw the **new Yellow Jacket;** those Saturday afternoon **cotton picking trips;** movies in the auditorium and how **hard those seats** got after two or three reels; the **swell football record** compiled by the '42 Jackets; Pete Watkins playing on the **All-Star Shrine team;** "One-barrel" leaving for the army; the **big** alumni dance with **no alum-**

(Continued on page four)

War Stamp Sale Great Success

There has been going on in Boyden this year a war stamp sale, conducted by Hillary Rink and Margie Munro, which has been a great success. This sale was begun at the end of last year and was thought then to be successful enough to continue. A goal of $10,000 was set at the beginning of the year. This goal was reached by midterm and a new goal of $25,000 was set for the whole year. This was more than doubling our first goal. As this story goes to press a total of $30,000 has already been sold.

BOYDEN GRADUATES GREATEST CLASS IN ITS HISTORY

FIRST TO GO

ROBERT MARION WINGATE

Boyden High School, for the first time, felt the grim reality of the current war Tuesday, February 23, when word was received here of the death of A. M. M., 3c, Robert Wingate, '42. Wingate was killed instantly when the plane in which he was flying failed to pull out of a dive while practicing dive bombing near the Norfolk Naval Air Station.

He was one of those responsible for the success of The Yellow Jacket as a printed paper. He served as its managing editor until he left for the Naval Air Corps. Outstanding in sports, Robert took part in football, basketball, and won his letter in golf. Wingate was a cheerleader during his last two years. He was also a member of the Senior Hi-Y Club and a member of the band.

School Likely To Close Due to Lack of Leadership

The night of May 28 will mark the biggest loss Boyden High School has ever had. The greatest class ever to graduate from Boyden will be walking down the aisle for the last time in their high school careers.

So great is the loss that the teachers and other students are pulling out their hair wondering what they will do for leadership next year. Never before in its history has Boyden had a graduating class that will take with it so many important school figures.

To help solve the problem, the administrators have called in several well informed men from Washington, D. C., to help train some of the underclassmen and rising seniors in leadership, to keep the school from falling completely apart. Also Dr. Z. R. Taylor from California, author of "High School Leadership," has accepted a position as instructor for a period of two months beginning August 1.

Dr. Taylor's course will include a series of lectures on "just what the leaders' responsibilities are and how to go about carrying these out." Dr. Taylor, who has been observing in Boyden, says: "I see that I have a hard job ahead of me. When I look at the leadership in the class of '43, I realize that there cannot possibly be any leaders left in the school after they are gone."

the call. Rebuffed a second time, the vestry considered a priest in Virginia before deciding in early August to send Dr. Frank B. Marsh and Ernest L. Hardin to Houma, Louisiana, a town south/southwest of New Orleans, to interview the Rev. Clarence Rupert Haden. Messrs. Hardin and Marsh returned with a favorable impression of Mr. Haden, and the vestry issued a call by telegram to him, knowing that he was considering a call from St. Paul's Church, New Orleans, as well. Before August was out, the church had received a third refusal. When members of the vestry considered a call to the Rev. J. Lawrence Plumley of Houston, they more thoroughly interviewed him and found him to be unavailable.

William Moultrie Moore Jr. (1916-1998), who came to St. Luke's in winter 1944, is seen here with his wife, Florence Muirhead Porcher, about the time of their departure from the parish in April 1952. Photograph by Judge James Allan Dunn.

St. Luke's Archives

The situation facing St. Luke's was difficult but not exceptional. When Bishop Penick came to Salisbury in October 1943 for a called meeting of the vestry on the subject, he noted seven vacancies in churches in the Diocese of North Carolina. Multiplying that across the nation one senses the very real shortage of priests during a war when many, like Mr. Guerry, were serving as chaplains here in the United States or abroad. The vestry next decided to issue a call to the Rev. Isaac Noyes Northup, who had become rector of All Souls Church, Biltmore Village, in 1941. To increase the chances of success, the offer of salary was increased from the $3,000 promised to Mr. Turner to $4,000. Mr. Northup, who had married Miss Josephine Gribbin, the daughter of Rt. Rev. Robert Emmet Gribbin, Bishop of Western North Carolina, in June 1943, declined the call in December and remained at All Souls Church until 1956.

Finally, in mid-December the vestry called the Rev. William Moultrie Moore, rector of the Church of the Epiphany, Leaksville (today's Eden), and St. Thomas Church, Reidsville. William Moultrie Moore Jr. (1916-1998), born in Mt. Pleasant, South Carolina, and the son of Mr. Moore Sr., and Jennie Verdier Edmonston, was graduated from the College of Charleston in 1937. He continued his education at the General Theological Seminary in New York, where he received an S.T.B. degree in 1940. In the mid 1930s, he began his path to ministry in the Episcopal Church by first assisting the Rev. D. N. Peeples with a summer boys' camp at Bluffton, South Carolina. In the later 1930s, when a postulant, he served as a lay reader in St. Andrew's Mission, Charleston, and assisted the Rev. Henry DeSaussure Bull, rector of Prince George Parish, Winyah, at Georgetown. Ordained a deacon on 5 June 1940, he officially began his ministry as priest-in-charge of St. Luke's, Andrews; St. Alban's, Kingstree; and St.

Stephen's Parish, St. Stephens, where Mr. Guerry had served from 1932 to 1935. After his ordination as priest in May 1941, Mr. Moore remained in South Carolina into summer 1942, when he resigned to accept a call as rector of the Church of the Epiphany, Leaksville, and St. Thomas Church, Reidsville.[29] He had been rector of those churches for 18 months when he accepted the call to St. Luke's.

During the year-long absence of a rector, the parish's worship and parochial activities were directed by the vestry and the church's several organizations. Further memorials embellished St. Luke's in 1943, and the chapters of the Woman's Auxiliary undertook service to the many sons, brothers and husbands at St. Luke's away in the war effort. Following the installation of three stained glass windows in 1941-1942 and the new hanging lanterns, memorial furnishings were added in 1943 to the chancel. In February Mrs. Edwin Clark (Mary Margaret Overman) Gregory's offer to donate a litany desk as a memorial to her son Lee Overman Gregory (1900-1941) was accepted. Four months later, the vestry received a request from her daughter-in-law, Mrs. John Tillery (Elizabeth Ragland) Gregory, to install a communion railing in memory of her mother, Mrs. William H. (Margaret Urquhart) Ragland (1868-1942). The proposal, made on behalf of Mrs. Ragland's children, was accepted pending the approval of its design, which was also made in June. Later in the month Mrs. William Hill (Frances Swink) Hardin's donation of an "Eternal Candle Light" was accepted. The new communion rail, the litany desk and a set of chancel Prayer Books, donated by Virginia (Cuthrell) Marsh as a memorial to her mother, Mrs. James F. Cuthrell, were blessed and dedicated by Bishop Penick during Sunday service on October 17th.

After Mr. Guerry's departure, the several chapters of the Women's Auxiliary at St. Luke's, including the recently-organized Mark Milne Chapter, took on the responsibility for writing monthly newsletters to servicemen stationed at camps and bases in the United States and those abroad. Exactly when the ladies began sending these newsletters is uncertain; however, the first known to survive was written by the St. Agnes Chapter on 23 January 1943. Breezy in tone, it shared news not only of the men in service, but also of Dorothy Wain and Elizabeth Price, who were members of the Women's Army Auxiliary Corps, and of Mr. Guerry's work at Camp Robinson, Arkansas. Ladies of the St. Luke's Chapter wrote to the parish's "Dear Boys" on 22 October 1943. "We are still jogging along without a Rector..." opened a letter that recounted Bishop Penick's recent visit and made mention of the crosses given by the church to each serviceman. The chapters kept up these welcome letters through April 1945, while Mr. Moore wrote the first of his own on 27 March 1944. By the end of May 1944, 65 members of the parish were in the armed services. Mr. Moore's Christmas greeting of 1944 was followed in January 1945 by a letter prepared by the Mary and Martha Chapter

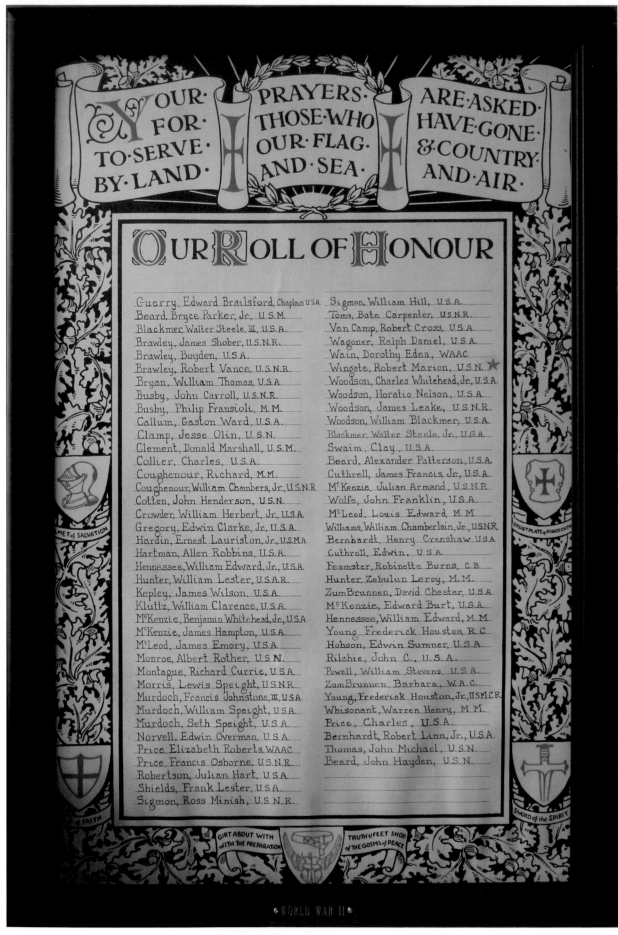

YOUR · PRAYERS · ARE · ASKED · FOR · THOSE · WHO · HAVE · GONE · TO · SERVE · OUR · FLAG · & · COUNTRY · BY · LAND · AND · SEA · AND · AIR ·

OUR ROLL OF HONOUR

Guerry, Edward Brailsford, Chaplain USA
Beard, Bryce Parker, Jr., U.S.M.
Blackmer, Walter Steele, III, U.S.A.
Brawley, James Shober, U.S.N.R.
Brawley, Boyden, U.S.A.
Brawley, Robert Vance, U.S.N.R.
Bryan, William Thomas, U.S.A.
Busby, John Carroll, U.S.N.R.
Busby, Philip Fransioli, M.M.
Callum, Gaston Ward, U.S.A.
Clamp, Jesse Olin, U.S.N.
Clement, Donald Marshall, U.S.M.
Collier, Charles, U.S.A.
Coughenour, Richard, M.M.
Coughenour, William Chambers, Jr., U.S.N.R
Cotten, John Henderson, U.S.N.
Crowder, William Herbert, Jr., U.S.A.
Gregory, Edwin Clarke, Jr., U.S.A.
Hardin, Ernest Lauriston, Jr., U.S.M.A.
Hartman, Allen Robbins, U.S.A.
Hennessee, William Edward, Jr., U.S.A.
Hunter, William Lester, U.S.A.R.
Kepley, James Wilson, U.S.A.
Kluttz, William Clarence, U.S.A.
McKenzie, Benjamin Whitehead, Jr., U.S.A.
McKenzie, James Hampton, U.S.A.
McLeod, James Emory, U.S.A.
Monroe, Albert Rother, U.S.N.
Montague, Richard Currie, U.S.A.
Morris, Lewis Speight, U.S.N.R.
Murdoch, Francis Johnstone, III, U.S.A.
Murdoch, William Speight, U.S.A.
Murdoch, Seth Speight, U.S.A.
Norvell, Edwin Overman, U.S.A.
Price, Elizabeth Roberts, WAAC
Price, Francis Osborne, U.S.N.R.
Robertson, Julian Hart, U.S.A.
Shields, Frank Lester, U.S.A.
Sigmon, Ross Minish, U.S.N.R.

Sigmon, William Hill, U.S.A.
Toms, Bate Carpenter, U.S.N.R.
Van Camp, Robert Cross, U.S.A.
Wagoner, Ralph Daniel, U.S.A.
Wain, Dorothy Edna, WAAC
Wingate, Robert Marion, U.S.N.
Woodson, Charles Whitehead, Jr., U.S.A.
Woodson, Horatio Nelson, U.S.A.
Woodson, James Leake, U.S.N.R.
Woodson, William Blackmer, U.S.A.
Blackmer, Walter Steele, Jr., U.S.A.
Swaim, Clay, U.S.A.
Beard, Alexander Patterson, U.S.A.
Cuthrell, James Francis, Jr., U.S.A.
McKenzie, Julian Armand, U.S.N.R.
Wolfe, John Franklin, U.S.A.
McLeod, Louis Edward, M.M.
Williams, William Chamberlain, Jr., U.S.N.R.
Bernhardt, Henry Crenshaw, U.S.A.
Cuthrell, Edwin, U.S.A.
Feamster, Robinette Burns, C.B.
Hunter, Zebulun Leroy, M.M.
ZumBrunnen, David Chester, U.S.A.
McKenzie, Edward Burt, U.S.A.
Hennessee, William Edward, M.M.
Young, Frederick Houston, R.C.
Hobson, Edwin Sumner, U.S.A.
Ritchie, John C., U.S.A.
Powell, William Stevens, U.S.A.
ZumBrunnen, Barbara, W.A.C.
Young, Frederick Houston, Jr., U.S.M.C.R.
Whisonant, Warren Henry, M.M.
Price, Charles, U.S.A.
Bernhardt, Robert Linn, Jr., U.S.A.
Thomas, John Michael, U.S.N.
Beard, John Hayden, U.S.N.

HELMET of SALVATION

BREASTPLATE of RIGHTEOUSNESS

FAITH

SWORD of the SPIRIT

GIRT ABOUT WITH WITH THE PREPARATION

TRUTH & FEET SHOD of THE GOSPEL of PEACE

WORLD WAR II

The names of 74 members of St. Luke's are listed below that of Mr. Guerry on the Roll of Honor for service in World War II.
Photograph by Charles Goldman, St. Luke's Archives

recounting the services and entertainments in Salisbury. These included the "Nativity Service" on Christmas Eve afternoon with Elizabeth Hardin as Mary, Mickey Thomas as Joseph, and a host of youngsters in the roles of angels, shepherds and wise men.

By Christmas 1944, Mr. Moore and his wife had been in the parish for 10 months and had happily settled into the life of St. Luke's and Salisbury. They were also the residents of a renovated rectory. While some modest improvements might have been made to accommodate tenants in the brick rectory during Mr. Guerry's tenure, the house had received relatively little attention since the later 1910s and the arrival of the Milnes. Faced in wartime with the need to provide a suitable residence for Mr. Moore and his family, St. Luke's decided against either renting a house or buying a more modern residence, and recommitted itself to refit the two-story brick house that had been occupied by the parish's priests from 1876 to 1938. As soon as Mr. Moore accepted the call to St. Luke's, the vestry set about a complete renovation of the rectory and the construction of a two-car garage. Work began in January 1944 and continued into early April, with J. Leo Campbell as the principal contractor. During this period the building was cleaned, its walls repainted, its floors sanded and refinished, and the heating, plumbing and electrical systems were replaced. When all was done, the R. W. Norman Company hung new white shades at the windows. The expenses totaled $8,167.87.

With the rectory repaired, a young energetic priest and his family at St. Luke's, World War II at an end, and the young—and not-so-young—men returned to Salisbury and the parish, a feeling of optimism spread through the church, and characterized work in the parish through the decade and up to the 200th anniversary of its founding in 1953. Although St. Luke's had seen a high number of its communicants enter service, it was blessed to have all of them return except for young Mr. Wingate. Those who had shepherded the church through the early 1940s welcomed the returning sons, brothers, husbands and friends back to the fold of parish life and appreciated the leadership and vigor which they brought to its renewal.

The successful refurbishment of the rectory prompted action at the church where a series of efforts, including memorials, improved the church fabric and enhanced worship. Two of these had occurred in the closing months of the war and were announced at the annual parish meeting on 4 January 1945. The boxwoods donated by Mrs. Murdoch Sr. in 1943 had been planted, at long last, on both the church and rectory grounds, and were described as "a very valuable as well as beautiful gift to the church." Both weather and shortage of labor had delayed their transfer from the grounds of the late rector's residence to St. Luke's. Communicants also learned that the E. W. Wagoner company would move the church bell from the frame tower standing near the Chapter House on Church Street, to the upper level of the church tower which

By January 1945 the wooden bell tower that stood at the gable end of the chapter house was found to be deteriorated. On 26 January 1945 the Salisbury Post carried an article informing its readers that E. W. Wagoner and Sons had relocated the bell to the belfry, above the vestibule. This photograph appeared at the top of the article under the heading "Landmark to be Razed." The April vestry minutes included a brief mention that the "old bell tower was soon to be torn down." St. Luke's Archives

was to be reinforced with steel beams. The old tower was to be taken down. Later, in April, Gilmer Martin was given a contract for concrete walks on the church grounds.

Memorials were also offered in 1945, approved, and installed in the church. Dr. Marsh expressed his desire to give "a new and larger Altar Cross." He donated both an imposing Altar Cross and a Processional Cross; although designs produced by the Geissler firm were considered, those produced by another major church furnisher, The Studios of George L. Payne, were selected by Dr. Marsh and the vestry. The Altar Cross was given in memory of his father, Thomas Benjamin Marsh (1863-1933); the Processional Cross was donated in memory of his mother, Agnes Neave Marsh (1872-1902). In the summer of 1946 the R. W. Norman Company laid new carpet in the church, largely at the behest of Mrs. Dave Oestreicher, its principal donor. The death of Eva Dornin Nicolson on 24 March 1945 prompted the gift of a memorial fund to honor her and her late husband, William Samuel Nicolson (1863-1925). Designs for bronze doors for the church by the Geissler company were vetoed in the summer of 1946 and those produced by the Payne-Spiers studio were declined in 1947. Finally, in the closing months of 1949, the E. W. Wagoner firm built and erected the present doors, and a few months later, in 1950, lanterns from J. & R. Lamb Studios were mounted on the church's outside walls flanking the doors. The lectern light, a memorial to Mr. Milne, is believed to have been installed during this period, when the Geissler company also submitted a proposal for a new pulpit light on behalf of an anonymous donor.

Attention was also focused on the Chapter House, erected in 1895 and now 50 years old, which had been used for meetings, Sunday School, as a parish hall and other church functions. With the recently completed parish house and Sunday School block fulfilling those important needs at St. Luke's, the decision was made to refit the Chapter House as St. Luke's Memorial Chapel. Virginia "Jennie" Gregory Sparks remembers from childhood her father's involvement with the project. Augustus S. "Bus" Merrimon Gregory (1907-1948) supplied lumber for the project from his farm near Salisbury, which probably included the beaded wainscoting in the chapel. Exactly when this occurred is unclear; however, in 1948 steps were taken to that end. On 9 April, Mr. Moore wrote to five leading church furnishing houses in the United States, including the Geissler, Lamb and Payne concerns, which had earlier supplied decorations to St. Luke's, seeking their assistance.[30]

> We are inclosing a picture of the East end of St. Luke's Memorial Chapel, with approximate measurements, for which we wish you to submit drawings for a stained glass window and an Altar. The mensa of the Altar will be six feet. The pews of the Chapel are of solid heart pine, natural finish, and are very old. The Altar, we feel, should be simple and of wood to conform with the pews.

> We should like drawings and approximate prices as soon as possible as we are very anxious to proceed with the furnishings of the Chapel.

The pews, which Mr. Moore later described as "having been given from a church which has been abandoned," came to St. Luke's from St. Jude's Chapel on the Sherrill's Ford Road.[31] St. Jude's had long ceased to be an active mission, and in the spring of 1948 St. Luke's took possession of its pews and other fixtures, subject to the bishop's approval.[32]

For many years a pageant was a special feature of the Christmas season at St. Luke's. This photograph, believed to have been taken in 1947 by James Torrence, features Mary Shaw Clement as Mary and Robert Fairley as Joseph.
St. Luke's Archives

The donors of the proposed window and altar had long associations with the parish. Elizabeth Brownrigg (Henderson) Cotten and her sister, Mary Ferrand Henderson of Chapel Hill, wished to donate a window in memory of their parents, John Steele and Elizabeth Brownrigg (Cain) Henderson. Designs for the Henderson memorial window, to rise above and behind the altar, were the subject of lengthy correspondence between Mr. Moore and the Henderson sisters. None of the design proposals satisfied Mr. Henderson's daughters, and the memorial was not erected.[33] Dr. Marsh, ever generous, donated the altar in memory of his mother Agnes Neave Marsh.[34]

With its altar and pews in place, and its walls painted in autumn of 1948, St. Luke's Memorial Chapel was ready for use. The following spring, the vestry adopted Dr. Marsh's motion to recognize the Daughters of the King with a bronze plaque that was subsequently erected in the chapel. Another project of this period was a proposed upgrade of the parish house kitchen, but as that post-war effort, if effected, was subsumed in later renovations and no known drawings or photographs survive, the extent of the improvement remains undefined.

The end of St. Jude's mission in Rowan County had also had its parallel in Salisbury, with the closing of St. John's Chapel. Services at St. John's had apparently ceased with Mr. Guerry's departure, and the building stood unused for some time. In 1945 the vestry tentatively agreed to sell the property for $8,500 to Cartex Mills, but it was not until late in 1946 that a quitclaim deed was obtained from the Henderson heirs and the property conveyed by deed to Cartex.[35] After the deduction for the street assessment the remaining funds were placed in the Mary Steele Henderson Fund.

William Stevens Powell (b. 1919) was a young historian, at the outset of a distinguished career, when he wrote a history of the parish for its 200th anniversary in 1953. He is shown here in the library of the North Carolina Collection, Wilson Library, Chapel Hill. Courtesy of Virginia Powell

The creation of St. Luke's Memorial Chapel proved to be among the most lasting contributions of Mr. Moore to the parish; however, 1951, the last full year of his rectorate, was marked by two events important in its history. The death of Eliza Marsh Murdoch on Tuesday, 6 February, brought to an end her long association with St. Luke's. With her marriage to Mr. Murdoch in 1884, she joined him at the center of parish life and held that position through his rectorate, and afterwards as his widow. Having served as an organist here and a member of the choir, she also taught the Woman's Bible Class for the last time the Sunday before her sudden death from a heart attack. On Thursday morning her body was taken to St. Luke's to lie in state in the chapel before her afternoon funeral service in the church; Mr. Guerry, assisted by Mr. Moore and the Rev. Carl Franklin Herman of Greensboro, conducted the service. Her grandsons and other kinsmen were pallbearers; William S. Murdoch, among them, remains a member of St. Luke's.[36] The chapel, built when she was president of the Bishop Lyman Chapter, Daughters of the King, was soon fitted with new doors in her memory.

In June 1951, Mr. Moore broached the celebration of the parish's 200th anniversary with the vestry, announcing that a member of St. Luke's had expressed interest in writing a short history to commemorate the event. William Stevens Powell was not a Salisbury native nor a long-time member of the parish; however, he was a devout Episcopalian, a historian and was anxious to contribute his talents to the bicentennial celebration. Born in Johnston County in 1919, he returned with his parents in the early 1920s to his mother's native Iredell County and grew up in Statesville, attending the Methodist Church. While a student at the University of North Carolina in the late 1930s, and again in the mid 1940s when he took his library science degree, he attended services at the Chapel of the Cross. He became a member of the Episcopal Church. When his parents moved from Statesville to Salisbury, he joined St. Luke's and gained the friendship of Mr. Moore. Although he maintained a residence in Raleigh while working as a research historian with the North Carolina Division of Archives and History, St. Luke's was his home church when he offered to write the history, afterward when he was librarian at the North Carolina Collection, and until his marriage in June 1952, after which he transferred his membership to the newly-organized Church of the Holy Family. Thus it came to be that the distinguished librarian, curator and professor who would become the most prolific author of North Carolina history and the acknowledged dean of its historians, would write the first history of St. Luke's.[37] But these accomplishments of Mr. Powell's long career lay ahead, when Ernest L. Hardin moved to accept the proposal at a vestry meeting on the 4 June 1951; the motion, seconded by Dederick C. Dungan (1899-1983), was passed.

Thom Williamson Blair (1920-2004) presided over the parish's bicentennial celebration in 1953. St. Luke's Archives

Mr. Moore, however, did not remain at St. Luke's for the parish bicentennial in 1953; he resigned effective 15 April 1952, having accepted a call as rector of St. Martin's Church, Charlotte. Mr. Moore returned to Salisbury and St. Luke's near the end of the summer to officiate at the wedding of Joan Lydia Ketner (1929-1988) to John Shelby Spong (b. 1931), a native of Charlotte, on 5 September. Miss Ketner, the daughter of James and Frances Ketner and a member of St. Luke's, was marrying a man about to enter Virginia Theological Seminary who would go on to become a leading theologian in the Episcopal Church and the Bishop of Newark (New Jersey).[38] Moultrie Moore remained at St. Martin's for 15 years, during which time he continued to serve on a number of diocesan committees, as a director of the Penick Home and as a trustee of the General Theological Seminary. In 1967 he was elected Suffragan Bishop of North Carolina and held that position until 1975, when he was elected Bishop of Easton (Maryland). He resigned that bishopric in 1983 and retired to his native Mt. Pleasant, South Carolina. There he served as Bishop-in-Residence at St. Andrew's Church. Bishop Moore died on 23 November 1998.[39]

The choice of a successor to Mr. Moore occupied a half year, from March, when Bishop Penick met with the vestry on the matter, until August, when a call was extended to the Rev. Thom Williamson Blair, then rector of St. Paul's and Immanuel churches, St. Paul's Parish, Hanover County, Virginia. He was born in 1920 in Haymarket, Virginia, the son of Captain Roswell Hadfield and Julia Williamson (Hall) Blair. His study at the University of Virginia, begun in 1937, was interrupted by service in All Saints Mission, Bontoc, the Philippine Islands, in 1939. Having returned to Charlottesville, where he received his bachelor's degree in 1942, he joined the United States Navy and served through the war. After his discharge, Mr. Blair studied for the ministry at Virginia Theological Seminary and received his bachelor of divinity degree in 1949. He then went as deacon-in-charge of the Hanover County churches, and remained as rector of both following his ordination to the priesthood in June 1950. He came to St. Luke's in October, and took charge of the parish on 13 October 1952.[40]

Mr. Blair's first year as rector was occupied with the usual congregational responsibilities and those attending the

A homecoming celebration on 12 April was part of the 200th anniversary festivities in 1953. It included a picnic lunch served by the ladies of St. Luke's and an address by Dr. Archibald Henderson that afternoon. This photograph, with the now-demolished court house annex in the background, is believed to have been taken during the day. St. Luke's Archives

You Are Especially Invited to the
HOME-COMING
CELEBRATION
OF
SAINT LUKE'S
EPISCOPAL CHURCH
SALISBURY, NORTH CAROLINA
Sunday, April 12, 1953
11:00 A. M.

200th Anniversary Celebration
1753-1953

FROM GENERATION TO GENERATION

much-anticipated 200th anniversary of the parish. In January 1953, he named James Shober Brawley as chairman of the 200th anniversary committee, which included Dr. Marsh and his wife Martha, Mrs. Dederick C. (Vivian Gregory) Dungan and William C. Coughenour Jr. The commemoration occurred over the course of two events, one in the spring and another in the autumn, on St. Luke's Day. On Sunday, 12 April, a homecoming celebration was held at St. Luke's with an "Old-Fashioned Picnic Dinner" served on the grounds after morning prayer. The afternoon program, beginning at 2:30 p.m., featured Dr. Archibald Henderson's address on the history of the parish. This was Dr. Henderson's second historical address to the communicants of St. Luke's; his first had occurred on 19 October 1924, commemorating the 100th anniversary of the parish's admission into union with the Diocese of North Carolina.

Bishop Penick presided at the second anniversary venue, on St. Luke's Day, when Mr. Powell's *St. Luke's Episcopal Church, 1753-1953*, was first made available. The 11:00 morning service included confirmation rites for 13 and concluded with the dedication of the additions to St. Luke's Memorial Chapel and the re-laying of its cornerstone. A covered dish luncheon was enjoyed afterward in the parish house. The work dedicated by Bishop Penick included the new brick veneer façade on the chapel and hyphen linking it with the church, its new doors installed as a memorial to the late Mrs. Murdoch, additions on the southeast side (consisting of a small office and the present men's lavatory) and improvements to the interior.

Rowan County's bicentennial celebration, which coincided with that of the parish, included a grand parade on Tuesday afternoon, 14 April. The float sponsored by St. Luke's Parish was photographed as it entered the crossing of Innes and Main streets. The Post *published this photograph, along with others of the parade, in the next day's edition.*
St. Luke's Archives

This kindergarten class of ca. 1954 included fourteen happy, smiling students who posed with their teacher Margaret Wain Bostian. First row, left to right: Juliette Johnston, Susan Sheneman, Donnie Clement, Susan Wear (Kluttz), Kelly Coughenour, Brantley Blair, Liz Collier (Goodman), Vaughan Earle. Second row: Cam Beard (Hall), Phillip Meares, Charles Welch, Dick Rendleman, Mary Starr Riddle (Shive), Jimmy Brawley, Mrs. Bostian.

St. Luke's Archives

Occurring in his first year at St. Luke's, the parish's 200th anniversary celebration and the publication of its history were among the principal events in Mr. Blair's five-year rectorate. Two other areas of church life—its staff and the relationship of St. Luke's to the Episcopal missions in Salisbury—also saw development under his guidance. A growing membership, especially of younger people, had steadily increased the Sunday School program, and in line with church staffing across the city's denominations, St. Luke's had engaged a part-time director of Christian education. This position took on an added import in parish life with the arrival of Miss Grace Brisbane in October 1953. Mr. Blair proudly introduced her to the congregation in his weekly newsletter for 31 October, welcoming her to the parish and encouraging parents and teachers alike to work with her and to take advantage of the skills she brought to St. Luke's. Miss Brisbane became a valued and long-serving member of the parish staff.

The arrival of an assistant to the rector coincided with the rearrangement of the relationship between St. Luke's and the surviving Episcopal missions in the county seat. With the closing of St. John's Chapel and the sale of its property, three Episcopal missions remained in Salisbury. Two of the group, St. Paul's and St. Peter's, dated to Dr. Murdoch's period, while St. Philip's was organized and first overseen by Bishop Delany. Their status and growth had fluctuated over the years, depending on the level of interest shown in them by the rectors of St. Luke's, their lay leadership, and the degree of support from the Convocation of Charlotte and the diocesan mission board. St. Paul's was the strongest of the three missions and with the largest membership it had erected a rectory at the corner of South Church and West Harrison streets in 1951.

In 1954 the decision was made to resolve concerns for the pastoral care of the missions, coincident with hiring an assistant to the rector of St. Luke's. The three parish missions were reestablished under the jurisdiction of the rector, Mr. Blair, with the proposed new assistant rector (or curate) responsible for

Having presided at the laying of the cornerstone of the completed parish house at St. Luke's, Bishop Penick laid the cornerstone for a new parish house at St. Paul's on 3 June 1956. He was assisted by Mr. Blair, left, and Urban Tigner Holmes III, then priest-in-charge of St. Paul's.
St. Luke's Archives

services at each. His salary and travel expenses would be borne by St. Luke's, the missions and the Diocese (in percentages that changed over time). As this matter was advancing, consideration was also given to reviving the mission at St. Joseph's in Spencer; however, the effort came to naught. Urban Tigner Holmes III (1930-1981), the first curate, came to St. Luke's in the late spring of 1954 and resided in the St. Paul's rectory. A man of exceptional ability and intellect, and a graduate of Philadelphia Divinity School, he was ordained priest on 27 December of that year at St. Luke's by the Rt. Rev. Richard Henry Baker, Bishop Coadjutor of North Carolina. "Terry" Holmes served the parish for two years. During this time, and in real part due to his attention, St. Paul's prospered, and on 3 June 1956 both Mr. Blair and Mr. Holmes were present when Bishop Penick laid the cornerstone for the new educational building at St. Paul's. That same day Mr. Holmes resigned his position, effective 1 September, to accept the office of chaplain at Louisiana State University, Baton Rouge.[41] With two months' notice, Mr. Blair was able to hire Claude Ward Courtney (b. 1911) as Mr. Holmes' successor.

Another matter of importance if not fruition in the mid 1950s was a proposal to establish an Episcopal mission in Milford Hills, the suburban residential park on the west side of Salisbury. James Allan Dunn (1894-1973), an attorney and member of St. Luke's, had been a resident of Milford Hills since building at 132 S. Milford Drive in 1927. In July 1955, cognizant of efforts to organize Milford Hills Methodist Church, Mr. Dunn broached the idea of a mission with Mr. Blair. He then wrote to Mr. Moore, in Charlotte, who was a member of the department of missions for the Diocese of North Carolina, and in 1956 would become its chairman.[42] While Mr. Moore, Mr. Blair and Mr. Dunn were all enthusiastic in regard to the prospects for the mission, and both a lot and a name—the Church of the Resurrection—were considered, the effort was unsuccessful, coming to an end in August 1956. The facts of the matter were simple enough: with three existing missions in Salisbury, St. Luke's was not in a financial position to support a fourth mission, and the department of missions did not have funds to support the purchase of a lot. The idea of closing St. Peter's and transferring its members to St. Paul's, put forth by Mr. Moore, might have encouraged prospects for the Milford Hills mission, but the time was not yet right for closing the mission in Salisbury's south ward.[43]

In May 1957, St. Luke's was host to the 141st Annual Convention of the Diocese of North Carolina; this two-day meeting was the first in Salisbury since 1918. Five months later, on 17 October, Mr. Blair and Mr. Courtney resigned as rector and curate, respectively. Mr. Blair's resignation was effective 2 December; he had accepted a call as rector of Christ Church, Charlotte. Thom Blair served as rector of Christ Church until 1969, when he became Dean of Christ Church Cathedral, St. Louis, Missouri. In 1974 he became rector of Trinity Church, Boston, whence he retired in 1981. From 1983-1984 he served as interim priest-in-charge of Trinity Church, New Orleans; and from 1984-1991 he was interim rector in succession at four churches: Calvary Church, Pittsburgh; Bruton Parish, Williamsburg; Holy Innocents, Atlanta; and Emmanuel Church, Staunton, Virginia.[44] Mr. Blair returned twice to St. Luke's, first to deliver a sermon on St. Luke's Day 1987, and last on 20 October 2002. His sermon on the 20th occurred one day past the 50th anniversary of his first sermon to the congregation as a young priest on 19 October 1952. The man, the church and the neighborhood had changed greatly since that long ago autumn day. But memories of his life here and his family's days in the rectory remained warm. Summersett Funeral Home, then the rector's nearest neighbor, had long since relocated to new premises on West Innes Street; however, Mr. Blair happily remembered his family's friendship with the undertakers.

> The old rectory was next to Summersett Funeral Home. After hours we took our 78 RPM records there to play, as we had no phonograph. Those were the first years of TV. We also watched the early shows there at the funeral home. Then Wilson and Frances Moser gave us a TV. Rochet (Mrs. Blair) says she and our youngest, Brantly, sat there and just watched the test patterns until a program came on.[45]

These light-hearted remembrances were followed by a more heartfelt appreciation.

> Most of all, Rochet and I remember the love and acceptance we received from the congregation, through thick and thin. That must be why after all these years we recall St. Luke's as a fine place to have been. We are still thankful for what you gave to us.[46]

1. Thaddeus A. Cheatham to William S. Powell, 8 July 1953, SLA.

2. At a vestry meeting on 21 November 1910, Mr. Cheatham reported "the circular window and a part of the large window have been shipped from the works in New York." This is the only significant reference to the windows to appear in the vestry minutes after that of 22 November 1909. In an article announcing Mr. Mallett's arrival as rector of St. Luke's, the *Salisbury Evening Post* on 10 January 1911 noted "several fine stained glass windows are now being installed" in the church. The Ascension, Henderson, Frercks and the "Madonna" windows were installed in a now unknown sequence as they arrived in Salisbury, beginning in late 1910 and continuing in 1911.

3. While various chancel furnishings have been replaced through the years by others, these paired brass candlesticks appear to be the first and only such important memorials to grace the altar at St. Luke's. Exactly when candles were first used on the altar during services is not known; however, an entry in the vestry minutes for the meeting of 7 January 1902 indicates they were not used prior to that time. "A request was asked by a party of ladies to place two appropriate candle sticks on the Altar & at occasional times to light them. It was discussed at length." How the request was answered is not now known; however, these pairs were in place by the end of the decade. Archibald Boyden Brawley was the first-born son of Robert Vance and May (Boyden) Brawley. Charles Price built a handsome Shingle Style house in the 300 block of North Fulton Street that was taken down and replaced by the Prince Charles Apartments. William Samuel and Eva (Dornin) Nicolson were the parents of the two Nicolson children.

4. JAC, 1910, 111.

5. Mabel Mallett to William S. Powell, 13 July 1953. SLA. Also *Stowe's Clerical Directory*, 1938, 215.

6. JAC, 1911, 110. The North Carolina Collection, Wilson Library, University of North Carolina, holds a copy of *Helping Boys*. Its catalogue cites the publication date as 1911, while the biographical entry in *Stowe's* gives it as 1913. Mr. Mallett was also the author of "Wit and Humor of the Parson" (1900); however, no copy of it was located.

7. JAC, 1912, 102. *The Carolina Churchman* of August 1913 published an account of the Junior Auxiliary's outing to Fulton Heights, where games and a picnic were enjoyed.

8. JAC, 1913, 109-112. Mr. Loflin was also minister in charge of six other missions established by Dr. Murdoch: St. Jude's, St. Mark's, St. Mary's, St. Matthew's, St. Paul's and St. Peter's.

9. JAC, 1915, 110. *Who Was Who in America*, Volume II, 1943-1950 (Seventh Printing, 1975), 561.

10. JAC, 1911, 110; 1914, 115; 1918, 114.

11. DNCB, 2, 50-51; ECNC, 326-28.

12. RCD, 90/370-71.

13. JAC, 1917, 117. Throughout its history the name of this congregation has been spelled as both St. Philip's and St. Phillip's. Hereinafter, St. Phillip's is used as that is the spelling used most often by members of the congregation.

14. For an account of Mr. Way's tenure as rector of St. Mary's see Martha Stoops, *The Heritage: The Education of Women at St. Mary's College, Raleigh, North Carolina, 1842-1982* (Raleigh: St. Mary's College, 1984), 204-239. *Also Who Was Who in America, Volume II, 1943-1950* (Seventh Printing, 1975), 561.

15. *Stowe's Clerical Directory*, 1938, 236.

16. "Former Mayor Is Dead," *Salisbury Evening Post*, 7 July 1920.

17. For Hobart Brown Upjohn's work in North Carolina see Davyd Foard Hood, *To the Glory of God: Christ Church, 1821-1996* (Raleigh: Christ Church, 1997), 169-75.

18. Henderson, Archibald. *Centennial Address: The History of St. Luke's Parish*. Privately printed, no date. Few copies of the 34-page booklet in paper covers survive. Dr. Henderson's address was reprinted also in the *Greensboro Daily News* on Sunday, 2 November 1924.

19. The settlement of Mrs. Boyden's estate was complicated by the deaths of three members of her immediate family in 1929 whose estates were moving to resolution: her son-in-law Robert Vance Brawley on 5 January; her daughter May Wheat (Boyden) Brawley on 11 February; and her husband Archibald Henderson Boyden on 19 June 1929. The Brawleys were the parents of three surviving sons: Robert Vance Jr. (1910-1989); Boyden (1913-1971), and James Shober (1918-1981).

20. The terms of Mrs. Frercks' will specified that the bequests to St. Luke's for the parish house and organ, and a third bequest of $7,000 to the Patterson School for Boys at Legerwood, be exempted from any necessary reduction that might be applied pro rata to the other bequests because of a deficiency. This was not honored. See Rowan County Wills, Book 9, pages 339-44. Also "Frercks Fortune Given to Church and Charity Here," *Salisbury Evening Post*, 19 May 1931. Mr. and Mrs. Frercks were the proprietors of the Mount Vernon Hotel in Salisbury.

21. Leslie N. Boney to Ernest L. Hardin, 15 April 1937, SLA. This letter is the earliest of a group documenting the construction of the parish house that survive; Mr. Boney makes reference to Mr. Hardin's letter of 13 April for which no copy appears to survive. The plans, mailed in mid May to Mr. Hardin, were noted in Mr. Boney's letter of 19 May 1937 to him.

22. SLA.

23. Among the items listed were "records of the memorial windows, pulpit, altar, etc., in the church." Whether these were original records is unclear, but if so, they would have enhanced the partial accounts and references to same in the vestry minutes and other church documents. They and all other contents of the cornerstone were lost to damage.

24. JAC, 1919, 99.

25. JAC, 1929, 136-37, 148-49.

26. The paperback cookbook was produced by the Rowan Printing Company. Although the book carries no publication date, it is believed to be 1937. In its advertisement, the Salisbury Motor Company "announces" the 1937 Buick.

27. A biographical sketch of William Alexander Guerry, Eighth Bishop of South Carolina, appears in ECSC, 712-714. Discussion of Edward B. Guerry's service in his native state also appears in ECSC, 152, 337, 342, 345, 364, 365, 395, 406, 682, 685 and 712. Mr. Guerry's brothers, Sumner and Moultrie, were also priests in South Carolina. For Mr. Guerry's service in South Farnham Parish, including the rectorate of historic St. Paul's Church, Essex County, see E. Lee Shepard, *A History of St. Paul's Church (2001)*, 204-10.

28. Rudolph Geissler was the proprietor of the company, located in New York City, which was in operation by the latter 1870s and still active when a design for the Milne window was sought. The firm's windows in St. Agatha's Church, De Funiak

Springs, Florida, is cited in the *Biographical Index of Historic American Stained Glass Makers*, 45. Dr. Marsh was chairman of the window committee comprising Julian Robertson, Donald Clement, Francis J. Murdoch Jr., and Ernest L. Hardin.

29. ECSC, 174, 221, 319-20, 344, 406, 682.

30. Mr. Moore also sent letters to the Conrad Schmitt Studios in Milwaukee, Wisconsin, and the Rambusch company in New York City. The Geissler firm also was located in New York City, while the Studios of George L. Payne occupied premises in Paterson, New Jersey, and the J. & R. Lamb Studios were located in Tenafly, New Jersey.

31. W. Moultrie Moore Jr., to The J. and R. Lamb Studios, 23 April 1948. SLA. He wrote, "We like the altar with the retable but we are wondering if it might not be possible to harmonize the altar with the pews which have been given from a church which has been abandoned. We are inclosing a sketch of these. We do not care for the design in the center of the altar. Could there be a different treatment here, or nothing at all?"

32. This was discussed at a vestry meeting on 6 April 1948. The Diocese of North Carolina held the St. Jude's property until 11 May 1964, when Bishop Baker and the diocesan trustees conveyed it to M. K. Overcash and Beatrice Treadway (RCD, 486/403-06). On 1 September 1965 Mr. Overcash, et al, sold the property to the trustees of Calvary Baptist Church (RCD, 502/9-10). The former St. Jude's Church, remodeled and overbuilt, is now the premises of Sherrills Ford Baptist Church.

33. SLA.

34. After protracted discussions, the contract for the altar was awarded to the Studios of George L. Payne and signed by Mr. Moore on 16 September 1948.

35. The quitclaim deed by the Henderson heirs, conveying their interest to the vestry of St. Luke's, was dated 9 November 1946, and recorded six weeks later on 24 December (RCD, 296/321-22). Meanwhile, on 16 December, St. Luke's vestry conveyed the St. John's property to Cartex Mills, Inc. (RCD, 301/173).

36. "Mrs. Murdoch Dies At Home," *Salisbury Post*, 7 February 1951. A short account of her funeral was published in the *Post* on 9 February. At the time of her death Mrs. Murdoch made her home with her granddaughter, Miss Margaret Balfour Bell, at 414 South Church Street.

37. Jane A. Bowden, ed. *Contemporary Authors, Volumes 69-72* (Detroit: Gale Research Company, 1978), 481. Telephone interview with Virginia Penn (Waldrop) Powell, 2 January 2004.

38. John Shelby Spong, *Here I Stand* (New York: Harper San Francisco, 2000), 56-57, 60-61.

39. Arthur D. Leiby to Davyd Foard Hood, 8 January 2004. Mr. Leiby, archivist of the Diocese of Easton, generously provided information on Mr. Moore's life as Bishop of Easton and a photocopy of his obituary that appeared in the *Eastern Shore Episcopalian* in January 1999. The bishop's remains were cremated and the ashes scattered in the bay of Mt. Pleasant.

40. Thom Blair to Israel Harding Hughes, 12 March 1953, copy in SLA.

41. DNCB, 3, 181. Mr. Holmes' two years at St. Luke's were the first stage of a distinguished but all too short career as a churchman and educator. He remained in Baton Rouge for 10 years, until 1966, when he joined the faculty of Nashotah House in Wisconsin. In fall 1973 Mr. Holmes became dean of the School of Theology at The University of the South. A prolific writer and contributor to professional journals, Mr. Holmes was the author of nine books, co-author of two, co-editor of three, and editor of another, all published between 1970 and 1981. He was at work on the manuscript of *What is Anglicanism* when he died of an aneurysm on 6 August 1981.

The book was published posthumously in 1982. In November 2001, some 80 educators, administrators, churchmen, theologians and writers convened at a conference at Kanuga to "Remember Terry." Their remembrances were published in a special edition of the *Sewanee Theological Review*, Volume 45, Number 3, in 2002. Also see *Who Was Who in America, Volume III, 1982-1985*, p. 194.

42. James Allan Dunn to W. Moultrie Moore Jr., 10 July 1955, copy in SLA.

43. W. Moultrie Moore Jr., to James Allan Dunn, 22 July 1955, copy in SLA.

44. After retiring, Mr. Blair moved to Fort Myers, Florida. His last residence was in Charlottesville, Virginia, where he died on 23 December 2004. See "Thom W. Blair," *Daily Progress* (Charlottesville), 26 December 2004, and "The Very Reverend Dr. Thom W. Blair," *Charlotte Observer*, 26 December 2004. Also *Episcopal Clerical Directory* (2003). In 1957 Mr. Courtney went to Charlotte as rector of St. Mark's Church, Mecklenburg County, and remained there until 1961. Since then he served other churches in North Carolina and Washington, D.C. until retiring in 1975.

45. St. Luke's service bulletin for 20 October 2002.

The resurrection of Christ has been interpreted in stained glass windows throughout history. The designer of the Frercks' memorial chose to portray the moment when Mary Magdalene; Mary, the mother of James; and Salome, who had come to the tomb to anoint Christ's body, learned of his resurrection. An angel, pointing heavenward, informed the Holy Women, "He is risen; he is not here." This image would have had special appeal to Mrs. Frercks, who donated the window as a memorial to her husband, Peter Augustus Frercks. On 14 June 1909, Dr. Murdoch officiated at the funeral and burial of Mr. Frercks. These were his last known acts as Rector of St. Luke's Church. Photograph by Robert Bailey

The appearance of the chapel reflects a series of improvements and enhancements carried out in the mid–20th Century that culminated in January 1965 with the installation of a group of stained glass windows created by J. Wippell and Company, Ltd.
Photograph by Robert Bailey

And God Saw that It Was Good

The Creation

Evermore Praising Thee

Prepare the Way of the Lord

The Lord Is Come

Lo, I Am with You Always

The six windows in the chapel, based on the theme of "The Unfolding Revelation of God," were designed by Claude A. Howard, an artist with J. Wippell and Company, Ltd. of England, and installed in January 1965. The transom over the Church Street entrance and the circular window in the gable above, representing "The Creation" and "And God Saw that It Was Good," are memorials to Harold Moses Goodman (1913-1963). The three larger windows in the northeast side of the chapel represent the Revelation of God the Father, God the Son, and God the Holy Spirit. The window interpreting The Revelation of God the Father, and titled "Prepare the Way of the Lord," features the figures of Noah, Moses, Isaiah and Amos; it is a memorial to the Clement brothers, Edward Buehler (1881-1948) and Louis Heyl (1902-1957). Titled "The Lord Is Come," the middle window represents the Revelation of God the Son and features events in the life of Jesus, including his calling to Simon and Andrew to give up their nets and "become fishers of men." It is a memorial to Edward Edson Proctor (1891-1964). The Revelation of God the Holy Spirit window, titled "Lo, I Am with You Always," illustrates the Pentecost and incorporates the figures of St. Augustine, Thomas Cranmer, Archbishop of Canterbury; and John Stark Ravenscroft, who was elected Bishop of North Carolina in Salisbury in 1823, as well as St. Luke's Church. This window is dedicated to John Steele Henderson (1846-1916) and his wife Elizabeth Brownrigg Cain Henderson (1850-1929). The Sanctus window, titled "Evermore Praising Thee," features the archangels Gabriel and Michael; it is a memorial to Myra Marguerite Fairley Brawley (1915-1963). Photographs by Robert Bailey

CHAPTER 7

Celebrating the Past and Meeting the Future

St. Luke's and the Challenges of the Modern Church 1958–2003

"Change" was surely the dominant leitmotiv in the life of St. Luke's Church in this near half-century of its long history as a parish of the Episcopal Church. During the period from 1958 through 2003, St. Luke's—its membership, its church facilities, its worship services and programs, and its character as a congregation—experienced both the transformations occurring in the national church and those in the Diocese of North Carolina, as well as changes in American society. These events were met at times with reluctance and resistance, as elsewhere, and with initiative, hope and joyful acceptance in other instances. Throughout this period a triumphant generosity of spirit saw the church through the adoption of the revised Book of Common Prayer and its new rites of worship; a new and welcome role for women as members of the vestry, wardens and assistant rector in the person of Virginia Herring; the provision of enlarged, renewed and restored facilities for worship and Christian education; and the issues of racial equality and human sexuality that remain concerns of the entire Christian Church.

The background and personality of St. Luke's clergy have paralleled this evolution. The first three of the parish's five rectors during this period enjoyed tenures at St. Luke's of 11 years or more, while their two successors, preceded by interim rectors, departed after relatively short terms here. O'Kelley Whitaker (b. 1926) brought particular skills as a minister and administrator to St. Luke's that benefited the congregation from 1958 to 1969, and saw fruition in his later positions as Dean of St. Luke's Cathedral, Orlando, Florida; Bishop of the Diocese of Central New York; and last as Assistant Bishop of Southern Virginia. Here in 1961, he became the first occupant of the new rectory on Mocksville

These events were met at times with reluctance and resistance, as elsewhere, and with initiative, hope, and joyful acceptance in other instances.

Avenue; oversaw the fitting up of the old rectory as the Canterbury House; witnessed the election of Marion Goodman in 1966 as the first woman on the vestry; and introduced the trial liturgy at the end of his rectorate. During that of his successor, Uly Harrison Gooch, the introduction of the Proposed Book of Common Prayer; the role of lay readers in worship services and as chalice bearers; the expanding role of women and other issues met with concern, struggle, resolve and, at last, acceptance. Mr. Gooch hired Father Kenneth Rosier Terry as his assistant, enjoyed the success of the needlepoint project, presided over the organization of the St. Luke's Episcopal Church Foundation in 1973, appreciated the support of Frances Moser, the first woman elected as senior warden at St. Luke's, and celebrated the 225th anniversary of the parish in 1978.

With the formal adoption of the new Book of Common Prayer at the 1979 General Convention and the resolution of other issues, a certain steady calm returned to the parish with the arrival of Ichabod Mayo Little Jr., in 1982. He enjoyed the collegial support of Paul Tunkle and Virginia Herring, two of the most respected and well-liked assistant rectors in St. Luke's history, and saw the successful completion of the parish's last major building project, and its dedication, in 1990. Gary David Steber, who came to the parish late in Mr. Little's rectorate as his assistant, served as interim rector for a year prior to the arrival of Clifford A. H. Pike in September 1994. Mr. Padgett's long service as organist and choirmaster ended early in Mr. Pike's rectorate, and he was succeeded by Dr. Phillip Edward Burgess in December 1995. Proposals for the interior renovation of St. Luke's, initiated during Mr. Pike's rectorate, continued after his departure and through the service of John Carlton Southern Jr., the interim rector in 1999-2000, and came to completion during the tenure of Stephen B. Morris. Mr. Morris's stay at St. Luke's, from December 2000 to 2003, among the briefest in its history, coincided with the 250th anniversary of the parish, and he presided over the ceremonies attending that celebration.

Following the departure of Thom Blair, the Rev. Israel Harding Hughes served as a supply minister at St. Luke's in the period from early December 1957 until 16 February 1958, when O'Kelley Whitaker held his first Sunday service in his new parish. The choice of Mr. Whitaker, then serving as minister-in-charge of St. Andrew's Church, Charlotte, was quickly made, proving to be a good decision for both the priest and parish; he remained at St. Luke's for just over 11 years. Born on 26 December 1926 in Durham, Mr. Whitaker was a son of Faison Y. and Margaret Louise (O'Kelley) Whitaker and a 1949 graduate of Duke University. In 1952 he received his divinity degree from Seabury-Western Theological Seminary in Evanston, Illinois. That same year he was made a deacon and ordained priest, in May and December, respectively, by Bishop Penick. Also in 1952, he became minister-in-charge of St. Andrew's Church, Charlotte, and served in that position until winter 1957-1958 when he was called to St. Luke's. Mr. Whitaker, married to Betty Frances Abernethy in August 1955, arrived in Salisbury with Mrs. Whitaker and their young son, William Faison Whitaker (b. 1956), and occupied the rectory on Council Street.

As events later proved, Mr. Whitaker had a strong, educated appreciation for music as a valuable part of the Episcopal liturgy and parish worship experience. And, as a young father, he also quickly determined that St. Luke's needed a new rectory. His energies were committed to the success of both efforts in the first years of his ministry here. His conversation with Robert C. Perkins in the sum-

O'Kelley Whitaker (b. 1926) came to St. Luke's in February 1958 and began an 11-year rectorate marked by numerous initiatives. St. Luke's Archives

Mrs. Nell Troxler and a happy, well-dressed kindergarten class posed for this photograph by James Torrence in about 1959. Seated, left to right: Lindsay White, Steve Perkins, Jim Kluttz, Jeanie Newman, Jim Wear, Charlotte Woodson, Susie Beaumont. Standing, left to right: Cleve Cox, Eva Bernhardt, Charlie Murphy, Mike Hodge, Lisa Taylor, "Miss Nelle," C. V. Roberts, Pete Green, Robbie Stone, Mary Lou Detty. Mrs. Troxler remained in charge of the parish kindergarten until resigning at the end of the spring session in 1973. St. Luke's Archives

St. Luke's second rectory, at 929 Mocksville Avenue, was completed and occupied by Mr. Whitaker and his family in spring 1961. The house was sold to Mr. Little and his wife in 1983 and remains the home of the rector emeritus and Mrs. Little.

Photograph by Jason Williams

mer of 1958, when Mr. Perkins was undertaking graduate work in the School of Sacred Music at Union Theological Seminary, came to fruition in the summer of 1959, when Mr. Perkins became the first full-time professional musician at St. Luke's, joining the church staff on 1 September.[1]

Developing plans for the new rectory, raising funds and completing the building occupied a longer period, but only by necessity and no lack of diligence. Before 1958 came to an end, Charles E. and Alma Brady, Hearne Swink and Edward Edson Proctor each gave lead gifts to the cause. Planning for both the rectory and improvements to the parish house kitchen advanced through 1959 in a committee chaired by Clarence Kluttz. Berta Allen Summerell's sketch for the kitchen was developed by W. D. Bolls; the improvements were completed, equipment was installed, and the new kitchen was put in use in January 1960. Planning for the rectory, a costlier venture, also came together in 1960, with Joseph John Summerell (1918-2005) as chairman of the rectory committee. For a period, thought was given to acquiring an existing house, but the die was cast in April when Samuel Mitchell Purcell Jr., offered the choice of two adjoining lots he owned on present-day Mocksville Avenue for the rector's new house.[2]

With a specific site in hand, plans for the rectory were developed by architect Robert Faires Stone Sr. (1926-1999) in the summer, approved by the vestry, and the contract placed with James Henderson Wilson & Sons in August. While Mr. Stone was the architect of record and supervised the construction of the rectory, the design of the house was a collaboration with Berta Allen (Russ) Summerell (1930-1998), who drafted the plans in Mr. Stone's office and later contributed her salary towards the landscaping of the rectory grounds. Mr. Whitaker and his family relocated from Council Street to 929 Mocksville Avenue in April 1961.

As plans for the rectory progressed, Mr. Whitaker addressed other needs and concerns of the parish. Among the first of these was a parish newsletter which followed on an initiative of Mr. Blair. "The Episcopal Family Newsletter," copies of which survive dating to September 1958, was renamed "St. Luke's Parish Paper." A contest to replace that prosaic title was held in late summer 1962. "St. Luke's Messenger," the winning entry submitted by Alda Furches, was adopted in October 1962 and continues in use to the present, although the design and frequency of publication has evolved. Worship services were enhanced in several ways. Late in 1959, Charles E. and Alma Brady made a contribution to St. Luke's for air conditioning in the church; the work was completed the following spring, in advance of the summer heat of 1960.

Not surprisingly, given his discerning interest in the Episcopal liturgy, Mr. Whitaker gave long-overdue attention to the communion vessels at St. Luke's. Since their arrival in the parish in 1889, the postbellum chalice, paten and flagon donated as a memorial to the Rev. John Thomas Wheat had been in constant use for the celebration of the Eucharist. Through the course of 70-plus years, this usage had affected both their appearance and condition. At the same time, increased attendance at Holy Communion occasioned the need for a ciborium to hold extra wafers. In 1961, Mr. Whitaker negotiated with Louis F. Glasier, a leading ecclesiastical furnishing house, for the purchase of a ciborium designed to complement the old St. Lazarus vessels; for repairs to those communion wares; and for the purchase of a second, paired chalice and paten of smaller dimensions for the chapel. The ciborium was given in memory of Justus Gilbert Daniel Jr. (1909-1961). The chapel chalice and paten were donated in memory of May Wheat Boyden Brawley, inscribed with the date of April 27, 1961.

The construction of the new rectory, the new parish house kitchen and the air-conditioned comfort of the church brought into discussion the use of the old rectory and improvements to other parts of the church plant. With some minor refurbishing, the old rectory was fitted up for Sunday School and meeting space, and in May 1962 it was renamed the Canterbury House at the request of the Canterbury Club, an association of Episcopal students at Catawba College who met there. The acquisition of a new chalice and paten for use in the chapel reflected its increasing use, and prompted renewed attention to its

St. Luke's newsletter began publication as "The Episcopal Family Newsletter," appeared briefly as "St. Luke's Parish Paper," and was renamed "St. Luke's Messenger" in October 1962.
St. Luke's Archives

May Wheat Brawley (1881-1929), whose name was first honored at St. Luke's in the naming of a guild in her memory, was remembered again in 1961, when the chalice and paten for the chapel were given in her memory.
Photograph by Jason Williams

appearance. Hanging lamps were installed in the chapel in memory of Francis Johnstone Murdoch Jr. (1886-1961), Sallie Barlow Bernhardt (1884-1959), Shirley Frances Ketner Buckingham (1926-1961), a sister of Joan Ketner Spong, and Minnie Porter Marsh (1882-1961), Dr. Marsh's stepmother. The English glass house, J. Wippell and Company, Ltd., was approached for the design of a complement of six windows for the chapel, and their coordinated design proposals were accepted in July 1964. Installed in January 1965, these modern memorial windows honored a group of parishioners whose lives in the church spanned the first half of the 20th Century: Harold Moses Goodman (1913-1963), a vestryman; brothers Edward Buehler (1881-1948) and Louis Heyl (1902-1957) Clement; Edward Edson Proctor (1891-1964), also a vestryman; John Steele Henderson (1846-1916) and his wife Elizabeth Brownrigg Cain (1850-1929); and Myra Marguerite Fairley Brawley (1915-1963), the wife of vestryman Boyden Brawley.[3]

Other efforts in the church reflected both Mr. Whitaker's role as chairman of the diocesan music committee and Mr. Perkins's success as organist and choirmaster, as well as somewhat cramped conditions in the chancel. At that time the choir was located on a level one-step below the altar with its seating extending from the apse out, under the arch, into the main body of the church. In short, as Mr. Whitaker described it, "the choir and their stalls in their present position provide a tremendous physical barrier between the congregation and the altar."

Mr. Whitaker's proposal of 20 June 1963 was to relocate the choir and the organ console to a position at the southeast end of the church in front of the Ascension window; to replace the window on the northeast side of the apse with a door in a larger opening to provide direct access from the chancel to the sacristy; to move the communion rail forward (toward the congregation); and to make minor adjustments to

This photograph of the Canterbury Club, an association of Episcopal students at Catawba College, was published in the college yearbook in 1956. In May 1962, the former rectory was renamed the Canterbury House at their request. Seated, left to right, are: Margaret Roseman, Gary Verell, Edward Wallace, Phyllis Roseman, Phares Coleman.
Standing, left to right, are: Dr. Richard Mears, Mr. Blair, the Rector, David B. Smith, Robert Marsh Cooper, Julia Harp, William Crosswhite, Patrick Carlisle, Mr. Holmes, assistant to Mr. Blair. Mr. Verell (b. 1933), now retired as a priest, was ordained deacon at St. Luke's in September 1959, and in December married Phyllis Roseman. Mr. Cooper (b. 1935), professor at the Episcopal Theological Seminary of the Southwest, was also ordained deacon in St. Luke's, on 29 June 1960. Herbert Stephenson Wentz (b. 1934), who grew up in St. Luke's, was also ordained deacon at the same service in 1960.

the position of the pulpit and lectern. Concurrently, the vestry was also considering the matter of expensive repairs to the organ that had been installed in 1936-1937. The proposed changes failed to gain the necessary support, and it was not until 1970 that the choir stalls were relocated to their present location, on level with the congregation, and the new organ acquired. Meanwhile Mr. Perkins, who had organized the children's choir and, no doubt, felt the potential of the size and character of the adult choir constrained by its location, left St. Luke's at the end of January 1965. He was succeeded by Kathryn (Wagoner) Koontz.

Disappointment on the one hand was balanced by other achievements. The need for an assistant to Mr. Whitaker was answered by Harvey Gerald Cook (b. 1933), who came to St. Luke's as a deacon in June 1965 and served into July 1968, when he was called up for active duty as a Navy chaplain. He was ordained priest at St. John's Church, Charlotte, on 29 June 1966, and presented with a private communion set by St. Luke's. The role of women in the life of St. Luke's reached a new milestone during these years, with the election in December 1965 of

The Men's Bible Class, taught by Dr. Douglas, was the largest Sunday School class of its day at St. Luke's. The group posed at the base of the Ascension Window for James Torrence on 23 April 1961. Front row, left to right: Donald Clement Sr., Ed Hobson, Capt. H. E. Grogan, J. Allan Dunn, Curtis Wyatt, Boyden Brawley, Donald Clement Jr., Mr. O'Kelley Whitaker, Dr. Charles H. Douglas, Mr. Herbert Wentz, Justin Uffinger, Jim Cox, Wendell Detty. Second row: James H. McKenzie, Edwin Norvell, Bill Coughenour, Wilson Moser, Albert Monroe, Frank Baker Marsh, William H. Hambley, Julian Robertson, Marvin Randall, Frank White, Floyd McSwain, Edward H. Clement, John Cole, Edward B. McKenzie, Charles Taylor, Charles Welch. Third row: Richard Messinger, A. N. Saleeby, Harold Newman Jr., Paul Green, Woodrow Miller, Samuel Purcell Jr., James Lyerly, James Riddle, Monroe Joseph, Charles Fisher, Vernon Wilkerson, Edward T. Taylor, John Wear, Ladd Johnston, J. C. Ritchie, Robert Manning Jr., Joseph John Summerell, Harold Devoe. Absent when the photograph was taken were: A. W. Alley, Charles E. Brady, John S. H. Burris, Warren Beaumont, Edward A. Brown, John Beard, Jesse Clamp, Leon Carroll, Gordon Earle, Ivey A. File, Harold Goodman, W. H. Hobson, Ralph Horton, Nelson Large, William Speight Murdoch, Steve Martin, O. Maynard Newman, Frank Parrott, Bate Toms, Russell Welborn, Charles Wentz. St. Luke's Archives

Marion Emerson Goodman (b. 1912), the widow of former vestryman Harold Moses Goodman (1913-1963), as the first female member of the vestry. Two years later, in December 1967, Blanche Williamson (Spencer) Robertson (1906-1993) became the second woman elected to the parish vestry. In spring 1966, between these two elections, St. Luke's hosted the diocesan convention of the Episcopal Churchwomen.

Frances Moser (left) and Marion Goodman appear together in this photograph published in the Salisbury Post *on 15 March 1970, in an article on the newly-opened gift shop in the Canterbury House operated by the women of St. Luke's.*
St. Luke's Archives

The physical fabric of the church was enhanced by gifts in the 1960s. A wrought iron trendle given by Hearne and Marian Swink was used for the first time during Advent 1965. Discussion concerning new bells for St. Luke's also advanced in 1965; however, it was not until spring 1968 that the four bronze bells, cast in Holland, were installed in the tower by the I. T. Verdin Company of Cincinnati. Dedicated on Easter Eve, 13 April 1968, the bells were memorials to Hayden and Clay C. Clement, Marian Cheney Swink, Robert Maxwell Brown Jr., and Bate Carpenter and Lily Bernhardt Toms. Mr. Brown Sr., also made a substantial contribution for the maintenance and servicing of the church bells. The death of Miss Louise Marvin Neave (1878-1966), an aunt of Dr. Frank B. Marsh, prompted the execution of the last stained glass window added to the decorative program of the church. In December 1967 the vestry approved the theme of the window, the conversion of St. Paul, but reserved final approval pending its design by J. Wippell & Company of England. Installed above the door opening from the baptistry onto the loggia leading to the parish house, it was dedicated on 29 November 1970.

While each year of Mr. Whitaker's rectorate was marked by one initiative or another, including the election of women to the vestry, the introduction of the trial liturgy was surely among the most momentous events of his 11 years in Salisbury. But now, 30-plus years later, the consternation that prevailed at the time had partially faded from the memory of many older parishioners and was almost unknown to younger communicants who had little experience with the 1928 Book of Common Prayer. In retrospect, St. Luke's stood in an enviable position in this matter, as Mr. Whitaker was chairman of the diocesan Commission on Worship and Church Music, renamed the Liturgical Commission as it introduced the new liturgy. He presided at a diocesan conference on the new liturgy held in Durham on 27-28 October 1967, and brought his insight and understanding to bear on the subject that formed the theme of his sermons in November.

The trial liturgy was first used at St. Luke's on Sunday, 2 December 1967, and again on the third Sunday of the month. Trial usage was continued through Easter 1968. Questionnaires on the liturgy were later distributed to communicants of the parish, and the results considered at a meeting of the vestry in October. Seventy of the 140 questionnaires returned represented the view of those "who felt we were not on the right track," with 65 of the total holding a positive opinion of the new liturgy. Five respondents were of uncertain view. Not surprisingly, younger members of the church favored the new liturgy, while the parish's older members favored the established 1928 version they had known for 40 years. These results may have had some real influence when another controversial issue, the matter of lay administration of the chalice, was discussed by the vestry in spring 1968, but no action was taken. It would fall to the next rector of St. Luke's to pursue that opportunity for the laity, which has since become established practice.

Through the 1960s the matter of Salisbury's mission churches, St. Paul's, St. Peter's and St. Phillip's; and St. Matthew's, Rowan County, had gained the periodic attention of St. Luke's and its clergy. This came largely at the instigation of the diocesan department of missions which sought to provide clergy to the small congregations. Of these, St. Matthew's had the largest attendance. Mr. Whitaker's final substantive efforts as rector of St. Luke's were a series of meetings on the future of the Episcopal missions. These began with a special called vestry meeting in November 1968, at which Bishop Fraser presented his views, noting that about 20 missions had been closed. Having closed St. Peter's in 1962, he was inclined to close others, including St. Phillip's and St. Paul's. He also suggested that St. Luke's might take on the pastoral care of St. Matthew's, with financial support from the Diocese. These matters remained open to consideration; however, in December letters were sent by St. Luke's senior warden Richard Dwight Messinger (1915-1998) to officials of St. Paul's and St. Phillip's, inviting their members to St. Luke's. In 1969, when St. Phillip's was closed, more than a dozen

This beautiful trendle, crafted by the Yellin metalsmiths, is one of the enhancements to worship used during the Advent and Christmas seasons. "Glory to God in the highest, and on earth peace, good will toward men" is inscribed on the ring base supporting 10 angels holding candlesticks.
St. Luke's Archives

Mary Ellen Brashears Brown, the mother of Robert Maxwell Brown Jr. (1944-1965) inspects the bell given in memory of her son with Mr. Whitaker while the complement of bells was being installed. They were dedicated on 13 April 1968. This photograph was published in the Post *on 4 April 1968.*
St. Luke's Archives

At Christmas 1950 St. Luke's Church presented a silver chalice and paten to St. Phillip's Church. With the closing of the church, and its deconsecration on 24 April 1970, the chalice and paten were returned to St. Luke's and became a part of the parish communion ware.

Photograph by Jason Williams

members of the church transferred their membership to St. Luke's, including the late Helen Leazer Wood (1917-2000) and her daughter, Dora Wood.

The closing months of Mr. Whitaker's rectorate were marked by the usual events in the life of the church and others of more import. At the congregational meeting in December 1968, Sarah Riddle (1918-1993) became the third woman elected to the vestry. When the vestry convened in January 1969, she joined Blanche Robertson and others to accept Kathryn Koontz's recommendation, authorizing the purchase of a complement of 37 handbells from the Whitechapel Bell Foundry of London. The body also approved the recommendation of the diocesan liturgical commission for the usage of the Trial Liturgy, on the second and fourth Sundays and Wednesdays, for a six-month period beginning in February. On 23 February Mr. Whitaker submitted his resignation as rector of St. Luke's, effective at the end of Easter Sunday, 6 April 1969, to accept a call as rector of Emmanuel Episcopal Church, Orlando, Florida.

For just over six months, from Mr. Whitaker's departure until October, St. Luke's was without a rector. Joseph John Summerell, the senior warden, served as chairman of the calling committee appointed to seek a new rector. In April a call was issued to the Rev. Charles Bledsoe, of Emmanuel Church, Bristol, Virginia; however, he declined the call. Near the end of the summer a call was extended to the Rev. Uly Harrison Gooch, then serving as locum tenens at St. Paul's Church, Richmond, Virginia. Mr. Gooch, born in Stafford, Virginia, on 14 May 1933, was the son of Mercer Ray and Agnes (Brooks) Gooch. He graduated from the University of Virginia in 1960 and Seabury-Western Theological Seminary in 1965. Mr. Gooch was ordained to the diaconate in June of that year and went as curate to Grace Church, The Plains, Virginia. In December 1966 he was advanced to the priesthood, and in 1966-1967 served as chaplain at the Medical College of Virginia and in a part-time capacity as priest-in-charge of St. Paul's deaf congregation. He became assistant rector at St. Paul's in 1967. His departure from that celebrated parish occurred contemporaneously with the arrival there of the Rev. John Shelby Spong, who would serve as rector of St. Paul's until being elected the eighth bishop of the Diocese of Newark (New Jersey) in 1976. Mr. Gooch, unmarried, came to Salisbury in October 1969 and was instituted rector on the 29th by a former rector of St. Luke's, the Rt. Rev. William Moultrie Moore, Suffragan Bishop of North Carolina. Three months later, in January 1970, Mr. Gooch was host priest when the Diocese of North Carolina held its annual convention in Salisbury.

FROM GENERATION TO GENERATION

Mr. Gooch's rectorate, begun on 1 November 1969 and extending through May 1981, was marked by important changes occurring in both the Episcopal Church and American society. Rising opposition to the Vietnam War, seen in the strength and size of protest marches, affected every strata of society up to the withdrawal of American troops in 1975—and afterward. The now-legendary Woodstock Festival, held in Bethel, New York, in mid August 1969, was another challenge to conventional values; its impact on social mores also would reverberate throughout the 1970s. In the church, revisions to the liturgy and the long-revered 1928 edition of the Book of Common Prayer were followed by trial usage and the adoption of the new Book of Common Prayer by the 1979 General Convention. The increasing role of women in the life, administration and ministry of the church paralleled the larger women's rights movement that challenged conventional notions of gender roles in America. Sexual politics of another nature, that of the rising visibility of gay men and women in both society and the church, also challenged convention. It simmered in the background as the Episcopal Church's more visible efforts focused on race relations and the hope for racial equality. During this period, the Episcopal Church and its ministers addressed problems with both alcohol and drug addiction. In varying degrees, all these issues affected St. Luke's and the life of the congregation.

Uly Harrison Gooch came to St. Luke's in fall 1969 and served as rector through the challenging decade of the 1970s. St. Luke's Archives

Simultaneously, the usual concerns in the life of a parish occupied the minds and efforts of its communicants. In the late summer before Mr. Gooch's arrival, St. Luke's engaged James H. Padgett, who had been assisting Kathryn Koontz in the parish music program, as organist. Mrs. Koontz continued in the parish as choir director. The church was also engaged in two real estate transactions. When Summersett Funeral Home vacated its historic premises on West Council Street, next door to the rectory, for its new building on West Innes Street, the property became available. After extended discussion, the vestry decided to purchase the property and the deed was executed in 1970.[4] This expansion of the church holding on both sides of Council Street was made possible through a generous bequest by Miss Sallie Hamlin Grimes (1892-1969), the daughter of Thomas Walter and Mattie (Dobson) Grimes.[5] Meanwhile, as these negotiations were in process, Mrs. Edgar (Elizabeth Urquhart Ragland) Neff (1906-1989) offered her house at 200 South Ellis Street to the church, with the provision that a memorial to her parents be made with the proceeds of its sale. Mrs. Neff's niece, Virginia "Jennie" (Gregory) Sparks and her husband, James Anderson Sparks, members of St. Luke's, purchased the house and live there to the present.[6]

In the time-honored tradition of St. Luke's, as elsewhere, gifts on the magnitude of these ladies' enabled the parish to both undertake long-desired projects and acquire important memorials. In this instance they supported the refitting and remodeling of the chancel and the purchase of a new organ. While neither the vestry nor the congregation approved of Mr. Whitaker's earlier proposal to relocate the choir to the rear of the church, their decision did not otherwise resolve the crowded conditions of the apse, which included both the chancel and the choir stalls. The sum of $30,000 realized from the sale of the Neff property, and an additional gift of $5,000 by Mrs. Neff, enabled St. Luke's to contract with Casavant Freres, Limited, of Quebec for a new organ.

The need for a new organ case and console provided the opportunity to address the problems in the chancel. In fall 1970 Robert F. Stone, an architect and communicant of St. Luke's, prepared plans for the chancel renovation that were approved by the vestry in November and completed in January 1971. This work effectively created the arrangements in place today. The choir stalls were located from the apse to their present location on the main level of the church. The former organ console was to be closed and a new console erected, as now, in the corner adjoining the choir and the pulpit. The chancel area was enlarged by moving the communion rail four feet forward, and the platform supporting the altar was enlarged in proportion. This work and smaller structural improvements, all funded by the Grimes bequest, enhanced the appearance of the church and provided a degree of physical comfort for the choir whose size could then increase. These changes also facilitated the movement of those taking communion. Once all was completed, new carpet was laid early in 1971. The capstone to the project came with the dedication of the organ during Festal Evensong on Sunday afternoon, 6 June 1971.[7]

Since the departure of Mr. Cook in 1968, St. Luke's had been without an assistant. Mr. Gooch took the initiative in spring 1970 to fill the

The Ragland Memorial Organ, the gift of Mrs. Edgar Neff in memory of her parents, was installed in a handsome case designed by Mr. Stone of the parish and dedicated at a service of Festal Evensong.
Photograph by Robert Bailey

FROM GENERATION TO GENERATION

position, approaching Kenneth Rosier Terry (1922-2005), then a member of the Order of the Holy Cross. Father Terry came to Salisbury as assistant rector in July 1970 and served the parish into 1977. In late summer 1971, following on Mrs. Koontz's resignation, the positions of organist and choirmaster were combined. Mr. Padgett, the organist, assumed the new duties and began his tenure as the longest-serving organist/choirmaster in St. Luke's history. As 1971 came to a close, two unrelated projects were completed. J. Wippell & Company of Fair Lawn, New Jersey, completed repairs to the stained glass windows and installed "protective glass." The firm of James Henderson Wilson and Sons partitioned and finished the second story of the rectory as two bedrooms and a bathroom.

Kenneth Rosier Terry, a highly respected and beloved priest at St. Luke's, came to the parish in summer 1970 as an assistant to Mr. Gooch.
St. Luke's Archives

Other capital improvements were implemented at St. Luke's in 1972, addressing a series of needs. The renovation and redecoration of the parish house, which had seen only periodic refurbishment since its completion, was the principal focus of attention. The second was the creation of a suite of offices, designed by Robert F. Stone, for the rector, associate rector, organist/choirmaster and secretary in the hyphen linking the church and the chapel. The large room now serving as the library was Mr. Gooch's office. St. Luke's staff offices remained there until the refitting of the Canterbury House in 1989. A third component of these coordinated physical plant efforts included the demolition of the former Summersett Funeral Home on 27 April 1972, and the paving of the site as an income-producing parking lot.

The renovation and redecoration of the chancel and the installation of the new organ gave rise to yet another project in 1971 that provided an extraordinary opportunity for members of the parish to work together creatively. This project was the creation of the church needlepoint, launched in the late summer and formally approved by the vestry in September. Berta Allen Summerell, described by Helen Cheney as the "fairy godmother who made the dream come true," spent countless hours studying the symbolism of the church, Biblical references and plants, and the history of St. Luke's before setting about the design of a coordinated series of cushions and kneelers for both the church and the chapel. In time the project swelled to 53 pieces of needlepoint executed by 63 women over the course of three years. It was dedicated on All Saints Day, 3 November 1974, when the altar hangings and vestments given in memory of the Rev. John Thomas Clark also were blessed.[8]

This photograph of Berta Allen Summerell, looking up from her desk at 3 Dogwood Road, was published on 20 October 1974 in a long article on the St. Luke's needlework written by Helen Cheney.
Courtesy of the *Salisbury Post*

A winged ox, the symbol of St. Luke, appears on the seat cushion for the priest's chair inside a border featuring other emblems of the physician and patron saint of artists whose name was adopted for the parish in 1753.
Photograph by James Barringer

While the women of the church were thus engaged, others in the parish undertook initiatives that strengthened the life of the church. For some time the matter of memorials, their administration and the investment of funds to benefit the church and its operations had been under discussion. In June 1973 the parish committee, headed by Henry Bernhardt, presented the proposed articles of incorporation and bylaws for the St. Luke's Episcopal Church Foundation, Inc., and they were unanimously adopted by the vestry. Two funds were established within the foundation. Income from Fund A is to be used "exclusively for periodic major maintenance, repair, preservation, restoration and capital improvements to the properties of St. Luke's Episcopal Church." Income from Fund B is to be granted "exclusively for Christian evangelism in the spread of Christ's church through missionaries or missions, health service, and education by institutions sponsored or co-sponsored by, or operating in close association with the Episcopal Church of the United States."

The first important funds assigned to the Foundation accounts came from the bequest of Allan Robbins Hartman (1906-1972) who had made St. Luke's, St. Paul's and St. Matthew's churches the beneficiaries, in equal shares, of one-half of his estate.[9] This gift in the amount of just over $35,000 was received by the church in winter 1975 and two-thirds was deposited in the Foundation's Fund B. Before the year was out a bequest from Hearne Swink was assigned in halves to the two funds. Over time, major undesignated gifts to St. Luke's would be assigned to these funds and a third one, Fund C. In 1980, a legacy from Sarah Stark (Jones) Gridley (1908-1979) was assigned to Fund A.[10] The Foundation made its first grants in 1976.

Other gifts to St. Luke's during Mr. Gooch's rectorate took the form of memorials that enriched the furnishings of the church and its altar. In 1974 a silver flagon was presented as a memorial to Walter Henderson Woodson Jr. (1903-1974). In 1977 Robert Maxwell Brown honored his wife, Mary Ellen Brashears Brown (1915-1976), with the gift of a chalice and paten of handsome ecclesiastical design and decorated with jewels.

While these and other activities reflect the conventions of parish life of the period, Mr.

This chalice and paten, the most imposing pieces among St. Luke's communion vessels, were the gift of Robert Maxwell Brown in memory of his wife Mary Ellen (1915-1976).
Photograph by Jason Williams

Gooch's rectorate was one marked by challenges and a certain degree of agitation in the mid to late 1970s. Liturgical issues, arising largely from the adoption of the proposed Book of Common Prayer and the increasing role of laymen, gave rise to animated conversation among the communicants of St. Luke's and between them and their rector. Similar exchanges were occurring in many churches throughout the Diocese; however, those at St. Luke's had a personal dimension that was particular to the parish.

The use of lay readers to administer the chalice during Holy Communion was a new concept and one being advocated throughout the Diocese by the Rt. Rev. Thomas Augustus Fraser Jr., Bishop of North Carolina. The matter was discussed here in 1974 and again in 1975, meeting resistance from both the vestry and the communicants. Then, in the fall of 1975, Mr. Gooch proposed Richard Messinger and David Setzer, both members of the vestry, as lay reader candidates for chalice bearers at St. Luke's. The vestry approved this recommendation and Bishop Fraser subsequently licensed Messrs. Messinger and Setzer as the first lay chalice bearers at St. Luke's. At its same meeting, on 10 November, the vestry accepted and unanimously endorsed the Bishop's request that Mr. Gooch serve as chairman of the Diocesan Liturgical Worship Committee. A year later a second pair of chalice bearers, Dr. Frank Marsh and C. J. Bradner, was proposed, approved by the vestry and licensed by Bishop Fraser. Meanwhile, in October 1976, St. Luke's had ordered 200 copies of the new Proposed Book of Common Prayer.

The 1928 Book of Common Prayer was held in high regard by many members of St. Luke's, and its replacement by the Proposed Book was greeted with both regret and resistance. The matter was aggravated when

Mr. Gooch, who had come to use the rites of the new book to the virtual exclusion of the earlier book, removed the 1928 Books from the sanctuary. That action and two lesser controversies forced a called meeting of the vestry in May 1977. In retrospect, the year was a "baptism by fire" for Frances Barbara (Sohmer) Moser (1917-2006), who had become the first female senior warden of St. Luke's in January of that year. At the end of September, Father Terry resigned, effective in October, to take up a somewhat cloistered life as editor of the Episcopal Book Club for the *Anglican Digest* and the refuge it offered from the gathering clouds.

David Setzer succeeded Frances Moser as senior warden in January 1978 and served as head of the vestry during a second year of troubled fortune at St. Luke's. Mr. Gooch's introduction of a freestanding altar prompted largely negative reactions, both spoken and written, whose consideration was taken up by the vestry but remained unresolved. Other efforts had positive results. The search for an assistant to Mr. Gooch was answered in the person of Jack Glenn Flintom (b. 1949) who had served as deacon at Grace Church, Morganton, was ordained to the priesthood in May 1978, and came to St. Luke's that summer. The year approached its close with the celebration of the 225th anniversary of the parish and the 150th anniversary of the building of the church, with ceremonies on 29 October. The order of the administration of the Holy Communion taken from the 1662 Book of Common Prayer, in use when the parish was organized in 1753, was used in the service. The Very Reverend O'Kelley Whitaker, Dean of the Cathedral Church of St. Luke, Orlando, Florida, was celebrant at the service, assisted by Thom W. Blair Jr., who preached the anniversary sermon. They were joined by Messrs. Cook, Guerry and Terry, who had been priests in the parish, along with Mr. Gooch and Mr. Flintom.

Issues which prompted concern and wide discussion within the parish remained unresolved in 1979, and although Mr. Gooch would remain as rector into 1981, his departure became inevitable. The resignation of Mr. Flintom in May 1979 was the first in a series of events that precipitated the vestry's turn to Bishop Fraser for counsel and guidance. He attended a series of meetings beginning on 3 October 1979, including one on 28 December 1980 at which Mr. Gooch's letter of resignation was read. When words had proven ineffectual in 1980, dramatically reduced pledges and contributions to St. Luke's had their consequence. Mr. Gooch's tenure as rector of St. Luke's would end as of 1 June 1981. As St. Luke's set about the process of seeking his successor, Bishop Fraser returned to the parish and continued to offer guidance, including the recommendation to hire an interim rector. At the close of a meeting in April 1981, Bishop Fraser offered words that serve as an effective benediction. Albert Rother Monroe (1910-2004), a conscientious servant of St. Luke's and then clerk of the vestry, recorded them at the close of his record of the meeting.

The 225th anniversary of St. Luke's Parish and the 150th anniversary of the dedication of the church were celebrated with ceremony on 29 October 1978. The participating clergy appear in the top left photograph by David Setzer. Front row, left to right: Edward Guerry, Bobby Smith, Charles Snellgrove. Second row, left to right: Thom Blair Jr., Father Terry, Jack Flintom, O'Kelley Whitaker, Uly Gooch, Gerald Cook. St. Luke's Archives

Mr. Setzer also captured other members of the parish on film. Mr. Whitaker (left) is seen talking with James H. Padgett, organist and choirmaster, and Henry Bernhardt (right), the first president of St. Luke's Foundation.

Julian Robertson Sr. (left-center) and his wife Blanche (center) are seen talking with Frances Swink Hardin.

Father Terry in conversation with Anne Hobson Murdoch.

Luncheon was held in the parish house following the service.

"Bishop Fraser emphasized that this is a new day and age for the clergy. Many cannot appreciate the strong feelings for the 1928 Prayer Book that some parishioners still have, and changes are not easy. In fact, for some, they come the hard way."

Mr. Gooch departed Salisbury. In 1982 he began a rectorate at St. Barnabas Church, in Richmond's southside and the Diocese of Southern Virginia, which ended in 1994. Mr. Gooch is a resident of Chesterfield County, Virginia.

For eight months, from June 1981 until February 1982, St. Luke's was served by supply ministers while the search committee considered candidates for rector, issued a call, and the parish awaited the arrival of its new priest. The search committee, formed in June with Edward Clement as chairman, went about its work with careful deliberation. Given the experience of recent years, a questionnaire was prepared and distributed to all members of St. Luke's, 17 years of age and older, concerning their expectations of the new rector and his service to the parish. By November the search committee had unanimously settled on the choice of Mayo Little as the new rector, and made its report to the vestry which, in turn, approved a call. Mr. Little, then rector of Calvary Church, Tarboro, moved with his family to Salisbury in January and began his rectorate on 1 February 1982.

Ichabod Mayo Little Jr., born on 24 October 1928 in Robersonville, Martin County, North Carolina, was the son of Ichabod Mayo and Ethel Doris (Bailey) Little. He received a bachelor of science degree from North Carolina State University in 1951 and a bachelor of divinity degree from Virginia Theological Seminary in 1960. Following his ordination as

Youth Sunday, 6 June 1982, was the occasion for this large festive gathering of the parish's children and teenagers. Mr. Little, recently arrived at St. Luke's, is on the left. St. Luke's Archives

deacon in June 1960 at the Church of the Advent, Williamston, he went as an assistant to St. James Church, Wilmington, where he was ordained priest in January 1961 by Bishop Thomas H. Wright. In July 1962 he was married to Elizabeth Howell Hill. That summer he also accepted a call as rector of St. Andrew's Church, Morehead City. Serving there from October 1962 until 1968, he then went to Winston-Salem as associate rector of St. Paul's Church. In 1972 he became rector of historic Calvary Church, Tarboro, whence he came to Salisbury. Mr. Little, his wife and their two children occupied the rectory on Mocksville Avenue, and in January 1983 they purchased it from the church.[11]

Mayo Little appears here in June 1986 with members of the Cub Scouts who had just received their God and Family awards. The scouts are, left to right: David Goodman, Andy Goodman, Neel Woody.
St. Luke's Archives

Mr. Little's rectorate, continuing through August 1993, was one of welcome tranquility marked by important increases in membership, the annual budget and the physical plant of the church. A major bequest by Frances Swink Hardin enabled St. Luke's to undertake the expansion and renovation of the parish house. Other sizable gifts, and the especially generous bequests of Dr. Frank Baker Marsh and his wife, raised the assets of St. Luke's Episcopal Church Foundation to impressive levels. During his tenure, Mr. Little and St. Luke's also had the good services of two able assistants: Paul Tunkle and Virginia Herring. These priests and lay volunteers enlarged St. Luke's services to the larger Salisbury community through both cooperative programs with other city churches and its own initiatives, of which the most important was the Loaves and Fishes Food Pantry. Within a year of Mr. Little's arrival, Miriam "Mimi" Parrott became the church's first female chalice bearer. In March 1992; as retirement was in the offing, the rector instituted the Lay Eucharistic Ministry to serve the spiritual needs of housebound communicants. The final project of Little's rectorate, the construction of a columbarium and memorial garden, was completed after his retirement and dedicated in June 1994.

In 1982, when Mayo Little came to St. Luke's, relatively little attention had been given to the physical fabric of the church beyond general maintenance and repairs. Similarly, the matter of improvements to the church and parish house complex, and a decision on the best use for the former rectory across Council Street, had been postponed. Maintenance and repairs were addressed first, and in June 1983 Charles Phillips, a Winston-Salem-based architect who specializes in historic restoration, was hired to assess the facilities and their needs. His report and recom-

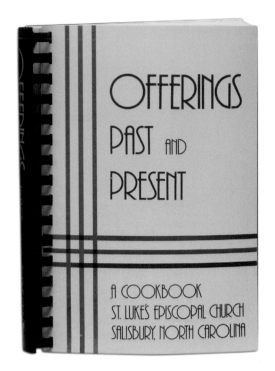

Offerings Past and Present,
St. Luke's second cookbook, was launched in September 1984 with a buffet luncheon featuring a wide array of items prepared from recipes published by the church women, including some from the 1937 cookbook.
Photograph by Charles Goldman

mendations, prepared in July 1983, were subsequently adopted and critical repairs to the walls, roof and coping of the church and parish house amounting to about $30,000 were made in 1984 under his supervision. Although the vestry endorsed the use of the Canterbury House for church offices in fall 1984, the larger question of upgrading and renovating the church buildings simmered until 1986, when an ad hoc building committee was formed. It sought preliminary proposals from Mr. Phillips, which were reviewed by the vestry in September and endorsed in principle in November, prior to their presentation at a congregational meeting on the 23rd. With the congregation's assent, building and development committees soon were formed. In April 1987, St. Luke's entered into a contract with Mr. Phillips for the preparation of plans for alterations and additions to the parish house, alterations to the office wing, alterations and additions to the Canterbury House, and landscaping and alterations to the grounds adjoining the church, chapel and parish house.

Over two years passed before the final drawings were produced and the project placed under contract. Delays in the production of the plans were exacerbated early in 1989, when local contractors declined to submit bids for the project. Through negotiation and revision, the scale of the plans and materials was reduced. In late April, a capital building campaign was launched to raise $1,025,000 of the expected $1.6 million cost of the work. It was chaired by Mrs. Patricia P. Rendleman and William Clarence Kluttz Jr. By the end of May, pledges exceeded the goal by about $85,000. Contracts were signed with Wagoner Construction Company with work to be completed first on the Canterbury House. The intention of this phasing was to enable the relocation of the parish's administrative offices to their new quarters prior to the major new construction linking the parish house and the chapel.

Work proceeded on schedule under the overview of Vernon Francis Wilkerson Jr. (1928-2000), chairman of the building committee. In October 1989, Mr. Little and the church staff occupied new and newly-furnished offices in the Canterbury House. A year later, on St. Luke's Day, the 18th of October 1990, the entire undertaking was dedicated with precedence given to the Frances Swink Hardin Parish House. The Rt. Rev. Huntington Williams Jr., Suffragan Bishop of North Carolina, was celebrant for the afternoon ceremonies. He was joined by two former rectors of St. Luke's: the Rt. Rev. O'Kelley Whitaker, Bishop of Central New York, and the Rt. Rev. W. Moultrie Moore Jr., the (retired) Bishop of Easton.

This splendid effort was the costliest building project undertaken by St. Luke's and the latest major improvement to the church except for the columbarium. It was also supported by the largest single gift in the history of the parish to that date. At her death on 6 January 1983, Frances

Swink Hardin left her house at 2 East Dogwood Road to St. Luke's; its sale to Mark and Barbara Perry realized a handsome sum which was wisely invested and had accumulated to more than $400,000 by 1989, when construction started.[12] The sum of $400,000, amounting to one-fourth of the total cost, was assigned to the parish house renovation and expansion. Mrs. Hardin's gift was recognized when the parish house was named for her and dedicated in her memory. Leading gifts were made by the late Julian Hart and Blanche (Spencer) Robertson, and Edward Tennent (1914-2002) and Elizabeth (Hardin) Taylor. These, respectively, funded the choir complex in the addition and renovation of the Canterbury House for the rector's staff and administrative offices. Mr. and Mrs. Robertson were honorary chairpersons for the capital campaign. Other major contributions to the project were also made by Mary and Richard Messinger, Katharine (Weisiger) Osborne, the Proctor Foundation, Richard J. and Patricia (Proctor) Rendleman and Ralph D. Wagoner.[13]

St. Luke's last major building project, initiated in 1986 and completed in 1990, included this major addition, incorporating lancet arch openings seen earlier in both the original church and the chapter house.

This photograph by Wayne Hinshaw was published in the *Post* on 16 October 1990.

Communicants of St. Luke's gave generously to the expansion and renovation of the Canterbury House, the parish hall and classroom building. Mr. Little's rectorate also saw other bequests and contributions that have supported individual projects and the larger work of the church. James Shober Brawley (1918-1981), a life-long communicant of St. Luke's and the author of *The Rowan Story, 1753-1953*, made a bequest of $5,000 to the church. This gift was set apart by the vestry for proposed revisal of William S. Powell's bicentennial history of the parish. Three additional gifts of note, separate from the capital campaign of 1989, also occurred in the period from 1989 to 1992. Dr. Alan Fulton Scott retired from practicing medicine in July 1989, and later that year he and Mrs. Scott donated his medical office at 715 Barker Street to St. Luke's Church. In 1990 the property was sold to Rowan Memorial Hospital.[14] This gift, made while the parish house renovation was underway, was applied to that project and recognized on a plaque in the St. Agnes Room. Dr. Fred Henry Chandler (1918-1990) left a bequest that was assigned in equal shares to Funds A and B of the

Foundation. In 1992 Edwin Overman Norvell (1920-2001) and his wife Judy (Proctor) Norvell donated funds to be used for the replacement of the pew cushions in the church when the need arose.

The circumstances of Mrs. Hardin's life enabled her generosity, and those of a couple who long figured in the life of St. Luke's prompted another splendid, larger gift. Dr. Frank Baker Marsh (1896-1991), a life-long member of St. Luke's, had a long and distinguished service as a layman in the parish. Serving many years as a member of the vestry, a frequent lay reader and as senior warden, he was ever anxious to contribute of both his time and means. Dr. Marsh remembered several members of his family with memorials in the church and chapel. He died on 19 March 1991; his wife Martha Louise "Bob" Jenkins Marsh (1906-1991) passed away five months later, on 29 August. They had no children. Except for some incidental bequests, the entirety of their estates was bequeathed to Fund B of the St. Luke's Episcopal Church Foundation. This gift amounted to about $3.5 million.[15] Their bequests have enabled St. Luke's to be the agent of enormous good will and service throughout the world, beginning in October 1993.

Dr. Frank Baker Marsh and his wife Martha Louise Jenkins Marsh, seen here on the lawn of their house at 725 Lake Drive, left bequests to St. Luke's that are the largest in its history.
Photograph courtesy of Ann Jenkins Anderson

Mayo Little's rectorate at St. Luke's was marked by an unusual harmony which owed in no little measure to his gentle character and even temperament. His success here and the church's service to its communicants and the community were also indebted to another personality trait: his ability to judge the capabilities of people, particularly those who came to join the parish staff. During his rectorate he was aided by two remarkable assistants. Except for the brief stay of Mr. Flintom in 1978-1979, the parish had been without an assistant to the rector since the resignation of Father Terry in fall 1977. Remembering the difficulty this had posed for the congregation, members of the vestry were anxious for Mr. Little to secure an aide. Paul Dennis Tunkle (b. 1950), the first person to hold that position, was a native of New York City and a graduate of the University of Maine. He received his master of divinity degree from General Theological Seminary in 1984 and was ordained to the diaconate in June of that year by the Bishop of Maine. He had visited Salisbury while still a graduate student, gained the unanimous approval of vestry members and was hired, with 16 July 1984 as his starting date in the parish.

In his energy, enthusiasm and intellectual curiosity, Paul Tunkle had had a counterpart at St. Luke's, in the person of Terry Holmes in the mid 1950s. Those qualities saw expression in his sermons and in his community outreach initiatives, including the Loaves and Fishes Food Pantry that opened at St. Luke's in fall 1986. Mr. Tunkle was ordained to the priesthood at St. Luke's by Bishop Estill in June 1985. He might then have sought his own parish, but that did not occur for two years. In fall 1987 he accepted a call to Holy Trinity Episcopal Church, South River, New Jersey, and left St. Luke's at the end of December. During 3½ years here, he had gained the respect and friendship of many people in the community which, in his liberal view, also embraced the parish he was called to serve. His departure occasioned regret and an editorial appreciation from Steve Bouser, the editor of the *Salisbury Post*, who wrote that "his has been a provocative and bracing presence, bringing a new vitality and forcing sometimes contented parishioners to re-examine a few of their values."[16] Mr. Tunkle had challenged the congregation and certain of its conventions, but avoided divisiveness.

Virginia Norton Herring (b. 1945), Paul Tunkle's successor as assistant rector, was also ordained to the priesthood at St. Luke's by the Rt. Rev. Robert Estill, Bishop of the Diocese of North Carolina. This ceremony occurred on 4 June 1989 and she, too, was gifted with a private communion set by the congregation. Her tenure at St. Luke's as the first female priest in the parish was not entirely a matter of choice, but one of good fortune. For one reason or another, the potential male candidates for the position of assistant passed out of consideration, and in September 1988 the vestry unanimously approved her hiring, effective 15 September. In a fashion she was not unlike Mr. Tunkle, who Steve Bouser described as a "Jew turned Episcopalian, accountant turned priest;" she came to the ministry in middle age and as the mother of six children. Born in Norfolk, Virginia, she was married to William L. Herring in 1967. Mrs. Herring received a bachelors degree from the University of North Carolina at Charlotte in 1985 and a master of divinity from Duke University in 1988. In 1987-1988 she was enrolled in Anglican Studies at the University of the South.

Paul Tunkle and Virginia Herring, both assistants to Mr. Little, figure among the series of priests who have served with the rectors of St. Luke's since 1954, when Urban Tigner "Terry" Holmes came to work with Mr. Blair.
St. Luke's Archives

Ginny Herring's ministry at St. Luke's was marked by interests and challenges that differed from those of her predecessor. Mrs. Herring quickly responded to the emerging AIDS crisis in the late 1980s, and in the summer after graduation from Duke she worked with an AIDS service ministry in Charlotte. After coming to Salisbury, she became a member of the Rowan County AIDS Task Force and gave inspired leadership to an organization that had been struggling, both to gain local support and to provide the necessary assistance to those with the disease and in need. Her efforts met with success and broad appreciation; however, the achievement came with a heavy cost. Her earlier work in Charlotte had gained the attention of bigots, and after her name and telephone number were posted by a "White Power Message Line," the vehemence directed against gays, lesbians and those with AIDS came her way through hate calls and obscene messages. Nevertheless, she persevered in her service to this local community, and gained admiration for her courage.[17] Early in 1990 Mrs. Herring took a leading role in establishing a parish friendship with the Church of the Heavenly Rest in Princeton, West Virginia. It began in Lent of that year, thrived for a period, but was discontinued after her departure from St. Luke's. Then, at the end of 1991, Mr. Little's illness and surgery for multiple myeloma in December placed larger parish responsibilities on her shoulders. Mr. Little's surgery proved successful and he assumed a full role in the parish; however, both Mr. Little and Mrs. Herring came to consider other possibilities in 1992.

Change came to the life of the assistant rector first. Having been an ordained priest for two years, Mrs. Herring considered a move to a new parish. In summer 1992 she accepted a call as vicar of St. Anne's Church, Winston-Salem; her last parish services at St. Luke's were on Sunday the 2nd of August. She remained at St. Anne's until 1999, when she went to Holy Trinity Church, Greensboro, as assistant rector.

Mr. Little's rectorate at St. Luke's had been successful and rewarding. Membership had grown from about 500 when he arrived, to about 560 in 1993. The church's annual budget had tripled in the same period, from about $100,000 to over $300,000 in 1993. The parish's physical plant had been enlarged and improved in its costliest building effort of record. This expansion provided facilities for a community-wide child care program, Mothers Morning Out, which opened with Betsy (Boyd) Cunningham as its director. In addition to the Loaves and Fishes Food Pantry, the church was involved with Meals on Wheels and other cooperative services through the Rowan Cooperative Christian Ministry and its successor, Rowan Helping Ministries. These social outreach programs involved both financial support and the invaluable contributions of many who volunteered their time. Parish programs likewise engaged communicant needs, including the Lay Eucharistic Ministry that was put in effect on 8 March 1992. Fund C was added in 1992 to the St. Luke's Episcopal

Church Foundation to provide Christian outreach in North Carolina and particularly in the Rowan-Salisbury community. With Mrs. Herring's departure and Mr. Little's likely resignation in the future, the vestry engaged the Rev. Gary David Steber (b. 1937), a nonparochial priest liv-

ing in Davidson to assist the rector, and Christopher Brown as director of Christian education. They joined the church staff in summer 1992.

In November 1992, Mr. Little announced his intention to retire effective 1 October 1993; however, 31 August would be his last day of service followed by a September vacation. In February 1993 Patricia Rendleman and William S. Murdoch were made co-chairs of the search committee, and Elizabeth Taylor was named chairman of the committee to celebrate the rector's ministry. A separate committee, chaired by Richard Mickelson, was named to select an interim rector. Having considered Mr. Steber's work in the parish and the qualifications of other candidates for the position, the committee in June recommended him as the interim rector to succeed Mr. Little. This recommendation was accepted and Mr.

Steber began his service on 1 September. Christopher Brown's contract was also extended into mid 1994. Mr. Little's devoted and exemplary service to St. Luke's was celebrated at a luncheon on 22 August and a picnic at the Warren Beaumonts' farm at Cleveland.

A final project of his rectorate, the first church columbarium and memorial garden in Rowan County, was completed after its end. Serious discussion on the project had advanced through 1991 and early 1992, when the vestry approved the concept of the facility in April. Robert F. Stone, an architect and communicant of St. Luke's, prepared plans that were refined through the next year, with the final drawing dated 18 August 1993. Wagoner Construction Company served as the general contractor, using locally-produced brick and Salisbury Pink Granite for the 280 niche shutters. Gates, benches and other memorial gifts by members of the

Hilarity continued through the evening at the picnic and roast for Mr. Little held at Warren and Gladys Beaumont's farm in Cleveland on 20 August 1993. Enjoying one of a series of "tributes" are, left to right: Betty Little, Mary Messinger, Mr. Little, Herbert Chen, Harriet Little Chen, John Little. Mr. Little and the party were also entertained by the "Banana Boat Singers," seen here with the honoree, left to right: Liz Goodman, Susan Kluttz, Mr. Little, Liz Alexander, Trudy Thompson.

*Vernon Francis Wilkerson Jr.
(1928-2000) and Mr. Little
(right) posed for this photograph
to accompany an article on the
columbarium written by the late
Homer Lucas and published in
the* Post *on 2 June 1994.*
Photograph by Wayne Hinshaw

Clement, Brier, Crawford, Joseph and Robertson families, enhance the Little-Wilkerson Memorial Garden.[18] It was named for the recently retired rector and Mr. Wilkerson, who oversaw its construction, and their wives. The Rt. Rev. Huntington Williams, Suffragan Bishop of North Carolina, returned to Salisbury for the dedication ceremony on 19 June 1994.

As anticipated, Mr. Steber served as interim rector of St. Luke's parish for a full year, through August 1994. Little effective change occurred in any of the parish's programs, committees or worship services during this period except in the matter of Christian out-reach. In October 1993, St. Luke's Episcopal Church Foundation was able to make its first major grants from Fund B for international work that had been so generously endowed by the Marsh bequests. Seven grants totaling $40,000 were awarded to both individual recipients and existing service entities, such as the Heifer Project International and the Presiding Bishop's Fund for World Relief that received $7,500 and $10,000, respectively. A second grant of $10,000 was critical in the restoration of the dome of the great 18th Century Russian Orthodox church of St. Sophia in Pushkin, Russia, which had been desecrated by unholy use since the 1930s and was being restored for Christian worship. In March 1994 a second series of Fund B grants contributed $18,000 to five projects.[19] The memory of Blanche Spencer Robertson (1906-1993),

*The post-Soviet restoration of
the Cathedral of St. Sophia at
Pushkin was supported by
generous grants from the St. Luke's
Foundation. The great church,
designed by the London-born
architect Charles Cameron for
Empress Catherine the Great
(1729-1796), was the centerpiece
of a model town, also called
Sophia, at the edge of the great
imperial summer palace complex
at Tsarskoe Selo.*
Photograph by Jane and John Riley

a long-time communicant and supporter of St. Luke's, who died on 28 December 1993, was honored by her son Mr. Robertson Jr., with an important gift which was assigned to Fund C of the foundation. Construction was also completed on the columbarium in spring 1994. Mr. Steber assisted the Suffragan Bishop in its dedication on 19 June.

The search committee completed work in mid 1994, recommending its choice of the Rev. Clifford A. H. Pike, rector of St. Peter's Church, Paris, Kentucky, to the vestry. The call was issued, accepted, and Mr. Pike and his family arrived in Salisbury in August to take up the rectorate on 1 September 1994.

Clifford Arthur Hunt Pike, the 25th rector of St. Luke's Parish, was born 9 September 1946 in Worcester, Massachusetts, the son of the Rev. Joseph Edison Colbourne Pike and his wife Louise Talbot. He received his undergraduate degree from Transylvania University in 1968 and his master of divinity degree from Virginia Theological Seminary in 1971. Mr. Pike was married in 1969 to Nancy Jane Geoghegan. In December 1971 he was ordained to the diaconate, and in June 1972 was ordained priest by the Rt. Rev. Paul Reeves, Bishop of Georgia. Mr. Pike began his ministerial career as assistant rector at Christ Church, Savannah, in 1971, and remained there as *locum tenens* in 1973. In 1974 he went to Memphis as associate rector of Calvary Church, and in 1977 he accepted a call as rector of St. Peter's Church, Paris, Kentucky. Some 17 years later, on 18 October 1994, the Rev. Henry Nutt Parsley Jr., Dean of the Charlotte Convocation, instituted Mr. Pike as the 25th rector of St. Luke's.

Clifford Arthur Hunt Pike was instituted rector in 1994 on 18 October, the Feast Day of St. Luke the Evangelist. St. Luke's Archives

Mr. Pike's rectorate at St. Luke's would extend to five years, through August 1999, and his taking up the call as rector of the Church of the Holy Trinity, West Chester, Pennsylvania. The course of this period was fairly typical. Mr. Pike spent the first year establishing himself in the parish, getting to know his parishioners, assessing needs and possibilities in the church and addressing parish staffing. Having come to a parish which had recently, handsomely refurbished its educational facilities, offices and administrative spaces, he quickly appraised the condition of the church itself, and particularly the interior. It had received little attention since the improvements attending the installation of the organ in 1970-1971. Now, with a choir steadily growing and improving under the direction of Phillip Burgess, new needs arose. In fall 1997 a committee was formed to evaluate space, maintenance, renovation and restoration issues. The committee presented its preliminary report in April 1998. Consideration of its various findings continued through the summer and

Sunflowers, cosmos, roses and zinnias bloom throughout much of the summer at the Canterbury House until being cut for altar arrangements.   Photograph by Robert Bailey

into fall, but effectively ceased in the winter of 1998-1999. By then Mr. Pike had come to consider other options, namely removal to a new parish, and an end to his stay in Salisbury. Meanwhile, another initiative had succeeded. Nancy Pike's idea of a cutting garden on the grounds of the Canterbury House was implemented by members of the flower guild, including Elizabeth Goodman and Carol Palmer.

Through these years parish life continued largely in its established patterns, with organizations, programs and activities continuing within the church, while Christian outreach addressed needs in the larger Christian community of which St. Luke's was a part. Church membership changed little from 1994 to 1999; however, the annual budget increased to just under $400,000 in 1999. Early in 1995 St. Luke's received two important gifts. David Tuttle Milne (1908-1995), the only son of the Rev. Mark Milne, rector of St. Luke's from 1918 to 1938, died on 3 January 1995 in Columbus, Polk County, North Carolina. Remembering his father's long, devoted service to the church and his own affection for the parish, he bequeathed $100,000 to St. Luke's.[20] This gift was assigned to the Consolidated Trust Progress Fund. Julian Hart Robertson Sr., a vestryman, senior warden and benefactor of St. Luke's, died on 22 February. His son and namesake honored his father, as he had

Now hanging in the chapel this beautiful icon was a gift to the parish in gratitude for the generous grants that enabled the restoration of the Cathedral of St. Sophia.
Photograph by Jason Williams

his mother, with a gift that was deposited to Fund C. In 1996 St. Luke's received a gift of an entirely different kind. St. Sophia's Church, which had received restoration grants from the St. Luke's Foundation in 1993 and 1995, expressed its gratitude with the gift of a 20th Century Russian icon which now hangs in the chapel. An anonymous gift of $100,000 for the parish youth ministry was made late in 1998 and announced in January 1999.

Mr. Pike delayed action in the matter of parish staff until spring 1995. The vestry approved hiring the Rev. Charles Roger Butler (b. 1932), the recently retired rector of St. Paul's Church, Watertown, New York, as an assistant to Mr. Pike. He began work in April on a part-time basis and served the parish until resigning 7 May 1997. Pike had a second assistant for a near year in 1997-

1998 in the person of John W. Gladstone, a deacon, who was honored with a farewell reception on 13 September 1998. James Padgett, the long-serving organist and choirmaster, resigned in spring 1995. The search for his successor came to an end a few months later, when Phillip E. Burgess was hired. He came to St. Luke's on 3 December 1995 and distinguished himself as a musician and choir-builder. His employment quickly proved to be a wise decision, for him and the church alike, and one of the lasting effects of the Pike rectorate. Mr. Burgess and the choir developed a new-found rapport, and he soon guided it to an unprecedented level of excellence. The adult choir, under his direction, has performed

twice in the National Cathedral, Washington, D.C., three times in Bruton Parish Church in Williamsburg, and on four different occasions at churches in Charleston and the city's Piccolo Spoleto Festival.

Since December 1995, the choirs of St. Luke's have been under the direction of Phillip Edward Burgess, who received the degree of Doctor of Musical Arts in Organ Performance and Church Music in 1992 from the University of Michigan. Mr. Burgess appears on the left of the photograph of the adult choir and in the center of the hand bell choir photograph.

Mr. Pike's second important, lasting contribution at St. Luke's, the initiative for interior renovations, did not bear fruit until after his departure. But that was not unintended. Mr. Pike's goal had been to complete the restoration of the church by 2003 as part of the 250th anniversary celebration. Following up on preliminary discussion, Mr. Pike asked Terry Eason, a well-known church architect and principal in the firm of Eason & Farlow Design, to come to St. Luke's in spring 1996, to appraise the condition and fabric of the church, and to prepare a report on its restoration. By March 1997, three firms had visited the church and studied its needs. Charles Phillips returned to St. Luke's and examined both the exterior and interior fabric. A representative of Schoenstein and Company, a major organ builder located in San Francisco, examined and evaluated the organ, and described it as ill-suited to Episcopal services. The damaged and deteriorated roof slates and their needed replacement

The cherub choir and the boy and girl choir (above) have also flourished under the leadership of Mr. Burgess.

was the one point on which everyone agreed. Thus, in September, the vestry approved a motion to replace the roof. The new roof was effectively completed in the winter of 1997-1998 at a cost of about $90,000. As this work was advancing in November, Mr. Pike announced the formation of a special interior committee at the annual parish meeting on the 16th.

During winter and spring of 1997-1998 the committee held a series of three meetings to gain the views of specialists in church music, architectural history and restoration architecture. These were attended by Phillip Burgess, Davyd Foard Hood and Charles Phillips, respectively. The committee's fourth meeting produced a preliminary report that was presented to the vestry on 20 April 1998. The committee recommended hiring Charles Phillips, a principal in the firm of Phillips and Opperman, to produce an interior plan, with options, for the renovation of the church. Four principal areas of concern were to be addressed in his study: improvements to choir seating; an improved, less visually intrusive sound system; the condition of plaster, paint and wood finishes and recommendations for cleaning, finishing and painting; and improvement to the lighting incorporating the reworking of the historic hanging lamps. The vestry approved the committee's report, and Mr. Phillips subsequently undertook his commission. However, 18 months would pass before the committee returned to the vestry with specific recommendations. By then Mr. Pike had departed the parish.

With Mr. Pike's resignation in July 1999, effective at the end of August, the vestry again decided to hire an interim rector while the search for a permanent rector was in process. Candidates for the short-term post were considered, and the decision was made to employ the Rev. John Carlton Southern Jr. He accepted and came to St. Luke's on the last day of October. Mr. Southern (b. 1946) was one of a small number of priests in North Carolina who had made themselves available for interim positions. Since his ordination as priest in June 1975, he had held positions in both North Carolina and Louisiana, including service at three churches in Asheville: St. Mary's, The Church of the Redeemer and Trinity Church. Mr. Southern served as interim rector until Stephen Morris came to St. Luke's in December 2000.

During this 13-month period, the church interior committee continued its work and a new project, the publication of a comprehensive history of the parish, was launched. Both efforts were the subject of special presentations to the vestry on 13 December 1999. Charles Phillips had presented an overview of the interior proposals in November, and in December Edward Clement, Barbara Perry and Patricia Rendleman, all members of the interior committee, presented their second report on the interior renovations. Recommendations were made in written form regarding the lighting and sound systems, the installation of new carpet compatible with the interior decoration of the church, new book racks on the backs of pews, historic paint colors, cleaning and polishing of the decorative woodwork and pews, removal of modern finishes and furnishings from the narthex and the installation of new partially-glazed doors linking it with the nave, cleaning of the stained glass windows, and a series of improvements to the church's tower entrance. The working estimates for these initiatives totaled about $331,000. General discussions on the recommendations and budget continued through 2000. That summer, Edwin and Judy Norvell donated the funds for new pew cushions and kneelers.

The matter of a new church history was presented to the vestry by Elizabeth Hardin Taylor, a life-long member of the church and the parish historian. In November 1982 Mayo Little had appointed her, together with Mary Nicolson, Edward Clement, James A. Dunn, Dr. Frank Baker Marsh and Edward Norvell, to a committee charged with updating the history of the parish. She and Mary Nicolson soon began working with William S. Powell on a revision of his bicentennial history. Although a draft manuscript was produced, it did not advance to publication. Mary Nicolson (1908-2002) then determined to underwrite the preparation of a new history by this author, and anonymously pledged $40,000 to the project, pending vestry approval. Robert Waddell's motion to approve the project, seconded by Juanita Bouser, was unanimously passed by the vestry.

During summer 2000 the search committee, co-chaired by Mary Blanton and Timothy Messinger, narrowed its purview to four candidates. After their visits to the parish in early October, the committee recommended the Rev. Stephen Morris, then priest-in-charge of a three-church station in Montana that included St. Mark's in Big Timber. The vestry issued the call in mid-October, it was accepted, and Mr. Morris and his family relocated to Salisbury to take up his work on 1 December. Mr. Morris did not come to Salisbury as a stranger, but as a friend already of Nancy and Edward Clement, who have a residence near Big Timber and attended St. Mark's on stays there. He was instituted as rector of St. Luke's on 24 January 2001.

Stephen Morris and his family were photographed walking in Milford Hills for a story written by Rose Post published in the Post *on 25 August 2001. Left to right: Henry, 5; Ellen, 6; Mr. Morris; Holly, almost 2; Jayne Morris, and Lee, 3.*
Photograph by James Barringer

Stephen Burnum Morris, the son of James Stephen and Dorothy Jean Morris, was born 4 May 1965 in Alexandria, Louisiana. He received his undergraduate degree in business administration in 1988 from Loyola University in New Orleans. After beginning a career in banking in Boston and marrying Jayne Ellen Laird in 1989, both he and Mrs. Morris decided to return to graduate school, relocating to Texas. There he changed courses again and transferred from Southern Methodist University to the Episcopal Theological Seminary of the Southwest in Austin. Having become a deacon in 1993, he received a Master of Divinity degree in 1994, when he was also ordained to the priesthood. For several years he held a range of positions and assistantships, including the chaplaincy of the Episcopal School in Dallas. In January 1999 he became priest-in-charge of the Episcopal Churches of the Upper Yellowstone.

Stephen Morris's arrival at St. Luke's was met with enthusiasm and high expectation, and he responded to his responsibilities as a parish priest with energy and a generosity of spirit. Arriving here at the age of 35, he brought the insights of a younger man to his office, one accepting of the long traditions of St. Luke's, while also guiding it on a path of continued Christian liberality. Working with the vestry, he instituted a new committee structure, addressing both the sacred and temporal matters of the church, which proved immediately successful and holds promise as a lasting legacy of a rectorate that was among the shortest in the history of the

The restoration of the faux painting in the chancel, a memorial to Edward Tennent Taylor, handsomely enriches the appearance of St. Luke's.
Photograph by Robert Bailey

FROM GENERATION TO GENERATION

parish. His tenure of just over three years saw the completion of important parts of the church renovation program initiated by Mr. Pike and the celebration of the parish's 250th anniversary over a weekend in October 2003. Soon after his arrival, he recast the appearance and purpose of "The Messenger." When the first issue of the revamped parish newsletter appeared in June 2001, it incorporated a lively, engaging mix of news articles, committee reports, columns from his pen and that of Phillip Burgess, as well as the expected monthly calendar of services and events and various schedules for laymen's work in the parish.

Initiatives in Christian outreach included the completion of two Habitat for Humanity houses, in 2001 and 2003, and participation in the Yadkin Valley Cluster of Churches to serve a growing Hispanic ministry. St. Luke's also continued its commitment to established programs of Rowan Helping Ministries. Mr. Morris was assisted by the Rev. Robert Bruce Cook Jr., for a year (2002-2003), and next by the Rev. Sarah Hollar, who came as an assistant in June 2003.

With a rector installed at St. Luke's, the efforts of the interior committee were rekindled and the project gained renewed momentum. However, over time, a program that rightly might have been described as a restoration of the interior, with admittedly contemporary enhancements, became a renovation except for the restored faux painting in the apse. In March 2001 consultant Julie L. Sloan completed a condition analysis of St. Luke's stained glass windows and submitted it to the committee. Donors for the lighting and sound improvements came forward in 2001, and the work was completed in 2002. Refitting of the historic hanging lamps and the supplemental lighting were underwritten in honor of Patricia Rendleman, a member of the interior committee, by her husband Richard and the couple's three children, Richard, John and Patricia. Mary Messinger and her family contributed funds for the new sound system.

The death on 29 October 2002 of Edward Tennent Taylor (1914-2002), a vestryman, senior warden and benefactor of St. Luke's, occasioned another act of generosity. His wife Elizabeth and their three daughters, Marye, Lisa and Kate, donated funds in his memory that enabled the restoration of the faux stone painting in the apse. Linda Croxson and Philip Ward, decorative finish specialists of Locustville, Virginia, whose work appears in the North Carolina State Capitol, the Treasury Building in Washington, and the John Steele House restoration in Salisbury, executed the decorative painting and renewed the finish of the reredos early in 2003.[21] Not unexpectedly, personal views on color influenced extended discussion on the paint selection for the plaster walls above the wainscoting and the carpet. These issues came to be resolved, the plaster was repaired, the church interior painted, and new carpeting was laid in the aisles. These enhancements and handsome new doors opening from the narthex into the church were completed in advance of the parish's 250th anniversary celebrations.

The 250th anniversary of St. Luke's parish was celebrated over three days, 17-19 October, in the presence of Bishop Suffragan Gloster and clergy who had formerly served here. John Rowan Claypool IV and the Rt. Rev. J. Gary Gloster are seen outside the church at the Sunday service on 19 October.

Father Terry (left), Mr. Gooch, and Mr. Little are seated in the church.

Photographs by David Setzer

By tradition the feast day of St. Luke the Evangelist, the patron saint of the parish, is honored by festivals and celebrations at St. Luke's. So it was with the 250th anniversary events held over the weekend of 17-19 October. The celebration was orchestrated by the parish's long-range planning committee, chaired by Barbara Perry.[22] The celebration opened Friday evening, the 17th, with a dinner at the Crystal Lounge, Catawba College, featuring an address by the Reverend John Rowan Claypool IV (1930-2005), author, theologian and retired rector of St. Luke's Church, Birmingham, Alabama. Saturday was set apart as family day, with games for children, lunch and the presentation of "We Are the Church." Mandy Monath wrote the script for the play, presented in two acts with choral accompaniment. Adults and children donned costumes and took on the roles of personalities in St. Luke's history from the colonial period to the present. Bryce Beard performed in the roles of his ancestors John Lewis Beard and his son, Lewis Beard (1755-1820), whose heirs set apart a tract of the Beard town property as the grounds of the church in 1827. Gary Thornburg played the role of the legendary Reverend Dr. Francis Johnstone Murdoch, the parish's longest serving rector. The Rt. Rev. Gary Gloster, Suffragan Bishop of the Diocese of North Carolina, guest of the parish through the weekend, was celebrant at the festival Eucharist on Sunday, the 19th, when he was assisted by Dr. Claypool, Mr. Morris and Ms. Hollar. An anthem commissioned for the anniversary from Kenney Potter, "Out of Your Riches," was performed by the choir.

The anniversary year was one of ongoing accomplishments, satisfaction and celebration; however, it ended on a different note. The improvements at St. Luke's enhanced both the physical appearance of the church and the services for worship. Members had joined together to build a second Habitat for Humanity house on Celebration Drive that

FROM GENERATION TO GENERATION

was dedicated on 17 May. They and others had volunteered for the RAIN ministry to AIDS victims, the Rowan Helping Ministries shelter and food pantry, Meals on Wheels, the Eagles Nest housing project, and the newly organized Yadkin Valley Cluster of Churches which ministers to the needs of a growing number of Spanish-speaking residents of the area. This work in Christian outreach was matched by programs within the parish, serving communicants of all ages and stations. Initiatives were also ongoing in regard to the possible expansion of the church plant through the purchase of the former Southern Bell Building and the Woodson law office, both on Council Street. These efforts reflected both prudent forethought and a response to the membership, which was increasing steadily during the Morris rectorate. Discussions on a needs and space study were also being held with an architectural planning firm. Thus, Mr. Morris' resignation in late November came as a real surprise to everyone in the church, and particularly those who had worked so closely with the rector to see the year's events to success. Mr. Morris had accepted a call to St. James Church, Ormond Beach, Florida. With his approaching departure at the end of December, Ms. Hollar assumed larger duties as the vestry undertook the search for both an interim rector and a rector for the second time in only five years.

1755 · We are the Church · 2003

A Musical Play in Two Acts
on the History of St. Luke's Parish

**Saturday the Eighteenth of October
11:00 o'clock in the morning**

St. Luke's Parish Hall

*Featuring: Singers, hunting dogs, wild beasts,
historical figures, and at least one deus ex machina*

Followed by lunch and more fun!

"We Are the Church," a pageant written by Mandy Monath, was performed by St. Luke's parishioners in the roles of personages important in the history of the parish. St. Luke's Archives

Sarah Louise Darnell Hollar (b. 1959) came to the parish in June 2003 and served St. Luke's with Mr. Morris, Mr. Holmes, the interim rector, and Mr. Hougland until accepting a call as rector of St. Mark's, Huntersville. St. Luke's Archives

ENDNOTES

1. Mr. Perkins was a native of Corning, New York, and a graduate of the School of Music, Syracuse University. He had served as organist and choirmaster at Calvary Church, Syracuse, and in North Carolina at St. Mary's Church, Kinston, and at the Church of the Good Shepherd, Rocky Mount, from 1953 to 1958, whence he departed for New York and graduate study. Prior to Mr. Perkins's arrival St. Luke's had enjoyed the services of talented musicians/organists including Mrs. Harry Ludwig, among others, who were usually paid on a monthly basis.

2. The vestry chose lot #15 of the subdivided lands of R. Lee Mahaley. RCD, 444/537-38. The conveyance to St. Luke's was made by Mr. Purcell and his wife Veda Irene ZumBrunnen Purcell.

3. *POST*, 24 January 1965. In her article, "Chapel at St. Luke's Sparkles With New Stained Glass Windows," Anne Murdoch names Claude Howard as the designer of the windows. They were ordered through the company's American agent in Fair Lawn, New Jersey, and installed by its artisans.

4. RCD, 545/608.

5. Rowan County Estates, #1520(1969).

6. RCD, 542/475-76. Mrs. Neff was first married to John Tillery Gregory (1901-1948), the brother of Mrs. Sparks' father Lee Overman Gregory (1900-1941). The sale realized $30,000 for St. Luke's. Mrs. Neff's second husband, the Rev. Edgar Ralph Neff, was an Episcopal priest.

7. The new organ was used for the first time at services on Sunday, 13 December 1970. The Frercks organ was conveyed to St. Francis Church, Greensboro.

8. *POST*, 20 October 1974. The memorial to Mr. Clark, a Methodist minister who died while in Salisbury in 1886 and was buried in the churchyard as a courtesy, was made by his granddaughter, Mrs. William C. Lukens, of Roanoke, Virginia.

9. Rowan County Estates, 72 E 211. St. Luke's received a direct payment from the executor of the estate, while the bequests to St. Paul's and St. Matthew's were made to the Diocese of North Carolina as trustee.

10. Mrs. Gridley was a native of Alleghany County, Pennsylvania, and the daughter of Frederick Herr and Katherine (Tift) Jones.

11. During the negotiations attending his acceptance of the call to St. Luke's, Mr. Little indicated his interest in acquiring and occupying his own residence in Salisbury. The Littles agreed to occupy the rectory, and if it suited them to purchase it from the church. This came to pass, and with the bishop's approval the rectory was sold to Mr. and Mrs. Little. RCD. 605/292-293.

12. RCD, 605/545. The property, comprising five assembled, adjoining parcels, was conveyed to the Perrys by Stahle Linn, the executor of Mrs. Hardin's estate. Frances Swink Hardin (1902-1983) came to the parish in 1924 with her marriage to William Hill Hardin Jr. (1894-1973), the son and namesake of the Archdeacon of the Charlotte Convocation. She had grown up in China Grove, the daughter of William Joshua (1853-1939) and Anna Swift (Hearne) Swink (18__-1946), where her parents had erected a small Episcopal church, the Church of the Ascension, that was effectively a family chapel. Mrs. Hardin and her husband had built the Dogwood Road house.

13. See the dedication program for the full list of donors to the project and the special spring 1989 edition of "The Messenger" which announced the capital campaign.

14. For Scott to St. Luke's see RCD, 651/290-291. For St. Luke's to Rowan Memorial Hospital Incorporated see RCD, 656/160.

15. Rowan County Estates, 91 E 288 and 91 E 698.

16. *POST*, 27 December 1987.

17. *POST*, 24 July 1992.

18. *POST*, 2 June 1994.

19. "All Things in Common," Vol. 1, No. 1, Fall 1996.

20. Polk County Estates, 95-E-6. Mr. Milne and his wife, who predeceased him, had no children. They had retired to Tryon.

21. *POST*, 24 February 2003.

22. Members of the parish long-range planning committee were: Phillip Burgess, William Comer, Donald Fortner, Elizabeth Goodman, Robert Monath, Mr. Morris, Barbara Perry, Patricia Rendleman, Elizabeth Taylor and Robert Ward.

With azaleas in full bloom, spring is the most colorful season on the grounds of St. Luke's.   Photograph by Robert Bailey

Epilogue

The presence of Ms. Hollar in the parish, and the good work of those charged with securing both the interim rector and a new rector proved fortunate to the life of the church in 2004 and afterward. Her steady leadership and counsel facilitated the transition from Mr. Morris's rectorate to the arrival of Douglas Lloyd Holmes, the interim rector, during the winter of 2004 and again, a year later, when Whayne Miller Hougland Jr., succeeded Stephen Morris as rector. During this period the programs and projects of the church continued without interruption. St. Luke's also initiated an important new mission project in Costa Rica, supported both by the volunteer efforts of many in the church and by a fall 2004 grant of $31,000.00 by St. Luke's Episcopal Church Foundation.

During this period the programs and projects of the church continued without interruption.

During the months of January and February 2004, when Ms. Hollar was effectively the spiritual steward of St. Luke's, two events brought joy to the parish and helped to lessen the sense of loss felt when Mr. Morris resigned. On 18 January, the Rt. Rev. J. Gary Gloster, Bishop Suffragan of North Carolina, came to St. Luke's and ordained Sarah Darnell Hollar to the priesthood. Stephen Morris returned to St. Luke's for the baptism of his goddaughter, Clara Linda Brown. His sermon that Sunday, 1 February, in the form of a letter to be given later to Clara, was

Tradition, celebration and renewal are all present in the rite of baptism, which reaffirms each individual's place in the heart of the church family. Bruce Ford, a happy grandfather, photographed his daughter Emily Ford and his granddaughter Clara Linda Brown with her godparents following Clara's baptism on 1 February 2004. Left to right: Mr. Morris, Jayne Morris holding Clara, and Emily Ford.
Courtesy of Emily Ford and Charles Brown

heartfelt in its instruction to the young girl, and a poignant valedictory to St. Luke's.

Sitting members of the vestry comprised the interim rector search committee, under the direction of Tim Messinger, the newly-appointed senior warden. Their choice was both quick and propitious. Douglas Lloyd Holmes came to St. Luke's on 1 March 2004, and served the parish until the arrival of Mr. Hougland in January 2005. Mr. Holmes (b. 1953) is a native of California and was educated at the University of Southern California and General Theological Seminary, whence he graduated in 1979 and 1985, respectively. He had served two churches in California before accepting the call as rector of St. John's Church, Cornwall, New York, in 1993. In 2002 he left New York and came south as associate rector at St. Margaret's Church in suburban Charlotte, a position he resigned in late 2003.

Mr. Holmes and Ms. Hollar enjoyed a collegial and effective tenure as priests at St. Luke's while the search committee, led by Richard Goodman and Mary Willis Page, worked to fulfill its responsibility to identify a successor to Mr. Morris. Existing parish activities continued on their successful course while a new project, a proposed five-year mission association with a parish in the Diocese of Costa Rica, garnered wide support under Sarah Hollar's enthusiastic leadership. Three fund-raising events were planned for the project by mid-September when Ms. Hollar, Barbara Perry and Robert Crum undertook an exploratory/planning trip to make arrangements for the larger parish mission trip in January 2005. They returned to share plans for work at the chapel of St. Philip and St. James, a day care center and a school, with those who attended a progressive dinner on 25 September and a cabaret on 16 October. Profits from the Episcopal Churchwomen's bazaar on 6 November were also designated in part for the Costa Rica work and the week-long new year mission.

The efforts of both the search committee and the Costa Rica mission saw success in January 2005. Whayne Miller Hougland Jr., began his tenure as rector on 1 January and held his first services at St. Luke's on the 16th. On 14 January Ms. Hollar and 16 members of the church departed for San Jose, Costa Rica, and returned on the 22nd. They also shared accounts of their experience as a team with the parish family in a variety of formats, including a Costa Rican night on 17 February with dinner, music and a slide presentation.

FROM GENERATION TO GENERATION

IGLESIA EPISCOPAL
CONGREGACION
SAN FELIPE Y SANTIAGO

Like Stephen Morris and Sarah Hollar, Mr. Hougland came to the priesthood after years in the business sector, and like Paul Tunkle, he was a convert to the Episcopal Church. Whayne Miller Hougland (b. 1962) was born in Owensboro, Daviess County, Kentucky, to Mr. Hougland Sr., and his wife Elaine Astoreca Hougland. His early years were spent in Versailles, where he attended Catholic parochial school through the eighth grade, and then entered public school. In 1986 he received his B. A. degree in history from the University of Kentucky. Meanwhile, in 1984, he was married to Dana Lynne Menges, and their first daughter, Erin, was born in 1985, the year he was received into the Episcopal Church. A second daughter, Leigha, was born to the couple in 1990. After a business career in sales, marketing and management that moved him and his family from Lexington to Philadelphia, to Chattanooga, and back to Lexington, Mr. Hougland decided to enter the ministry. In 1995 he enrolled in the School of Divinity at the University of the South, where he graduated with a master's degree in 1998. Mr. Hougland was ordained to the diaconate on 13 June 1998 by Bishop Wimberly, and six months later, on 19 December, Bishop Wimberly ordained him to the priesthood. Both ceremonies occurred in Christ Church Cathedral, Lexington, where he had joined the staff after graduation from seminary.

During St. Luke's first mission trip to San Jose, Costa Rica, members of the team dismantled partitions in a former commercial building and refitted the space as the Church of St. Philip and St. James. In left photograph, left to right: Robert Crum, Sarah Hollar (behind post), Michael Mills, George Dischinger IV.

Photograph above, left to right: Tommy Page, Robert Crum, Michael Mills, Greg Kaufmann, Dowd Temple, John Hartpence.
Photographs by Lynn Mills

The Rev. Whayne Miller Hougland Jr., came to St. Luke's Parish in January 2005 and was instituted rector on 18 May 2005.

In 1999 he was promoted to the office of Canon Evangelist, where he served until accepting the call to St. Luke's in November 2004. Mr. Hougland was instituted rector on 18 May 2005.

During his first year as rector of St. Luke's, the parish continued existing programs in Christian education, outreach and volunteer service, laid plans to erect and built a third Habitat for Humanity house, made plans for a second mission trip to Costa Rica in January 2006, and completed the repair and restoration of stained glass windows in the chapel. The three large windows in the northeast side wall had serious problems of bowing, caused by deterioration of the lead cames and the intense buildup of heat between the windows and the unvented protective glazing. After an examination of the work of several repair and restoration studios, the work was placed with Guarducci Stained Glass Studio in Warrenton, North Carolina. The windows were removed in April 2005, taken to Warrenton, where the glass was cleaned and the windows fitted with new lead cames. The newly-repaired windows were reinstalled in the chapel on 14-15 July. On 7 August groundbreaking was held for the parish's third Habitat house, and on 10 September a crew of volunteers assembled to begin raising the house on its newly-built foundation and flooring. Two weeks later, on the 24th, the parish held its second progressive dinner to support the second-year mission team's trip to Costa Rica. Summer 2005 also marked the end of Sarah Hollar's tenure at St. Luke's as assistant to the rector. She had accepted a call as rector of St. Mark's Church, Huntersville, and departed the parish at the end of July.

Members of the 2005 Habitat House building team began raising the walls of the parish's third Habitat house on 10 September.
Photograph by Melissa Graham

Now, in the second year of Mr. Hougland's rectorate, continuity, challenge and change continue to define parish life and service, whether here in Salisbury or in Costa Rica or at other points where the grants of St. Luke's Episcopal Church Foundation, totaling just over $148,000 in 2004-05, extend the reach of the church. But what of the church itself? And its future? In a sermon preached on the occasion of the baptism of his goddaughter, Clara Brown, the Rev. Stephen Morris wrote these words:

St. Luke's is a great church. The people care for one another…it is an historic church that values tradition. It is comforting to know that…in our world there remain places that remind our souls of a long time ago. (It is also) a parish church that responds readily to the changing needs of the community and world around it… St. Luke's works to evangelize the unchurched and strengthen the faith of those who believe.

In its ministry through the years, each generation of St. Luke's continues to answer the call that the Virgin Mary heard from God.

> My soul magnifies the Lord,
> and my spirit rejoices in God my Savior,
> for he has looked with favor on the
> lowliness of his servant.
> Surely, from now on all generations
> will call me blessed;
> for the Mighty One has done great
> things for me
> and holy is his name.
> His mercy is for those who fear him
> *from generation to generation.*
>
> (Luke I: 46-50. New Revised Standard Version)

With services oftentimes canceled few enjoy the remarkable scene when snow covers the lawn at St. Luke's and presents a strong counterpoint to the dark brickwork of the church.

Photograph by Robert Bailey

Addison, James Thayer. *The Episcopal Church in the United States, 1789-1931*. New York: Charles Scribner's Sons, 1951.

Agner, Martha W., and Mary Jane Fowler, eds. *The Old Lutheran Cemetery, Salisbury, North Carolina, Since 1768*. Salisbury, NC: The Old Lutheran Cemetery Committee, Historic Salisbury Foundation, 1981.

Agner, Martha Withers, and Martha Hines Morehead, eds. *The Heritage and History of St. John's Evangelical Lutheran Church, Salisbury, North Carolina, Through 1983*. 2 vols. Salisbury, NC: St. John's Evangelical Lutheran Church, 1988-1995.

Walker Anderson to Duncan Cameron, 14 February 1825, Cameron Papers, Southern Historical Collection, Chapel Hill, NC.

Walker Anderson to Thomas Ruffin, ___ March 1825, Ruffin Papers, Southern Historical Collection, Chapel Hill, NC.

Atkinson, Thomas. *The Old Paths: A Sermon, Preached in St. Luke's Church, Salisbury, by The Right Reverend Thomas Atkinson, D.D., Bishop of North Carolina, at the Ordination to the Priesthood of the Rev. Messrs. Benjamin Swan Bronson, George Badger Wetmore, William Murphy, and Thomas Goelet Haughton, on Whit-Sunday 1857,....* Fayetteville, NC: Edward J. Hale & Son, 1857.

Aull, Sara, and Mary Brandon. *Dr. Josephus Wells Hall: A Man of Energy and Enterprise, Salisbury, North Carolina*. Salisbury: Historic Salisbury Foundation, Inc., 1994.

Barrett, John G. *The Civil War in North Carolina*. Chapel Hill: University of North Carolina Press, 1963.

Beard, Christine, "Diary," photocopy of transcript copy prepared by Mary Jane Fowler ca. 1986 from hand-written abstracts made by Francis Johnstone Murdoch that are held in the St. Luke's Archives. Original diary is believed to be lost.

Beard, John, and others. *A Misstatement in the "Episcopal Journal" of Bishop Ravenscroft, Corrected*. Salisbury: Philo White, 1827.

Block, Susan, *The Wrights of Wilmington*. Edited by Frederick L. Block. Wilmington, NC: Wilmington Printing Company, 1992.

Brawley, James Shober. *The Rowan Story, 1753-1953: A Narrative History of Rowan County, North Carolina*. Salisbury: Rowan Printing Company, 1953.

Brown, Louis A. *The Salisbury Prison: A Case Study of Confederate Military Prisons, 1861-1865, Revised and Enlarged*. Wilmington, NC: Broadfoot Publishing Company, 1992.

Brydon, George MacLaren, "The Ministry of the Reverend Robert Johnston Miller in North Carolina," unpublished typescript essay, Diocese of Virginia Papers, Virginia Historical Society, Richmond, VA.

The Carolina Churchman, Raleigh and Greensboro, NC. 1909-1935.

Carolina Watchman, 21 September 1858, "Died...Rev. J. H. Parker..."

_____. 11 May 1863, "An Appeal."

_____. 1 June 1863, "Died...William Campbell Lord."

_____. 9 May 1864, "Died...Mrs. Sarah Jane Martin."

_____. 7 May 1866, "Gov. Ellis' Remains."

_____. 16 September 1867, "New Residences."

_____. 7 June 1872, "Local and State Items."

_____. 28 June 1872, "Local and State Items."

_____. 20 April 1876, "A Working Church."

_____. 14 October 1880, "Death of T. G. Haughton, Esq."

_____. 19 July 1883, "The Episcopal Church."

_____. 17 November 1887, "Local."

_____. 2 February 1888, "Death of Dr. Wheat."

_____. 18 June 1891, "Local."

_____. 1 June 1893, "The funeral train, containing the remains of the South's great leader in the 'Lost Cause'."

_____. 1 July 1908, "Deaths, Samuel R. Harrison."

Carter, Hodding, and Betty Carter. *So Great A Good*. Sewanee: The University Press, 1955.

Chamberlain, Hope Summerell. *This Was Home*. Chapel Hill: University of North Carolina Press, 1938.

Charlotte Observer, 25 February 1940, "Salisbury Communion Service Has Rare History."

_____. 26 December 2004, "The Very Reverend Dr. Thom Williamson Blair."

Thaddeus A. Cheatham to William S. Powell, 8 July 1953, St. Luke's Archives.

Chesnutt, David R. and C. James Taylor, eds. *The Papers of Henry Laurens*, vol. 15. Columbia, SC: University of South Carolina Press, 2000.

The Church Intelligencer (Raleigh, NC), 13 June 1861, "A Prayer For Those Who Have Gone Forth to War...," and 28 November 1862, "Two of the occasional prayers, by Bishop Atkinson,...."

Clark, Walter, ed. *The State Records of North Carolina*. Vols. 23 and 25. (1904, 1906). Reprint, Wilmington, NC: Broadfoot Publishing Company, 1994.

Clerical Directory of the Protestant Episcopal Church in the United States of America. New York: Church Hymnal Corporation for the Church Pension Fund, 1956-1968.

Collins, Donald E. *The Death and Resurrection of Jefferson Davis*. Lanham, Maryland: Rowan & Littlefield Publishers, Inc., 2005.

The Columbia (SC) Record, 10 January 1933, "Death Claims Aged Minister."

Corbitt, D. L., ed. "The Robert J. Miller Letters, 1813-1831," *North Carolina Historical Review* 25, no. 4 (Oct. 1948): 485-521

Corbitt, David Leroy. *The Formation of the North Carolina Counties, 1663-1943*. 1950. Reprint, Raleigh: North Carolina Division of Archives and History, 2000.

Crist, Lynda Lasswell, et al, eds. *The Papers of Jefferson Davis*, Vol. 11. Baton Rouge: LSU Press, 2003.

Currin, Beverly Madison. *The Search for the Lost Rectors: Reflections on the History of Old Christ Church and Pensacola in the Nineteenth Century*. Pensacola: University of West Florida Foundation, 1999.

Daily Union Banner (Salisbury, NC), 7 October 1865, "Sacrilege and Disloyalty."

Davies-Rodgers, Ellen. *The Great Book, Calvary Protestant Episcopal Church, 1832-1972, Memphis, Shelby County*, Tennessee. Memphis: Plantation Press, 1973.

Davis, Burke. *The Long Surrender*. New York: Random House, 1985.

[Davis, Jefferson.] "The Late Mr. Jefferson Davis." *The Illustrated London News*, 14 December 1889, 751-52.

Davis, Thomas Frederick. *A Genealogical Record of the Davis, Swann, and Cabell Families of North Carolina and Virginia*. N. p.: 1934.

Davis, Varina Howell. *Jefferson Davis, Ex-President of the Confederate States of America, A Memoir*. 2 volumes. New York: Belford Company, 1890.

Duncan, Norvin C. *A Pictorial History of the Episcopal Church in North Carolina, 1701-1964*. Asheville: Miller Printing Company, 1965.

Eavenson, Howard N. *Map Maker & Indian Traders*. Pittsburgh: University of Pittsburg Press, 1949.

Episcopal Clerical Directory. New York: Church Hymnal Corporation, 1972-2003.

Ervin, Samuel James Jr. *A Colonial History of Rowan County, North Carolina*. The James Sprunt Historical Publications, vol. 16, no. 1. Chapel Hill, 1917.

Escott, Paul D. *Many Excellent People: Power and Privilege in North Carolina, 1850-1900*. Chapel Hill: University of North Carolina Press, 1985.

Etheridge, Elizabeth H. *St. Andrew's Episcopal Church: The Sesquicentennial, 1840-1990*. Salisbury: Diversified Graphics, 1990.

Fish, G. Stowe, ed. *Stowe's Clerical Directory of the American Church 1932-33* (and subsequent vols.). Northfield, Minn.: G. Stowe Fish, 1932.

Fries, Adelaide L., ed. *Records of the Moravians in North Carolina*. Vols. 1-3 (1922-). Reprint, Raleigh: State Department of Archives and History, 1968.

Gatling, Eva Ingersoll. "John Berry of Hillsboro, North Carolina." *Journal of the Society of Architectural Historians* 10, no. 1 (March 1951): 18-22.

Grant, Daniel Lindsey. *Alumni History of the University of North Carolina*. Chapel Hill: General Alumni Association, 1924.

Green, William Mercer. *Memoir of Rt. Rev. James Hervey Otey, D. D. LL. D., The First Bishop of Tennessee*. New York: James Pott and Company, 1885.

Greensboro Daily News, 2 November 1924, "The History of St. Luke's Parish: The Beginnings of the Episcopal Church in Rowan County."

_____. 6 October 1957, "Jewelry Used In Making Old Communion Service."

Harrison, Fairfax, ed. *Aris Sonis Focisque, Being a Memoir of an American Family, the Harrisons of Skimino*. N. p.: De Vinne Press, 1910.

Henderson, Archibald. Centennial Address: *The History of St. Luke's Parish*. N. p.: n.d.

Mrs. Archibald Henderson's Diary, Henderson Family Papers, Southern Historical Collection, Chapel Hill, NC.

John Keais Hoyt to Clara Hoyt, 10 September 1865, John Keais Hoyt Letters, North Carolina State Archives, Raleigh, NC.

Jones, Robert O., comp. *Biographical Index of Historic American Stained Glass Makers.* Raytown, Missouri: Stained Glass Association of America, 2002.

Joslin, Allen Webster. *The One Hundredth Anniversary of the Organization of St. Paul's Parish.* Salisbury: Aull Printing & Photocopying, 1987.

Journal of the Annual Convention of the Protestant Episcopal Church in the State of North Carolina, various printers, 1819-1930.

Kirkland, Thomas J., and Robert M. Kennedy. *Historic Camden, Part Two: Nineteenth Century.* Columbia, SC: The State Company, 1926.

Krider, Josephine Kluttz. *History of the First Presbyterian Church, Salisbury, North Carolina, 1821-1971.* N.p., 1971.

Life Sketches of Lutheran Ministers: North Carolina and Tennessee Synods, 1773-1965. Columbia, SC: State Printing Company, 1966.

Linn, Jo White. *First Presbyterian Church, Salisbury, North Carolina, and Its People, 1821-1995.* Salisbury: privately published, 1996.

London, Lawrence Foushee, and Sarah McCulloh Lemmon, eds. *The Episcopal Church In North Carolina, 1701-1959.* Raleigh: The Episcopal Diocese of North Carolina, 1987.

Mallett, Frank James. *Helping Boys: A Handbook of Methods for Sundays and Weekdays.* New York: American Church Publishing Company, 1911.

Manarin, Louis H. and Weymouth T. Jordan Jr., compilers and editors, *North Carolina Troops, 1861-1865, A Roster.* 15 vols. Raleigh: State Department of Archives and History, 1966-2003.

The Mary and Martha Guild Cook Book. N.p., n. d. [1937?].

Milburn, Frank P. *Book of Designs, Frank P. Milburn, Architect, Michael Heister, Associate.* Columbia, SC: The State Company, 1905.

_____. *Designs From the Work of Frank P. Milburn, Architect, Columbia, S.C.* Columbia, SC: [?The State Company], 1901.

_____. *Designs From the Work of Frank P. Milburn, Architect, Columbia, S.C.* Columbia, SC: The State Company, 1903.

_____. *Examples From the Work of Frank P. Milburn and Company, Architects, Washington, D.C.* Washington: National Publishing Company, n.d.

_____. *Examples From Work of Frank P. Milburn and Company, Architects, Washington, D.C.* Washington: Gibson Bros., n.d. [ca. 1906].

_____. *Selections from the Latest Work of Milburn, Heister & Co., Architects, Washington, DC.* Washington: National Publishing Company, n.d. [ca. 1913].

_____. *Selections from the Latest Work of Milburn, Heister & Co., Architects, Washington, D.C.* Washington: National Publishing Company, n.d. [ca. 1920].

Miller, Robert Johnston. *An Introduction to the Knowledge of Christian Religion.* Salisbury: John Martin Slump at Michael Brown's printing-office, 1799.

Morning Herald (Salisbury, NC), 31 January 1938, "Bishop Edwin Penick Dedicates St. Luke's Church Parish House."

Murdoch Family Papers, Collection of William Speight Murdoch, Salisbury, NC.

Murphy, Walter. "Hinton Rowan Helper." *The State* 10, no. 23 (7 November 1942): 6, 16.

The North Carolina Churchman. Various places of publication: Diocese of North Carolina, 1936-1978.

Offerings Past and Present: A Cookbook. Salisbury: Episcopal Churchwomen, St. Luke's Episcopal Church, 1984.

The Old North State (Salisbury, NC), 21 June 1866, "The Young Ladies of St. Luke's Church…"

_____. 26 June 1866, "City and State Items: Ladies' Entertainment."

_____. 26 April 1867, "Pastoral Letter To the Parishioners of St. Luke's Church…"

_____. 20 August 1869, "The new suburban residence of Saml. R. Harrison, Esq…"

Owens, Robert B. *Christ Church, Rowan County: An Historical Sketch, 1921.* Reprint, with a supplement by W. Preston Barber, n.p., n. d. [1951?].

Peatross, C. Ford, and Robert O. Mellown. *William Nichols, Architect.* Tuscaloosa, AL: University of Alabama Art Gallery, 1979.

Powell, William S. *Dictionary of North Carolina Biography*, 6 volumes. Chapel Hill: University of North Carolina Press, 1979-1996.

_____. *St. Luke's Episcopal Church, 1753-1953.* Salisbury: St. Luke's Church, 1953.

Ramsey, Robert W. *Carolina Cradle: Settlement of the Northwest Carolina Frontier, 1747-1762.* Chapel Hill: University of North Carolina Press, 1964.

_____. "James Carter: Founder of Salisbury." *North Carolina Historical Review* 39, no. 3 (Spring 1962): 131-39.

Rowan County Deeds, Office of the Register of Deeds, Rowan County Building, Salisbury, North Carolina.

Rowan County Estates Records, North Carolina State Archives, Raleigh, North Carolina.

Rowan County Wills, Office of the Clerk of Court, Rowan County Court House, Salisbury, North Carolina.

Rumple, Jethro. *A History of Rowan County, North Carolina, Containing Sketches of Prominent Families and Distinguished Men.* 1881. Reprint, with a new index by Edith M. Clark, Baltimore: Regional Publishing Company, 1974.

St. Luke's Archives, St. Luke's Episcopal Church, Salisbury, NC.

Salisbury Post, 21 May 1907, "Church Plans Drawn."

_____. 22 June 1909, "A City in Sorrow: Dr. F. J. Murdoch Dead."

_____. 23 June 1909, "Dr. Murdoch's Funeral."

_____. 3 July 1909, "Tribute of Respect."

_____. 5 July 1909, "Resolutions of Respect."

_____. 9 July 1909, "In Memoriam."

_____. 17 February 1917, "Episcopal Church Notices."

_____. 19 February 1917, "Episcopal Churches Consecrated."

_____. 7 July 1920, "Former Mayor is Dead."

_____. 20 October 1924, "Interesting and Valuable Loan Exhibit."

_____. 27 October 1924, "The History of St. Luke's Parish…"

_____. 8 April 1925, "Mrs. Mark Milne Died Tuesday P. M."

_____. 15 May 1931, "Mrs. Frercks Dies Today at Age of 85 Years."

_____. 19 May 1931, "Frercks Fortune Given to Church And Charity Here."

_____. 25 September 1932, "Reminiscences Of Harrowing Days in Salisbury."

_____. 23 June 1934, "Rev. William Hill Hardin Dies In His Sleep At His Home Here; Funeral Will Be Conducted Sunday."

_____. 24 June 1934, "At The Close Of Day," and "Hardin Funeral at 5 P. M. Today, Cleveland Church."

_____. 31 January 1938, "St. Luke's Parish House Corner Stone Laid Sunday."

_____. 29 December 1938, "Rev. Mark Milne Died Last Night Following a Sudden Heart Attack."

_____. 1 June 1941, "Stained Glass Window to Be Erected at St. Luke's Church to Honor Rev. Mark Milne."

_____. [10 or 11] November 1941, "Bishop Penick Pays Tribute to Memory of Milne at Dedication."

_____. 17 May 1942, "Interesting Old South Main Street Building Begins New Era."

_____. 26 January 1945, "Historic St. Luke's Church Bell Moved from Old Tower to Church."

_____. 7 February 1951, "Mrs. Murdoch Dies at Home."

_____. 11 April 1953, "St. Luke's to Observe Its 200th Birthday Tomorrow."

_____. 12 April 1953, "Henderson To Make Address Here Today," and "First Textile Plant Formed Here in 1836."

_____. 20 June 1953, "St. Luke's Chapel Cornerstone Opened."

_____. 29 September 1957, "St. Luke's Communion Set Created of Abiding Love."

_____. 18 January 1958, "The Rev. O'Kelley Whitaker To Be New St. Luke's Rector."

_____. 15 November 1964, "Episcopal Women Are Ready For Their Best Bazaar."

_____. 24 January 1965, "Chapel at St. Luke's Sparkles With New Stained Glass Windows."

_____. 10 December 1965, "St. Luke's Elects Woman To Vestry."

_____. 25 September 1966, "Chapel Project May Lead Way to Addition of Hospital Chaplain."

_____. 13 November 1966, "Bazaar Lists Outlet Stores."

_____. 15 October 1967, "A Century-Old Rectory Has Been Saved For Use Today."

_____. 2 December 1967, "St. Luke's Will Begin Trial Use of New Liturgy."

_____. 31 March 1968, "New St. Luke's Bells Will Ring On Easter."

_____. 4 April 1968, "The Bells of St. Luke's."

_____. 15 March 1970, "Something New Added To Canterbury House."

_____. 8 November 1970, "St. Luke's Church Women Ready For Bazaar's Opening Wednesday."

_____. 17 January 1971, "Bachelor Priest Spreads Influence Beyond Church."

_____. 11 July 1971, "Father Terry Likes Secular World, Cuts Monastic Ties."

_____. 13 July 1972, "Rediscovered Letter Tells Origin of Communion Service."

_____. 12 November 1972, "St. Luke's Episcopal Church Women Work Long."

_____. 16 September 1973, "Rumple and Murdoch Distinguished Ministers."

_____. 20 October 1974, "St. Luke's Needlepoint: Dream Come True."

_____. 10 November 1974, "St. Luke's Church Bazaar Pretties Ready."

_____. 20 October 1976, "St. Luke's Church Women Plan Festive Fall Bazaar."

_____. 7 November 1976, "St. Luke's Bazaar On Wednesday."

_____. 10 April 1977, "St. Luke's Episcopal To Be Re-Landscaped."

_____. ___October 1978, "St. Luke's Episcopal celebrates 225th year."

_____. 4 February 1984, "St. Luke's tree has experts stumped."

_____. 27 March 1984, "Tree mystery takes root."

_____. 30 March 1984, "For the last time: It's a cedar."

_____. 19 September 1984, "St. Luke's mixes old and new in cookbook."

_____. 18 October 1987, "History in making: Blair brings new ideas to old churches."

_____. 27 December 1987, "Tunkle's journey enters new phase."

_____. 21 May 1988, "Pastor ordained by 2 denominations."

_____. 11 June 1988, "Francis J. Murdoch: Minister at forefront of industrial growth."

_____. 18 June 1988, "Murdoch: successful with ministry to the soul and to the pocketbook."

_____. 16 October 1990, "St. Luke's to dedicate new areas."

_____. 20 March 1991, "Physician Frank B. Marsh dies at 94."

_____. 24 July 1992, "Goodbye to St. Luke's AIDS ministry."

_____. 27 October 1992, "Deaths: Rev. E. B. Guerry."

_____. 2 June 1994, "St. Luke's adds columbarium."

_____. 17 October 1994, "St. Luke's plans celebration for new rector Tuesday."

_____. 26 November 1994, "Time to thank a giving woman."

_____. 25 August 2001, "Father Stephen preaches what he experiences—healing."

_____. 24 February 2003, "St. Luke's bringing back the old."

_____.18 October 2003, "St. Luke's begins weekend of events."

Saunders, William L., ed. *The Colonial Records of North Carolina*. Vols. 5-10. (1887-1890). Reprint, Wilmington, NC: Broadfoot Publishing Company, 1993.

Shepard, E. Lee. *A History of St. Paul's Episcopal Church*. N. p., 2001.

Sloan, Julie L., "Stained-Glass Window Condition Analysis, St. Luke's Episcopal Church, Salisbury, NC." Julie L. Sloan, Stained Glass Consultant, North Adams, MA, 2001. Photocopied.

Spong, John Shelby. *Here I Stand*. New York: Harper San Francisco, 2000.

The State (Columbia, SC). 11 January 1933, "J. H. Tillinghast Dies At His Home."

Stoops, Martha. *The Heritage: The Education of Women at St. Mary's College, Raleigh, North Carolina, 1842-1982.* Raleigh: St. Mary's College, 1984.

Thomas, Albert Sidney. *A Historical Account of the Protestant Episcopal Church in South Carolina, 1820-1957.* Columbia, SC: R. L. Bryan Company, 1957.

Trow's New York City Directory, 1882-1883, 1883-1884. New York: Trow City Directory Company, 1882, 1883.

Uray, Richard M., and Elizabeth D. Bernadin, eds. *A History of St. Peter's Church.* Columbia, SC: St. Peter's Parish, 1990.

"Urban T. Holmes III: Remembering Terry," *Sewanee Theological Review* 45, no. 3 (2002), 223-334.

Way, William, and Virginia Kirkland Donehue. *By Grace, Through Faith: A History of Grace Church, Charleston, 1846-1999.* Columbia, SC: R. L. Bryan Company, 2000.

Way, William. *The History of Grace Church, Charleston, South Carolina: The First Hundred Years.* Durham, NC: Seeman Printery, Inc., 1948.

Western Carolinian (Salisbury, NC), 15 April 1823, "Episcopal Convention."

_____. 22 April 1823, "The Convention."

_____. 5 August 1823, "Pastoral Letter of the Bishop of North Carolina."

_____. 23 September 1823, "The Rev. Mr. Green."

_____. 30 September 1823, "Lutheran Church."

_____.8 November 1825, "Bishop Ravenscroft."

_____. 26 December 1826—27 February 1827, "Contract for a Church."

_____. 13 March—10 April 1827, "To Brick Makers."

_____. 22 July 1828, "Consecration."

_____. 12 May 1829, "Notice is hereby given…"

_____. 4 October 1834, "A Fair in Salisbury, By The Fair."

Who Was Who in America, Volume II, 1943-1950. Chicago: Marquis Who's Who, 1975 (seventh printing).

Williams, George W. *St. Michael's, Charleston, 1751-1951.* Columbia, SC: University of South Carolina Press, 1951.

Wilson, Samuel Jr. *The Buildings of Christ Church.* New Orleans: Louisiana Landmarks Society, 1997.

Wodehouse, Lawrence. "Frank Pierce Milburn (1868-1926), A Major Southern Architect." *North Carolina Historical Review* 50, no. 3 (July 1973): 289-303.

Wood, Helen Leazer, edited by Marguerite Rogers Howie, "Remembering St. Phillip's Episcopal Church, unpublished typescript, 1993.

Wood, John Taylor, Diary, vol. 3 (1865), John Taylor Wood Papers, Southern Historical Collection, Chapel Hill, NC.

Thomas Wright to Mary Wright, 13 June 1831. Wright/Cotton/Douglass Family Papers, 1798-1990, W. S. Hoole Special Collections Library, The University of Alabama, Tuscaloosa.

The Yadkin and Catawba Journal (Salisbury, NC,), 22 July 1828, "Consecration."

FROM GENERATION TO GENERATION